They Loved to Play

For

Susan and Barby

They Loved to Play

Memories of the Golden Age in Canadian Music

Murray Ginsberg

eastendbooks
Toronto 1998

Copyright © Murray Ginsberg, 1998

All rights reserved. No part of this publication may be reproduced, stored in a retrieval system, or transmitted in any form or by any means, electronic, mechanical, photocopying, recording, or otherwise (except brief passages for purposes of review) without the prior permission of eastendbooks. Permission to photocopy should be requested from the Canadian Reprography Collective.

Care has been taken to trace the ownership of copyright material used in the text. The author and publisher welcome any information enabling them to rectify any reference or credit in subsequent editions.

Printed in Canada by Metrolitho

Canadian Cataloguing in Publication Data

Ginsberg, Murray, 1922–
    They loved to play : memories of the golden age in Canadian music

Includes index.
ISBN 1-896973-14-0

1. Musicians — Canada — Biography. 2. Music — Canada — History and criticism. 3. Ginsberg, Murray, 1922– — Friends and associates. I. Title.

ML394.G49 1998   780'.92'271   C98-931517-7

eastendbooks is an imprint of Venture Press
45 Fernwood Park Avenue
Toronto, Canada M4E 3E9
tel. (416) 691-6816   fax (416) 691-2414
e-mail eeb.ven@sympatico.ca

Contents

Acknowledgements	*6*
PRELUDE: Memories of the Way It Was	*7*
PART ONE: In the Beginning	*13*
PART TWO: Coming of Age	*35*
PART THREE: The Last Days of Swing in Toronto	*71*
PART FOUR: At the CBC	*115*
PART FIVE: Hooked on Classics	*177*
PART SIX: Silver Threads Among the Gold	*223*
CODA: Where Is Music Going?	*261*
List of Interviews	*268*
Index	*269*

Acknowledgements

I have incurred many debts in my work on this book. I wish to thank my daughter Susan, and nieces Sharon Ginsberg and Ruth Ann Beales, who assisted so much in transcribing dozens of taped interviews (a laborious task if ever there was one). And I particularly want to thank the irrepressible tenor saxophonist Hart Wheeler, one of the most intelligent individuals I've ever met, who went out of his way so many times to help.

Others, too, assisted with the transcriptions: at one point as many as fifteen students from University of Toronto were working on the interviews. They had to catch every word on the tapes, through a maze of coughs, door slams, and dog barks. Once or twice we had to guess at the final results; was it a crucial word or just the dog?

I am deeply indebted as well to the musicians I interviewed. Everyone I contacted gave freely of his or her time. A complete list of those involved appears at the end of the book. Their taped interviews remain intact and can be checked for accuracy. Their words (with a little judicious editing) are their own. In the profiles of musicians who died years ago — and could not, therefore, be interviewed — my stories are based on anecdotes and other material provided by younger people who knew them. Much also comes from my own memories of having played and otherwise associated with so many talented individuals over a period of some fifty years.

I should also say that all of us who have loved to play are indebted to all those who have loved to listen. I am, myself, someone with a foot in both camps. And this book has been written at least as much for those who love to hear good music as for those who love to play it. The writing itself, in any case, has been a labour of love, and I am grateful to everyone who has shared in the labour, particularly the publishers, eastendbooks — Jeanne MacDonald, Nadine Stoikoff, and Randall White — all lovely people who worked tirelessly and bent over backwards many times to bring a lengthy project into the light of day.

Murray Ginsberg
August 1998
Toronto

PRELUDE

Memories of the Way It Was

NAT CASSELLS, THE WIZARD OF THE SAXOPHONE, 1930s. At the Manoir Richelieu Hotel in Quebec. *Courtesy Nat Cassells*

This book would never have been written had I not driven to Kingston, Ontario, in July 1990 to interview Albert Pratz, the renowned former concertmaster of the Toronto Symphony. I had to get Albert's story for an article I was writing for the *International Musician*. Retired from the Toronto Symphony Orchestra, Albert was teaching members of the National Youth Orchestra of Canada during the summer months on the beautiful campus of Queen's University.

After a stimulating three hours with the violinist, I returned to my Toronto home where I found a message waiting for me from Erica Goodman, harpist daughter of another celebrated Canadian violinist, Hyman Goodman. "Dad's in town from California," she trilled on the telephone, "and we'd like you to join us for dinner this evening."

When she turned the phone over to her father, I told Hyman I had just interviewed Albert Pratz. Would Hyman mind if I brought my tape recorder for an informal interview with him, also for the *International Musician*, between bites of food?

The evening went smashingly — full of Hyman's interesting and hilarious anecdotes about life in the world of symphony orchestras, conductors, and soloists. When I was bidding him adieu he asked me, "Instead of writing articles about Albert and I for the *International Musician*, why don't you write a book about the dozens of musicians you've played with? I'm sure their stories would fascinate readers and music lovers across Canada."

By the time I'd reached my home a half hour later, I'd made up my mind. A book was a great idea, and I immediately set about making a list of appointments with friends and colleagues with whom I had worked on every level of the music business over a fifty-year career. In the end, the task turned into a great adventure of some seventy interviews — most of which were conducted over a six-year period, beginning in 1990. Inevitably, the adventure also took me back into my own memories of life as a musician in small jazz groups, big dance bands of the swing era, studio orchestras, and eventually the symphony itself.

With a cautious glance backwards at one type of music critic at least, I should make clear at the start that the book I've finally wound up writing is a kind of nostalgic memoir, rather than a work of history in any formal or especially serious sense. I don't mean by this that I have been hasty in my writing, or that the book is just about my own story. I have taken some pains to be accurate, allowing that, as in all oral history, both my own and my informants' recollections may not always be clinically exact. I have tried to let the musicians I have interviewed tell their own stories as much as possible. To distinguish their words from mine, without vast numbers of repetitive quotation marks, I've put passages drawn directly from the interviews in italics. And a lot of what follows appears in italics.

I have in fact tried to tell the story of a certain time and place and community of people. I hope that Hyman Goodman was right, and that the story will fascinate more than a few readers. But it is the story as seen from my own angle of human vision. What I have written about are memories of the golden age in music, and while I think you can learn from memories of this sort — if that's really what you want to do — they do not quite add up to a learned book. What I have aimed at is a more lively treatment of the subject.

I should very quickly make clear at the start as well that while Toronto, Canada, has a great deal to do with what I've written, this book isn't just about Toronto. Too many people in Toronto, some say, still think the most important things that happen in Canada, in a business like music at any rate, happen in Toronto, and this is, of course, just not true. But it is true that the great majority of musicians who worked out of Toronto in my own time originally came from many other parts of Canada (and even a few other parts of the world). And more than a few musicians who worked in Toronto at some point in their careers eventually wound up working in places like London or New York or Los Angeles.

Mart Kenney, for instance, was probably the most successful of all distinctively Canadian bandleaders during the golden age in music. His Western Gentlemen were the toast of the Royal York Hotel in Toronto during the years that immediately followed the Second World War, and the featured attraction at the Mart Kenney Ranch near Woodbridge, Ontario, in the fifties and sixties. But the Kenney band had forged its style at the Alexandra Ballroom in Vancouver, and Waterton Park in southern Alberta. And Mart himself had moved to Mission, BC, by the time the sixties came to an end.

At the other end of the country Cy McLean, leader of the band that finally brought black Canadians into the Toronto musicians' union in the earlier 1940s, originally came to Toronto from Nova Scotia, in the early part of the thirties. And, on another kind of variation on the theme again, two musicians who had a lot to do with the early history of the Canadian Broadcasting Corporation in Toronto, Percy Faith and Robert Farnon, eventually wound up working in Los Angeles and London, respectively.

Though my own parents came to Canada from eastern Europe in the earlier part of the twentieth century, I was myself born and raised in Toronto, and spent most of my professional career there. Inevitably, my nostalgic musical memories do have more than a little to do with the way it used to be in what has subsequently become Canada's most populous metropolis. But I have travelled from one end of the country to the other in the course of earning my living — and to various other parts of the world, proceeding east from the Atlantic coast and west from the Pacific. I have worked and become friends with people from many different places. Now, in my later years, I spend a good part of each year outside Canada altogether (though for me, as for others, there's still no place quite like home). And, of course, there is nothing particularly "Canadian," in any narrow sense, about the music that all of us have loved to play and listen to. It is something that all of Canada shares with various other parts of the world today.

In the end, I have written about the part of the Canadian music business that has been based in Toronto, simply because that is what I know best. Yet even with this kind of self-imposed limitation, I have finally had to accept that I had neither time nor space to write about everything and everyone I find interesting and significant myself. I have tried to concentrate on those musicians who seemed to me either the most exceptional or the most representative of their day. But even here constraints of space have meant that far too many good stories (and important musicians) have unhappily wound up on the cutting-room floor. To all those involved, I can only apologize and express my deep regrets.

I also discovered that although I had worked with musicians for most of my life, I knew surprisingly little about the details of their own marvellous lives until I actually interviewed them. For readers who may not have bothered to consult my formal acknowledgements up front, I should just say again that I am deeply indebted to those who have so generously shared the details of their experiences with me — from Nat Cassells, the "Saxophone Wizard" of the 1920s; to saxophonist Bert Niosi, who held forth at the Palais Royale on Lake Shore Boulevard West for eighteen years; to violinist Albert Pratz, who had played with the famed NBC Symphony Orchestra under the baton of the legendary Arturo Toscanini (and to all those other marvellous artists with whom I eventually played in the Toronto Symphony); to Bobby Gimby, whose song "CA-NA-DA" swept across the country during its 100th anniversary in 1967 (and who, sadly, has recently passed away on June 20, 1998); to my very good friend, bassist Murray Lauder, with whom I shared wartime experiences and a lifetime of laughs; and to all the other wonderful musicians whose stories grace these pages.

The task of even putting together the stories I could finally find room for raised some other difficult questions of judgement as well. Was it okay to print an anecdote about a recording session with the celebrated Igor Stravinsky on the podium, during which a loud rude noise exploded from somewhere in the orchestra? Should the book always adhere to good taste, or include the odd obscenity if the story is funnier than hell? Especially to Canadians and even more especially to Torontonians of my own generation, perhaps, I should confess that I have not always erred on the side of good taste.

In any case, the book I have ultimately come to lay before the reader contains accounts of many of the musicians who came from every corner of Canada and elsewhere in the world to play in Toronto, in what most people of my own generation still do see as a musical golden age. The book is at least my own nostalgic version of a master score for the period, from the jobbing one-nighter and steady engagement players, to the jazzmen, symphony artists, teachers and educators, arrangers, composers, vocalists, and those who performed on radio and television and in the recording studios, and all the others in-between who had stories to tell and, above all else — who loved to play.

End of an Era

There is one last note I want to sound, by way of prelude, before getting into the main theme. Early on in my adventure of interviewing musicians, I discovered that writing a book of the sort I wanted to write was almost as difficult and arduous as learning how to play a musical instrument. It wasn't until I had consulted the eldest of my interview informants — the saxophone wizard Nat Cassells — that I really began to get some sense of how to go about constructing my master score.

When Nat let me into his apartment on Broadview Avenue, in Toronto, one day in June 1992, I was taken aback by his appearance. Although he was more than twenty years my senior, and three days away from his ninetieth birthday, I was surprised to see how much his condition had deteriorated. To me he had always been one of those immortals who seemed indestructible, who never grew old. But to see him walk with difficulty back to his armchair and slump into it with a sigh of relief was almost too much to bear.

I had played with him on different occasions at the Royal York and King Edward hotels and (I guess because I was a dreamer) I always found myself awed by his presence. The stories of his past career were, to me, like mythical tales from another age. He had played with Luigi Romanelli's orchestra at the King Edward Hotel in the 1920s; he had been a member of the Dumbells vaudeville troupe that toured Canada during the First World War; he had played with Alexander's Ragtime Band in Detroit; and he had a tone on his saxophone so beautiful that (so it was said) people across Canada used to invite him into their homes after concerts to hear him play again, just to prove to themselves that he indeed was the wondrous musician they had heard earlier that night.

Today there are saxophonists who, because of technically improved instruments and advanced teaching techniques, may play as well as Nat Cassells did in his heyday. But, during his hour in the sun there were few who performed on the artistic level achieved by the Wizard of the Saxophone.

From almost the first of my interviews, I was acutely aware that some of my informants were experiencing varying degrees of deterioration, suffering from an assortment of old-age related maladies: a quivering thumb, a throbbing artery, or haziness of memory. Most, however (like the Wizard of the Saxophone, himself), still had their mental faculties and recounted their experiences with clarity. But Nat Cassells, at ninety, I felt, was tired, waiting for Fate's knock on the door.

I visited him again a week later to return a couple of photographs of Romanelli's orchestra, which I had borrowed to have copies made for this book. He seemed genuinely glad to see me and we spent a happy hour talking about his career. When I finally rose to leave we shook hands, both knowing we would never meet again.

On October 15, I read in the *Globe and Mail* that Nathan Cassells, ninety, had passed away in his sleep on October 12, 1992.

For me it was the end of an era.

Part One
In the Beginning

DON ROMANELLI AND HIS ORCHESTRA, 1920s.
Courtesy Benny Paul

When I was four years old, in 1926, my father took me to a Saturday matinée at the Gaiety theatre, on Richmond Street in downtown Toronto. And although that was many years ago now, through the haze of time my recollections summon up visions of acrobats, handsome tenors in military uniform, and Gallagher and Sheen, the celebrated comedy duo of Zeigfield Follies fame in New York:

"Were you in the boat when the boat tipped over, Mr. Gallagher?"

"No Mr. Sheen, I was in the water!"

(That one had the audience rolling in the aisles: at four years old, I still couldn't quite understand what was so funny.)

My father wore a straw hat, the fashion of the day adopted by most of the gentlemen who came to the Gaiety that summer afternoon. Dad and I sat so high up in the top balcony that I was sure I could reach up and touch the ceiling. Admission for my father was twenty-five cents and, I think, ten cents for me.

At Claxton's Music Store — Where It All Really Began

Of course, the Canadian music business in Toronto began some considerable time before my first visit to the Gaiety theatre with my father, in 1926. And I have thought quite a lot about just where and when it all got started.

As Fate would have it, I spent the last few decades of my own musical career working for the Toronto Musicians' Association. And I've concluded that the origins of this particular organization come as close to a real beginning as anyone can point to.

What is popularly thought of as the present professional musicians' "union" in Toronto started on December 2, 1887, when a dozen musicians paid one dollar each to form the Toronto Orchestral Association, during a meeting held above Thomas Claxton's music store on Yonge Street. Ultimately, a growing demand for musical and theatrical entertainment in the city had prompted the meeting. Instrumental musicians were required to provide accompaniment for opera and theatre, and to entertain in their own right at concerts, indoors and in the park. As many as sixty-seven individuals in the city of Toronto had reported their occupation as "musician" in the Canadian federal census of 1881. And they were all at a disadvantage, individually, when negotiating fees for their work.

The initial president of the new organization was Thomas Claxton himself. The first order of business was "to wait on eminent musicians of the city to become honorary members of the association." By the end of 1888, 100 membership cards had been issued. According to the new fee schedule in 1889, six nights of theatre work with the option of two matinées earned a musician twelve dollars per week. Sleighing parties paid four dollars per musician. A few years later, the association proudly proclaimed a bank balance of $308.60, which prompted a motion to be passed which approved the purchase of "one blackboard and six spitoons" for the meeting room.

In 1894 the organization's official name was changed to the Toronto Musicians' Protective Association, allowing non-orchestral musicians and the ubiquitous local militia-regiment bandsmen to join. By this time the association was providing membership sick benefits, and had hired auditors to oversee the books.

Over the next few years an influx of musicians from Buffalo apparently threatened to encroach on the local Canadian (or "British North American") talent. The association was faced with the decision of either proceeding alone, or joining the more broadly based American Federation of Musicians. It no doubt wisely decided on the safer course, and in 1901 the Toronto Musicians' Protective Association became Local 149 of the AF of M. The local organization's name remained the same, however, until 1952 when it was shortened to the Toronto Musicians' Association, the name by which it is known today.

Toronto, Canada, and the Great Boom

Happily enough, the growth of the local entertainment business, which employed members of the Toronto Musicians' Protective Association, received a big shot in the arm from the great Canadian economic boom of the late nineteenth and early twentieth centuries. The boom sparked the "last best west" on the Canadian prairie, and put Toronto on the map as an emerging big city back east. During the first three decades of the twentieth century, the Toronto metropolitan region would triple its population. And it attracted musicians from virtually every other part of Canada (and other parts of the world as well).

In 1899, just as the boom was getting under way, a new City Hall opened at the north end of Bay Street, on Queen. It was built of buff sandstone, and had a handsome clock tower, soaring above the city streets.

By this point several generations of migrations from the United Kingdom had made "Toronto" (which is actually a North American Indian word) an especially British North American place. It was dominated by people of English, Scottish, and Irish stock, and still gave a certain special status to the narrow world of the Protestant Orangeman, and the old aspiring local aristocracy of the "Family Compact." The early twentieth century would start to change all this, as new Jewish migrants from eastern Europe, some Italians, and even a few people of Chinese origin began to arrive, gently opening the door to the very culturally diverse and "global" Toronto we know today. But Toronto would remain a kind of Anglo-Saxon haven for some time yet ("the citadel of British sentiment in America," as even a local book of the 1930s would say).

In the 1890s the city limits extended north on Yonge Street from Lake Shore Road to Summerhill Avenue, west to Dufferin Street, and east to Coxwell Avenue. The main downtown intersection was King and Yonge streets. Most of the traffic on the roads was still made up of horse-drawn carriages and wagons, although the appearance of the odd new-fangled automobile made the pedestrians stop and stare, as horses not yet used to the chugging contraptions would rear and whinny.

Two miles west of Yonge, Queen Street crossed the lines of the Grand Trunk

Railway and ran into Lake Shore Road, which continued west across the Humber River. By 1912 the city's northern limits along Yonge Street extended to Lawrence Avenue, which bordered on farming country. Downtown, on Front Street, a few blocks west of Bay, the Queen's Hotel, erected in 1862 and renowned for its elegance and fine cuisine, was the stopping place for those who could at least pass as visiting British (and European) aristocracy. And musicians of suitably high calibre provided soft music for the hotel's eminent guests while they dined. On occasion, at just the right moment, the leader might signal the players to launch into a rag, "to liven up the place and get some toes tapping."

Three miles west of Yonge Street, on a few hundred acres of land extending north from Lake Shore Road, stood the grounds for what had begun in the middle of the nineteenth century as an annual fair for Ontario family farmers. Then the farmers' fair turned into the Toronto Industrial Exhibition. By 1912 it had become the Canadian National Exhibition, soon to be the largest annual event of its kind in the world.

From the time its gates opened in mid-August, until they closed at midnight on Labour Day, people from all over North America and abroad visited the CNE to view the best in farm produce and livestock, the latest in industrial machinery, and to enjoy the beautiful flowers. Kids got sticky trying to shove gobs of candy floss into little mouths, while entire families tried games of chance and watched fat, bearded ladies in the sideshows on the midway. Local militia bands paraded through the grounds and performed on bandstands daily. The price of admission was a mere twenty-five cents.

At the turn of the century, Sir Henry Pellatt's private company had brought electricity to Toronto by harnessing the power of Niagara Falls, and carrying it over transmission lines to a grateful city. But it took Adam Beck and the Hydro-Electric Power Commission of Ontario another decade to establish the public system which finally brought electric power into most Toronto homes. Ever since 1891 electric trolley cars had been carrying passengers down Spadina Avenue. They clanked east along King, then north on Sherbourne past many fine mansions and the Horticultural Gardens, and westward along Bloor Street to Spadina again, on their rectangular route around the city's core. The trolleys dropped passengers off in front of the leading hotels and restaurants, where music and musicians softened the rough edges of the emerging big-city hustle and bustle.

By 1914 Sir Henry Pellatt had completed the construction of Casa Loma, his too extravagant imitation of a European medieval castle, built on a hill just north of Davenport Road. Little did he realize at the time that, just fifteen years later, his castle would briefly become a hotel that served as the birthplace of the famous Casa Loma Orchestra (the first white big band in America that played jazz). Later still, Sir Henry's castle would become the meeting place for thousands of young high-school and university couples, who would dance the evenings away to the music of some of Toronto's best big bands, until the urbane and elegant age of jazz and swing finally gave way to the quite different age of rock and roll.

The Dumbells and Nat Cassells (as a very young man)

A recession in 1913 and then the Great War of 1914–1918 put an end to the great boom that launched the twentieth century in Canada. Unlike the neighbouring U.S.A., Canada was in the war from start to finish. And Toronto's still very close ties to the British Empire turned the conflict in Europe into something of a horrific local ordeal. But people forgot their troubles by going to the movies in the city's numerous cinemas. From the largest theatre emporiums such as the Pantages on Yonge Street to the most insignificant neighbourhood Bijou, music to establish the proper mood for the action on the silent screen was supplied by anyone from a solitary piano player to large pit orchestras, like the ones Jack Arthur conducted at the Winter Garden.

Other theatres featured legitimate plays or vaudeville, and often a combination of movies and live entertainment on stage. The Grand Opera House, on Adelaide, and the Princess, on King, featured everything from light opera (*The Merry Widow*) to the latest London and New York musicals (*Choo Chin Chow, La La Lucille*). The Star, on Temperance Street, was one of several burlesque houses that presented ladies who took their clothes off (well, almost) while dancing behind large feather fans. In "Toronto the Good" the morality squad was always on hand to see that certain parts of the female body were never really exposed.

While entertainment thrived in the theatres of Toronto, across the Atlantic Ocean on the battlefields of Europe, another kind of entertainment was taking root. Captain Merton Plunkett, a native of Orillia, Ontario, was acutely aware that the combat soldier desperately needed a diversion from the horrors of the trenches, and so he began conducting sing-alongs among the troops on leave. With songs such as "Mademoiselle from Armentières" and "Pack Up Your Troubles in Your Old Kit Bag," the sing-songs became so popular that, under Plunkett's direction,

THE DUMBELLS, 1922.

Courtesy Benny Paul

the amateur entertainment was soon organized into a variety show called the Dumbells. The show had everything a soldier needed: singers, dancers, comedy sketches, and even female impersonators, whose acts were so true to life that after each show a line of soldiers would wait at the stage door to meet the "ladies."

By the spring of 1917 the group, which had taken its name from the 3rd Division "dumbell" insignia, was cheering the soldiers of that division. When Captain Plunkett began his sing-alongs, he had no idea that the Dumbells would in a few years become a polished stage production — and ultimately the toast of Broadway in New York.

All of this was, of course, before my own time, so I never saw any of it myself. But, as I've already mentioned, quite a few years later I did work with Nat Cassells, and he had been a part of the Dumbells at one point. When I interviewed him in 1992, he also told me about his own earliest days in the music business in Toronto:

Do you remember Professor Glass, the music teacher? He organized a band for kids which he called Professor Glass' Juvenile Band. Glass taught every kid who was admitted to the group.

Only kids sixteen years old and under were allowed to join, and when I was ten years old, in 1911, Professor Glass brought me in as a clarinet player. He was my first teacher. We practised a lot and actually got good enough to be able to play the Poet and Peasant Overture, *and played a concert at Scarborough Beach Park.*

I stayed with the band until I was sixteen and then left to join the 110th Irish Regimental Band. I knew even though I was sixteen I'd learned a lot about the clarinet from Professor Glass, including the ability to read music easily. I practised a lot while I was with the Irish Regimental Band. I played a number of parades and concerts with them, and it was good experience for me."

One day a fellow who lived near my father's tailoring store on Queen Street saw me on the streetcar, carrying my clarinet case. He played the saxophone and had heard me play clarinet. "Why don't you get a saxophone?" he said. "What for?" I asked. I was seventeen years old at the time. "I'm working with this band at Mosher's Arcadia Ballroom on College near Grace Street," he said. "I've got so much work that I can't handle it all." His name was Harry Foss.

So I bought a saxophone from the R.S. Winnings music store on Yonge Street, below Richmond. And I started to practise, without lessons, using my knowledge of the clarinet, since there is a similarity in playing both instruments. I took the saxophone to Harry Foss' house where he played records on his Edison gramophone. We listened to a lot of Ted Lewis records. Remember "Is Everybody Happy?" We thought he was wonderful, his clarinet was wonderful, his saxophone was wonderful.

Foss said to me, "I want you to come to Mosher's Arcadia and sit next to me. Maybe you can help me." When I showed up and sat next to him I was so bad that they sent me out for fish and chips.

Harry Foss played the sax well enough but he couldn't get a vibrato. So he tied a string to his heel and the other end to his hand, and when he tapped his foot in rhythm

PROFESSOR GLASS' JUVENILE BAND, 1911. Cassells is fourth to the right of the bass drum, front row. *Courtesy Nat Cassells*

it would cause the string to pull on his hand which held the saxophone, and that way he got a vibrato. It may have been a little broad but good enough for Frank Whiteman, the orchestra leader.

I began practising a lot, but at first it was hard for me. Then I decided to take lessons from a fellow who did all kinds of work in Toronto. I can't remember his name, but he was one of the top sax players in the city. After I took a couple of lessons he said I didn't need any more. I was playing correctly. Then he surprised me by asking whether I could play with his band for a couple of weeks. That job led to other jobs around the city until I was offered the job at the Dardanella Ballroom in Wasaga Beach. But I had to join the union. That first union job was in the summer of 1918.

The New Symphony Orchestra

The Great War in Europe also had some impact on a Toronto musical organization that would much later come to play a quite prominent role in my own career. In 1908 the city's first symphony orchestra had been founded, with some seventy to eighty players under the direction of Frank Welsman. The story of this aggregation now seems a bit obscure. In any case, it soon disbanded under the stress of the 1913 recession and then the Great War.

Several years after the war had ended, in 1922, a group of Toronto musicians, who wanted to rehearse and perform symphonic music as a diversion from their regular employment as theatre pit players, persuaded Luigi von Kunits to organize a New Symphony Orchestra in the city. The musicians, a number of whom were students of von Kunits', knew he could train an orchestra. He had emigrated to the new world from Vienna in the late 1890s to become concertmaster of the Chicago Festival Orchestra. In 1912 he came to Toronto to head the Canadian Academy of Music, which went on to become locally celebrated for its string playing.

Von Kunits was confident that, especially with his students in tow, Toronto had enough skilled players for the New Symphony Orchestra. But all its musicians actually earned their living playing afternoon and evening performances in the theatre pits. The only time the orchestra could present concerts was between theatre performances, from 5:15 to 6:15 PM (after which the musicians would return to their respective theatres).

The musicians were assembled in late 1922 and rehearsals began. For the players it was a joyous time: at last they were able to play their beloved Mozart, Beethoven, and Brahms. Playing accompaniment to vaudeville acts or music to the flickering images on the silent screen seemed less onerous, as long as they could spend some happy hours with von Kunits and the New Symphony Orchestra.

Von Kunits rehearsed them well. On April 23, 1923, the sixty-musician aggregation, with the maestro on the podium, made its debut in Massey Hall (erected in 1892, as a gift to the people of Toronto from its famous family of agricultural machinery manufacturers). Playing to a half-filled auditorium, the orchestra offered a program consisting of:

> Overture to "Der Freischütz," Weber
> Slavonic Dance, Dvorak
> Two Hungarian Dances, Brahms
> Symphony No. 5 in E Minor, Tchaikovsky

According to Arnold Edinborough, in his excellent *A Personal History of the Toronto Symphony*, the critics were impressed. The *Mail and Empire* reported that "the opening performance ... was highly reassuring ... the orchestra played with marked refinement and freshness of tone." As the *Globe* explained to its readers: "The performance was surprisingly effective, the various parts being played with excellent technical finish and a good quality of tone." And Augustus Bridle of the *Star* wrote that "the players invested the work (Tchaikovsky's *Fifth Symphony*) with a power and a colour and an authority that one seldom hears surpassed by the best touring orchestras."

Two more concerts were given in May. Then at summer's end the first full season of Twilight Concerts was announced: twenty hour-long performances, to take place every two weeks, from September 25, 1923, until May 27, 1924. Though responsive, the early audiences were not large. But by its fifth season the orchestra had finally found its patrons. During the 1926–27 season, the name Toronto Symphony Orchestra became the official title of the growing organization. In 1931 Ernest MacMillan would succeed Luigi von Kunits as conductor. And, unlike its obscure predecessor before the First World War, this Toronto Symphony Orchestra has endured, without interruption, down to the present.

The Jazz Age in Toronto

By the time of the New Symphony Orchestra's first concert in 1923, the fabled and much more popular Jazz Age had descended upon English-speaking Canada's largest big city. And it had its own particular local ambience and style.

In 1922, for instance, Sunnyside Amusement Park, half a mile west of the CNE, opened to the public. It replaced Scarborough Beach Park in east Toronto, which had attracted Torontonians for decades. Sunnyside included games and rides, a ferris wheel, merry-go-round, roller-coaster, hot dog stands, and schemers who, for twenty-five cents, would try to guess your weight within three pounds. If they failed you won a prize worth pennies. If they guessed right they pocketed your quarter.

Two hundred yards to the west, Sunnyside boasted a new bathing pavilion that had a couple of high diving boards in constant use. Much to the delight of the awed bathers, daredevil youngsters soared from the highest board to pierce the water below. Outside on the beach other bathers chose to dip their toes in Lake Ontario, then quickly withdraw. (Why was the water always so cold?)

A wooden boardwalk ran along the beach, from Sunnyside to the Humber River. On Easter Sunday everybody dressed in their finest clothes and, if the day was sunny, they promenaded along the boardwalk in the annual Easter Parade.

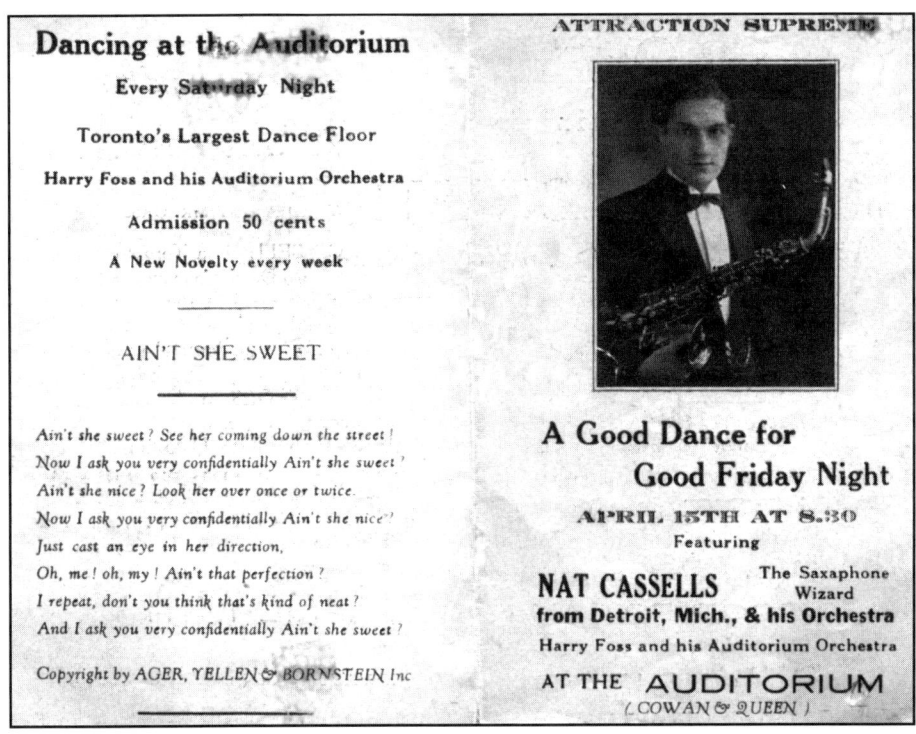

NAT CASSELLS AT THE AUDITORIUM, COWAN AND QUEEN, 1925.
Courtesy Nat Cassells

In the Beginning

Around the same time the Toronto Islands, about a mile off shore, were an enormous attraction for much of the citizenry, who would take the ferry boats *Trillium* and *Bluebell* from the foot of Bay Street across to Ward's and Centre islands and Hanlan's Point for picnicking and swimming. On Sundays the Toronto islands always presented band concerts, to the delight of the visitors.

Aware that in the springtime a young man's fancy turns to thoughts of love, the owners of the steamers *Chippewa*, *Cayuga*, and *Northumberland* ran excursions to Lewiston, at the mouth of the Niagara River in western New York, leaving Toronto every day at 5:35 PM and returning around 11:00 PM. Those wonderful spring and summertime trips attracted young romantic couples, who loved to dance under starry skies to the lilting strains of Don Romanelli's and Ed Culley's orchestras.

By the middle of the 1920s the Jazz Age was in full roar, with everybody dancing the new steps — the charleston, lindy hop, and two-step. Young couples, seduced by the strains of "Dardanella" and "Down Among the Sheltering Palms," couldn't wait to get on the dance floor. Dance halls and pavilions began to spring up in the most unlikely places.

The Auditorium at Queen and Cowan featured Nat Cassells (the Saxophone Wizard), and Harry Foss and the Auditorium Orchestra. Another spot, Mosher's Arcadia, was on the second floor of a building over an automobile sales room, on College Street near Grace. Still another was the Arcadian, on Danforth Avenue, which featured dining and dancing, with music supplied by various local dance bands.

On St. Clair Avenue, near Oakwood, the Robina Gardens provided employment for musicians who played "the best dance music in Toronto" (not necessarily for union scale) for couples who wanted to try the new steps. The Jazz Age in Toronto, however, also had its limitations. There were nights when the only people in the hall were the musicians. Such were the fortunes of amateur entrepreneurs who wanted to make a lot of fast money, but didn't know how to attract customers. Sometimes in English-speaking Canada's largest big city, in the Roaring Twenties, some musicians went home without being paid.

Radio Days and the Birth of the CBC

I was born in Toronto at the start of the Jazz Age in 1922. This was the same year that the Sunnyside Amusement Park opened to the public. And, I would later discover that 1922 was also the year when Toronto's first radio station, CFCA, began broadcasting from a plant in the offices of the *Daily Star* newspaper, which, at that time, was employing an aspiring young writer from Chicago named Ernest Hemingway.

As with so much else, a great many of the early radio stations that Torontonians and other Canadians listened to were based in adjacent parts of the U.S.A., and paid virtually no particular attention to Canada (and/or the British Empire, or "Empire and Commonwealth," as it would later be said). Very early on, eminent local leaders expressed concerns about the need to ensure that some form of

TORONTO RADIO ORCHESTRA BEFORE THE AGE OF CBC, 1931. Some of the musicians are: front row, left to right: (1st) Sam Hershenhorn, (2nd) Cecil Figelski, (4th) Benny Paul, (5th) Charlie Green, (6th) Percy Pasternak. Back row: (1st) Vaughan Sturn, (3rd) Max Greenberg, (5th) Bruce Campbell, (7th) Dave Caplan. *Courtesy Benny Paul*

"Canadian voice" be available on the new air waves.

In 1924 Canadian National Railways began a primitive programming service in both English and French. Its Toronto outlet was known as CNRT. And it was on this early CNR radio "network" that "Hockey Night in Canada" first began.

As with so much else, again, however, the Canada of the day ultimately looked to the experience of the imperial metropolis in the United Kingdom for a more enduring model. In 1927 the publicly owned British Broadcasting Corporation was formed.

A Canadian royal commission appointed to investigate the matter ultimately recommended something somewhat similar for Canada. And in 1933 the Canadian Radio Broadcasting Commission (or CRBC) was established. In 1936 the Commission was reorganized and its name shortened to the Canadian Broadcasting Corporation (CBC).

The CBC's French language services were headquartered in Montreal (Canada's largest big city at this point which, along with a substantial English-speaking minority, also had a French-speaking majority). But even then Toronto was Canada's largest English-speaking big city. It became the headquarters for the CBC's English language services.

This would have a big impact on the music business in the city. Percy Faith, for instance, joined the staff of CRBC Toronto almost as soon as it was established in 1933. And it was his experience there that provided the springboard for his subsequent more illustrious career with NBC Radio and with Columbia Records in New York City.

The Romanelli Dynasty

I was a mere eleven years old when CRBC Toronto first got under way in 1933. At that point my own musical career had yet to begin, and I knew very little about Percy Faith.

I also knew very little about the real king of the Canadian music scene in Toronto during the 1920s, and most of the 1930s. But when I did start to get involved in the business, I heard a lot of stories about Luigi Romanelli. (And even when I was only eleven years old, I suppose, I did know something about the public reputation of the Romanelli brothers.) Much, much later still, when I began doing my interviews for this book, I heard a lot of these old stories again. Here, for instance, is sax player Lew Lewis on the subject:

Luigi Romanelli was a man who made it his business to be impeccably dressed. In the morning he would wear morning clothes — tailcoat, ascot tie, striped trousers, everything. He was immaculate, soft-spoken, and appeared the fine gentleman at all times. A remarkable man with a gospel background, Luigi was soft-hearted as well. If anybody was in trouble of any kind he would always help as much as he could, quietly and graciously.

When we were at the Manoir Richelieu he liked to go riding, I suppose to impress the hotel guests, but he liked the exercise as well. He'd wear the proper riding jacket, ascot tie, breeches, and the derby perched on his head at the proper angle. He looked absolutely stunning. At that time he was close to sixty, but he was still quite athletic.

One day we were out at the rear of the hotel somewhere and who comes riding up on a beautiful charger but Sir Luigi himself, wearing the ascot, derby, breeches, everything, and carrying a riding crop, and looking absolutely elegant.

We all greeted him. "Louie, how are you? So nice to see you."

And he answered, "Is everybody enjoying themselves? Just thought I'd come by and say hello." A real democratic gesture.

When he signalled the horse to turn, it heaved and threw him to the ground. We all rushed over to help him up. He must have hurt himself: he really took a hard fall. But he got up on his own steam, brushed himself off, got back on the horse, and rode away as though nothing had happened. A remarkable man.

As a teenager Luigi Romanelli played the violin on Toronto streets for a young dancer, George Weitz (later to become George White of George White Scandals fame). At this point he also made his stage debut as an actor, with a Toronto child actress known as Gladys Smith, later to become "America's sweetheart," Mary Pickford, the famous silent film star. Around 1910 he was studying the violin with Jan Hambourg (one of several Hambourg brothers who had come to Toronto from Europe, and made a great contribution to the growth of music in the city).

After 1910 Romanelli became an orchestra player in various Toronto theatres. Then, after studying in Europe, in 1918 he became music director of the Allen

Theatres chain. His theatre orchestra was one of the first to accompany silent films with descriptive music. And the Romanelli orchestra at the Victoria Theatre, at Richmond and Victoria streets, was the first to broadcast on CFCA radio in 1922.

From the early 1920s on — virtually until his death on July 29, 1942 — Luigi Romanelli presided over the music at the King Edward Hotel in Toronto. For four summers he took an eleven-piece orchestra to the exclusive Manoir Richelieu, at Murray Bay in Quebec. In the 1930s Romanelli's Monarchs of Melody were heard on both CRBC and CBC radio, and occasionally on NBC's Blue Network in the United States.

Two of Luigi's brothers were also violinists and orchestra leaders in Toronto. Don organized bands as early as 1918 for the Lake Ontario cruise ships Cayuga and Chippewa, and Leo joined the Monarchs of Melody at seventeen, and later became assistant director. Over the years other members of the "Monarchs" would include pianist Johnny Burt, saxophonist Nat Cassells, trombonist/arranger (Seymour) Red Ginzler, singer Jimmy (later to be known as Trump) Davidson, bassist Gurney Titmarsh, saxophonist Gordon Day, and drummer Gene Fritzley.

In 1992 Nat Cassells told me about some of his particular experiences with the fabled king of the early music scene in Canada:

Sometime in 1921, Luigi Romanelli invited me to play for his sister's wedding, but first I had to go to brother Don's house for a rehearsal. The musicians couldn't get over the fact that I had no problem reading the sheet music of "Carolina in the Morning." In those days a lot of musicians who played dance jobs couldn't read music, something that doesn't exist in the 1990s. My ability to read, of course, developed during my early years with Professor Glass' Juvenile Band.

Well, we played the sister's wedding. Pianist Jack Curry was on that job, as was violinist Cecil Figelski, bassist Ben Seth, harpist Larry Cortese from London, and drummer Gene Fritzley. We were recognized as the top players in Toronto, and it all came together. So Luigi said, "Fellows, we're all starting at the Oak Room in the King Edward Hotel next week." That was in 1921 and it was the beginning of the Romanelli dynasty. And that group of players was the original King Edward Hotel orchestra, which sounded wonderful. They were so versatile that all I had to do was step off the bandstand and the remaining players would become a chamber music ensemble — two violins (Luigi and Don), a harp (Cortese), and piano (Curry). They could play anything: classical, Strauss waltzes, Palm Court music — anything.

In an orchestra of that calibre one might expect that all the musicians were schooled players. But pianist Jack Curry could not read music easily or quickly, which gave the others a lot of trouble. Although he was highly respected and could play anything in the best of taste, he would have to take new sheet music home and practise it. The other musicians, all proficient sight readers, could never understand why Curry found reading so difficult. Still, each was receiving anywhere from $75 to $100 a week, depending on how valuable each musician was to the leader. And that was a lot of money in 1921.

The King Edward directors knew what they were doing when they hired Romanelli. By this point the King Eddie had supplanted the Queen's Hotel as the place in Toronto that catered to those who passed as visiting British and European aristocracy. In this atmosphere the man who led the orchestra in the Oak Room had to be a person of charm and integrity, who presented himself to the public at all times as a figure of refinement. Charismatic Luigi Romanelli was such a man.

He conducted the affairs of his orchestra like a business. He had an office in the hotel, with several secretaries, a manager, and an assortment of personnel to attend to the business of the organization on a daily basis.

Once he became established at the King Edward, it didn't take long before the maestro was in great demand by every corporation, institution, and influential family in Toronto. Many times when the Oak Room evening came to an end, around 1:30 PM, some of the musicians would pack their instruments and proceed to the Eglinton Hunt Club, or a debutante party in Rosedale, and play until the small hours of the morning.

The Luigi Romanelli name became so popular that, for years, the organization was able to place orchestras in a great number of hotels, restaurants, and theatres across the city. Brother Don had an orchestra in the Royal York for several months, and brother-in-law Enrico del Greco led the pit orchestra in various theatres for a number of years.

As drummer Jimmy Cooke put it to me in one of my interviews:

Before Horace Lapp went into the Royal York we were jobbing around the city. Horace told us about an important job in the Crystal Ballroom of the King Edward Hotel, but the job didn't belong to Horace.

LUIGI ROMANELLI'S ORIGINAL ORCHESTRA AT THE KING EDWARD HOTEL, 1921.
"The best musicians in Toronto" left to right: Romanelli (standing), violinist Cecil Figelski, pianist Jack Curry, saxophonist Nat Cassells, harpist Larry Cortese, drummer Gene Fritzley, and bassist Ben Seth. *Courtesy Nat Cassells*

Since Luigi controlled the music in the hotel, the job was really his. In fact, Luigi Romanelli controlled almost all of the music in Toronto in those days. "If you didn't work for Romanelli then you didn't work in Toronto," was a common saying among the musicians.

The affairs of the orchestra took top priority. New arrangements of the latest songs had to be written. Red Ginzler, Jimmy Davidson, Johnny Burt, and even the highly respected Percy Faith contributed to the Romanelli library, which was reputed to be worth more than $50,000. Rehearsals were an important item on the weekly agenda. When a vacancy in the orchestra occurred, the staff made sure that all the musicians in the city were notified well in advance that auditions would take place on a certain date. And the auditions themselves could be a bit of a trial. As Lew Lewis would much later explain:

I got to play with Luigi Romanelli's orchestra through Gordon Day, who had been a member of Romanelli's sax section for some months. One day Gordie told me that Romanelli needed a tenor saxophonist. "There's going to be an audition soon and I want you to try for the job," he said. "I know what he likes — a lot of pathos and emotion when you play a solo. I know that'll do it."

So I went down to the Oak Room to try for the best job in Canada. That was some time in 1937. When I walked into the Oak Room, the orchestra was playing and I saw every sax player in Toronto was there. When I saw Gordon Evans I knew I wasn't going to get the job. Gord Evans was one of the best sax players in the city, really terrific. Then I saw Luigi with his staff. He always had his cohorts and yes-men around him.

Romanelli called out to one of the sax players. "All right there, you. Up! Up!" and pointed to the stage. The player climbed onto the bandstand and sat in the audition hot seat. Then Romanelli called out a tune and everybody scrambled with his music folder to find the correct arrangement. They would play a little and then Luigi would ask the sax player to play a couple of solos. Then he'd say, "All right, take his name!" and ask for the next player. "You, there. Up! Up!" There must have been three or four players who auditioned ahead of me. Then he turned to me: "Now you," he said.

I got on the stand and sat next to Gordie Day. As we picked the music from the music folder I whispered to Gordie, "Jesus Christ, Gord ... I didn't know ... " But Gordie said, "Remember what I told you. Ham it up as much as you can."

So we played, and I tried to do what Gordie had said. I hammed it up. Next came a tune that had a tenor solo in it and Gordie whispered to me, "Give it all you got." Well, I played my heart out. It ended up with Romanelli standing in front of me with his baton. He was just standing and listening. Then pretty soon he was conducting — conducting only me. And Gordie had a big smile on his face.

Then Romanelli asked for another tune. "I want to hear this again," he said. So we played another number with a tenor solo, and when we finished he said to his cohorts, "Send everybody home," and then said to me, "Come with me." He took me up to his office with his arm around my shoulder and told me what a great future I had with him. That's how I got hired.

In twenty years of successful music-making, was there ever a time when something went wrong, when the gods on high decided it was time to throw a monkey wrench into the works? Apparently there was, and Toronto's formidable trumpet player, Ellis McLintock, has a particular story to tell here:

We were playing an automobile show in Oshawa. They were introducing the newest cars for 1939 (it was October 1938, I think) and everybody who was anybody in the corporate world, as well as politicians, movie stars, radio personalities, and tons of money were there; very formal white-tie affair. Of course, Luigi was impeccable in his attire: white tie, top hat, and tails. His orchestra was the biggest thing musically in Canada and we were providing the music on stage for the show. For the people in the audience Romanelli's orchestra completed the picture.

Finally the house lights dimmed, the orchestra started with a fanfare, and the curtain — a roll-up curtain — slowly began to rise. On stage Luigi was conducting, standing in front of the orchestra as the curtain rose, and as it did, his tails got caught in the curtain as it rolled up. In no time Luigi was dangling about three feet above the stage in full view of the audience, as they roared with laughter while he struggled to be free. The stage-hands immediately brought the curtain down and poor Louie, embarrassed beyond belief, ordered the musicians to pack up and leave the theatre. The musicians, of course, did everything to suppress their laughter, each one moving swiftly out the stage door and into their cars in record time. What a shocker! He was lucky he didn't get killed.

According to accounts from other musicians who knew about the incident, a lawsuit was filed against the theatre people, but after a cooling down period, the matter was dropped, and Luigi, gentleman that he was, was able to laugh about it.

In the very end, according to virtually all the musicians I came to know when I started in the business myself (and all those old enough to remember, whom I later interviewed for this book), the key to Luigi Romanelli was that he was a man of great integrity. He helped to set standards for the music business in Toronto, and in Canada at large, that would go on to shape the future, long after he and his brothers and all the Monarchs of Melody had left the scene.

Ooh Duckie: The Song of Horace Lapp

There is one other giant of the Canadian music scene in Toronto during the earlier twentieth century who somehow seems to me to belong at the beginning of the story (even though his long and active career stretched on well past the Second World War). And that's the bushy-haired orchestra leader, Horace Lapp.

Horace Lapp was successful in virtually everything he did, and respected by Canadians from coast to coast to coast. There are dozens of anecdotes about him, but drummer Jimmy Cooke, who played with Horace for years and became his right-hand man, tells a story that seems to sum up the sort of person he was:

> Horace was a character and he loved it. He was a screwball but at the same time a tremendous person. And he was funny, as funny as anyone can be. One time we were doing fashion shows at Eaton Auditorium, and I always used to take my chimes, because Horace always liked things dressed up. We were in the orchestra pit where I was busy packing the chimes into individual slots so they wouldn't hit each other and scratch when Horace came along and said, "Oh Cookie, you damned old fool (he had special names for everybody), that's not the way you do it. You do it like this," and he pulled a chime out of its slot just as Lady Eaton, who loved him, came by.
> As he tugged on the chime it hit her on the noggin. "Ooh, I'm sorry Duckie," he said, and she held her head and replied, "Oh my goodness, Horace, I was just coming down to tell you how lovely the music was." Poor Horace said, "I didn't know you were there, but maybe we can make amends." And away she went, holding her head.

Born in Uxbridge, Ontario, on March 3, 1899, Horace was a church organist who later played piano with Luigi Romanelli. As a member of Jack Arthur's several theatre orchestras from 1924 to 1935, he composed and conducted music for stage shows at Shea's Hippodrome on Bay Street and the Imperial Theatre (formerly the Pantages) on Yonge Street. He also led a dance band at the Royal Muskoka Hotel from 1934 to 1936, and at the Royal York Hotel from 1936 to 1944. Later on, he was the regular organist at Maple Leaf Gardens, and a producer of shows at the CNE Bandshell in the 1960s. As one of the last surviving silent film accompanists in Canada, he also recorded soundtracks for CBC TV's 1969 series of the thirty-seven existing Laurel and Hardy movies.

Throughout all his activities in Toronto, among local musicians Horace is best remembered for his years as an orchestra leader at the Royal York Hotel (which opened on Front Street in 1929 as "the largest hotel in the British Empire"). After a few years of unsuccessfully trying supper dances in the Imperial Room with several bands, none of whom knew what it took to attract people, in 1936 the Royal York approached Horace Lapp to bring in his orchestra. The prestige of the Royal York was at stake. If the Oak Room of the King Edward Hotel was successful, then the same must apply to the Imperial Room. As with the charismatic Romanelli, the leader of the Imperial Room Orchestra had to present himself to the public with flair and vitality.

Lapp agreed to bring his band into the Imperial Room under certain conditions. "I'll come in with the proviso that I can have a say in the bandstand being revamped," he said (as legend has it). "I want a brand new stage with lots of flowers, and I'll only come in for three months to see if I like it; or if you like us. If not, I don't want people to say, 'Oh, Horace Lapp went in and he didn't make it.' I want that clearly understood."

The hotel management knew Lapp to be a very proud person, who was 'in' with the Toronto social set of the day. The social set were the very people the management wanted to attract, and they went for it.

They left the planning to Horace. He designed a beautiful bandstand, tiered to show off each instrumental section. Horace himself sat at a grand piano on the stage or first level, along with the saxophones. The trombones sat on a second level and the trumpets on a third. A top tier was reserved for Denny Vaughan, a marvellous musician and singer who sat at another grand piano, just like the one Horace played.

When the stage was finished, it had indirect lighting and spotlights (especially one shining down on Horace), and a beautiful theatre curtain that opened on an oval-shaped track when the band played the opening theme song. As Jimmy Cooke relates:

Horace laid down the band rules before the job started in the fall of 1936. The deportment of the musicians was something to see. You didn't talk about your golf game or anything else while on the stage. "Save your chats for intermission," he told the musicians, "and don't turn around to talk to the man behind you."

Horace was all showmanship. We had five sets of band uniforms, all made by Ed Provan of Yonge Street, one of Toronto's most prestigious haberdashers in his heyday, who provided suits and uniforms for many of the city's musicians. No cutting corners. We had white tails, dark tails, coats without tails, and blue and red jackets (not jazzy red, but tasteful red), and we changed uniforms at intermission.

We also had to be inspected each night before we went down to the Imperial Room to make sure the boutonnière in everyone's lapel was in place. It was a very unique organization. We even took tap dancing lesson. Horace would announce, "Ladies and Gentlemen, we now present our floor show!" And the guys would get down on the floor and do a tap dance routine which always drew a lot of laughs from the crowd. Horace travelled first class all his life.

Flair and vitality? Horace Lapp and his orchestra stayed in the Imperial room nine years. And they played at the Banff Springs Hotel during the summer months for three of those years. This job was more than just a summer engagement. In the heart of the beautiful Canadian Rockies, in the wild rose province of Alberta, the hotel attracted famous people from all over North America and Europe.

According to many of the musicians from the various orchestras who played the Banff Springs Hotel, there were always important guests staying for a week or two. It was quite common to see famous Hollywood movie stars, such as Ginger Rogers, Barbara Stanwyk, Jack Benny, and Kate Smith; renowned jazz musicians, including Benny Goodman; Broadway actors, world politicians, and personalities of one sort or another on the golf course, in the dining room, or in the cocktail lounge.

The large hotel staff — the waiters and the waitresses, the bell boys, clerks and

HORACE LAPP AND HIS ORCHESTRA AT THE ROYAL YORK HOTEL, 1936. Musicians on the bandstand of the Imperial Room, before the tiered bandstand was built. Front row (second from left) saxophonist Gordon Day, (fifth from left) violinist Isadore Desser. Back row: bassist Peter Sinclair, drummer Jimmy Cooke (standing to the right of the chimes). *Courtesy Jimmy Cooke*

receptionists — all worked hard to cater to the visitors. Horace always felt these people should be rewarded for their efforts. And Jimmy Cooke tells another story:

Once a month our gesture towards the Banff staff was to play a dance for them in the ballroom after all the official duties had been performed for the day. The dance was a volunteer gesture from the musicians. On this particular night we took our instruments over to the ballroom at just after midnight and got set up to play. Horace ran in to tell us that he had an important meeting with the Reynolds cigarette people, who had been making a fuss about him being a great leader and musician and wanted him to come to their private room. "You get started without me, Duckie," he said. "I've got to see these people. I'll be over later."

So we switched Freddie Treneer from saxophone to piano (Fred was a competent pianist) and we were all set to go. We picked out all the good arrangements of the old dandies, which Horace didn't always choose and began to play. The staff were on the floor having a ball and we were enjoying playing those wonderful arrangements, many having been written by top New York arrangers, when all of the sudden we saw Horace at the door of the ballroom, stopped by the security doormen and bouncers. Since they had never seen him perform in the dining room, they didn't know who he was. They wouldn't let him in.

"That's my band," he shouted. "I've got to get to the bandstand."

But the doormen were adamant. "I don't give a damn if you're Mickey Mouse," one said. "You're not getting in so forget it, and that's it!"

So he left in disgrace and went up to his room and pouted. The next day he gave us hell because we didn't come to his aid. There were repercussions also for the bouncers and doormen who were put on the carpet. Horace went to the manager, whom he knew from the Royal York Hotel:

"Ron, we're going home," he said.

"You can't go home, Horace," Ron replied.

"Goddamn right we can," Horace said. "I went to see my band last night and they wouldn't let me in."

"Who wouldn't let you in?"

"Those guys at the door, they wouldn't let me in."

"Well, we'll certainly rectify that!"

"No, I wanna go home!" He then told one of the band members to tell everybody to pack up. "We're all going home."

He did that a number of times. When I first started working with Horace, I often thought, "This is the guy I'm going to work for?" The slightest provocation and he was always going home or quitting.

Another time he went to Ron and said, "Ron, I'm not having a nice time. I don't like it here at all. I miss my car." Ron said, "Horace, we can get you a car here."

"No, I like my own car."

So Ron said, "Would you be happy if we had your car sent here?"

"Yes, I would like that very much. And send out four bicycles while you're at it. They're at my place. I want one for Cookie, I want one for Sandy, and the others for some of my other musicians."

Believe it or not, they sent the car and bicycles from Toronto to Banff by CPR freight. That's the kind of pull he had. The hotel people loved him.

Another time when he heard that the mother of one of the musicians was dying of cancer, Horace got him a railway pass to get him home to be with his mother, and when she improved he came back. He made four trips. That was the side of Horace you never forgot: very kind, very generous. He was a character, but always so respectful — a very decent person.

Indeed, when the occasion called for it, Horace Lapp would spare no expense. On one particular coast-to-coast tour that included radio broadcasts, he added four of Toronto's finest violinists — Albert Pratz, Hyman Goodman, Isadore Desser, and Paul Sherman — to enhance the lustre of the orchestra. The violinists only played the radio broadcasts. He didn't care how much the extra players cost.

As Jimmy Cooke said, Horace Lapp was all showmanship: anything to add to the entertainment. He always included the musicians in the nightly floor shows. There would always be a guest star to headline the show, but the musicians had to learn six different tap-dance routines, taught to them by Louise Burns, a well-known dance instructor who gave them lessons once a week. One routine was a Hawaiian hoola dance with grass skirts. Another was a soft-shoe dance. Another had the musicians playing violins, still another playing guitars. Of course, they had to be taught how to hold a violin and how to draw the bow across the strings. The playing was not very good, but that added to the humour of the act. According to the musicians who participated in the floor shows, Horace Lapp was a genius who had everything — vision, presentation, a marvellous sense of humour.

Horace's magic touch even rubbed off on some of the people that he treated rather harshly. One night his guitarist, Ted Andrews, came to the job half an hour late (he had slept in) and Horace fired him on the spot. Andrews, who was also a trained singer, then moved to England, where he got into the movies. (He flew Hudson Bombers in *Captains of the Clouds*, and appeared in other films as well.) In England Ted met and married a screen actress who had had a child, Julie, by a former marriage. As the story goes, Ted Andrews coached the young Julie, who took his surname when her mother married Ted. And — thanks to Horace Lapp — that's how the British movie star Julie Andrews (perhaps most famous for her roles in *The Sound of Music* and *Mary Poppins*) first got started on her own long career.

HORACE LAPP AT THE ORGAN IN LATER LIFE, circa 1970. *Courtesy Horace Lapp*

After leaving the Royal York Hotel in 1944, Horace Lapp continued performing as a pianist and organist. But he still regularly found himself in absurdly comical situations. The pianist Earl Parnes remembers one in particular, from after the Second World War:

> For a number of years each October I had been providing dinner music for the annual Lumbermen's Association Convention at the Royal York Hotel. Since the Lumbermen's entertainment committee knew me well, they understood that from time to time if I couldn't make the two-hour job myself, I would send in a competent substitute to play the piano in my place, which was okay with them. And who was better able to play the gig than the master pianist himself, Horace Lapp. So I called him one day, a couple of weeks before the engagement, to ask whether he would be available for the

In the Beginning   33

evening of Thursday, October 9. I told him he would be required to play from 7:00 to 9:00 PM *and then leave.* "All you have to do is do what you do best — play anything that comes to mind, Horace," I said. "You'll be in the ballroom on the convention floor. And I know they'll love you. I'll put a cheque in the mail to you today."

"Don't you worry about paying me now, Duckie," Horace said. "I'll be there with bells on," and hung up.

"Two days before the appointed night I called Horace to remind him of the date. When he picked up the phone and heard my voice he gushed about the wonderful people he'd played for last week. "Simply marvellous, Duckie," he said. "Absolutely wonderful response. People were coming up and shaking my hand all evening. Can't thank you enough for the job."

"But Horace," I said. "The job is this Thursday, not last week."

A moment of silence. "Ooh, Duckie, I think I've made a horrible mistake," he said. "Oh dear, I'll be sure to be there this Thursday. Don't you worry one bit."

When I checked with the Royal York to find out who Horace had actually played for the week before, the manager chuckled: "That was the night Aluminum of Canada had their convention. When I saw Horace at the piano I thought they had purchased him. And apparently Aluminum of Canada thought Horace automatically came with the Royal York Ballroom. I couldn't understand why everybody was thanking me so much."

Whatever else, it seems clear to me now that Horace Lapp carried something of the unique spirit of the beginnings of the Canadian music scene in Toronto on into the later part of the twentieth century. He was irrepressible. And, in one way or another, he kept on performing until his death on January 28, 1986, a few weeks before his eighty-seventh birthday.

Part Two
Coming of Age

MURRAY AND FRIENDS AT THE STANDISH HALL HOTEL, DECEMBER 1941. Standing around piano, left to right: Leader Trump Davidson, saxophonist Paul Hebert, drummer Sid Perl, trombonist Stan Wheeler, bassist Sam Levine, trombonist Murray Ginsberg, saxophonist Willie Delaurentis, pianist Harvey Silver, saxophonist Reg Saville. *Murray Ginsberg, private collection*

At age fourteen, on the third Saturday in January 1937, I took my first trombone lesson. And thus began my own life as a professional musician. My teacher was Harry Hawe, principal trombonist with the Toronto Symphony (by this point under the direction of Sir Ernest MacMillan, who had succeeded Luigi von Kunits of the New Symphony Orchestra). Harry Hawe taught many of the young aspiring trombonists in the city during the 1930s and 1940s. We learned our scales, practised long tones and staccato tonguing, and prepared our assignments for the coming week, when Mr. Hawe would give another lesson.

Soon enough I stumbled across others, more or less my own age, who were also starting their musical careers. We played in school orchestras and youthful rehearsal bands in someone's home, generally on Saturdays and Sundays. We played trios and quartets in attics and basements and in churches — anywhere — just to be able to make music. We were bitten by the music bug right from the start.

I will always be grateful to Harvey Perrin, the director of music for Toronto elementary and secondary schools, who got me into Eldon Brethour's Secondary School orchestra, which rehearsed every Saturday morning at Jarvis Collegiate. I can't remember meeting a kinder man, a true teacher in the absolute sense, dedicated to bringing music into the lives of young children. (To think of the thousands of Toronto children who were influenced by this man!)

It all came about for me when I was invited by a music teacher called Mr. Hague to join the Harbord Collegiate orchestra, which was preparing to present Gilbert & Sullivan's *Pirates of Penzance* for their forthcoming Show Night. They needed a trombone player to fill the gap in the brass section.

Although I was attending Central Technical School, a number of blocks away, I lived only three houses south of Harbord — a matter of two minutes to cross Harbord Street and get to the rehearsal in time. After a while Mr. Hague brought my name to Mr. Perrin's attention, and Mr. Perrin guided me into Eldon Brethour's Saturday morning orchestra at Jarvis Collegiate, which brought together more advanced players from all the local high-school groups in the city.

These Jarvis Collegiate sessions not only benefitted our individual musical development, but they also provided us with the opportunity to meet young musicians from across the city, who within a few years would become close friends.

As teenagers most of us were too naive to think that anyone else might play better than us. But then we heard the likes of Teddy Roderman, one of the finest trombonists Canada ever produced, or Ellis McLintock, the formidable trumpet player who at seventeen played principal trumpet in the Toronto Symphony while still going to high school, and it didn't take us long to realize who the stars were — those musicians blessed with an abundance of talent the rest could never match.

This was the beginning of the maturing process for many. It may have bruised some egos, but we persisted. We took our weekly lessons and practised until our lips were sore, while our mothers and fathers and brothers and sisters would often yell, "Stop already, I can't stand the noise."

We Were Just Kids Starting Out

Of course, everyone who starts out in the music business has their own particular story. Some way down the road in my own Toronto career, it was often said that as many as two-thirds of the musicians working in the city had originally come from some place else. Like a lot of my own early friends, I started out in Toronto and finished there as well.

Much later still, however, when I was interviewing musicians for this book, it struck me that there are certain common threads to almost all stories about getting started in the music business in Canada in the 1920s, 1930s, and 1940s. Jimmy Cooke, the drummer who was Horace Lapp's right-hand man, remembers:

I began studying the drums with Harry Nicholson when I was fifteen. I used to take my lessons in his apartment every Sunday morning. I was his first pupil, and I know he didn't teach too many people at any time. I started to play around with other kids in amateur bands and I remember auditioning for summer jobs, particularly at the Island, Centre Island, Hanlan's Point, and other places. It got so that I auditioned with so many bands that the manager of one place thought I was the only drummer in the city.

Gordon Evans, whom I've already briefly mentioned in connection with the intimidating auditions held by Luigi Romanelli in the 1930s, has a somewhat different story that, at the same time, also sounds a bit the same:

I got started when I was eleven years old. My brother bought a ukulele at the corner store. The ukulele included a few free lessons. So I heard him playing these chords, and I wanted to try playing it as well. I was really interested. My brother said, "You should have a saxophone." From then on I bugged my parents for a saxophone. So for my twelfth birthday my dad took me down to Whaley Royce and I got my first saxophone and ten free lessons. My teacher was Leo Johanus. I think he lived on Ontario Street, just below Dundas. Anyway, I took the ten lessons. Then he went away on a summer job and I had to wait until the fall to take more lessons. I was a kid taking lessons and my feet couldn't even touch the floor when I sat on a chair.

Leo had a Sunday morning saxophone class. I remember eight kids playing saxophones. Boy, that was a big deal for me. There was a fellow named Harold Ross who played clarinet. One day Leo said, "I want you to hear Harold play clarinet." I couldn't believe how great he sounded. I thought, "My God, am I ever going to play like that?"

Then I started to listen to records with Coleman Hawkins and other big-time players on them. I was only twelve or thirteen, and I tried to copy them. I began buying all kinds of records to listen to, with Roy Eldridge and Chu Berry on them, and Andy Kirk and his Clouds of Joy and Fletcher Henderson's band. I must have been fifteen then, because I was working at a place called the Silver Slipper at the west end of Sunnyside, north of Lake Shore Road. I can't remember the leader, Henry Kelnick, I think.

Hart Wheeler, who began to play the clarinet in 1937, has a similar tale:

I got started when I was fifteen years old. My rich aunt recognized some sort of latent talent because I was playing bones and harmonica in public school. So she went to Whaley Royce, the music store on Yonge Street, but didn't know what to get me. The decision she finally made was one which affected my whole life. She was trying to decide what kind of instrument I should play: a trombone, trumpet, or clarinet. She chose the clarinet, which was the cheapest at $26.50. It was an Albert System clarinet and you're in the hands of Fate in such circumstances. Who knew what an Albert System was?

But I got the Albert System clarinet and at the same time I discovered Benny Goodman. The first thing I wanted to do was play Benny Goodman solos. Of course, that didn't entail taking lessons or learning notes or how to read, or anything else. I just wanted to play. There were ten lessons that came with the clarinet, but the teacher lived on Dufferin Street, just north of Bloor, and when you're fifteen years old in 1937, a teacher who's fifty looks ninety. He looked like an old man and his house smelled of moth balls. It was a real turn-off. Anyway, he showed me where to put my fingers, and from then on I got Benny Goodman records and learned Benny Goodman solos all by myself.

Of course, I didn't know what I was doing. But now I know what I was doing then — I was learning all those chords, I was learning all those fingerings, I was learning all those tunes, teaching my ear to pick notes from the records. That was right from the beginning. That was how I got started.

Inevitably, some of us were more prodigious and started earlier than others. And violinist Bill Richards' story has something to say here:

I was born in Ottawa in 1923. When I was five years old my mother arranged for me to take piano lessons, which went on for several months until the teacher moved away, providing me with a good reason for going to another instrument. When I was six I began taking violin lessons, and after some months my teacher thought I was doing well enough to have me play a little solo in his next recital for his pupils.

When I was eight I played on a radio station whose call letters were CNRO, which stood for Canadian National Railways, Ottawa. Later it became the Canadian Radio Commission, and in 1936 the CBC. I guess you might say I was one of the first musicians to play on the CBC. I began appearing regularly on radio during those childhood years, but every time I did, the union stepped in to stop the performance. They said I was taking work away from the professionals who, by the way, were grown-ups. When I was ten I would get four shows under my belt and the union would complain.

Even so, others had already become still more successful when the rest of us were just starting to get on. And this was the classic story of Ellis McLintock:

In 1937 I was seventeen and going to Parkdale Collegiate and bringing home about $100 a week. I was making seventy dollars every two weeks with the Toronto Symphony, which wasn't too much, but I was also teaching at the Conservatory and doing radio shows with Percy Faith, which all added up to that salary. I guess the principal of

Parkdale was sort of proud to have one of his students with the Symphony; so in order for me to be able to do all that work, he had my classes rearranged.

One day I was driving a brand new car and pulled up beside my Latin teacher, Scotty McGuiness. Everybody at Parkdale who took Latin spoke it with a Scottish accent. But whenever I played a solo at the school I would always include Bonny Mary of Argyle, and little Scotty would be in heaven. Then I flunked a Latin test. So Scotty said, "You know you flunked your Latin test," and I told him, "I didn't have time to study." I explained what I was doing with my trumpet. He knew that I had put in for a teaching certificate, thinking that I would teach one day. Scotty said, "Ellis, teaching is an honourable profession," and I said, "Yeah, but what does it pay?"

"Well, you know I'm the head of the department. It was $6,200 last year."

I said, "Is that all?" and showed him my datebook. He saw fifty dollars today, seventy-five dollars tomorrow, seventy dollars the next day.

"Laddie, you stick to your trumpet," he advised.

In my own case in Toronto, there were other important sides to the early musical education that my friends and I acquired. When we were sixteen or seventeen, for instance, we took streetcars to the corner of King and Roncesvalles, climbed down those 400 steps to Sunnyside (they don't exist anymore), and clung to the high chain-link fence that enclosed the Sea Breeze — the open-air rectangular dance floor located at the east end of Sunnyside on Lake Shore Boulevard West, between the Palais Royale Ballroom and Sunnyside Bathing Pavilion. Whatever was playing, to our ears the music was always exciting, and we wished to God we were up there on the bandstand, playing a hot solo with the band.

We always liked Jack Evans' band which played for "jitney dancing." They were set up on the stage of a bandshell at one end of the marble floor, and to us kids the musicians looked great in their white jackets and black bow-ties. (Many other bands besides Evans' played the Sea Breeze: most of them weren't that good, but our young ears didn't know it yet.) While we watched, glassy-eyed, couples paid a nickel to dance three minutes, then exit through the east gate, hurried along by two men stretching a rope across the floor, which allowed another crowd of dancers to enter through the west entrance.

Playing jitney dances was extremely hard work for the musicians, who barely had enough time between numbers to pick the next tune and begin again. A Sea Breeze job lasted four hours and many brass players' lips buzzed aplenty during the last hour of the job. Among the tunes they played in those years — the late 1930s and early 1940s — were "Curse of an Aching Heart," "The Gang that Sang Heart of My Heart," "Dardanella," "Darktown Strutters Ball," "All of Me," and "Dinah" (is there anyone finah ... in the state of Carolina).

We also took those 400 steps down to the Palais Royale whenever the Palais' owners, Cuthbert and Deller, brought in a big band from the U.S.A., like Artie Shaw or Jimmy Dorsey. We could never buy a ticket (usually $1.50), but we'd stand

ORCHESTRA LEADER JACK EVANS, circa 1938.
Courtesy Evans family

outside all night trying to catch snippets of the music. How great those bands sounded! We knew the names of all the musicians who played the Palais: they were our heroes (quite equal to our other heroes — Charlie Conacher, Joe Primeau, Busher Jackson, and the other players with the Toronto Maple Leafs hockey team).

We waited outside, hoping to hear Artie Shaw play "Begin the Beguine," which started with that wonderful introduction — pop! da dada da - dahh da - bop, pop! - da dada da - dahh da — "Indian Love Call" (with tenor saxophonist Tony Pastor singing the scat chorus), and "A Man and His Dream," sung by Helen Forrest, to us the most beautiful band vocalist in the world, except when Jimmy Dorsey was at the Palais and Helen O'Connell, the other most beautiful band vocalist in the world, was singing "Green Eyes."

Back at home we listened to Dick McDougal on CKEY radio, who played records of all the bands all day long. Who can forget the brilliant trumpet solo by Billy Butterfield at the opening of Artie Shaw's "Stardust." Or Bunny Berigan's "I Can't Get Started With You." After school we would rush home, take out our instruments, and play along with Tommy Dorsey, Benny Goodman, Fats Waller,

40 They Loved to Play

Duke Ellington — all the famous bands, a different band every half hour. We got to know the tunes played by every orchestra so well, that just by groping for the chord changes we learned to play every song in every key.

McDougal also featured the "sweet bands," like Guy Lombardo and Sammy Kaye, which we shunned. You'd never find us playing that Mickey Mouse crap, no sir. (Of course, there were musicians who *liked* that kind of music and actually *tried to play* like Carmen or Lebert Lombardo. We were unaware and too stupid to realize just how rich and famous Guy Lombardo from London, Ontario, would become. He did rise to heights undreamed of even by Luigi Romanelli and the Monarchs of Melody at the King Edward Hotel.)

In the 1940s when the Canadian National Exhibition opened each August, we hurried down to a huge tent near the midway to catch the American bands that played in the huge tent, which had a hardwood floor large enough to accommodate 10,000 dancers. I vividly remember seeing Tommy Dorsey with a young Frank Sinatra, Duke Ellington, Bunny Berigan, Cab Calloway, and all the others who came through every August. And we cursed the CNE managers when they cancelled the event a few years later.

On Saturday afternoons some of us would jam at the Elm Grove, a club (originally a store) on Queen Street West, near Dufferin Street. Because it was a so-called private club, it was allowed to sell beer to club members. Anyone who came into the Elm Grove could become a member by paying a fee of fifteen or twenty cents, thereby entitling that person to buy beer.

Though it actually ended outright "prohibition" some half a dozen years before the U.S.A., Ontario in those days was still at least something of a dry province, meaning no cocktail lounges or booze sold in restaurants, the same as it was in the rest of Canada, with the exception of Quebec. The Liquor Control Board in Ontario had a tight grip on the sale of booze and beer to the public. Only certain affluent private clubs were allowed to sell spirits. Taverns which sold beer did exist but they had strictly segregated sections for "Men Only" and "Ladies and Escorts."

At the Elm Grove we met musicians from across the city who came to join the fun. Guitarists Stan Wilson and Dick O'Toole, trumpeters Jimmy Reynolds, Bill Saila, and Bob Pier; clarinetist Bubs Reed; saxophonists Phil Antonacci and Lew Lewis; and pianists Johnny Burt, Carl Gleiser, and Tiny Perkins were among the more-or-less established players you'd see there on most Saturday afternoons.

As kids just starting out, we looked for other places to play. And if they paid you a couple of dollars for your efforts, so much the better. A number of Catholic churches — Circolo Columbo, St. Agnes, St. Francis, and others — held dances on Sunday nights. And during those formative years when we developed our skills, if your playing impressed the other musicians you might find your phone ringing later in the week, and a leader you never heard of booking you for a job. ("I heard you played some good stuff at that Catholic church, what's it called, the 'Cherkaloh Columboh?' How are you for next Saturday night?") Of course every new connection was flattering. That's how we began.

The Sunday night church dances were organized by the priests, "to keep our young people off the streets." One priest I recall, Father James Dale, would speak to the dancers during the band intermissions at Circolo Columbo, stressing the benefits of remaining celibate until marriage. It was sound advice that was generally accepted respectfully.

There was, of course, always the possibility of a lucky strike presenting itself, in which case, to hell with the priest's lousy advice, because an unquenchable fire burned in every young man's loins. In Toronto the Good in those years, on the other hand, the shame and embarrassment of an unmarried pregnant girl was a fate worse than death. Usually the young people did just come and dance. And we just supplied the music.

The Jobbers

Soon enough we began booking a greater variety of jobs, including school dances, New Year's parties, conventions — all sorts of affairs. We also played at summer resorts, working weekends at Minet's Point, Port Elgin, Bala, Port Colborne, anywhere the Model T Fords would take us. Those non-union jobs paid from fifty cents to two dollars. The money may have been important to us, but our real reward came just from playing that beautiful music. God, how we loved to play!

My own first job came very early. I only cringe a little when I remember it now. At the age of fifteen Jackie Kane (an alto sax and clarinet player, somewhere on the order of Benny Goodman), Earl Freeman (a drummer with a full head of hair like Gene Krupa and a ton of equipment [bass drum, tom-toms, cymbals, snares, high hat, woodblock, cowbells, for example], somewhere on the order of Gene Krupa), and myself (somewhere on the order of Miff Mole, Jack Teagarden, and Tommy Dorsey, but with a twenty-five dollar made-in-Czechoslovakia Wallace trombone, held together with elastic and plumber's tape) got a New Year's Eve job at the Tri-Bell Club, a second-story meeting hall over a store on College Street, near Bathurst. The gentlemen who hired us were kind, respectful, sports aficionados whose interests in thoroughbred racing, hockey, gambling, and poker brought them together several times a week.

New Year's Eve, of course, was the night to celebrate. We were promised $1.50 each to play dance music, from 9:00 PM to 1:00 AM. It was our first professional engagement and we'd practised diligently for weeks to be ready for the big night.

At the appointed hour the trio, each decked out in black tie, assembled on a makeshift stage in a corner of the room designated as the "ballroom," ready to go. Jackie Kane, who informed us that he would be the leader, beat off the tempo for the first tune, "Christopher Columbus," a popular Fats Waller composition. The Tri-Bell men and their ladies stood around, fascinated by the music, some with their mouths open. A couple tried to dance but were so taken with the lilting strains of the performers that they decided to stand and listen instead. Boy, we gave it all we got!

LLOYD "STEVE" RICHARDS BAND, 1938. Bass player is a young Murray Lauder, Howard Gallagher is on piano, with Mary Moir as vocalist. Leader Richards was then, as today, a fine trombone player. *Courtesy Murray Lauder*

When the trio played the last chord of "Christopher Columbus", the crowd muttered something indecipherable. We took that to mean they wanted more of the same. Kane thought it was time to show off our improvisational skills. Standing up with his clarinet tucked into his armpit, à la the King of Swing, he called out "Bugle Call Rag" and beat out a tempo so fast that the opening bugle call was an imbroglio of pots and pans dropped from the roof of a three-story building.

The next ten choruses played by everybody in cacophonic free-style featured some red-hot solos interspaced with some incredible ensemble work, which to the listeners was probably a nightmare, but to us the next thing to being in heaven.

At the end of "Bugle Call Rag," Mr. Foster, one of the Tri-Bell leaders, approached us, counting out $4.50 in quarters, which he doled out to each musician. "Thanks a lot boys," he said. "You have surpassed our wildest dreams. We would like you to pack up and take the rest of the night off, so you can enjoy New Year's the way it should be enjoyed."

We respectfully told him that we were prepared to play until 1:00 AM, that we wouldn't think of taking advantage of the guests by leaving early, but he persisted. "No thanks, fellows. I can't thank you enough for this amazing experience. I wish you each lots of luck in your chosen professions." (Some fifteen years later, in fact, Jackie Kane had become the Jack Kane who wrote superb arrangements for CBC television shows, including his own "Music Makers" program, until his unfortunate death in 1961.)

Coming of Age *43*

In the late 1930s and 1940s, very few of us owned cars (and many were too young to drive in any case). To get to a job we took the public system, operated by the Toronto Transportation (later Transit) Commission, sometimes to the outreaches of the city. It was one thing to climb on a TTC streetcar on the way to the Royal York Hotel with a saxophone or trumpet case, but when a drummer had to get on with all his equipment — bass and snare drums, a case filled with sticks, mallets, cowbell, triangle, wood blocks, cymbals, high hat stand, and so on — the conductor would often order the embarrassed clown to move down to the rear, even when there was no room to move anywhere.

Of course, every double-bass player getting on a crowded streetcar has also been the butt of every joke and insult, from "Let's see you put that fiddle under your chin and play us a tune" to "Couldn't you have brought a piccolo instead?"

Not only could getting to the job be a chore, but getting through the main doors of a posh hotel could also be intimidating. Quite often musicians were not even allowed to carry their equipment through the lobby, or get on an elevator with civilians on their way to the same function as the musicians. They had to enter by the hotel workers' entrance — usually at the rear of the building, through an alleyway — and take the service elevator.

Even journeymen musicians were, I suppose you could say, just workers after all. In any case, at this point we became the journeymen musicians, the "jobbers" who played for the dozens of bandleaders who booked conventions, club dances, floor shows, all sorts of affairs at the Royal York Hotel, the "King Eddie," Masonic Temple, Arcadian Court, Hart House, and Palais Royale. Everywhere we went we were told to show up on time, ready to play (sometimes even in barns). Dress was the Toronto musician's tuxedo — black suit, white shirt, black bow-tie, black shoes, black socks. Not brown — black.

Toronto was a jobber's Friday and Saturday night town, which meant most jobs took place on those nights. Not much doing the rest of the week, except in December when Christmas parties almost every night of the week became a bonanza for musicians. And although we made what we thought was good money then, the leaders who had not booked their best players early enough were often saddled with the leftovers — the misfits who came to the job with instruments they could barely play. How those nights dragged! One bad musician could turn an evening of otherwise joy into a night of misery.

"If you ever hire that sonovabitch again don't call me," we would tell the leader, but we soon dropped our objections when the phone rang a few weeks later. We were glad to book anything and everything because of the opportunity to play. The money only became important if we had bills to pay, or we needed to buy a 'jar,' or the leader took longer than the usual month and a half to mail the cheque.

We played for Eddie Stroud, Jimmy Fry, Russ Barraca, Ferdy Mowry, Jack Evans, Rudy Spratt, Bennie Louis, Jimmy Amaro, Don Gordon, and anyone else who phoned us to do a job — even a sideman who happened to book a cousin's wedding or a company dance on his own. (The nature of the business in Toronto during those years was such that Friday's sidemen could become Saturday's leaders. And the musicians' union was the only union in the world that admitted employers and employees into its membership, and charged the same union dues to each, to receive the same protection.)

In the winter of 1940 at age eighteen, before I joined the union, I dropped out of Central Technical High School to play with Don Blackburn in Barrie — then a small rural town about fifty miles north of Toronto, whose main street was just a wide spot in the road. The job was at a place called Town Hall, where soldiers from nearby Camp Borden came every evening, to dance with the town girls (and sometimes try their luck in other ways).

The band included: bassist/leader Blackburn; Lew Paisley, a much-older-than-the-rest-of-us trumpet player; Bill Carter, a nice guy who played tenor sax; Bill Carney, a very good piano player; and Charlie Carlyle, a drummer with a carbunkle on his cheek, who left his job as an undertaker's apprentice to play in Barrie, and who had a Model T Ford that would drive us home to Toronto every Saturday night, and pick us up on Mondays to get us back again in time for the job. It was a very good band for a bunch of kids (plus one adult who probably needed the money more than the rest of us). We played arrangements of the latest tunes, written by most of the guys, and the job was a lot of fun. Barrie was a nice town with a lot of friendly people, who treated us like big shots for a change.

We used to eat in the Harmony Grill, a diner owned by a handsome Greek named Jack Stanwyk. He spoke with a heavy accent which always fascinated me. He was very friendly, and after he got to know us well enough he would give us fatherly advice on saving our money. He would warn us as well: "Watch out forrr bahd gerrls. Dey get you in trrrouble." And we often heard a baby crying upstairs. Jack proudly told us the baby's name was Alan. Twenty-five years later I played on CBC television shows with a very fine trumpet player and a wonderful guy who gave us a lot of laughs — the same Al Stanwyk we heard crying upstairs in the Harmony Grill that winter of 1940 in Barrie.

My having left school during my third year at Central Tech didn't go over too well with my father, who only six years earlier was still using the strap to beat some sense into me whenever I pulled a brilliant stunt, like dropping out of school. But this time Dad was resigned to the inevitable: Since I wanted to play so badly and had lost all interest in continuing my studies to become a cartoonist, there wasn't much he could do about it. I would be earning thirty-five dollars a week, not bad during those Depression years, and I would be coming home every Saturday night with the money (which I would otherwise squander) to be with the family Sundays and Mondays, until I would leave again Monday afternoon to return to my new six-nights-per-week occupation. And, besides, at eighteen I was too big for Dad to pull his belt off and give me one for the road.

Every evening that Town Hall job was not really complete unless and until the soldiers had been embroiled in several bloody fist fights (usually over who owned the rights to a girl). The fights finally had to be quelled by the five or six military policemen who, at the pleading of dance hall entrepreneur Charlie Johns, had to be present in the dance hall every night from 9:00 PM to the midnight closing. By the time the soldiers returned to Camp Borden every night, there was blood on the Town Hall floor that had to be cleaned up. And there was often some similar blood in a few of Barrie's restaurants and other meeting places as well.

I left the Don Blackburn band in March 1941 because I had fallen in love with a girl named Pat, with whom I had taken my "maiden voyage." Soon enough, however, this turned out to be a disaster. And, spurned by my girl, I returned to Toronto. After I'd been back awhile, somebody told my father: "It was good experience for the boy." I think my father agreed. But he said nothing about it to me.

Back in Toronto, I returned to the big-city musical routine. Although the place was still a Friday and Saturday night town at this point, some among my old crowd of journeymen musicians had begun to play for Stanley St. John, a society orchestra leader, in great demand by the wealthy Rosedale crowd. Stan would often book two and three jobs on the same night, and not necessarily Fridays and Saturdays. When that happened he would appoint one of the older musicians he could trust: one who knew how to manage an engagement, pick the right tunes at the right time, smile at the crowd, make the correct announcements, act just right, like a leader.

There was no fooling around on these jobs: no drinking, no talking — only professional behaviour. But if he liked you, you could do a lot of work for Stan. The music might not be to your liking (no jazz or other "far-out" fare) but, what the hell, it was pretty good money. You would play waltzes, fox-trots, the latest popular songs, like "Red Sails in the Sunset," "Did You Ever See a Dream Walking," "Cocktails for Two," all on stock arrangements bought at local music stores (Whaley Royce on Yonge Street or Eaton's Music Department), for seventy-five cents or one dollar. To liven up the crowd, just at the right time Stan (who played piano) would count off a bright tempo, and the band would launch into "Doing the Hokey Kokey." Stan's drummer, a smiling leprechaun named Bert Meechim, bounced up and down behind his drum set as he beat out the rhythm, and the crowd usually went wild.

Some of us auditioned for Stan in his home on Cortleigh Boulevard in north Toronto. He would show off his home with pride. I remember him taking me through the rooms of his magnificent house, pointing out the exquisite wallpaper in each room even before I opened my trombone case. He even showed me the wallpaper in the bathroom: it, he said, had come from Belgium (and, of course, being a wallpaper man, I understood enough to express profound admiration).

The audition consisted of playing the second trombone part of a stock arrangement which kept the trombonist playing melody usually in the lower register. (Not the best way to show off your extraordinary ability, and I was still quite young and not a very good player, but I must have gotten by.) Then Stan would take out his little book and tell you where he wanted you to show up for the job. His jobs were always in the best places: the Granite Club, Eglinton Hunt Club, or in one of the Royal York or King Edward Hotel ballrooms. He didn't specify the dress, but you knew it was the Toronto musician's tuxedo: black suit, white shirt, black bow tie, etc.

The people we would play for on Stan's jobs were different from those we'd find on other jobs. These were the city's wealthy folks, mainly from North Toronto or Rosedale. They dressed beautifully, never behaved badly, never made too much noise, and always acted in the best of taste. They also drank a lot.

Stan St. John himself was not only a busy orchestra leader, with dozens of jobs every month, but a rather wealthy man in his own right. He invested heavily in the stock market, always seemed to know which stock to buy, and was always free with his advice — always willing to share his good fortune. The alto sax player Hank Rosati, remembers a particular case of Stan's generosity:

> Stan was always talking about all the money he was making. One night his bass player, Freddie Ford, said, "Hey Stan, I've got a fair bit of money stashed away in the bank. I could sure use some advice on what kind of stock I could put my money into. Can you recommend something?"

STANLEY ST. JOHN CONDUCTING CBC ORCHESTRA, circa 1940. The "Good Year Hour" rehearsal and broadcast, seen above, took place at the McGill Street studios. Some of the musicians are trumpeter Jimmy Reynolds, trombonists Ken Houston and Alfie Wood; horn player Cliff Spearing; saxophonists Lew Lewis and Ben Paul; violinists Blaine Mathe and Bobby Steinberg; and cellist Charles Mathe. *Courtesy Stanley St. John*

Always quick to help his musicians in any way he knew, Stan recommended a couple of sure fire items that couldn't miss. He recommended two, which we'll call A and B. "These two stocks are great ones," he told Freddie.

Freddie, who always wore a serious expression on his face, who hardly ever joked about anything, said, "Are you sure, Stan? I've never invested in the market before, and I'd hate to lose any money."

Stan assured him. "Nothing to worry about, Fred. If I tell you to buy these stocks, you'll thank me many times over."

The next week we were playing somewhere and Freddie asked, "Stan, did you buy any of those two stocks you told me about last week?"

Stan said, "Yes, as a matter of fact I did."

Freddie asked, "Which one did you buy?"

Stan said, "I bought A. The minute I bought it, it went zooming up through the ceiling. Made a killing, if I say so myself. Why do you ask? Which one did you buy?"

Fred said, "I bought B. It went zooming down through the floor. Thanks a lot."

"Play by the rules: the Union'll look after you ... "

Of course, even beyond the upscale world of Stanley St. John, the best jobs were the steady engagements which offered security for those who could find weekly employment in a night club or hotel dining room, anywhere.

Happily enough for us, customers who sought escape from the problems of the Great Depression years (and even the early part of the war) often found it in an evening of dining and dancing at a favourite night spot.

During the 1930s and early 1940s a number of Toronto bands enjoyed steady seasonal employment at such places — Ferdy Mowry at the Club Embassy at the north-east corner of Bloor and Bellair; Trump Davidson at the Club Esquire in Sunnyside; Frank Busseri at the Hollywood Hotel on the Queensway at Royal York Road; Henry Kelnick, Ozzie Williams, and others at the Silver Slipper (that special club located on Riverside Drive, just north of Lake Shore Boulevard, on the east bank of the Humber River); Nelson Hatch at the Old Mill; and Bobby Cornfield in Simpson's Arcadian Court.

And (as I've already talked a bit about) the cream of steady engagements were with Luigi Romanelli in the Oak Room of the King Edward Hotel, and Horace Lapp, Mart Kenney, Frank Bogart, Johnny Linden, Moxie Whitney, Howard Cable, and others in the Imperial Room of the Royal York Hotel.

We also played for Trump Davidson, Bert Niosi, Earl Hawkins, Sam Silver, Jimmy MacDonald, and various others at the Balmy Beach Canoe Club, the Boulevard Club, Toronto Badminton and Racquet Club, the Savarin, the Hollywood Hotel, Bloor Casino, Fallingbrook Pavilion, Casa Loma, Club Top Hat (formerly Club Esquire), and the Sea Breeze in Sunnyside. (Almost all these places no longer exist — at least as they did then — but for people like me they still conjure up memories of magic moments.)

One way or another, as the months and years of lessons and playing passed and our skills improved, we ultimately found ourselves playing more prestigious jobs than the ordinary three- and four-hour dance gig. One in particular stands out for me. Because I was still in my teens, an emotional juvenile in love with the music that engulfed me, I especially remember the Toronto Skating Club's annual ice show at Maple Leaf Gardens in 1940. It featured two orchestras: Puff Addison's Toronto Symphony Concert Band, and Jack Jardine's forty-piece orchestra, which played music a concert band would never touch (popular swing and dance tunes, for example). Both were located up in the old blue-seat section at the west end of the Gardens, side by side.

ELLIS MCLINTOCK IN MID-CAREER.
Courtesy McLintock family

As the skaters went through their colourful choreographed routines on the ice, one of the pieces Addison's Concert Band played was Tchaikovsky's *Cappricio Italien*. And it was on that particular week-long job that I first came to realize the true extent of Ellis McLintock's enormous talent, when he played the dramatic trumpet fanfare in the slow introduction (based on bugle calls heard by Tchaikovsky at the barracks of the Royal Cuirassiers on a visit to Italy in 1880).

It became clear to me that the great composer wrote the fanfare with only an Ellis McLintock in mind. When Ellis held his trumpet high and played the solo, pearl-like notes flew from the bell of his instrument with machine-gun staccato precision, piercing the cool Gardens' air. Every time he played it, the blood froze in the veins of every musician in both orchestras. "How was it possible for a mere mortal to execute the difficult passage with such ease?" we muttered. Or was Ellis more than just a mere mortal?

From a more practical point of view, playing engagements like the Toronto Skating Club's show at Maple Leaf Gardens could never have taken place unless even we mere mortals had joined the Toronto Musicians' Protective Association.

Walter Murdoch was the union's president, and Arthur Dowell its secretary. After collecting the twenty-five dollar initiation fee, Dowell swore in new members. One of the questions he always asked was, "Have you ever played a non-union job?" Some conscientious individuals such as Hank Rosati told the truth and admitted they had. This automatically brought a fine that took months to pay off, and dampened the early rewards from one's new and now altogether professional career. Most of us just gulped and said we hadn't. But we did wonder: how was it possible to break into the business without playing non-union jobs first?

In any case, Arthur Dowell's question remained indelibly burned in our brains for the rest of our lives. When you join the musicians' union you do not violate the key commandment: "Thou shalt not play with non-union musicians." Playing with non-union musicians, Dowell explained, was unfair to the musicians who were union members who knew they must work for union scale, not a penny less. At the end of the swearing-in ceremony, Arthur Dowell's final words were prophetic to our young ears. "Play by the rules, boys," he said, "and the union'll look after you." (And most union members would heed almost all Dowell's commandments, throughout their subsequent careers.)

The world was our oyster as we stepped into the big time. But it soon came crashing down when we found an unscrupulous leader or employer paying less than scale. When that happened we learned that the Toronto Musicians' Protective Association was indeed our saviour. Murdoch or Dowell always went to bat for us with a vengeance, and we usually got the money we were promised. Whatever else he may or may not have been, President Walter Murdoch was so convincing, his personality so strong, that he was often referred to in the newspapers as "Canada's Music Czar."

Being in the union, on the other hand, did not automatically solve all your problems. Drummer Jimmy Cooke (who would eventually wind up with Horace Lapp) remembers some odd parts of his early experience as a complete and now-certified professional:

I joined the union in 1932 and worked with Russ Barraca in a number of Catholic churches. Not only church dances but a lot of Italian weddings too. Then I graduated to Jack Evans. I was with Jack for two and a half years, which wasn't easy because Jack was particularly hard on drummers. Two and a half years was a record but I stuck it out. We had many an argument, many a battle. I would quit every night, and he would phone my mother, who thought he was great. Jack would say, "That Jeemy walked out on me again." And she would tell me to go back to him.

Jack played at Columbus Hall on Sherbourne Street, a block below Bloor. Columbus Hall was a mecca for dance bands in those days. In those days there was nothing more popular than a music battle, a battle of the bands — Jack Evans against Jimmy Barber, or against Jimmy Fry. I didn't only play with Jack but with other bands too when I wasn't playing at Columbus Hall.

On one particular battle, I didn't realize until it was too late (when I booked them) that I was playing with two bands on the same night. It was at Columbus Hall, where I had one set of drums on the stage and another one set up on the dance floor. I would play one number with Jack, then jump down on to the floor and slide along to my other drum set, and play with that band. This went on all evening, and I wasn't very popular because I had double booked. Both leaders fired me. Each one said I played better with the other band than with them.

Another time we were playing a music battle against an all-girl band. We were all set to hear them play when their drummer took sick and couldn't play. So they asked me if I would sit in for her. You can imagine the ribbing I got when all the musicians who were scheduled to battle later in the evening came in and saw me playing with the girls' band. Boy, it took me a long time to live that down. They kept ribbing me for weeks.

Hart Wheeler tells another story that has something to do with girls' bands — and also shows how your ultimate union destiny couldn't protect you from quite everything in a young Toronto musician's life:

One afternoon in 1938 the gang I was in decided to go to the Silver Slipper, which was on Riverside Drive, east of the Humber River, just north of Lake Shore Boulevard. We'd heard that an all-girl band was rehearsing there, and the guys didn't need any encouragement to pay the band a visit ... I always carried my Albert System clarinet in my windbreaker. The clarinet, really two sections joined in the middle when you played it, was separated inside the jacket; it was easier to carry it that way. Whenever the mood hit me I'd put it together and play a Benny Goodman solo, no matter where I was. I guess you might say I was kinda nuts, carrying that clarinet day and night.

When we looked through the windows we saw that there weren't any girls at all. It was a band full of guys. So the gang faded but I stayed. I was so interested in hearing the band play. I was enthralled because they were good musicians, especially this tenor sax player, whom I'm sure must have been Phil Antonacci.

All of a sudden I heard a noise behind me. I looked around right into a glaring searchlight coming from a big long flashlight held by a giant cop and I went rigid. "What are you doing here, kid?" he said. "What do you have here?" and opened my windbreaker and saw the clarinet. "What's this?" he yelled. "Where'd you get it?"

"It's mine," I said.

"Oh yeah?" he yelled, and grabbed me by the collar and dragged me out to the front of the building. By now I was covered with white stucco dust from leaning against the window, and being pushed and dragged up the steps of the Silver Slipper. The cop had the clarinet in one hand and me in the other.

He pushed me through the doors and ordered, "Get into the office" and closed the door and locked it, leaving me shivering, while he took the clarinet to the bandstand.

The musicians, of course stopped playing when they saw the policeman. "Who owns this?" he asked, holding up the clarinet. When the musicians said it didn't belong to them (and besides, who in his right mind would own an Albert System anyway), the cop came back to the office, accompanied by the manager and the musicians. "Is this really your instrument?" he asked again. When I said it was mine, that my aunt bought it for me, he said, "Okay, let's hear you play it."

All of a sudden the Hollywood lights went on. The cameras started to grind away, and I had a command performance. I put the mouthpiece between my lips and played my very best Benny Goodman solo. When I finished everybody applauded. "Well, I guess it is your clarinet after all," the cop said, and left.

Mr. Hawe and His Friends

My own coming of age in the Canadian music business in Toronto, during the late 1930s and early 1940s, had almost everything to do with the strictly popular music of the time. But other students, those who played string instruments, were directed towards classical music, the music of the great composers. In the 1930s and 1940s there were many more fine violinists emerging in Toronto than a city of its size should normally produce. What were the conditions during those early years that allowed the extraordinarily large number of top calibre violinists such as Albert Pratz, Hyman Goodman, Sam Hershenhorn, and others to surface? Was it the fierce competition to be the first to reach the pinnacle of recognition? Or was it anxious insecurity to clamber over ghetto walls in order to earn society's respect?

Whatever the reason, even though the local symphony orchestra was far from internationally famous, English-speaking Canada's largest big city was already becoming known in the world's musical communities for its excellent string players. And the later celebrated conductor Victor Feldbrill has some intriguing memories here, from the early days of the Second World War in Toronto itself:

In 1941 when I was an eighteen-year-old violinist, Sir Ernest MacMillan gave me the chance of a lifetime. He asked me to conduct the Toronto Symphony for twenty minutes of a rehearsal. Twenty minutes to rehearse a six minute piece! He sat with a smile on his face as he watched from the balcony of Massey Hall.

So George Bruce, the personnel manager, came to me and said, "Young man, you've got a future, but be careful how you speak to these violinists."

I revered all those guys. I'd heard that all the international conductors who conducted the Toronto Symphony said the first violin section was on a par with any in the world. They were all top professionals. (I was studying with one of them.) "There's no better first violin section anywhere," they said. Imagine this little punk getting up and telling them how to play! But I was careful and we got along well.

Successful symphony and studio musicians advise students that the surest way to success lies in following the teacher's instructions to the letter, taking the latest lesson to your study room and practising long hours, a discipline of repetition and self-appraisal, of constant listening to the sound and technique of professional soloists and comparing what you hear to your own performance, of concentration and playing with enthusiasm and determination. Slowly but surely, the students who persist and seize every opportunity ultimately find themselves in the ranks of the top professionals. Still, there were those among the emerging top players who were never satisfied with their performance. Hyman Goodman told me:

I wished I had been lucky enough to meet a great teacher, because then I would have been a better fiddler. How much can a teacher show you how to make a warm and full sound? Plenty, because seventy percent of fiddle sound is in the right arm. Taste is personal, that is true. But intonation is a must, and sitting down and working on the Carl

Flesch scale book which was my Bible, as it was David Oistrakh's, too, and the Kreutzer exercise book. I played forty-two études every day, and loved them.

When I think about the few really great musicians Toronto produced in the 1930s and 1940s, I can't help but think about Teddy Roderman. I first met Teddy in 1937, when I was coming out of the house he lived in with his parents and relatives on Bellwoods Avenue, after having taken an arranging lesson with his Uncle Lou Little. I was fourteen and had just begun learning to play the trombone. A sweaty, ratty-faced twelve-year-old kid, wearing a baseball glove and cap, came up the veranda steps and we shook hands. He also had begun trombone lessons with Mr. Hawe, who was due to arrive any minute. Soon enough it would be clear to everyone that Ted was a natural — and certainly one of the finest trombonists who has ever come out of Canada.

THE TROMBONE SECTION OF THE MODERNAIRES, 1942. In the Masonic Temple, Yonge and Davenport. Trombonists are Murray Ginsberg, nineteen, and Teddy Roderman, seventeen.
Courtesy Mary Burns(Bates)

Mr. Hawe used to tell us: "That young Roderman boy thinks he's fooling me when I give him his lesson. Most of the time I see a swollen circle on his lips, not from intense practising, but from pressing the trombone mouthpiece against his mouth for a few minutes. He wants me to think he's been practising for hours." Many years later, however, when Harry Hawe died, he left his trombone to Teddy.

My War in England

From the summer of 1939 to the spring of 1945, the biggest event in Canada, even for young and obsessed professional musicians, was the Second World War. The war finally caught up with me on September 20, 1942. I joined the band of the Royal Canadian Ordinance Corps and was shipped off to Barriefield, near Kingston, Ontario.

We marched about the base and played stirring military music (which, because of the peculiar physiography of the area, could be heard for miles around). Then, on December 4, 1942, I was transferred to the Royal Canadian Army Show. At first we were in Montreal, and then we moved to Toronto to rehearse for a tour of military camps and bases across Canada. For most of 1943 we travelled around the country with a Broadway-type production, featuring the then quite young comics

Johnny Wayne and Frank Shuster, and assorted other entertainers, accompanied by a forty-piece orchestra.

When we reached Port Arthur, Ontario, a new bass player from the Camp Borden 48th Highlanders Band joined the Army Show orchestra. His name was Murray Lauder. I can't exactly remember if we'd met before, or just how we met in the Army Show. But Murray and I became very good friends, and he figures in almost all my wartime memories. Whether it was at a jam session or a band rehearsal, the first thing I noticed about Murray's bass playing was his pure sound. To me, there is nothing more beautiful than the pizzicato sound of a bass violin — probably the most important instrument in any jazz band. When Murray plucked a string on his double bass the pure sound boomed out to fill the room. What joy his playing brought to the musicians who played with him!

Rather late in 1943, after the Army Show tour had played the west coast and returned to Toronto, we had a couple of weeks leave. Then we met again to rehearse a new show (or so we thought). Quite unexpectedly, however, our commander, Colonel Victor George, walked out on stage one morning in the middle of rehearsal at the Victoria theatre in Toronto, in late November 1943, and announced: "An order from Ottawa: This new show you have all been working on is cancelled. The Army Show will be broken up into five concert parties and will be moving to England within weeks." The five units were: A and B (orchestra shows); C (the tall girls, I think); D (short girls — if I'm right about C); and E (Wayne and Shuster). We began writing and rehearsing new material immediately. Everyone pitched in. We had to be ready as soon as we landed in England.

We arrived in Liverpool on December 21, 1943, and boarded a train to Aldershot that same day. Our Unit A band show included: trumpeters Art Oakley and Denny Farnon; myself and Jack Madden on trombones; saxophonists Brian Farnon (later replaced by Eddie Graf), Bob Kinsman, and George Leech; pianist Denny Vaughan; drummer Fred Powell; and bassist Murray Lauder. Our strings were: violinists Jack Groob and Leonard Hershenhorn; viola player Steve Kondaks; and cellist Tadeus Konjalava. May Mends sang, Betty Mason, Stan Tasker, and Frank Cassidy danced, contortionist Penny Brander contorted, and Don Hudson was our magician. Sgt.-Maj. Bill Charles conducted and drank all of our booze.

We played jazz, and we featured a very funny Tramp Band (four musicians who wore silly costumes and clowned around), and we entertained the Canadian and British troops in southern England and on the continent. Before the June 6, 1944 invasion of France we performed throughout Surrey, Sussex, Kent, and the rest of the south: all beautiful English countryside. The soldiers (and the few civilians who were able to see a performance) loved the show. We met many nice Brits who showed their gratitude by inviting us in for tea and cakes. We sometimes played as many as ten shows a week — generally from Monday to Friday, with the odd show on the weekend.

On most weekends most of us went to London where we stayed at special hostels provided for Canadian servicemen on leave. ("Show your weekend pass to the desk clerk and get a free bed for the night.") On one such weekend in April 1944, Murray Lauder and I checked into the Cartright Gardens hostel on a Saturday. After taking in the sights, which included a pub or two and grabbing a bit of supper at one of the Lyons Corner Houses in the west end, we walked into the Feldman Swing Club, 100 Oxford Street, at eight o'clock, where we'd been told nightly jam sessions took place.

We'd been told right. On approaching the club we heard the lively music out on the street. When we entered the packed room, an overflow of American, Canadian, and British musicians were blowing the roof off of "Sweet Georgia Brown." I recognized the great American tenorman Sam Donahue, and Tommy Dorsey's clarinetist Johnny Mince playing alongside the wonderful British trombonist George Chisholm and trumpeter Kenny Baker.

We looked for an empty table. Nothing in sight. Lauder spied a few RCAF musicians and said, "I'll see you later." I discovered a table with two pretty girls.

"Mind if I sit down?" I asked.

"Please do," said the dark-haired one, a beauty.

"I'm Murray Ginsberg," I said.

"I'm Myra Rosengarten," and pointing to her blonde friend, added, "and this is Mavis."

ARMY SHOW ORCHESTRA IN FEBRUARY, 1943. Rehearsing the stage show at the Victoria Theatre before the cross-Canada tour of army camps and war bond rallies. Some of the musicians are violinists Bill Charles, Jack Groob, and Eddie Sanborn; cellists Tad Konjalava and Charlie Dojack; bassist Peter Sinclair; guitarist Tony Bradan; accordionist Ned Chiaschini; pianist Denny Vaughan; saxophonists Brian Farnon, Moe Weinzweig, and Lew Lewis; trumpeters Babe Newman and Denny Farnon; trombonists Jack Madden and Murray Ginsberg. Conductor (back to camera wearing braces) is Frank Fusco, seen here rehearsing the male chorus. *Murray Ginsberg, private collection*

"Can I get you a Coke or something?" I asked. But they both already had their drinks. In any case, despite the marvellous music, I spent the next half hour falling in love with Miss Rosengarten. She had a gentle voice, and when she spoke her words flowed mellifluously, like honey. When she wasn't looking at me, I studied her dark eyes, the delicious curve of her cheeks, her luscious red lips. And her trim figure. Oh me, oh my.

I learned that both Myra and Mavis worked in an office close by. They'd "just nipped in for a bit to hear the music. Smashing, wot?" (Smashing? I wasn't used to the strange jargon. God, they speak funny over here, wot?) The half hour was over in a flash. The girls grabbed their purses and rose to leave.

"Where are you going?" I asked. "Please don't go so soon."

"We promised our mothers we wouldn't be late," Mavis replied.

"Yes, I'm already late," Miss Myra Rosengarten added. God, what a beautiful voice, what a lovely face.

"Well then, can I see you home?" I asked.

"No thank you, I'll be alright," smiled Myra.

"Please let me call you. Can I have your telephone number?"

"Well ... I ... I suppose so. It's 954-7388."

They moved through the maze of tables and disappeared through the door into the night. I called her alright. Many times. And we saw each other a lot after that. Until her Aunt Betty stepped into the picture. Then it seemed something wonderful had ended. Much later I would know that something had really only begun.

Meanwhile, the war continued. On August 15, 1944, a corvette took Unit A of the Canadian Army Show across the channel, delivering us onto the beach of an apple orchard in La Deliverande, Normandy. A sign there declared: "Allied troops, you are entering France as liberators. You are expected to behave as liberators."

For the next six months as we performed, we followed the fighting soldiers up through France, Belgium, Holland, and Germany. When we crossed the border into each country the same sign greeted us: "... you are entering as liberators ... " But when we crossed into Germany, the sign changed: "Allied troops, you are entering Germany as conquerors. You are expected to behave as conquerors."

From time to time Unit A found itself in areas that came under fire (as did the other shows), either from German artillery, buzz bombs, or V2 rockets. To write at all seriously about our experiences, however, would fill volumes. While in England and on the continent we ate together, slept together (a few times on rat-infested floors in a thousand-year-old castle on the Isle of Wight), drank together, and laughed together. Despite the ravages of war and the constant real threat of catching the shell or bomb with your name on it, we did have a lot of laughs. Murray Lauder and I went through it all. And if you want to know about our trip back to Canada in January 1946, on the HMS *Scythia*, the ship that only went up and down while our stomachs went in the opposite direction — don't awsk!

Today in our seventies, Murray Lauder and I still see each other and often talk on the phone. And we laugh when he says, "Hey Mur, d'ya remember the time when Jack Groob organized a show put on by a couple of hookers in Benay Sur Mer in France?"

Jack Groob (one of our violinists) marched all the guys — left, right, left, right, no talking! — to the house, where we were admitted into a bedroom to view the two ladies of the evening tell bad jokes wiz a Frawnsh aug-sant, cavort around on the bed (each wore high rubber boots to keep from getting bruised), and smoke cigarettes and blow smoke rings — but not by placing the cigarettes between their lips. The next day as we were getting ready to do a matinée at the theatre, Denny Vaughan kept looking through a peep-hole in the curtain to see who was in the audience, when all of a sudden he blurted, "The girls are here! The girls are here!" He referred, of course, to the two hookers from ze night before.

Nowadays, thinking about the war also reminds me of the trumpet player, Babe Newman. I'd first met him back home in the summer of 1940 on a job at Minet's Point, on the south shore of Kempenfelt Bay, near Barrie. Before I laid eyes on him I heard a magnificent trumpet warming up behind a wall in the exact style of Bunny Berigan, the fabled New York jazz trumpet player. Babe's ability to produce the same sound as Berigan, the same inflections, licks, and variations was uncanny.

Then I saw Babe himself. He had a pleasant chubby face but was otherwise

UNIT A, SWING PATROL, ARMY SHOW BASE IN GUILDFORD, SURREY, MAY 1945.
While a new show was rehearsing, the war in Europe ended on May 7, 1945. With Jack Groob conducting, Swing Patrol played its first engagement in Amsterdam's City Theatre before an invited audience that included Amsterdam's city officials and the top brass of the Canadian and Dutch armies. Swing Patrol performed in Oldenburg, Germany, while the "non-fraternization-with-the-enemy" edict was in effect. At the time, Canadians (as well as other Allied soldiers) were free to walk into any store in Germany and receive goods and services free. *Murray Ginsberg, private collection*

trim. He was attired in the uniform of the 48th Highlanders Regiment stationed at Camp Borden — kilts, Glengarry cap, and tunic. "Babe" Velmour Newman, born in Prince Albert, Saskatchewan, had joined the 48th band after the war broke out. He remained with it until he was transferred to the Army Show in Montreal, and there I bumped into him again. As with a number of other musicians when the chemistry was right, we became close friends. We enjoyed playing together (his jazz was spectacular), and with Murray Lauder, Hank Rosati, and all the other guys. We enjoyed hanging out together. And we had our laughs.

Babe was Destiny's child, landing wherever the wind blew him. When he tired of sounding like Bunny Berigan, he switched to sounding like Roy Eldridge — just like that. An amazing musician. And the stories of his escapades and love affairs were the sort one reads in a *True Confessions* magazine — like the drama one sees (or used to see) on the silver screen.

Some Giants Who Left Toronto

Some things about the Canadian music scene in Toronto had changed when I got back from the war. And one of them was that some of the best talent had departed for greener (and bigger) pastures. The tenor saxophone player Georgie Auld was a case in point. I heard a story about him when I was doing my interviews.

Georgie went to the States. He played exciting tenor with a couple of name bands. Georgie never wanted to be a saxophone player. He wanted to be a gangster like his brother. He was incredibly good-looking, like a movie star, and he had ladies coming out of his ears. He had a great swinging band. I even played with him for four weeks. That was in January and February of 1946.

I went to New York as a music student. I told the U.S. immigration authorities, who asked about my trumpet, that I was going to take lessons from Charles Colin. I also carried a message from Benny Winestone, written on a serviette to give to Georgie. It read: "Georgie, I want you to hear this kid play." I went to this restaurant about midnight. The band didn't start to play until ten o'clock. I didn't know that. I was from Winnipeg, right? In Winnipeg everything closes at midnight. I handed the serviette to Georgie and said, "Benny Winestone asked me to give this to you." The minute he heard me say "Benny Winestone," he said, "Benny Winestone? How is he? Where is he?"

When he read the note, he said, "Listen, I can't hear you until we're through," and pointed to a couple of booths. "That's where the band sits when they're not playing. When they're on the stand you sit there and listen." So I sat there and heard the band. There were four trumpets and every one of them was a bebopper. Each one played all of Dizzie's licks, all that fast stuff. Oh my God, I thought, I knew I couldn't play that fast. I had no idea of what he was going to ask me to play. I assumed it would be a fast blues or some bebop song like "What Is This Thing Called Love" or "Groovin' High."

Then, three other guys came in with trumpets. Apparently they were going to try out too. Finally around 3:30 the place empties and he tells the rhythm section to stay. He

58 They Loved to Play

calls out, "Hey Canada, you were the first one here, so get your trumpet out. Get up here and play me thirty-two bars of 'Body and Soul.'" So that's exactly what I did. I didn't go too far from the melody, I wanted him to hear my sound and my attack, but I did play a few embellishments. I didn't think of F minor 7th or go in that direction at all. Just as I went into the bridge, Georgie says to the guys, "I've heard enough. See the manager, you're in." Then he said to the three trumpet players, "Look, I've heard what I wanted to hear. I'm sorry you had to come down. Thanks for coming."

I had bumped into another Toronto talent who was no longer around after the war, during my time with the Army Show and Unit A. As I've already noted, two of the three Farnon brothers — Denny (trumpet) and Brian (saxophone) — were actually in the Unit A band, along with Murray Lauder and Jack Groob and Denny Vaughan and myself and everyone else. The most talented of the trio, Bob (or, as it would most often be put later, Robert), had already played a key role in putting together our 1943 Army Show tour across Canada.

Nowadays, it's clear that Bob Farnon has left a legendary legacy. He is regarded by many fellow musicians as the greatest living arranger for strings, in ballads such as "Laura," "A Nightingale Sang in Berkeley Square," "A La Clair Fontaine," and in his marvellous medley from *My Fair Lady*. Rob McConnell, leader of the superb Boss Brass in Toronto today simply says that Robert Farnon is the "world's greatest arranger." And, whatever else, he is certainly one of the greatest musicians who ever came out of Canada.

Born in Toronto in 1917, Bob came from a musical family. His father played violin and his mother played piano. As I've just mentioned, older brother Brian wound up as an excellent alto saxophonist, and younger brother Dennis became a trumpet player. Bob himself first played drums and then trumpet. But he also got into his first love, arranging, at a very early stage in his remarkable career.

By the time he was twenty he became a household name through the many early CBC radio programs he played on, particularly the long-running "The Happy Gang," which came on every weekday afternoon, right after the CBC news. That show, with pianist Bert Pearl as its leader began in 1937 as a two-week summer replacement and ran for twenty-two years. Bob had also been a member of Percy Faith's trumpet section on such CBC shows as "Music By Faith," and on shows conducted by Sam Hershenhorn, Geoffrey Waddington, and others. As a member of Faith's orchestra he would write the choral arrangements, sometimes during rehearsals when he had a few bars "tacet" (or did not have to play).

Bob remained with "The Happy Gang" at the CBC until 1943, when he left to become Capt. Robert Farnon of the newly formed Royal Canadian Army Show. I first met him when he rehearsed the orchestra at the Victoria Theatre for the show's cross-Canada tour. But he took what proved to be his decisive journey across the water under somewhat different circumstances than I did.

A special broadcasting contingent of the Canadian Army Show, with Bob at its helm, landed in England in July 1944. Here they joined American Maj. Glenn

ROBERT FARNON, 1957. With Arthur Jackson, of the Chappell Recorded Music Library.
Courtesy Robert Farnon Society

Miller and British Sgt.-Maj. George Melachrino. And the three orchestras, at the behest of Gen. Dwight D. Eisenhower of Supreme Headquarters, Allied Expeditionary Force, broadcast morale-lifting entertainment to the Allied Forces around the world, via the BBC's armed forces network.

The present-day Toronto broadcaster and big-band enthusiast Glen Woodcock has recently master-minded a CD of the Canadian parts of these old wartime BBC broadcasts, entitled *The Lost Recordings: Capt. Bob Farnon & the Canadian Band of the AEF*. In fact it's a mix of various old radio broadcasts, and it's been pointed out to me that I'm playing trombone on a few of them myself, including a jazz octet version of "Between the Devil and the Deep Blue Sea."

After the war ended, alas, Bob Farnon remained in England. Since then he has worked on over 100 scores for major British and Hollywood films, recorded dozens of albums with the world's major popular, jazz, and classical singers and musicians, won several Ivor Novello and Grammy awards, and been acclaimed by musicians in Britain and North America for his wonderful arrangements.

In January 1997, Robert Farnon was (finally!) named to the Order of Canada. As I write today he still lives with his wife, Pat, on Guernsey in the Channel Islands. Although he has resided in the United Kingdom since the Second World War (and his vocabulary now includes words like "garden" instead of backyard, and "lounge" instead of living room), he still carries a Canadian passport and speaks with a very recognizable Toro'no accent. Not too long ago the magnificent American singer Tony Bennett told a Toronto press conference that "the people of

Canada should build a statue to Robert Farnon for his unparalleled and magnificent contribution to music this century."

Very early on in the war itself, another great Toronto arranger, Percy Faith, had also left town for greater opportunities elsewhere. In this case, the pot of gold was not in the United Kingdom but in the neighbouring United States. Percy Faith was born in Toronto in 1908, and began his musical career as a pianist. The trumpet player Morris Isen remembers:

> Our families lived next door to each other when I was a teenager on Palmerston Avenue, in west Toronto. Percy's mother would complain that her son couldn't practise the piano properly when I practised my trumpet. She said I was too loud."

Both, nonetheless, succeeded in music and rose in the professional ranks — Morris as a CBC studio player and Percy as one of the world's most brilliant arrangers.

In the 1920s Toronto movie theatres cried out for good pianists: every cinema had to have music to dramatize the action on the silent screen. The days of amplified recorded music were still light years away. The better the piano player, the easier it was for him or her to grab a good-paying job. And Percy Faith was one of the best. He had studied piano with Frank Welsman at the Toronto Conservatory of Music. In 1923 he was considered good enough to appear as soloist with the Conservatory orchestra, playing Liszt's *Hungarian Fantasy* at their annual concert in Massey Hall. According to Morris:

> Percy was a "natural." When he wrote his first arrangement for Geoffrey Waddington, it was so good that his future as an arranger was assured.

In fact an injury to Percy's hands, which took place when he was a teenager when he rescued his sister from a fire, had placed at least certain limitations on the ultimate future of his piano playing. Percy went on to study with Louis Waizman, who would become the librarian at the CBC, and he patiently honed his arranging craft. Soon enough he was writing arrangements for anybody who was willing to pay for a magnificent orchestration by Faith — for Luigi Romanelli, Rex Battle, Geoffrey Waddington, Percy Pasternak, and many, many more.

He conducted his first radio show in 1931, and he joined the CRBC (and later CBC) network when it was first established in 1933, as a conductor and arranger. Between 1938 and 1940 he arranged for and conducted "Music by Faith," which also went down to the U.S.A. on the Mutual Broadcasting System. (Some listeners in Canada, who didn't have a clue as to who or what Faith was — thought "Music By Faith" was a religious show.) TSO violinist Harold Sumberg recalls:

> I played on his very first show. In fact, I did all his shows. His string writing was so

spectacular that only the best violinists could play the parts. And he had the very best of Toronto's fiddlers, mostly from the Toronto Symphony.

When I finally did get to know these players, every one said that Percy Faith was a genius. His arrangements were brilliant and colourful and made effective use of counterpoint. And they were years ahead of their time. Later on, American conductors and arrangers such as Andre Kostelanetz and Morton Gould would use symphony-sized orchestras comprised of classical woodwinds, brass, and percussion to perform popular songs.

In 1940 Percy Faith accepted a position in Chicago to conduct the "Carnation Contented Hour" radio show. Somewhat less than overjoyed with the budget cuts and other treatment he had been receiving from some of the executives at Canada's national radio network (who probably weren't aware of his enormous talent), he was happy enough to get the new job in the U.S.A. and said goodbye to the CBC.

In the U.S.A., his fortunes rose dramatically. The "Carnation Hour" (on NBC radio) lasted until 1946. Percy then moved to CBS, where he conducted the Coca Cola show known as "The Pause That Refreshes." In 1950 he was appointed arranger-conductor for Columbia Records in New York City. Then he moved to Los Angeles in 1959, as arranger-conductor for Columbia Records there. And this job carried on right up to his death in 1976.

Faith returned to Canada a number of times to direct Victory Bond Drive shows during the Second World War, and later to conduct concerts and CBC TV specials. I played for him myself on two occasions — once when he conducted the Toronto Symphony at the Forum at Ontario Place, and again when he was brought to Toronto to do a Canada Day telecast. On that second show his arrangement of our national anthem, "O Canada," was so stirring and colourful, with the bass instruments playing an extraordinary descending counter melody to the main theme, that producer Norman Campbell ran excitedly out of the control booth yelling, "That's the greatest arrangement of 'O Canada' I've ever heard!"

From 1950 to 1976 Percy Faith also enjoyed considerable success writing for films, such as *The Love Goddess*, *The Third Day*, and *Love Me or Leave Me*. In the 1970s I actually ran into him a few times when he returned to Toronto to visit family and friends. We shook hands and exchanged a couple of "H'ya doings" in a nice neighborhood restaurant (I forget the name) on north Bathurst Street. On our last such meeting he seemed to be suffering from some illness, but he was all smiles nonetheless. He died in Los Angeles on February 9, 1976.

The Girl Who Never Smiled Again

At about the same time that Percy Faith left for the United States, a beautiful young Toronto woman was making another kind of contribution to North American popular music. And this short but sweet story takes me along several other paths of my own life in the city (and, ultimately, even my musical career).

For me this story starts when I was fourteen years old, and still living with my family at 542 Euclid Avenue, in west-central Toronto. This was where Harry Hawe would come every Saturday at 1:30 PM to give me my first trombone lessons. Across the road and down the street, I used to see two very pretty girls come and go out of another house on Euclid Avenue. At fourteen I always fell in love with every girl I saw, but I was too shy to approach these particular objects of my affection. (Besides, they were a few years older than I was.)

Somehow, however, I learned that they were Ruth and Mickey Lowe. Ruth, the older one, was breathtakingly gorgeous. And, as if that wasn't enough, within a few short years she would become famous, as a pianist and the composer of a lovely song about lost love. Soon enough Ruth Lowe, the piano player, left Euclid Avenue to join Ina Ray Hutton's all-girl orchestra. She toured around North America, playing theatres, ballrooms, and concert halls. In the days of big-band machismo, really successful all-girl orchestras were a rarity. Phil Spitalni's fine group, Ivy Benson's excellent orchestra in England, and Ina Ray Hutton's on this side of the great pond were among the few that thrived.

Ruth Lowe also wrote songs for Ina Ray Hutton's band. Then she met Harold Cohen, a handsome publicist in the music business who showed an interest in her songs. They fell in love, married, and lived in Chicago for a few very happy years, until he died suddenly in 1939 of a kidney ailment. The broken-hearted twenty-four-year-old widow returned to Toronto where she got a job playing on the radio and, to ease her pain, wrote as many songs as she could. One of them was "I'll Never Smile Again," a plaintive lament about her loss of Harold Cohen. Ruth played it on her radio broadcast. Percy Faith was in the studio at the time and asked if he could use it on his show. According to the musicians in the Faith orchestra, his arrangement of the piece was one of the most beautiful they had ever heard.

At this point, the Canadian National Exhibition was bringing in famous American bands to play in a huge tent near the midway — with a portable hardwood floor, large enough to hold 10,000 dancers. In the late summer of 1939, Tommy Dorsey was performing there, and Ruth Lowe took a copy of "I'll Never Smile Again" to him. He was impressed, but held off recording it until 1940 when, with the prospect of the U.S.A. eventually entering the war growing stronger, he felt the time was now right.

Soon enough again, however, Tommy Dorsey's arranger came up with another wonderful setting for Ruth Lowe's song. Dorsey took his band, his Pied Pipers backup singers, and principal vocalists Jo Stafford and Frank Sinatra, into the recording studios and produced a smash hit. With Sinatra singing the melody and the others supporting him, "I'll Never Smile Again" soared to the top of the charts and stayed there for months. Although America was still not yet in the war, the mournful melody touched the heart of the nation.

With the success of her song, Ruth Lowe moved to New York where she came into contact with adulating singers and songwriters. And she also became friendly with Dorsey and Sinatra. When Sinatra announced that he was leaving the Dorsey organization to strike out on his own, Ruth asked him if she could take a crack at writing a theme song. With the help of two other songwriters who wrote the melody, Ruth wrote the lyrics to "Put Your Dreams Away" — another smash hit, and Sinatra's theme song for twenty-five years. (Only when Paul Anka, from Ottawa, wrote "My Way" did the great crooner switch to a new signature tune.)

In 1943 Ruth, tired of the Big Apple, returned home to Toronto. She married investment broker Nat Sandler and they had two sons, Stephen and Tom. Today Stephen is an investment broker and Tom a photographer. He remembers his mother playing the piano every day.

Every night the house was filled with happiness and joy because of Mom's playing. She played all the time.

RUTH LOWE IN HER PRIME, circa 1940.
Courtesy Sandler family

In 1958 Dorsey's recording of Ruth Lowe's "I'll Never Smile Again" was chosen the second greatest popular song recording of all time. ("A-Tisket, A-Tasket," sung by Ella Fitzgerald, was number one.)

Still further down the road, in the late 1960s and early 1970s, I had the band at the Northwood Golf and Country Club on Sheppard West in Toronto. The band, comprised of tenorman Phil Antonacci, pianist Jimmy Coxson, drummer Acey Howard, bassist Jack Richardson, and myself, played for dinner-dancing every Tuesday and Saturday nights. We would also play at the club for private parties on other nights of the week. Quite often Nat and Ruth Sandler would be there as guests of members. I also remember seeing the couple at private parties around the city. On one occasion I was introduced to them, and took the opportunity to tell Ruth that we both lived on the same street years ago. (Yes, she remembered Euclid Avenue, vividly; and no, she didn't know that I lived up the street.) She was unassuming, sincere, and gracious in her compliments about the band.

Even if Ruth had never written songs, I think, she would have been a compelling person. Every time she came into a room, all eyes turned in her direction. At fifty, she was one of the most beautiful women I have ever seen. After I got to know the Sandlers, I was pleasantly surprised when they hired me to play a family affair. Ruth herself died in 1981 at the age of sixty-six. A year later, "I'll Never Smile Again," recorded more than 100 times, was inducted into the American Recording Hall of Fame.

Mart Kenney (the Western Gentleman) and Norma Locke

Toronto was bound to lose some very talented musicians after the Second World War. But it also gained some very talented ones from other parts of the world — and especially from other parts of Canada. Quite a few came from Western Canada. It could even be said that the most successful Canadian big band that ever worked out of Toronto originally came virtually intact from the Canadian West.

In fact, of all the steady engagements enjoyed by Canadian musicians in the mid–twentieth century, the one with Mart Kenney and his Western Gentlemen, endured for the longest time. Kenney was a household name from Victoria to Halifax, and his organization was a Canadian institution. From January 1931, when he took his first band into the Alexandra Ballroom, at Hornsby and Robson Streets in Vancouver, until 1969, when he announced his retirement, and moved from Woodbridge, Ontario, to Mission, BC, there has never been another Canadian group that can claim so much uninterrupted musical history.

Even now it is doubtful that Mart Kenney (even in his eighties) has ever really retired. He still leads a band on dance engagements, and appears as soloist for special functions. Between 1931 and 1976 he and his band travelled across Canada many times and performed in more than 220 different cities, towns, and resorts from Nanaimo, on Vancouver Island, to Charlottetown, Prince Edward Island.

From the end of the war, to the late 1960s, Mart Kenney's band was more or less based in Toronto. Its most authentic roots, however, were in the Canadian West of the Dirty Thirties. The musicians from the 1931 band that opened at the Alexandra Ballroom in Vancouver were: Jack Hemmings, trumpet; Glen Griffiths, trumpet and piano; Bert Lister, tenor and baritone sax; singer/saxophonist Art Hallman (later become an important bandleader on his own); Ed Emel, drums; Hec MacCallum, bass; and Mart Kenney himself, who played the saxophone.

In his son's Toronto apartment in November 1992, he told me how it all began:

We started playing stock arrangements. But as soon as the band got going, I started writing arrangements. I was able to get all of the musicians to write arrangements, which worked out very nicely. Almost everyone played more than one instrument. Art played piano, but when we learned that he played clarinet, we got him a saxophone, since there is a similarity in playing both instruments. When Glen Griffith wasn't required on trumpet, he played piano. At the Alexandra we had a piano at both sides of the bandstand.

Mart and his musicians played the Alexandra until the following spring. In 1931 the country had just begun to suffer through the Great Depression.

The manager said things were so bad that he wanted me to cut scale. As it was, scale was seventeen dollars a week for three nights. The band played Tuesdays, Thursdays, and Saturdays. I got twenty-three dollars as leader, the sidemen earned seventeen dollars. But I had to pay for the music. We tried every gimmick in the book to get people into the ballroom, like charging thirty-five cents admission for ladies before 9:00 PM.

Kenney had chosen his musicians not necessarily for their ability as much as for their eagerness to improve. And improve they did. Under the leader's inspired direction, the band began to develop a distinctive sound.

We auditioned for the Hotel Vancouver, as a summer replacement. The musical supervisor for the Canadian Pacific Hotels liked the orchestra and was ready to sign a contract. But when I told him where we were currently playing, he almost choked on his false teeth. Apparently, the Alexandra Ballroom wasn't the place for a respectable orchestra. It simply wouldn't do to flash posters all over the city announcing, "Direct from Vancouver's gonorrhea racetrack, the Alexandra Ballroom, Canadian Pacific Hotels brings to the Hotel Vancouver for your dancing pleasure, Mart Kenney and his Orchestra." I realized we had to get out of Vancouver to clean up the image.

Since we were doing remote broadcasts for CJOR Radio in Vancouver, I went to station manager, George Chandler, and said, "I would like to audition my orchestra for a job in Waterton Park, but the owners live in Lethbridge. Is there any way we could be sure that they could hear one of our broadcasts?" Lethbridge, Alberta, was just too far away from Vancouver to hear one.

George thought a minute, and said, "I'll tell you what we'll do. We'll wait until after midnight some night, and then boost our power a little bit. We can't do it earlier because there are too many stations on the air. If you write these guys and tell them to tune in to our wavelength on a certain night, I'm sure the broadcast will carry that far." (I think George was as interested as I was to see if we could be heard in Lethbridge.)

Kenney wrote the McLean brothers, the owners who lived in Lethbridge, and asked them to listen to the broadcast. Waterton Park, is located on the Canadian side of the Waterton Glacier International Peace Park, at the south-west corner of Alberta, in the foothills of the Rocky Mountains. On the appointed night, the McLeans heard the high quality of the music and wasted no time in contacting the leader. They were hired for the summer at Waterton Park.

It's not surprising that the McLean brothers were so quick to hire the Kenney orchestra. Kenney had put to good use the meticulous instruction on playing his own chosen instrument that he had received years earlier from the well-known Vancouver saxophone teacher Harry Karr:

Every morning we would begin with a half hour of scales to make damn sure we were in tune … I'd realized you could get away with a lot of things in a ballroom that you couldn't get away with on radio. With the many radio broadcasts that we soon found ourselves doing, it was imperative that the band be perfectly in tune at all times.

In the summer of 1934 at Waterton, Horace Stovin, the Western Regional Director of the Canadian Radio Commission, put Mart Kenney's orchestra on Canada's coast-to-coast network.

Stovin recognized the quality of sound and intonation of the band, particularly since we were playing mostly waltzes at Waterton Park. It all added up to music that was compatible to broadcasting and to listening.

This was also the point at which Mart Kenney's orchestra finally discovered its ultimate winning identity in the Canadian market. Some weeks before the band started the 1934 season at Waterton Park, Kenney had thought a lot about a theme song to open and close the radio broadcasts. He had taken a trip to eastern Canada and the United States, to check out such famous orchestras as Ted Lewis' and Wayne King's. He wanted to learn how they presented their broadcasts. He noted the importance of a theme song, and realized that his band ought to have a western connection, since the broadcasts would be originating from Western Canada.

Finally, coming back on the train I remember searching my memory for hours, trying to think of a suitable theme song. Then I suddenly remembered a sheet of music my mother had kept on her piano for years called "The West, A Nest and You, Dear." I knew immediately that that was the song I needed.

The night before the group opened in Waterton Park in 1934, it had picked up a few extra dollars on a one-nighter at Henderson Lake in Lethbridge. Everyone arrived in the afternoon, early enough to have a rehearsal and try Bert Lister's new arrangement of "The West, A Nest, and You, Dear." Now that they had their theme song, the musicians suddenly knew the band also needed a name, or even an image; something to distinguish it from other orchestras. As Mart remembers:

While we were searching through our folders for suitable numbers to present on the forthcoming broadcast, Bert suddenly called out, "How about The Western Gentlemen?" We all stared at him. Bert repeated, "I'm suggesting Mart Kenney and his Western Gentlemen. How about it?"

When the broadcast finally went on the air, the orchestra opened with tom-toms followed by a short brassy fanfare. The announcer bawled, "Rugged Rhythm from the Land of Rugged Peaks!" The band floated into "The West, A Nest, and You, Dear," as the announcer declared, "From beautiful Waterton Park, in the heart of the Canadian Rockies, it's the music of Mart Kenney and his Western Gentlemen." With a signature tune and an appropriate title in place, that night in 1934 probably marked the real beginning of the Mart Kenney dynasty.

The series of coast-to-coast broadcasts that followed brought us fan mail from all parts of Canada and the American border states. When the CP hotel people heard the first broadcast, they offered us not the Hotel Vancouver, but the Hotel Saskatchewan the following winter.

The success of the radio show led to a summer engagement at Lake Louise — one of Canada's most beautiful resorts in the Rocky Mountains. This was a happy time for the band, Kenney remembers, because when the summer ended they were booked into the Hotel Vancouver. During that job, the band also became a hit with the general manager of the hotel chain operated by the Canadian Pacific Railway.

Mr. Matthews liked the music so much that he took a keen interest in placing the band in other important CPR hotels. Those two gentlemen, Stovin and Matthews, were very helpful to me.

The following summer the Western Gentlemen were sent to the Banff Springs Hotel (the bigger-sister establishment not far to the south-east of Chateau Lake Louise). Then they went back to the Hotel Vancouver. In 1937, they took their first trip east, for an extended engagement at Toronto's Royal York Hotel.

From the moment when Canada joined the Second World War in September 1939, family life across the land was disrupted. The departure of Canada's young men into the services took a heavy toll on the personnel of all manner of businesses and organizations. Like everyone else, Mart read the newspapers to keep up with the war's progress. Much of the time the news was bad, telling of Nazi victories in Norway, Belgium, and France. Kenney's band was, in fact, the first to regularly tour and perform for the Canadian Armed Forces, from coast to coast to coast:

In 1940, I investigated the idea of our band joining the services as an entertainment unit. But four of us were turned down on medical grounds. So I contacted Brigadier Foster who was in charge of Auxiliary Services in Ottawa, and offered our services for the troops. Auxiliary Services wrote back to say that I should get in touch with the camps myself.

This didn't go down too well with Kenney. He wrote back to suggest that the various camp commanders contact him if they were interested. That did the trick.

As a result, on our tour east that September, when we arrived in Saskatoon at noon, army vehicles were waiting at the station to transport us out to Camp Dundurn.

The show that afternoon brought thunderous applause from the young soldiers, who were overjoyed to hear a band that came from their neck of the woods. More tours followed to army camps and air force bases across the country.

From 1943 to 1945, on the Coca Cola company's "Victory Parade of Canada's Spotlight Band," they entertained over 400,000 soldiers, sailors, airmen, and war workers, in some 200 radio performances. Every week on the Trans-Canada Network, audiences shared Mart Kenney's music with loved ones and friends stationed in navy centres, army camps, air force bases, and war factories across Canada. By the end of the war the band really *had* become a Canadian institution.

Just at the edge of this fame, Mart's own personal life began to take a twist. Sometime in 1944, Norma Locke, a singer from Ottawa, caught his attention:

In 1940 when radio personality Byng Whittaker heard the sixteen-year-old singer at the Ottawa High School of Commerce annual concert, he realized she had the voice and personality to become a star. He knew she had been gaining experience jobbing around Ottawa, and she sounded so good that he immediately booked her for a series of CBC shows called "I've Got a Right to Sing the Blues."

Whittaker and his wife moved to Toronto that same year. Norma followed them a year later, and lived with the couple for a while. As Kenney tells it:

The first thing she did was to enroll in the Royal Conservatory of Music to study singing. It was there that she learned the importance of correct breathing, voice technique, and all the other crucial elements required to become a trained singer. Eventually she had enough knowledge of music that she could sit down and sketch out an arrangement on the piano keys — sort of a work sheet, so that someone like Lucio Agostini or Howard Cable could pick it up and go with it. Ultimately, Norma did a couple of Victory Parade Coke shows for us and I was impressed. I invited her to lunch to ask whether she would be interested in joining the band. She said that one of her goals was to sing with our band, but she was concerned that I might hold her to an exclusive contract. I explained that but there would be no objection to her performing outside engagements, providing they didn't interfere with the band's itinerary.

As a result Norma Locke joined the band on February 4, 1944, and it didn't take Kenney long to learn respect for the determined young lady:

In her pursuit of excellence ... Norma approached each song with careful attention to diction and phrasing and sang with flawless intonation and much feeling. She also earned the respect of many of Toronto's top-calibre studio musicians. Later on, "Dream Street," one particular CBC radio show, led by Gino Silvi, called for her to not only sing but to act as narrator. Her clear, warm speaking style set the mood for each new weekly scenario and made that show one of the most popular on the network.

Not long after Norma became part of the band, the leader was so taken with her talent, personality, and intelligence, that he began to look at her with more than just professional interest. In 1952 Mart and Norma were married. And they lived a happy life for almost forty years — until her unfortunate death in 1990.

After the war and so much travelling, in 1946 Mart Kenney and his Western Gentlemen returned to the Royal York Hotel for three years. Then in 1949 Kenney opened the Mart Kenney Ranch in Woodbridge, a small town a few miles northwest of Toronto. The Ranch accommodated over 1,000 people, and many nights the place was packed. It was an open-air nightclub with no roof, and its patrons danced dreamily under the stars.

After more than a few successful years with the Mart Kenney Ranch, the bandleader and his bride began to feel that they'd had perhaps enough of life in the fast lane. They found themselves yearning for some peace and quiet. Finally, in 1969, they sold the Woodbridge dance property and moved to Mission, BC.

MART KENNEY AND NORMA LOCKE, 1980s
Courtesy Mart Kenney

In some respects Mart himself has never quite retired. He will still perform anywhere in the country, whenever he is asked. And when he does, the Western Gentleman still holds firm to his priorities, even today. As he explained to me at the very end of my 1992 interview:

Every time I pick up my saxophone I try to play it better than I played it the last time.

Part Three
The Last Days of Swing in Toronto

TORONTO MUSICIANS PLAYING A SUMMER JOB, circa 1950. This is probably Centre Island, judging from the small bandshell. The day must have been a hot one. Except for the unidentified trumpet player at extreme left, Art Oakley, Fred Davis (trumpets), Steve Richards, and an unidentified player (trombonists) have their shirts off. Saxes are Bob Muse and Mark Mortimer. The other two are unidentified. Drummer is Al Blue. *Courtesy Fred Davis*

At the end of the Second World War in 1945, great waves of refugees scrambled to seek the security of North America. Between 1946 and 1960 Canada admitted close to two million new migrants from other places. A new "baby boom" in the country itself added still more to a growing population. Villages soon became towns; and towns became cities.

People who had worked in wartime factories had lots of money jingling in their pockets and looked for ways to spend it. A building boom exploded across the land. In Toronto the growth of the suburbs exploded as well. In 1953 the Ontario government turned the old city of Toronto and its surrounding suburbs into the Municipality of Metropolitan Toronto, which stretched from the Rouge River on the east to Etobicoke Creek on the west, and from the Lake Ontario waterfront north to Steeles Avenue. The old city had been home to about 630,000 people in 1931. The new Metro Toronto had more than a million people when it was created. By 1971 it would have more than 2 million.

With so much money lying around, the country went on a buying spree. Houses, furniture, cars, and lakeside cottages were snapped up in the 1950s and 1960s. Still more to the point, in 1946 the new Progressive Conservative government of Ontario had liberalized the province's liquor laws. Cocktail bars and lounges sprouted up in the growing Toronto metropolis. The CBC added a television branch to its Canadian radio network in 1952. The Toronto Musicians' Association now had about 2,000 members. Work was plentiful for weekend jobbers, steady hotel orchestras, and studio musicians.

The old British or Anglo-Saxon side of the city had already begun to change between the two world wars. The new migrations after the Second World War just kept changing it more and more. Out of the mixture came many new talented musicians from Toronto, from other parts of Canada, and from the world at large.

They played the night clubs, ballrooms, jazz clubs, concert halls, radio and television studios, and other venues spread across the length and breadth of the city.

New places sprung up particularly in the city's downtown core. The Colonial Tavern on Yonge, and the Towne Tavern on Queen Street, just east of Yonge Street, brought American jazz stars like Billie Holiday, Sarah Vaughan, Jack Teagarden, Phil Napoleon, Coleman Hawkins, Lester Young, and Harry "Sweets" Edison to town. (And in the 1950s the world's greatest bebop saxophonist, Charlie Parker, made a historic recording at Massey Hall.)

Local bands played the Club Norman, Cork Room, Pilot Tavern, Savarin Restaurant, and the Park Plaza Hotel, to name just a few. On most nights after our jobs finished, and especially on Fridays and Saturdays (still the nights most Toronto musicians worked), players from more than a dozen bands would congregate at Bassel's restaurant at Yonge and Gerrard streets, for a hot beef sandwich and a cup of coffee, with friends who might have played at the Chez Paris or Park Plaza Hotel on Bloor Street, or downtown at the Royal York or King Edward hotels. The get-togethers usually began at 1:00 AM or later. They would continue until 3:00 AM, or sometimes as late as 5:00 AM, when the birds would begin to chirp.

THE MODERNAIRES AT THE SEA BREEZE BANDSHELL, 1941. Over the years, the band experienced several personnel changes. Here the musicians, left to right, are: trumpeter Vern Graham; saxophonists Cliff Flaherty and George Naylor; trumpeter Harry Freedman; saxophonist Ken Adamson; vocalist Mary Bates; pianist Roy Patterson; trumpeter Bob Pier; saxophonist Bob Muse; drummer Russ Farr; bassist Vic Goring; trombonist Homer Watson. *Courtesy Mary Burns (Bates)*

Like our counterparts everywhere else, we Toronto musicians had our own language. We would exchange stories about who we'd played with, perhaps book a job for the next weekend, discuss the latest jazz group to hit Toronto, or pass on the latest wisecrack to fly from the lips of Trump Davidson, Local 149's eternal funny man, who held forth at the Palace Pier on Lake Shore Boulevard.

When Bassel's closed its doors for the last time in the 1960s, we started meeting at Joe and Willie Delaurentis' Dell Restaurant on St. Patrick Street, for a bowl of minestrone, a plate of spaghetti and meat balls, and the same latest gossip. By this time, a lot of things had begun to change. And for a lot of people in Toronto the fate of Sunnyside on the west-end waterfront had been a straw in the wind.

By the start of the 1950s, automobile traffic had become so heavy that the city fathers were faced with a series of impossible traffic bottlenecks in many parts of the city. The worst was the one at Sunnyside, created by the hordes of cars and trucks emptying onto Lake Shore Boulevard, as they left King and Queen streets, on their way west towards the Humber and other points. Something had to be done to ease the burden.

Thus, only thirty-four years after the place had been established by the Toronto Harbour Commission, the decision was made to dismantle the famous amusement park. By February 1956, Sunnyside Park had been demolished to make way for the new Gardiner Expressway. From that moment on, things were never quite the same again.

Our sons and daughters never really got to know Toronto as it was during those unforgettable years. Today they seem to accept the heavy metal bands and disco joints as part of the musical landscape of the new metropolis, as though the present has existed since time began. They find it hard to believe that their parents danced to irresistible music played by a lot of swinging bands in such great entertainment emporiums as the Palace Pier, Club Kingsway, Fallingbrook Pavilion, and under the starry skies of the Sea Breeze. And now all these places have just vanished into a nostalgic golden past.

Bert Niosi and the Palais Royale Ballroom

Back when the golden age was still alive, from the 1940s to the 1960s, Yonge Street boasted so many clubs, restaurants, and dives where music was the main item on the menu, that it resembled a mini Greenwich Village or Broadway and 52nd Street, loaded with jazz joints. Every night music blared from every doorway.

Down on Lake Shore Boulevard, at the west-end waterfront, the Palais Royale Ballroom and the Palace Pier had large followings of dancers and music lovers who had patronized both venues for years (even stretching back to the later days of the time between the two world wars). Bert Niosi was a big part of the history of the Palais Royale. Memories of the eighteen magic years when Canada's King of Swing reigned supreme at the Sunnyside Ballroom remain in the hearts and minds of thousands of dancers, many senior citizens today, who often reflect on life as it was at the Palais more than five decades ago. To this day married couples who met and danced to Niosi's music when they were single in their twenties and thirties still talk about those heady times.

Originally built in 1921 as a boathouse, the Palais Royale, under a succession of owners, was a failure not only as a boathouse, but also as a restaurant, night club, and a ballroom-grill. In 1932 its fortunes changed when Bill Cuthbert and George Deller, two concessionaires from Sunnyside Amusement Park, bought the white clapboard building. They hired Whispering Harry Bedlington and his Whispering Orchestra to play for dancing. For the first few months, however, not many people were interested in dancing in the refurbished hall with the special spring-supported wooden dance floor. And the owners turned to talent agent Joe Broderick to see why there were no takers.

"Your price of admission is too high," he said. "Twenty-five cents a person plus ten cents a dance might have been all right ten years ago, but we're going through a depression right now and nobody has any money." What to do? "Lower the entrance fee to ten cents and charge five cents a dance," Broderick replied. "And get a band with some life in it. That should do the trick."

Cuthbert and Deller took Broderick's advice and hired a young Bert Niosi to see if his brand of music would attract crowds. They didn't intend to keep him on for more than one season. Their original plan was to bring in different groups at the beginning of each season, to offer patrons a variety of the best local bands. That was good marketing strategy, they felt. But with the lower admission fee and Niosi's swing music, the crowds began to pour in — as many as a thousand a night. Broderick, Cuthbert, and Deller soon decided on a change in policy: You don't argue with success. As long as Niosi attracted huge crowds, there was no reason to look for replacements.

Eventually, business became so successful and the crowds so large that the partners decided to raise the prices. Cautiously and judiciously, admission went to twenty-five cents, then thirty-five, then fifty, and ultimately, after a period of years, to a straight seventy-five cent charge for men and fifty cents for women. Charging a fee for every dance was abolished. And bouncers still had to control the crowds.

Bert Niosi's first band at the Palais included brother/drummer Johnny, pianist Harold Gray, bassist Johnny Dobson, guitarist Doug Hurley, trumpeter Tony Ferrano, trombonist George Guerrette, alto saxes Gav Morton and Max Fink, and tenor sax Teddy Davidson. Johnny Dobson wrote many of the arrangements, as did Bert. Some songs they played were "Stardust," "Moonglow," and "Smoke Gets in Your Eyes." They did up-tempo tunes as well, especially one of the big hits of the day, "The Music Goes Round and Round" ("I blow the air in here, and the music goes round and round, oho oh ho, oh ho, and it comes out here"). For a while, dancers even performed a cute ring-around-a-rosy routine called the "Big Apple."

When Gav Morton left the band in 1939, a seventeen-year-old Phil Antonacci took his place and blew everybody away. The young jazz musician was so good that he became an integral part of the band and was featured on every tune. In fact, because he was so taken with his new tenorman and wanted to present him to the public as much as possible, Niosi organized a band-within-a-band, with Phil as the centrepiece. And it became a highlight of the Palais' entertainment every night.

The happy union was not all one-sided. For Phil Antonacci the chance to play with the great Bert Niosi was a also godsend:

When I heard Bert play alto I knew that was it. He played it like a violin, beautifully technical. That's where I learned to play at the top register of the horn, which on tenor sax is very difficult. He didn't actually teach me, but I watched him play those beautiful ballads every night and saw how he did it.

At first, house rules were strictly enforced: men had to wear suits and ties; women wore their best dresses. Ladies of the evening were barred from the premises. The emphasis was definitely on dancing cheek to cheek, no breaking apart, no truckin' on down, and no jitterbugging. Short of frisking everyone who entered the ballroom, liquor of any kind was strictly forbidden. The only drinks allowed to be consumed were ginger ale and Cokes. Bouncers patrolled the areas where the people sat at tables and often peeked under a table to see if a brown paper bag containing a bottle was hiding there. Bottles were often confiscated and the offending couple ejected.

Even so, there were those who concealed tiny flasks which went undetected as they paid their way into the hall. The careful ones tippled in the privacy of the washroom cubicles. The sap who was caught putting a bottle to his lips was soon accompanied to the front door and sent from the premises.

If a single male was foolish enough to try to cut in on a dancing couple, which ultimately led to a ruckus, the culprit soon found himself sailing through the Palais Royale doors onto the pavement. The bouncers at the Palais were the toughest in Toronto. As one of my interview informants much later explained:

Despite the tight crowd control practised by the bouncers, on some nights fights broke out more than once during the four-hour evening. Enter the bouncers: one named Frosty, five feet, eight inches of dynamite, usually got to the culprit first. If the offender wasn't too tall, Frosty would reach up, grab the guy by the back of his head, and bring it down on his own head with such force that the poor guy would sink to the floor, out cold. If the villain was six feet or more, his head beyond reach, Frosty would let loose with a right cross to the jaw and the result would be the same. The bounder would usually come to in the parking lot.

In 1933, manager Joe Broderick, eager to raise the growing profile of the Palais Royale even higher, had asked New York society pianist and bandleader Eddie Duchin to bring his band to the ballroom for just one night. A reluctant Duchin inquired, "Why me? Nobody in Canada has ever heard of me." But Broderick knew better. Over 3,000 paid to dance to his Park Central Orchestra that night.

With the success of the Duchin night, Broderick began to bring in other big name bands. When Paul Whiteman brought his famous orchestra to the Palais, admission for the one night leaped to seventy-five cents a person. That was the beginning of the golden days of the big band era. Soon, Cab Calloway, Duke Ellington, Bob Crosby, Louis Prima, Count Basie, Jimmy Dorsey, The Casa Loma Orchestra, and most of the other famous American bands came to call. On those special nights, the enthusiastic crowds packed the ballroom to overflowing. Many people came from as far away as Niagara Falls and Buffalo.

The first fans inside the ballroom established their territory early, pressed against the bandstand from the beginning. Lines of latecomers took up positions behind the front line, and sometimes stretched back fifteen and twenty rows deep, with everyone clambering for a vantage point when the visiting band played. On those nights there was very little space left for dancing. Little matter. People came primarily to listen, not only to the guest bands, but also to the intermission music of Bert Niosi, who was advertised by the managers as Canada's King of Swing.

In 1937 Artie Shaw and his band played to a packed house. His hit record, "Begin the Beguine," was just sweeping North America. When Shaw told Cuthbert and Deller that he had no more dates that week, the partners kept him on for two more nights, which saw business continue to flourish. (When the bandleader expressed his gratitude for the two extra nights, the pair returned the compliment.)

During the six long years of the Second World War a great many soldiers, sailors, and airmen at one time or another came through the doors of the Palais, to dance every dance with girls from the munitions factories and offices — often it was their last dance before being shipped overseas. All too many did not return.

When the war finally ended, with the exhilaration of victory in the air, the boys who did return reappeared from the conflicts in Europe and the Pacific. Business at the Palais Royale, along with business in every other dance hall and night club in Canada, boomed as never before.

In 1946 the Bert Niosi band underwent a dramatic change. With the discharge from the services of so many fine musicians now back in Canada, Bert decided to improve the quality of his orchestra. In came Babe Newman and Paul Grosney, two fine jazz artists, to join Ferrano on trumpets; on trombones Ross Culley, an excellent lead player, along with Ted Everett and myself; tenorman Pat Riccio; altoist Hank Rosati; and baritone player Larry Martin joined Phil Antonacci in the saxophone section. The rhythm section — with Johnny Niosi on drums; Johnny Dobson (for a few months) on bass, followed by Howard Morris; Doug Hurley on guitar and vocals, and newcomer Jimmy Coxson, one of the country's top jazz pianists — was recognized as one of the best in Canada. Pat Nixon was the band's beautiful vocalist.

With postwar styles in clothing changing, the Palais dress code was also allowed to relax. Men could now enter as long as they wore a jacket, slacks, and a tie. Women were admitted in trouser suits as well as in dresses (and even pork-pie stetson hats). With the new band filling the ballroom to capacity six nights a week, dancers were now allowed to jitterbug, twist and leap, and jig, jog, jostle, and jounce to every new step. In 1946 dancers without partners began the new choreography of line dancing. Lined up in a row, each dancer would execute identical steps to tunes like "Jersey Bounce" and "Up the Lazy River."

The crowds kept pouring in. They were particularly large on New Year's Eve, literally hanging from the rafters 'round midnight.

When the Palais Royale was constructed in 1921, the roof and walls of the clapboard building were secured not only with metal brackets, but also with lengths of three-quarter inch lead pipe, that stretched across the room from wall to wall. When we musicians in the trumpet and trombone sections sat on the upper levels of the tiered bandstand, which was, itself, four feet above the ballroom floor, the three-quarter inch pipe was at our eye level, about ten feet above the floor. When the clock struck the midnight hour and we played "Auld Lang Syne," a huge roar went up from the thoroughly inebriated crowd, everybody hugging and kissing and shaking hands — including the dozen or more idiot daredevils we saw hanging upside down from the rafters, wailing like banshees, their legs wrapped around the pipes. (How those jokers got up there remains a mystery to this day.)

While I was playing with the band after the war, I learned that bandleader Bert Niosi's career had begun way back in the 1920s when, as a fourteen-year-old, he played a summer engagement with Guy Lombardo and his Royal Canadians in

Cleveland. That was also the beginning of Lombardo's climb to success. The Cleveland job led to a fall engagement in Chicago, and Bert was all set to go until his mother ordered him back to his native London, Ontario, where he had been studying saxophone and flute while attending high school.

While still a teenager Bert had also toured the Lowes vaudeville circuit with the McPhillips Buescher Boys Orchestra. He formed his own nine-piece band in 1931, and played the Club Embassy at the corner of Bloor and Bellair in Toronto for about a year, just before Bert expanded the group and moved to the Palais Royale.

At the Palais, Bert established himself early on as a consummate professional. All the music in the band's folders was arranged for the Bert Niosi Orchestra: stock arrangements were taboo. There were regular weekly rehearsals, generally on Thursday afternoons when Bert would hand out the parts of the latest Johnny Dobson, Bert Niosi, and (later) Pat Riccio, creations. Although many of these charts were difficult, the bandleader always kept intelligent control of the rehearsals. When the results were introduced to the crowds, fans who often showed up two and three times a week would congratulate Bert on just how great the new charts sounded. And the band swung every night. "To be good, an orchestra must have a solid rhythm section that will give the band a lift," Bert used to say, "but there must always be good arrangements."

The policy at the Palais was to have continuous music all night — music that suited every taste. Thus, when the time came for the musicians to take a breather, the band-within-a-band would play for fifteen or twenty minutes on a small stage at the opposite end of the ballroom. Then the focus went back to the big band for a couple of sets, after which Bert or Pat Riccio would play the piano, while another musician would double on drums, and others would play their trumpets or saxes for fifteen minutes of waltzes.

Most of the musicians in the 1946 band were top-calibre players, many of whom went on to become recognized, award-winning jazz artists, or seasoned recording-studio musicians. Niosi himself was an amazing player. With a beautiful sound equally matched by a phenomenal technique on his alto saxophone, Bert was an even better clarinetist. No matter the tune or the tempo, the quiet, shy gentle man was an articulate giant when he played. For us, one of the joys of playing in that band was to hear the same incredible sound of Bert's performance, night after night.

Frank Bogart, who had his own Toronto orchestra of the day, remembers:

In the 1940s, when Bert was at the Palais, he came on my show at the Club Top Hat and played all the instruments. A few years later, Percy Faith told me he had heard that broadcast. It was the first time he had heard Bert play and was impressed. Prior to that time he only knew Bert Niosi had a jazz band at the Palais, but didn't know anything else about him. After he heard him play all those instruments, he wasted no time in getting Bert to play with his own CBC orchestra. From that time on, Bert worked a lot at the CBC.

Although the Palais remained open all year round, the Bert Niosi Orchestra also played at Crystal Beach during the summer of 1946. For those of us in the band at the time it was a welcome holiday. Located on the north shore of Lake Erie, Crystal Beach was primarily a summer resort with a beautiful sandy beach. The park itself included a very large ballroom where the band played for dancing, as well as a roller-coaster, ferris wheel, electric automobiles, shooting galleries, and the usual games of chance found in such parks. A miasma of frying lard from the hot dog and hamburger stands greeted visitors to the area.

During that summer the management of the ballroom also brought in the bands of Les Brown, Stan Kenton, Sammy Kaye, and others every two weeks — which always attracted large crowds from Buffalo and other U.S. towns across the border. For us in the Niosi band, life was a joy ride. We spent long sunny days on the beach, where our bodies baked a cordova brown, enjoyed playing four-hour gigs six nights a week (and hearing the fine solos of Phil, Pat, Jimmy, Babe, and Paul, as well as Bert himself), and rejoiced in the likes of Les Brown and His Band of Renown. We didn't have a care in the world. (And, oh yes, in the late afternoon

BERT NIOSI IN HIS LATER CAREER, APRIL 1981. Playing solo with Paul Grosney's Orchestra at the Scarborough Town Centre, April 1981. Gordon Evans is seen at left playing his alto sax, Sam Noto at right (rear) on trumpet, and Phil Antonacci on tenor at right. *Courtesy Paul Grosney*

most of us would take a couple of hours out from the beach to practise our instruments. Everyone had to be in top shape when we were on the bandstand.)

The day after Labour Day, the first Monday in September, which signalled the end of summer, we returned to the Palais Royale on the Toronto waterfront for another season of ballroom dancing. On opening night our return was greeted by hundreds of fans, glad to see their musical conquering heroes back home.

Inevitably, our days in the sun just after the Second World War would wane. A new kind of music — rock and roll — would begin to emerge in the 1950s. Only a few years after the war ended, crowds at the Palais Royale gradually began to grow smaller. With the increasing demand for Bert Niosi's services at the CBC, in 1950 the bandleader reluctantly quit the *palais de dance* which had been his home for almost two decades.

In 1952 he became a member of Bert Pearl's "The Happy Gang" radio show on CBC, a stint which lasted seven years. During that time he was also one of the busiest musicians at the CBC studios, both as a player and as a leader. Then, when he left "The Happy Gang" in 1959, he moved to CBC television, as a musical director of "Four for the Show," "Cross-Canada Hit Parade," "Country Hoedown," and "The Tommy Hunter Show."

Wherever he turned up, Bert Niosi was a very versatile musician — proficient not only on saxophone, clarinet, and flute, but also on trumpet and trombone. Accompanied by brothers Joe, on bass, and Johnny, on drums, he once appeared on CBC television playing all these instruments. At an earlier benefit during the Second World War, he had played every instrument in his fourteen-piece band except the bass fiddle. To mark his great talent and many accomplishments, he was honoured at a CNE Bandshell concert in Toronto in 1978, later seen on a 1979 CBC special devoted to his career. And, in the very end, Bert Niosi left a legacy of musical excellence when he died on August 3, 1987, at the age of seventy-seven.

Black Music in Canada

When Fats Waller wrote "Black and Blue," the opening lines of the song told the story in a nutshell. He was commenting on the struggle all black people had to cope with, every day of their lives:

Cold empty bed, springs hard as lead,
Pains in my head, feel like old Ned,
What did I do ...
To be so black and blue?

There was a lot about the golden age of popular music in North America that owed some very large debts to black (or African-American) musicians. And in Toronto, as in other parts of Canada, we had to take in a great deal of this at second hand.

It has been said that in the first-half of the twentieth century there were so few people of African descent in Toronto that when one of them saw another, anywhere in the city, they would wave.

Even in those days, however, there were some local black musicians in town. The more historic "Toronto the Good" had not really been a very hospitable place for them, but after the Second World War things began to change. There is a story to be told here, and in doing my interviews for this book, I turned to the musical Wright brothers — Henry and Frank — to help me get it told.

Guitarist Henry Wright got started in the 1930s through another musical brother, Bill, who played drums with Reg McLean's band. Reg was a piano player, brother of Cy McLean, who also played piano. Reg and Cy had both moved to Toronto from Nova Scotia in 1934. Since work for black musicians in Toronto and elsewhere in Ontario was rare, most worked for the railroad, if they were lucky.

Reg McLean's ten-piece band rehearsed once a week in Mrs. Wright's house at 4 Sullivan Street, near Spadina and Dundas. Mrs. Wright was the mother of four boys — Bill, Henry, Johnny and Frank, and two girls — Alice and Minnie. Henry explained to me:

Every time the phone rang, Bill would leave his drums to answer the phone. I would sit on the drums and keep time until Bill came back. This went on for so long that as a result I got to know all the orchestrations. When the band got booked out of town and Bill couldn't make it (he worked on the railroad), they would pass me off as him.

Eventually, the leadership of the group passed from Reg to his brother, Cy, who took an eight-piece band into Fallingbrook Pavilion, on Toronto's east-end waterfront. Some of the musicians were trumpeter Roy Worrell, saxophonists Wilf Williams and Lloyd Salmon, drummer Sammy Richardson, bassist Vivian Roberts, guitarist Henry Wright, and trombonist Albert Marsden. As the years progressed — before, during, and after the Second World War — other musicians, such as drummers Bill Wright and Al Mayers, and saxophonists Raymond Coker, Ollie Wagner, and Don Carrington would join the band.

One summer, we got a job playing for a lady who ran a dance hall in Crystal Beach. We found rooms in a nearby rooming house, where we parked our bags and slept. I used to do the business for the band, so after our first week I went to the lady and asked for the money. She said she didn't have any; it had been a bad week.

The war was on and earlier that week the main ballroom at Crystal Beach had brought in the Horace Heidt Orchestra. And it was that orchestra that attracted all the people.

I knew she didn't have money, but it meant that we had worked the entire week for nothing.

Henry returned to the rooming house and called a meeting of the musicians. He explained that even though the dance hall owner didn't do any business that week, he felt she couldn't be trusted and suggested leaving Crystal Beach as soon as possible.

We had an offer to play at a place on Lake Chemong near Peterborough, and since we had no money to pay for the rooms, we decided to sneak out of the rooming house.

The band had a friend, Daddy Klein, who had a Cadillac. On occasion Klein would transport the musicians to a job. When the band went to Crystal Beach he followed them and took a room near their rooming house and stayed all week. Henry went on with the story:

At first, we were going to tie bedsheets together and let ourselves out the window in the middle of the night. But we had to abandon the idea because Albert Marsden, our trombonist, weighed about 350 pounds and there wasn't a sheet that would hold him. So we decided to sneak down the stairs. Our instruments were in Daddy Klein's trailer hitched to his Cadillac, but we had to carry our bags down the stairs.
So we're sneaking down the stairs as quietly as we could, and who should be waiting for us at the bottom but the woman's husband with a shotgun over his arm.
"Where you boys going?" he asked.
"Oh, we'll be back next week," we said.
"Well, leave your bags in this room here," he said, pointing to a room on the main floor. He was gonna make sure we would be coming back to pay. The rooms were seven or eight dollars per musician.

The shotgun convinced the musicians to abandon their plans and call another meeting. After further discussion they decided to leave a couple of bags with the man downstairs, but only after they'd removed the most important items and placed them in a suitcase that would be going with a musician. As Henry put it:

That was the only way we got out of there. Daddy Klein drove the instruments in the Cadillac trailer and we drove in our car to Peterborough and played the full summer on Lake Chemong. That job paid the musicians a percentage of the night's business — 60 to 40 percent: The house got 60 percent and we got 40 percent. It was a jitney job, ten cents a dance. No intermission.

One reason black musicians were treated so shabbily was their exclusion from the Toronto Musicians' Protective Association, which might otherwise have given them protection. President Walter Murdoch, who ruled the union with an iron fist, made it clear at more than one general meeting of the union that (in language which even people like Walter Murdoch would not use nowadays) "niggers are not allowed here."

As time went by Cy McLean's band, nonetheless, found employment in a number of places:

We played the Fallingbrook Pavilion, the Parkside Tavern, a few dances in Gravenhurst and other Muskoka towns ... a show at the Standard Theatre on Spadina for the TriBell Club ... and a tour of Ontario resorts during the summer of 1946 for Lever Brothers, promoting Lifebuoy soap.

The Lifebuoy tour paid each musician an unusually handsome eighty dollars a week. When they weren't playing for a percentage of the business somewhere, the musicians typically made thirty to forty dollars a week in other, kinder places. But as Henry explained, as far back as 1936 he had started a day job with the Canadian Pacific Railroad:

We had more dry spells than pay days. I couldn't earn enough money as a musician playing in non-union halls.

I told Henry that I could remember, when I was sixteen or seventeen, seeing black people going into a house on the south side of College Street, near Spadina. On some summer nights we would hear screeching brass and cymbal crashes coming out of a top floor window. Henry said the music came from the Universal Negro Improvement Association Hall:

The U.N.I.A. at 355 College Street was the meeting place for Toronto's black community. They hired us on Thursday nights and we used to have jam sessions on Sundays.

The U.N.I.A. was the brainchild of Marcus Garvey, a native of Jamaica. And although he lived in Jamaica, he travelled all over North America trying to organize a Return to Africa movement. Conditions in America were too harsh, and Garvey felt that Africa would be more hospitable to the "freed" descendants of slaves. Until not too long ago, almost every North American city and town with a black population had a U.N.I.A. meeting place.

One Sunday night in 1941, Pat Riccio, his brother Jimmy, and I were invited to the U.N.I.A. Hall in Toronto, though I didn't quite know the name of the place at the time, or understand exactly what it was. We saw Cy McLean and some of his musicians playing Count Basie tunes on a small stage. Almost everyone in the packed room — men and women, boys and girls — participated in the entertainment. They came right out of the audience to sing, tap dance, or tell funny stories. Even in the very small Toronto black community of the day, the wealth of talent we saw on stage that night was extraordinary.

Yet even though the city had elected its "first black alderman" as long ago as 1894, Toronto the Good was still very prejudiced in the earlier parts of the twentieth century. When bands like Duke Ellington or Cab Calloway came to town

CY MCLEAN AND HIS ORCHESTRA, 1940s. Left to right: back row: Sam Richardson, drums; Vivian Roberts, bass; Cy McLean, piano. Second row: Albert Marsden, trombone; Roy Worrell and Clyde Jemet, trumpets; Henry Wright, guitar. Front row: Bobby Brown, Lloyd Salmon, and Wilfred Williams, saxophones. *Courtesy Henry Wright*

they couldn't stay in the top hotels. Only certain hotels allowed blacks into their rooms. If they were lucky they would stay in local people's homes. Henry remembers how his mother let a twelve-year-old Sammy Davis, Jr., sleep in their house when he performed with his father and uncle as the Wilf Marsden Trio:

Sammy Davis, Sr., and uncle Wilf Marsden stayed at the Statler Hotel downtown but they didn't want the kid with them because they probably had chicks running in and out of their room. So Sammy Davis, Jr., stayed with us when they played the Shea's Hippodrome or the Casino Theatre. The kid used to play in the street with Frank who was a couple of years younger.

Henry's brother, Frank Wright, remembers himself that:

We'd be playing ball out in the street and the taxi would pull up. And Sammy would say, "Well, gotta go," and he'd get in the cab and go to the theatre. Then he'd come back. Whenever the Wilf Marsden Trio was in town Henry and our older brother Bill would bunk together so Sammy could sleep in a separate room.

I can myself remember that, even though in those days visiting black musicians from the U.S.A. always drew large crowds in places like the Palais Royale and the Silver Slipper, it was understood that black audiences were usually barred from Toronto entertainment venues. But the Second World War, on the heels of the Depression, had stirred up a lot of things.

In September 1944, Cy McLean and his band went into the Club Top Hat (the former Club Esquire), on Lake Shore Boulevard, and played there off and on until 1947. That job was a turning point for black musicians in the city because, at last, due to pressure brought by the Top Hat management on the musicians' union, Cy McLean and his band were allowed to join the Toronto Musicians' Protective Association — Local 149 of the American Federation of Musicians of the United States and Canada.

Despite the band's new status and its popularity in the club, however, it would still be a long while before conditions in the street really began to change. What I can report, sadly but with complete confidence, today, is that Cyril G. "Cy" McLean died October 29, 1986, at age seventy, after a heart attack in his Port McNicholl, Ontario, cottage. Henry Wright died in Toronto, May 21, 1995, from complications following a stroke.

Vibraphonist Frank Wright (Henry's younger brother) has been a highly respected jazz musician in Toronto's musical community almost from the beginning of his career. Even though he began to study music in 1950 at nineteen, an age later than when most musicians begin, he was an intelligent student who learned quickly, and he was soon recognized as an able improvisor:

When I started, it was just on the spur of the moment. I'd been working for the railway at the CPR Roundhouse on John Street, near where the CN Tower is now. I was living at home with my mother.

That Roundhouse serviced locomotives which pulled passenger trains. I worked on boilers. After the fires were dumped outside, the locomotives would be brought into the shop and I'd climb into the fire box and change the grates. Boy, it was all heavy work, and hot. They would have blowers on in there but it was still hot. I worked on that box for five years, from 1946 to 1952.

In 1950 I had no more notion of buying vibes than the man in the moon until I went down to the Colonial with my brother Henry and caught the Red Norvo Trio, with Charlie Mingus on bass and Tal Farlow on guitar. From the minute I heard them I was knocked right out. I'd never heard anything like them before.

Up to that point, all Frank knew about music had come from listening to his brother Henry play guitar, and hearing bands on the radio. But Red Norvo was the inspiration he needed to get him going. He purchased a small set of vibraphones from Long and McQuade, and picked up lessons whenever and wherever they were available. He sought out David Fonger, a percussionist who played in the Royal Alexandra Theatre pit orchestra:

He showed me how to hold mallets, how to alternate, and other things about the vibraphone. Then Peter Appleyard came to town. He joined the union as soon as he arrived, but because of a six-month union waiting period before he could work, he came to our house in the afternoon to have tea with my mother. Then he gave me lessons.

Frank also studied theory and harmony at the Royal Conservatory for some months. Then, when George Shearing came to the Colonial, he brought vibraphonist Cal Tjaeder with him. And Frank took advantage of the opportunity.

I told Tjaeder I was just starting out so he took me up to the third floor where he got some manuscript paper and wrote out some exercises in about five minutes. He said, "Just practise these in every key and that'll get your technique up." He was a nice cat.

Meanwhile, Frank Wright, the vibraphonist, was still working on railway boilers in west Toronto. In 1952, after five years of heavy toil, he found himself in line for a promotion to fireman:

Two Irish fellows and myself were in line for the promotion. We went to Union Station to have our eyes tested, to make sure we weren't colour-blind. A fireman had to be able to read all the signs on the road.

The next step was to write an examination. Each candidate passed it easily. Frank was sent to the CPR freight yard at Runnymede and Dundas. When one engineer saw Frank he complained: "You guys should be porters." And Frank's name was removed from the fireman's list.

I made an appointment to see the president of the CPR, Frank explained. When I complained that I should have been given the fireman's appointment, the president said, "If you had fought in the war, maybe I could do something, but under the circumstances there's very little I can do." He said he was sorry, it was just one of those things.

So I went back to the old shop and boilermaking. The boss I worked for was a bastard who got satisfaction from being nasty. I would work with the boilermaker who would teach me welding, then would watch me to see if I was doing it right. Whenever the boilermaker was giving me a lesson, the boss would walk by and see me standing there watching him work. The boss would always say, "That's all you got to do?"

One day he said it once too often, so I told him where to stick his job, and I quit. That was in 1952, just at the time Bill Lee, a piano player, formed a quintet and asked me to join him.

Bill Lee's group emulated the George Shearing style which went over well with the fans. They started doing a lot of engagements, particularly high school and university dances. (When they played Oakville High School, a student named Hagood Hardy stood at the front of the stage all night long listening to Frank play. He was so impressed that he later told others, "I saw a fellow by the name of Frank Wright playing vibraphone and that's the instrument I'm going to play.")

In 1953 the Bill Lee quintet landed a teenage radio show at CFRB which went for twenty-six weeks. Frank explains:

We taped the show on Mondays, one week before it was broadcast on Tuesday nights. It was a good show; Lloyd Percival was on, and Miss Canada was giving beauty tips to the kids. The show was sponsored by Orange Crush and we used to play a mystery song, and whoever mailed in the winning title got a case of Orange Crush sent to them. And we made a lot of money.

In the late 1950s the jazz musicians of Toronto played a benefit for ailing Clem Hambourg, who had become a legend because of his jazz and coffee club known as the House of Hambourg. (Clement Hambourg was a classically trained pianist. He and his two brothers came from Russia to perform and teach in Toronto, around 1910. For a number of years between the two world wars the brothers ran the highly respected Hambourg Conservatory of Music on Sherbourne Street. In the early 1950s, eccentric Clem developed a liking for jazz and started the House of Hambourg.)

Every jazz musician in Toronto, it seems, played that benefit, and Frank Wright was among them:

Some time after midnight Friday night we had just finished our set and I was moving my vibes off the stand to make way for Joe Williams and his trio. Williams was appearing at the Towne Tavern and agreed to play the benefit after the Towne gig was finished. At the benefit he had finished one song when Dave Caplan came to me with a message: "Joe Williams would like you to sit in with his group." I was elated: Holy jeez! Joe Williams wants me to play with HIM? I started to shake. Joe Williams was one of the greatest jazz singers alive. I moved the vibes back on stage and wound up playing a couple of tunes with some of the greatest musicians in the world.

As the years progressed, Frank also played radio and television shows. And Frank has also performed for visiting dignitaries in Ottawa.

In 1985 we played dinner music for Prince Philip and Lt.-Gov. Lincoln Alexander. Wray Downes was on piano, Archie Alleyne on drums, Steve Wallace on bass ... The band looked great and sounded good. We all wore tuxedos.

When the dinner and speeches were over the party, led by Prince Philip, moved towards the doors. But the prince made a point of stopping at the bandstand to speak to the musicians. When he stopped, his entourage stopped as well. The prince came right over and started talking to me. "Are you going to play some more?" he asked. I didn't know what to say, so I said, "Yes, sir."

"I really enjoyed the music," he said. "Nice for listening and nice for dancing." And he smiled and walked away, followed by the party of dignitaries.

Then a reporter from the Sun *jumped up and asked, "What did the Prince say?" I was going to say he wanted to know if Moe Koffman was at George's Spaghetti House this week, but I thought twice and didn't.*

Towards the end of our interview, Frank talked about his early childhood:

My father used to work for Abe Orpen, a gambler who ran a gambling house near the Humber River, beside the location where the Palace Pier later stood. The big brown house was advertised as a tourist home, but it was really a front for an illegal gambling operation. My father cleaned up the place late on Saturday nights after everyone left.

One fateful day during the Second World War, Frank's father left the "tourist home" and was killed while crossing the road.

He had finished work and was heading for the median from where he would get a streetcar. There was a bridge there, which doesn't exist today, and a guy came flying over the bridge and when his brakes failed he hit my father. He just went over the car and coughed and died. I was twelve years old.

Frank had seen his father alive for the last time, on New Year's Day 1942, a short time before the accident.

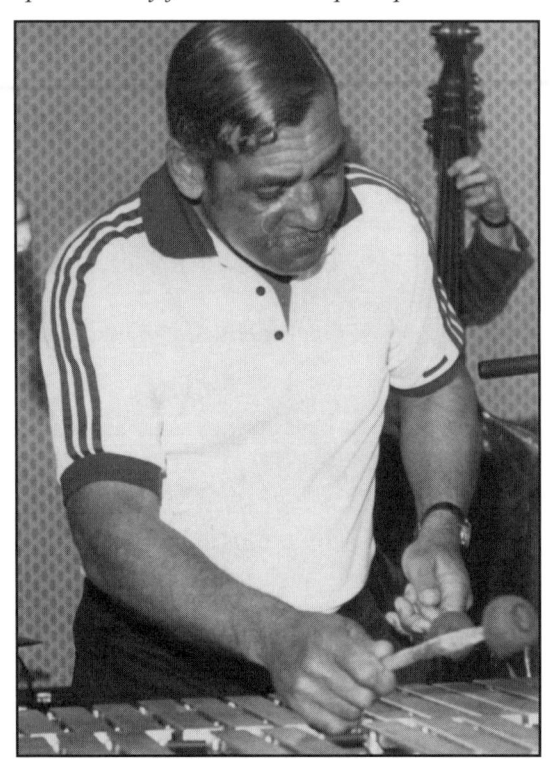

FRANK WRIGHT AT HARBOURFRONT, MAY 1985. *Courtesy Frank Wright*

Frank Bogart

On May 26, 1996, Toronto's exclusive Granite Club hosted a unique event, in celebration of something equally unique, that had its beginnings some fifty-six years before (even some two years, in fact, before the unhappy death of Frank Wright's father). The letter of invitation read: "In appreciation for all the happy times I have had at the Granite, I'm inviting all my friends to an afternoon of dancing and fun."

The letter was sent by pianist and bandleader Frank Bogart to every member of the club, whose membership lists the who's who of Toronto's most influential families. The event drew just about every individual who pays dues to the august curling/social organization. Appearing with Bogart was his fifteen-piece All-Star Band, with vocalist Ruth Powell, also the bandleader's wife. It was all Bogart's way of thanking every family whose members had danced to his music for over five decades, and whose sons and daughters had celebrated hundreds of birthdays, and, a few years later, their own weddings, to the same music. Although the Granite had periodically shown its appreciation for the services of the Frank Bogart organization, Frank insisted that this party was on him.

A generous man, Frank always made sure that the musicians who played with him found little gifts and tokens of appreciation (such as their paid-up union cards) on their music stands at Christmas time, on birthdays, and for other personal celebrations. As best as I can remember at least, Frank Bogart is one of those rare individuals who has never had a word of criticism or anger cast in his direction: indeed, a man loved by all.

One of Canada's most successful musicians, Frank has made it his business to be on top and in control of whatever job he has done, having the tunes of the day at his fingertips, as well as a large collection of standards to please everyone's taste. In his long career he has been applauded time and again for the way he has handled the evening's music.

His first appearance at the Granite was on the first Saturday in October 1940. Over the ensuing years, Frank left the club for three years and went to the Club Top Hat. Later on there was another extended intermission, at the Imperial Room of the Royal York Hotel. Then Frank Bogart and his Orchestra went back to the Granite Club again, and settled in for a very extended stay.

What do musicians do when they reach retirement age? They hang up their gloves and take it easy; perhaps indulge themselves in a hobby or two. Not so for Frank Bogart. "As long as the fingers hold out and people want me, I'll be there."

A lot *has* changed since the days when Frank first began to put down roots at the Granite Club, at the end of the Second World War. But he still keeps busy enough playing private functions at Toronto's golf and country clubs. (And did I forget to mention Frank's other love? He teaches karate once a week. In fact, at the May 26 party, Frank presented a display of martial arts by ten of the finest Black Belts in Canada. Frank, a 4th degree black belt himself, also participated, and from all reports he broke the board with the classic karate chop. Not bad for a man who also celebrated his eighty-first birthday on the same day as his big party. And it all goes to show: It ain't over 'til it's over.)

I knew that Frank Bogart's story just had to figure in my interviews for this book. I had gotten together with him at his Toronto penthouse apartment, after his big eighty-first birthday party in 1996. And I started by asking him how it all began.

It all goes back to the Lombardos who were born in London, Ontario, he explained. My mother came from London and she used to tell me how her father used to walk home at noon with the Lombardos' father. That was in the early 1900s. The elder Lombardo would talk about his boys and their interest in music.

Frank's mother also told him about the Niosi family.

A lot of good bands came out of London, Frank explained. There was a large Italian community in that city that brought a Professor Venuti over from Italy to teach them. I guess that's where Bert Niosi became such a tremendous musician. In my opinion, he was a giant in the business.

Young Frank took an immediate interest in Guy, Carmen, and Liebert Lombardo, who as teenagers played violin, flute, and drums, respectively, before each settled on his permanent instrument (Guy continued on violin, Carmen turned to alto sax, and Liebert to trumpet). The band had adopted a style of playing that was to become their landmark. And Frank was taken with that style. For years he followed the Lombardos' career while they jobbed around London, and after they became a hit in the United States. Whenever he heard their particular "sweet" style, he became more convinced that he would one day lead his own orchestra, playing the same kind of music.

Born in Woodstock, Ontario, on May 26, 1915, as a young man Frank lived in Galt, Ontario, where he learned to play the piano.

My mother played piano; so the influence on me to play the same instrument was strong right from the start. I began lessons when I was seven years old. When I was fourteen, we moved to Hamilton and I took lessons from another chap who showed me how to read a piano part that had only the melody line and chord symbols above each bar.

While attending Hamilton Central High School, he joined Fred Sweeney's dance band as pianist; a relationship that lasted until he graduated. Then he moved to Toronto and joined Ferde Mowry's band, one of the city's best orchestras:

During those early Ferde Mowry years, I heard a marvellous piano player on the radio named Eddie Duchin, who played with Leo Reischman's orchestra at the Central

FRANK BOGART, AUGUST 22, 1978. His Orchestra played the Granite Club for more than fifty years, a record for any orchestra. *Courtesy Frank Bogart*

Park Casino in New York. They came on at five o'clock in the afternoon every Saturday, and as far as I was concerned that was exactly the type of piano I wanted to play.

Unlike most bandleaders whose piano players just played rhythm or light fills, Reischman gave Duchin a lot of flexibility to do whatever he wanted:

Eddie would play a simple thing that sounded so effective. He'd cross his hands and play the melody in the bass, which people thought was tremendous. It added a certain elegance to the Reischman style of music.

The year was 1931, and the Great Depression was taking its toll on businesses of all kinds, and this included hotels. The management of the Central Park Casino asked Reischman if he could cut his band of fifteen musicians down to a more manageable number for economic reasons. But, at the time, Reischman had a chance to go to the Waldorf Astoria where he had played a few years earlier. So they asked Duchin if he could bring his own band into the Central Park Casino.

Up to that time, all piano players just played rhythm or light fills. Bandleaders never thought the piano important enough to feature it in their arrangements, except in the odd solo. When Duchin began his new stint, almost overnight he changed the whole concept of dance band music. Free to do his own thing, the pianist was all over the keyboard. He not only played in the bass, but he had a special introduction on the piano which was followed by the trumpet, which killed the people.

OPENING DAY, CLUB ESQUIRE, NOVEMBER 26, 1936.

Courtesy City of Toronto Archives, G&M, SC 266-42039

92 They Loved to Play

As I've noted earlier, in 1933 Joe Broderick, manager of the Palais Royale Ballroom in Toronto, brought Eddie Duchin in for a one-nighter. The crowd was the largest in the Palais Royale's history. Frank Bogart was there, too:

I was so impressed that I've tried to play that style ever since.

When Frank joined Ferde Mowry in 1934, the band was in its third year at the Club Embassy. After six years with the organization, Frank decided it was time for him to lead his own group. In the summer of 1940 he took his new band into the beautiful Brant Inn, on the Burlington lakeshore. The music he played and the special way he handled the evening made him an immediate hit with the crowd.

They played six nights a week — a good job for all the musicians. But the summer would soon be waning, and Frank knew he would have to vacate the club to make way for another band:

I had to come up with another six-night per week job, so I looked around. I wandered into the Granite Club on St. Clair and asked for the general manager. I remember he was at the end of a long table and I was at the other end.
"What can I do for you, boy?" the manager asked. It all seemed so ridiculous.
"Well, I've got a dance band," I said. "I'm out at the Brant Inn and I'll be finishing up in another month. I wondered if you ever need a band. I want you to come out and hear us." I left some tickets and that was the end of the interview.
Come that Friday night, we're outside playing at the Sky Club (an outdoor venue), and who's at the front table but the general manager of the Granite Club, his wife, and the Club's president. And that's how it started.

Within a few months Frank was back in Toronto playing at the prestigious club on St. Clair Avenue. The opening date was Saturday, October 5, but although the Granite Club was the perfect venue for Frank, who always wanted to play for high society, the job found the band playing Saturday nights only:

We played that winter and spring. But we still needed six nights a week. Then suddenly I got the chance to go into the Club Top Hat.

Originally called the Club Esquire, this place had been built in Sunnyside on the north side of Lake Shore Boulevard, near the Palais Royale. It was run by Bill Beasley (who later had most of the CNE midway concessions). His plan was to open the club seven nights a week for dining and dancing, and to feature top-flight acts brought in from New York and Hollywood — a revolutionary departure from the way night spots in Toronto were operated until then. Beasley was no ordinary entrepreneur. This club was to be a replica of the best New York nightclubs, complete with two bands, a master of ceremonies, floor shows featuring a line of chorus girls, comedians, and a different big name headliner every week. Because the Ontario liquor laws didn't allow the sale of alcohol in public places, Beasley's people said they'd handle that situation later. The year was 1936.

Beasley knew Jimmy Davidson and felt this man had everything to front a band in a club like his. A good-looking six-footer, who caught the eye of every woman who laid eyes on him, Jimmy was not only a distinctive singer, but a marvellous jazz cornetist and arranger, and had the ability and confidence to lead the band through complicated floor show acts. Besides, he was a man with an extraordinary sense of humour. All that Davidson needed at this point was a catchy name. After some thought, Beasley decided on "Trump" for trumpet playing Jimmy.

Club Esquire, needless to say, enjoyed considerable success. The shows were marvellous, exactly like the New York shows. The dance music was lively, and the food was excellent, particularly the coffee, which you could order before, during, and after dinner. Beasley did everything he could to get a liquor licence and when it became clear that the licence would not be forthcoming, the club finally closed.

Frank Bogart continued the story:

Some chaps at Tip Top Tailors took it over and renamed it the Club Top Hat. I was offered the job so I informed the Granite Club management that I had a chance for a steady job, and went in there for a few years. The year was 1941.

For musicians whose influences were the great jazz players of the day, the Club Top Hat was terrific. Bogart's men were in heaven:

What a job that was! Some of the tremendous artists that came through were Fats Waller, Coleman Hawkins, Red Norvo, and a fine little band out of Boston called Savoy Lewis. He had Cat Anderson on trumpet, the great screech trumpet player who played with Duke Ellington in later years.

What about the men in Bogart's own band? As Frank remembers:

I had some excellent musicians work for me over the years. Teddy Roderman, who played fine trombone, was with me for a short while before he went into the service; Cokey Campbell played saxophone; and of course, the legendary Benny Winestone. I also had Jackie Kane on sax when he was sixteen or seventeen. Both played the Top Hat along with trumpeter Gordon Delamont, trombonist Floyd Roberts, tenorman Gordie Bell, bassist Art Huston (whose claim to fame was that his uncle, Walter Huston, the great screen actor, would phone him every time he appeared on stage in Toronto), and drummer Al Blue.

Benny Winestone made Jackie Kane's life a hell, because although he played excellent clarinet, on alto he played out of tune. Benny used to make his life a torture, always reprimanding him to pull his mouthpiece out or push it in, whatever was necessary for the young musician to correct his intonation. And Winestone would never let up. "Tune up, goddammit. Ya cawn't play laak thaat. Yo'rre merderr t' play weth." And Jackie would come crying to me. "I can't stand it," he'd say. "I can't stand it anymore."

But Benny kept up the barrage. "Why don't ya take some lessons?" he'd yell. "Yo'r the werrst playerr I ever werrked with."

So what did he do? On a Sunday he flew down to New York and took a lesson from Hymie Schertzer, who'd played lead alto with Benny Goodman and Tommy Dorsey. Of course when he came back he didn't play any better. But Jackie was with me until he, too, went into the service.

I know myself that, several years later, after Jackie Kane had returned from the service and was working in Toronto, he went to New York as the bandleader on a summer TV show featuring Edie Gormé and Steve Lawrence. When he looked over the band (a New York contractor had hired the musicians), he saw the lead alto was Hymie Schertzer.

"Do you remember me?" Jackie asked.

"No," Schertzer replied. "I only know that you're going to lead the band."

Jackie said, "I took a lesson from you six years ago."

Schertzer could hardly believe it. This fellow who took a lesson from him only six years ago was now the orchestra leader conducting the band for one of the top shows on American television!

As for Benny Winestone, stories about him continue to be told, over and over to this day by the musicians who knew him. His appearance may not have had all the classic features of a Scottish Highland bagpiper, but the burr in his accent, as thick as porridge, left no doubt where he came from. Frank Bogart remembers:

Benny used to do this one tune with us, a novelty piece. It was called "Sam, You Made the Pants Too Long." We got him a pair of oversized pants which he put on and would come out to the mike. When he sang it in that heavy Glasgow accent, it would kill the people. They'd ask for it every night.

Many years later in his penthouse apartment, Frank began to finish his story:

After our first year at the Club Top Hat, management was approached by the CBC to see whether they would be interested in featuring a Saturday afternoon jazz show for radio. Would they? You bet your life they would! Particularly when it would provide free advertising every week, with the Top Hat name repeated many times during the hour broadcast by CBC jazz aficionados Byng Whittaker and Elwood Glover, who handled the announcing chores. That's what really got it started. Top American jazz stars, like Coleman Hawkins and Fats Waller, who came to the Club to do their week's engagement, would make a special appearance on the broadcast by playing one number.

For the live concert Bogart added a second trumpet, Trump Davidson, and guitarist Merve Johnston. In addition to the Americans, a lot of local jazz musicians were featured every week — players such as Bert Niosi, trumpeters Paul Grosney and Gordon Braun, and saxophonist Lew Lewis. Singer Norma Locke also appeared as a guest. Frank recalls as well that:

Denny Vaughan, who became a TV personality in England, also guested on the show, not as a pianist but as a singer, although he did play some piano. Denny was a powerhouse who died much too young. When he left England and settled in New York for a while, he played with Lester Lanin, and saw how successful Lanin was doing in society work. Then when he came to Toronto he started to do a lot of society dates.

In the end there's a tale behind Frank's ultimate route back to the Granite Club:

At the Top Hat, there was an outside part of the club, nicely laid out, that after a couple of years the owners thought they would open for the summer months. The idea was certainly sound; during the hot summer months, the cool breezes off beautiful Lake Ontario created just the ambience the owners had hoped for. The setting seemed perfect. So they advertised the "new" outdoor room, which on opening night and successive evenings filled with patrons.

And then the unexpected happened with a vengeance. The owners forgot that trains ran just behind the club several times a day, including the evenings. Well, the room didn't last long, because when the trains rumbled by, the smoke and black soot that belched from the smokestacks came down on the guests, who ran for cover.

That's when I decided I'd had enough and phoned the Granite Club to see whether they would have me back. So I went back there for a couple of years, and managed to build up a jobbing connection which worked out pretty well for me. After I left, other bands followed, and the Top Hat did good business and remained open for many years.

In 1949 the Bogart band went into the Imperial Room for a couple of seasons. Then they returned to the Granite Club yet again.

While we were in the Imperial Room there happened to be a convention of broadcasters up on the mezzanine floor. When they finished their meetings they used to come down for dinner and listen to the band play. An NBC representative came to the bandstand on one of those evenings and said how much he liked our music.

"Would you be interested in going on a weekly NBC broadcast?" he asked.

"I certainly would!" I responded. And that was all. I didn't hear anything after that.

Then one day I got a call from CBC saying NBC wanted to pick us up, that the broadcast would go through CBC from coast to coast and down into the States. Elwood Glover was the announcer, and the show went out Friday nights at ten o'clock. It went on for quite a long time and for us it was very exciting.

After the show was on a couple of weeks, I was inundated with dozens of song-pluggers who used to fly up to Toronto every week to try to get me to play their songs.

From here on, as they say, the rest is history. A lot of other things on the Toronto music scene would change. But Frank Bogart and his Orchestra played the Granite Club for more than fifty years, at both the club's St. Clair Avenue site and, after 1972, at its new Bayview Avenue location. A record for any kind of band.

"Trump"

There is another kind of record in the annals of the golden age in Toronto — more on a par with the saga of Bert Niosi at the Palais Royale Ballroom. Trump Davidson's tenure at the Palace Pier (not far west of Niosi's palais de dance) lasted eighteen years. And like his counterpart at the Palais, the magnificent Sudbury-born jazz cornetist left an estate containing musical riches and humour that is talked about and quoted to this day.

At the height of his career, "Trump" brought a fourteen-piece band, plus vocalist, into the Queensway Ballroom in September 1944 (the name was changed two years later to the Palace Pier), and stayed until the building burned down in 1963. During the life of the band, many changes in personnel took place, mainly during the war years when almost every available young man was called into the service. Yet Trump's musicians were always reliable players, some particularly fine jazz artists. Over his career they included saxophonists Moe Zene, Howard (Cokie) Campbell, and brother Teddy Davidson; trombonists George Guerette, Teddy Roderman, Stan Wheeler, Bill McCauley, and Lloyd "Steve" Richards; pianists Johnny Burt and Harvey Silver; drummers Reef McGarvey and Jimmy Paul; and bassists Pete Sinclair, Sam Levine, Joe Niosi, and Sam "Bozo" Weiner.

Located on the west bank of the Humber River at the western boundary of Sunnyside, the Palace Pier, a huge 300-foot-long structure built out on the lake in 1931, was used at first as a dance pavilion, a roller rink, and a fight arena (anything to make money). As the years went by it became strictly a dance hall, which catered to thousands. From its opening a number of local bands played for dancing, but none were good enough to attract major crowds until Trump Davidson brought his musicians on stage in 1944. From that time onward, with so much activity generated by masses of servicemen and factory workers searching for entertainment, crowds constantly filled the Palace Pier.

The band started playing four nights a week. Wednesdays, Fridays, and Saturdays were for dancing. Because of the local Lord's Day Act, which prohibited dancing on the Christian Sabbath, Sundays were a sing-along. Price of admission included cake and coffee. If anybody wanted soft drinks and extra glasses and maybe a bowl of ice, the waitresses would oblige — for a price of course.

Though there was no dancing on Sundays, shows were allowed, with Doug Romaine as the MC. The shows typically included a guest artist — a singer, dancer, comic, or magician. Although Romaine was a master funnyman who could entertain a crowd for hours, he also led the audiences in sing-alongs of the latest tunes. One night when a little seventy-eight-year-old lady asked to come on stage to sing

"There'll Always Be an England," the crowd of over a thousand went wild. Everybody stood and sang along with her.

The Palace Pier stage was an elaborate tiered affair. The floor of the bandstand on which the saxophones sat was five feet above the ballroom floor. The trumpets and trombones sat on the next level, and the drums and bass were on the top level. On both sides of the stage were stairs that could be moved into place (casters on the stair bottoms), in order to allow the musicians to climb to their respective perches when they played. From the audience's viewpoint, the stage was like something out of Hollywood.

For the Sunday night shows both sets of stairs were always in place, because various musicians would come down to the mike when playing a solo. After the band played an opening piece to launch the entertainment, Trump announced, "And now for the moment you've all been waiting for. Let's have a big round of applause for your master of ceremonies, Doug Romaine!" And Romaine would come charging down the left stairs to the microphone to welcome everyone with a few ribald jokes. A very good opening.

On one particular Sunday, no one seemed to notice that the stage hands had for some reason forgotten to roll the stairs into place. When Trump said, "Let's have a round of applause for Doug Romaine," the popular master of ceremonies, not knowing the stairs were not in place, dashed from his hidden backstage pinnacle into full view of the audience, which saw him fly screaming into the air, arms and legs flailing, and drop several feet to the bandstand floor. The audience gasped in horror, but when Romaine got up and limped to the microphone to deliver his ribald jokes, they concluded it was only a gag and yelled for more. (Romaine and the management subsequently agreed that repeating all this would make a sensational opener, but after it had been talked over a number of times, the idea had to be scrapped as unworkable.)

As a feature at the Pier, Trump always included his six-piece Dixieland band, which took centre stage in front of the microphone and played the Dixieland standards "Way Down Yonder in New Orleans," "Muskrat Ramble," and "When the Saints Go Marching In." On occasion Trump would sing such classics as "Nobody Knows You When You're Down and Out" and "Hard-Hearted Hanna, the Vamp of Savannah, GA." In its heyday the sextet included pianist Harvey Silver, drummer Reef McGarvey, bassist Peter Sinclair, clarinetist Cliff MacKay (later replaced by Jack Wachter), and myself (after I left Bert Niosi at the Palais Royale).

In 1953, the group was featured on a CBC coast-to-coast half-hour radio show. The show proved so popular that it became a regular Saturday night series which lasted for six years.

Although Trump's band was initially engaged for only four nights, before long the Palace Pier management had every other night of the week booked for private parties. The ballroom could hold thousands of people, and the Pier welcomed large corporate affairs and the many celebrations among Toronto's increasingly dazzling variety of "ethnic groups" as well. Soon enough, with a few exceptions, the band was playing seven nights a week. Then someone discovered a law that said an establishment couldn't dictate to a prospective client who it must use to provide the music for its party. If a client wanted someone else, the Davidson band found itself with a free night.

At times like these, it didn't take long before some jazz club, like the Colonial Tavern or the Edison Hotel, would bring Trump Davidson's Dixieland Band in for a week. Those jobs always attracted large crowds, entirely different from the Palace Pier party crowds. At places like the Colonial or the Edison, people came to hear some very good jazz, particularly when played by The Man himself.

A man of extraordinary talent, Jimmy "Trump" Davidson had taught himself to play the cornet while still a teenager. Why cornet and not trumpet? Because from his teens he had been smitten with the cornet style of Bix Beiderbecke, the great 1920s jazz-age musician from Davenport, Iowa, who'd played with Paul Whiteman's orchestra — even though he couldn't read a note of music. At first Davidson's efforts involved trying to emulate Beiderbecke's easy-rolling riffs on cornet. Then he taught himself to play the piano, so he could copy Bix's piano stylings in such pieces as "In a Mist" and "Flashes," which greatly influenced Trump in some of his own compositions.

And Trump could sing as well. As I've noted earlier in this book, he had originally been hired by Luigi Romanelli as a vocalist. The cornet playing came after-

TRUMP DAVIDSON'S DIXIELAND BAND, 1963. The sextet, with Harvey Silver (piano), Trump, Joe Niosi (tuba), Reef McGarvey (drums), Jack Wachter (clarinet), and Murray Ginsberg) (trombone) has been enlarged to include Hank Monis on banjo and Teddy Davidson on tenor sax. Here, the band is appearing in Walter Hall, University of Toronto Faculty of Music, for the 10th Century Concerts, a series of chamber music concerts that went on for six years. *Courtesy Harvey Silver*

The Last Days of Swing in Toronto 99

ward, when Trump inveigled Romanelli into letting him sit in the brass section at the King Edward Hotel in 1929. All through his career, Trump Davidson's husky-voiced singing style embodied a dash of elegance, particularly on ballads such as "Embraceable You" and "You'd Be So Easy to Love." The ladies especially loved it.

In his heyday, Trump was also one of the best jazz singers in Canada. His voice, steeped in tradition, recalled the glory days of the early jazz singers. Songs like "Ace in the Hole," "Ragtime Rufus," "I Found You Out" (When I found you in someone else's arms), and "Sunday" were some of the gems in his vast repertoire.

At the same time, it was Trump's playing — oh, that magnificent cornet, ultimately not at all similar to Bix Beiderbecke's — that was in a class by itself. When he placed the mouthpiece to his lips and blew, everything — from "Maple Leaf Rag" to "Fidgety Feet," and through all those exalted songs of the 1920s and 1930s, to "Nobody Knows You When You're Down and Out" — became a miniature history of jazz. Charlie Shavers, the great black American trumpet player who worked in John Kirby's spectacular sextet in the 1940s and who came to the Palace Pier with Tommy Dorsey in the 1950s, once told us: "Do you folks realize what a great jazz musician you have in Trump Davidson? Had he been born in the United States he would be world-famous, right up there with the best of them."

As Toronto's own sax player Lew Lewis also told me in one of my interviews:

Trump could put more emotion into sixteen bars than anyone I know. And working with him night after night, for so many years, he never repeated anything, always in the best of taste, sheer utter music. You weren't bedazzled by a flow of technique that obscures all. He was essentially a musician, playing music. One time when Phil Napoleon was playing at the Colonial Tavern, we were sitting and chatting during a break, and I said, "You've played all over the States and Canada and heard the best players in the world. Of all those players, which one knocks you out the most?" He said, "Trump Davidson. He's the boss. If he lived in the States he would be world-famous."

Davidson was the musician's musician. Everyone gravitated towards the good-looking six-footer with the hilarious sense of humour. And it became a badge of honour to say, "I play with Trump." His music, with most of the arrangements written by him, along the lines of the Bob Crosby Band, was so seductive that everyone wanted to play in his band.

As piano player Harvey Silver explained in another of my interviews:

Trump was just amazing. He would write his arrangements quite often when he was sitting in the car while I was driving somewhere. He would pull out some manuscript paper, and when he had an idea, he would begin to write, part by part. He didn't bother preparing a master score first. He'd just begin by writing the first trumpet part, then the second trumpet part, and all the way through each instrument part for a fifteen-piece band. And those arrangements were always right. He never really studied arranging or composition until the end of his career, when he couldn't play any more.

Then he studied with Gordon Delamont, and the arrangements he wrote then were incredible. All the best musicians in town had difficulty playing them. He wrote things that he would have liked to play but never could. I guess he wanted to make sure Erich Traugott or Arnie Chycoski couldn't play them either. But of course those guys could play anything.

Trump's band did have a reputation for drinking. Unlike other high-calibre orchestras in Toronto, where liquor was taboo, every night a number of the musicians brought their own mickeys of booze to the job. If someone happened to be without a bottle, no problem. The gentleman would simply ask for the loan of a drink. Cokey Campbell, a fine saxophone player who often didn't get to the liquor store in time, was known to ask friendly tenorman Moe Zene, "Can I borrow a drink from you? I'll pay you back tomorrow."

Fine. The following night, Zene usually got his drink returned with a little interest. If payment wasn't made on time, there would be hell to pay, and the whole world heard about it. (Cokey Campbell's appellation, by the way, didn't come from sniffing the white powder, but from his obsession with Coca Cola). But the band was a happy one most of the time. And a lot of that happiness was generated by the leader's sense of humour.

As the night progressed, Trump, with a twinkle in his eye, would make tongue-in-cheek announcements to the crowd: "We'd like to dedicate the next song to Miss Sylvia Stitz who is celebrating her twenty-first birthday." Or, "The next number we are about to play is Duke Ellington's immortal 'Black and Fat Testicle.'"

On the annual St. Patrick's Day Ball, when every slightly stoned, rosy-cheeked son and daughter of the Ould Sod was celebrating, Trump would announce, 'For your dancing pleasure we now present 'Feel the Fluter's Balls," and then in a rollicking 6/8 time, sing "Hennessy Tennesny played with hi'self, while the music went round and round." The couples dancing by would look up at Trump, not sure just what they'd actually heard. "What did he say?" a guy would ask his partner, sticking a finger in his ear to clear it out, "Did I hear right? Surely he didn't ... "

There was always so much going on at the Palace Pier. Taking the lead from the success of the Palais Royale, Bill White, the manager, began to bring in famous American bands. Jimmy Dorsey, Tommy Dorsey, and Harry James all came to the Pier. (James drew the biggest crowd — forty-five hundred people. Frank Sinatra was with James then and as legend has it, making seventy-five dollars a week.) Gene Krupa, Benny Goodman, and Hal MacIntyre drew crowds as well.

Louis Prima was always a favourite, along with Les Brown (impeccable musicians, impeccable arrangements). On the night the exciting Stan Kenton band played the Palace Pier, and transported the crowd of more than fifteen hundred to Cloud Nine by playing all his renowned arrangements, namely, "Peanut Vendor," "Artistry in Rhythm," "Across the Alley from the Alamo," Trump's band came on stage to play the intermission. Trump's first words to his musicians were, "Okay, now let's show these guys how to drink."

Earlier in his career, when Trump was at the Club Esquire in 1936, he not only conducted the sometimes difficult music for the acts with finesse, but he was also perfectly at ease with most of the name acts. Often he would invite groups like the Mills Brothers (or Ray, Prince, and Charles) to an afternoon of golf.

One afternoon Trump and his musicians went to hear Ray Noble, who was appearing at Shea's Hippodrome on Bay Street. British-born Noble had been a member of the weekly (George) "Burns and (Gracie) Allen" American radio show, on which he both led the orchestra and took part in various humorous sketches, usually playing the part of a buffoon. When the radio series ended, Noble went on a tour of the United States and Canada with a band that was made up of a number of the finest American musicians (Claude Thornhill, Bud Freeman, Charlie Spivak, and others). After the performance in Toronto, Trump went backstage to meet Noble and compliment the band on their fine playing. He invited Noble to the Club Esquire.

Trump Davidson, circa 1960. *Courtesy Harvey Silver*

At the time Noble had a tour of the British Isles lined up for 1937 and desperately needed a band. American musicians were out of the question, he explained, since the British musicians' union disallowed American musicians from working in the United Kingdom. Members of the British Empire were okay, however, and when Noble heard the Club Esquire band, he said he didn't have to look any further. Since Canada was part of the empire on which the sun, it was said, never set, would Trump like to bring his band to the United Kingdom? It would have to be under Noble's name, but Trump would receive top billing as featured soloist. The musicians, of course, readily agreed.

On that four-month tour Noble and the Canadian musicians played to packed houses throughout the United Kingdom. On returning to Canada, Trump jobbed around Toronto, either as a sideman or leader, whenever booking agent Bert

Mitford called him to play the Boulevard Club, University of Toronto, the King Edward and Royal York hotels, and other lucrative engagements. On occasion the band played out of town.

In the summer of 1940 Trump took his fifteen-piece group to the Dardanella Ballroom in Wasaga Beach, on the south shore of Georgian Bay — the Toronto vacationers' paradise. In November 1941 he took a nine-piece group into the Standish Hall Hotel in Hull, Quebec, for four months. Since Quebec had much less stringent liquor laws than Ontario, most government office workers in Canada's federal capital city of Ottawa, Ontario (just across the Ottawa River from Hull), as well as a substantial part of Ottawa citizenry patronized the Hull watering holes nightly. Because the Standish had an excellent restaurant and a marvellous band, the crowds filled the place to capacity every night.

When trombonist Joe Carny was called up to the air force, and very few available trombone players remained, I, at the tender age of seventeen, was asked to join the band. Sam Levine got me the job and met me at the railway station in Hull on Saturday, November 29. That's how I first got to play with the great Trump Davidson. God, I was shy and nervous. That afternoon, Leila, his wife, lost her purse with the band cheque inside — about $600. So when we started that night, Trump wasn't in a good mood. He didn't even look at me, which made me feel doubly awkward. At that point he didn't like me either. (I guess he didn't like seventeen-year-old punks.) But Jack Wachter, the sax player, took me under his wing.

The Standish Hall Hotel dining room was a huge rectangular ballroom with linen-covered tables on either side of the dance floor. On the second storey overlooking the dance floor, a balcony also containing linen-covered tables ran around the four walls. When filled, the room held 2,000 people on both levels.

On entering, the bandstand, which was the focal point of the room, could be seen at the far end. Like most bandstands, the Standish Hall's was tiered — saxes Reg Saville, Willie Delaurentis, and Wachter on the lowest level; brass players Stan Wheeler and myself on trombones, and Trump on cornet on the second level; and drummer Sid Perl, pianist Harvey Silver, and bassist Sam Levine on the third level.

Because he confessed to having what he called a tin ear, and couldn't improvise, Harvey Silver, an otherwise accomplished pianist (during his lifetime he taught hundreds of young beginners), had trouble playing the correct chords for songs he didn't know. When Trump called out a tune which we would improvise, while playing his cornet he would call out the chords to Harvey, two bars ahead! How he did it we never knew, but he was always like that. He could call out the chords two bars ahead of time out of the side of his mouth and never go wrong. That was the measure of the man.

After the Palace Pier burned down in 1963, Trump went into semi-retirement. But when the phone rang, he and his favourite musicians would perform as always. In 1986, he was preparing to play the annual Eastern Star dance in Sudbury with a six-piece group, as he had done many times before. Two days before the engagement, Trump drove to his sister's home in Sudbury where he stayed until the other musicians showed up. Harvey Silver remembers the ensuing sad events:

That evening I was setting up the music stands in preparation for the dance when I was suddenly called to the phone. It was brother Teddy, who said, "I've got bad news. Jimmy fell this morning and cracked his skull. He's in the hospital." We went on that night without Trump and we managed to get by, but it wasn't a happy evening for any of us. He died in the hospital two days later.

Trump had been taking a lot of sun because he wanted to look good for the dance. To make his tan look impressive, he was going to wear a white suit. After a few hours in the sun, he got up to go inside and fell backwards and cracked his skull. That was the beginning of the end for him. He was sixty-nine when he died.

The Job At Toronto's Last Authentic Burlesque Theatre

Three years before Trump Davidson's Palace Pier burned down in 1963, another great institution from the golden age of music in Toronto had closed its doors. And just thinking about it fills me with a bitter-sweet nostalgia.

Look west along Queen Street today, from old City Hall, and try to imagine that thoroughfare sixty years ago: rows of seedy stores, a few cheap eateries, a couple of fleabag hotels, the odd cleaning establishment. Plopped in the middle of the sorry stretch on the south side of the street stood two theatres; the Roxy, a third-rate movie house, and the Casino, Toronto's last authentic burlesque theatre.

During the day that part of Queen Street usually bustled with lawyers from Osgoode Hall, or shoppers on their way to Eaton's and Simpson's. In the evening much of the bustle disappeared, but the street had its share of winos and derelicts, shuffling aimlessly along the sidewalk, and garish hookers who prowled the shadows hoping for a customer. The people who roamed those few blocks by night were part of the godless scenery, unloved and alone.

Before Nathan Phillips Square, new City Hall, and the Sheraton Centre were built in 1965, Elizabeth Street ran south from Grosvenor Street, a block north of College, down to Queen. In 1939 if you walked down Elizabeth below Dundas, you would pass rows of unflattering second-storey Chinese restaurants and stores that displayed made-in-China goods for sale — porcelain teacups, chopsticks and fans, and prints of smiling girls whose cheeks always seemed to be painted too red — and you would wind up at the box office of the Casino Theatre (if you could get in, that is, without having to stand in line).

From the day it opened, on Good Friday 1936, until its closing in 1960, the Casino did good business, most of the time. It began as a burlesque house, a thorn in the side of Toronto the Good, and in 1949 it switched to vaudeville (and Toronto's virtuous citizens breathed easier). In 1960 the house was renamed the Civic Square Theatre and operated under that name as an actor's legitimate showcase until it closed in 1962. Then the site, as it were, vanished altogether.

Saxophonist Archie Stone led the pit orchestra at the Casino from 1940 straight through to 1960. It was a six-piece group: two trumpets, one trombone, piano, drums, and the leader on sax. After some years with this combination, the demand for a bass violin became insistent, particularly when top-calibre acts were featured. A new contract was negotiated that called for a seven-piece band with a full-time bassist.

Although playing in the pit of a burlesque house was not the most respectable of engagements in the eyes of a punctilious musical community, the Dirty Thirties of the Great Depression didn't offer much to choose from for discriminating musicians. The lucky ones wound up with a solid, steady job, even if it did involve playing eight shows a week in a "den of iniquity." Besides, very few musicians would turn the Casino job down even in the best of times. However you looked at it, a steady paying job was far better than waiting at home for the telephone to ring.

The acts that appeared at the Casino read like a who's who of show business: Phil Silvers, Buster Keaton, Red Buttons, Chico and Harpo Marx (as singles), Henny Youngman, Victor Borge, Blackstone the Magician, and many others. Even the so-called exotic dancers, each with their own speciality, were among the most famous: Georgia Southern, Sally Rand, Ann Corio, Lily St. Cyr, and Gypsy Rose Lee. The theatre also boasted a chorus line of twelve girls (count 'em).

Periodically the presence of strippers within the city's confines sent shock waves reverberating through the upper echelons of the local churches. But attempts by the police commission to close the theatre constantly failed. According to Murray Little, manager of the Casino from its opening in 1936 to its closing in 1960:

Ironically, a short film about Africa created the loudest furor. The appearance of bare-breasted women was too much for the righteous citizens and a hearing was called. But it didn't go anywhere. By today's standards, the film could serve as a geography lesson for our school kids without anyone batting an eyelash.

Another time an ordained minister, who used to attend matinée performances to see that Toronto's morality laws were not violated (so he said), lodged a complaint with the police force's morality department because the word "hell" was uttered in a sketch. As Murray Little remembers:

They called us for an explanation. The titillating aspect of girls stripping was the focal point of the complaint. Joseph Sedgwick, one of Canada's most brilliant lawyers, represented us. When I went up there with him in front of the Board on College Street — not in a courtroom, it was just a hearing — he suggested we have the sketch acted out right there, and leave it to the Board to decide whether it was a violation of the morality laws.

The sketch involved a woman seeking a doctor's advice on how to avoid getting pregnant. The doctor prescribed orange juice. "It's a wonderful prophylactic," he tells her. A couple of months later she visits the doctor again. This time her waistline reveals she is pregnant. "I took orange juice before I got into bed like you told me to," she says. "Look at me, I'm pregnant. How the hell should orange juice keep me from getting pregnant?"

The doctor replies, "I didn't tell you to take orange juice before you got into bed. I told you to take orange juice instead *of getting into bed." That was the punch line. The Board had a good laugh and threw the hearing out. But the pious citizens cried foul.*

When the Casino's policy switched to vaudeville, all the famous bands appeared regularly, including Tommy Dorsey, Duke Ellington, Count Basie, George Shearing, and Cab Calloway. Barry Little, Murray's son, has kept a scrapbook, which he consulted with enthusiasm during my interview with him and his father.

A number of beginners, tried their routines on the Casino stage in those years. Jerry Lewis, nineteen years old, mugged to a record that played backstage until stopped by the musicians' union. Walter Murdoch, the union's president, insisted that either the pit band play the accompaniment live, or the management hire a large orchestra to back the comic on that number, which was ridiculous because the record featured a large orchestra playing a special arrangement which would be impossible to duplicate with the seven-piece pit band.

That was before Jerry Lewis and Dean Martin were a team. Murray Little also noted that a twelve-year-old Sammy Davis, Jr., appeared with his father Sammy Davis, Sr.. Together, with Uncle Wilf Marsden, they were billed as the Wilf Marsden Trio in song and dance numbers. (And I was reminded of Frank Wright's story, about playing ball with Sammy Davis, Jr., on Sullivan Street, and the taxicab coming, and Sammy saying, "Well, gotta go," and getting in the cab and going to the theatre.)

Others who appeared at the Casino in the 1950s were singer Vic Damone, Jimmy Dorsey (with a young Moe Koffman in the sax section), Kay Starr, Dorothy Lamour, and Mel Torme. Barry Little remembers:

Torme had brought his own piano player and he insisted that the pit band not play one note while he was doing his routine. The band wasn't even allowed to move their heads from side to side; Torme said it disturbed him.

It's not known just how Casino band leader Archie Stone reacted to this particular incident. In any case, his band had different musicians playing during its twenty years in the pit. But one of the mainstays was drummer "Nibsy" Silver, who was with Archie from the beginning. Nibsy was a rarity. In the pit of any burlesque theatre it was highly unlikely that drummers would need music for a striptease number, which was usually four beats to the bar, or three-quarter time with light brushes on the cymbals. But Nibsy had to have a sheet of music to guide him through the routine.

On the other hand, it's often said that Archie never rehearsed the band for any act, and that was unusual. According to Murray Little:

Archie would only talk the arrangements through with the acts. Of course some of them protested they would never go on stage without a rehearsal, but Archie was adamant. "Don't worry," he'd say. "I promise you it'll be okay." The Ames Brothers were particularly disturbed. "How can you let us go on without a rehearsal?" they complained to me. But I told them, "Take my word for it, Archie's a very special musician." They were very uneasy when they went on stage. After the first show, which of course went well, they came downstairs, delighted by what happened. "How the hell do you do it?" they asked Archie. "Absolutely amazing!"

(I remember that Archie, himself, once explained to me what it takes to play in a pit band: "Pit bands must have complete flexibility playing anything and everything on sight, being able to change tempo or key as often as every five bars. Our phrasing must be perfect to fit every movement of the performer, be they singer, juggler, or dancer," he said. "I always keep one eye on the stage.")

As Barry Little remembers things, there was in fact some rehearsal for Casino shows, but not very much:

The chorus line used to rehearse in the sign shop on the top floor of the Roxy. The producer was Chuck Gregory, a very talented choreographer from the States who was present at all rehearsals, even for the individual acts. I was always intrigued to see how he would get the girls to do certain dance patterns. The musicians were very good readers and only needed a moderate amount of rehearsal time. Sometimes performers would show up late, having driven their cars to Toronto. Then the rehearsal would be a talk-through. They'd say, "We'll do this, and we'll do that," and then snap their fingers — one, two, three, four — and add, "This is about the tempo." That would be the end of the rehearsal. They'd hand out the music and the musicians would read it right off.

Over the twenty years, Archie's musicians included trumpeters Vern Gooch and George Beck (later replaced by Gordie Goldhawk and Peter Samborsky), trombonist Jack Katz, pianist Nathan Lustig (replaced by Maurice Winston), drummer Nibsy Silver, and bass player George Clements. Barry Little also remembers that:

We had a problem with Maurice Winston. He couldn't swing. He was a wonderful reader; both he and Archie could read an act's arrangements cold turkey. They'd transpose anything in any key, no problem. But when Maurice accompanied certain singers we'd get complaints. Both Archie and Maurice weren't jazz musicians. They simply could not play that idiom. They were pit musicians, classically trained, and played everything straight ... which doesn't work with a jazz act.

What about the local musicians who came to the theatre to take in the shows (as quite a few of us did)? To start with we knew that Archie's trumpet players were more than adequate for the job, certainly able to play four shows a day, six days a week, and an extra show after midnight on Sunday, without hitting any sour clams.

In fact, a lot of us in the local music business would take advantage of every opportunity we had to visit the Casino. Was it because of the strippers? Maybe, but frankly, I think not. The only people who drooled when the strippers performed were the bald-headed oldsters, who brought sandwiches and sat in the front rows and whistled at the ladies all afternoon. (One ticket admitted you to the theatre, and there was no such thing as clearing the crowd out to make room for the next audience.)

There was so much going on in that sub-culture — from the girls, to the comics, to the MCs singing their opening numbers, even to Archie's band — that if one act didn't please, some of the others would. One thing that fascinated many Toronto musicians of the day was the trombone playing of Jack Katz. One of the kindest gentlemen in the business, Jack had a sound on his instrument that was difficult to duplicate (or believe).

In every burlesque pit band's repertoire were several particular girl-oriented songs that the band usually played as accompaniment to the strippers — songs like "Little Girl, You're the One Girl for Me," "Did You Ever See a Dream Walking?" and "My Little Alice Blue Gown." The song that really killed us at the Casino was Jack Katz's rendition of "A Pretty Girl Is Like a Melody." His sound lay somewhere between that of a muted bedpan with a severe head cold, and the last quart of water gurgling down the bath-tub drain. Yet it was interesting. One of the reasons many of us took in the shows was to hear Jack play a solo piece. And no one dared criticize his playing. If some poor sap was foolish enough to make fun of his style, Jack would turn from being the nicest guy on earth into a raging bull. When he died his funeral procession was one of the longest I can ever recall. So many friends and colleagues came to pay their respects to the memory of their special friend.

Then there was trumpeter Pete Samborsky. Much of the music emanating from the pit was "faked," or improvised. When Pete faked anything, his beautiful sound and amazing technique turned many a trumpet player in the audience green with envy. It seems there wasn't anything he couldn't do on his horn, and he was another reason many of us visited the Casino.

Maurice Winston, not a spectacular piano player at the best of times, was a remarkable scholar whose real talents lay elsewhere. In-between stage shows, when the movie was showing, the musicians generally went out on the street to breathe fresh air. Holed up in the dungeon-like dressing rooms in the basement of the theatre day and night could lead to health problems. But Winston had little regard for the confining quarters.

With his nose deep in some thick encyclopaedia, the bespectacled pianist was always engrossed in a philosophical or scientific subject. Playing those four shows a day was just a means of getting to his studies. Ultimately, he left the theatre job to work in Toronto's Connaught Laboratories, organizing the blood bank for the Canadian government as part of the war effort. Later he joined the faculty of the

AD FOR THE CASINO, DECEMBER 6, 1950. The *Telegram*

Massachusetts Institute of Technology, as professor of mathematics.

When the policy of the theatre switched to vaudeville, the chance to see Tommy Dorsey or Duke Ellington or any of the other marvellous name bands was for us the same as winning the Irish Sweepstakes. And the comedy sketches! Ah, those predictable, double-entendre, and oh-so-suggestive sketches.

There'd always be the corpulent sugar-daddy with a buxom young girl on his arm — both standing at the reservation counter in front of the hotel clerk, while the old guy would tremble in anticipation of the joy to come as he signed the register as Mr. and Mrs. Smith. And the punch line would invariably show the old guy getting something he didn't bargain for, like the hotel clerk phoning him at the penultimate moment to say the real Mrs. Smith was in the lobby with a couple of detectives and an army of reporters and cameramen, on their way up to the room. This was immediately followed by a blackout on the stage, with the band playing the rousing chaser. Then a spotlight would pick up the sugar-daddy, struggling to get his pants on as he tore down the fire escape, but stopping long enough to face the audience and say, "The real Mrs. Smith? Who the hell is the real Mrs. Smith?" Then there would be another blackout, and a roar of laughter from the audience.

Every burlesque theatre had an MC to sing the opening number, tell a few jokes, and introduce the acts. And the Casino had some very good ones: Rex Doyle, Bobby Goodman, and Robert Alda (who had come to Toronto from the U.S.A., and later went to Hollywood to star in a movie about the life of George Gershwin, called *Rhapsody in Blue*.) Murray Little remembers Bob Alda coming to the theatre every day, with his beautiful blond wife and their baby son, Alan. This was the same Alan Alda who would later become famous on the "M.A.S.H." TV series. As a little boy he was apparently so cute that the girls in the Casino chorus would fight over who was next in line to bounce him on their knee backstage, while daddy was out front introducing the Irish skits, the Dutch skits, and the Jewish skits. Alan was about ten years old before the family moved back to the States.

Somewhere around this time, there was a fire at the theatre one Friday night, when a curtain too close to the hot lights in the wings began to smoulder. A stagehand walked out on stage and asked everyone to clear the place. Twelve hundred people quietly walked from the theatre as firemen battled the gathering blaze, which produced an enormous amount of smoke. Almost everything backstage — curtains, scenery, props— was destroyed. In response to Murray Little's pleas, the staff at the nearby Eaton's department store remained on the job, while an army of seamstresses, carpenters, and painters sewed, hammered, sawed, and painted new scenery. Twenty hours later, in the true tradition of the theatre, the show went on.

Of course, not everyone who played the Casino was famous. Red Marshall and Bob Ferguson were two lesser-known comics who were every bit as funny as the reigning giants of the day, but never made it to the top. One time Ferguson stopped in the middle of a story to tell a heckler, who had yelled that Bob Hope was much better, "If Bob Hope had my material, he'd be here too."

Other acts that appeared were Bora Minevitch and the Harmonica Rascals and Steppin' Fetchit, the black comic character who appeared in so many movies in those years: his act wouldn't be tolerated by either black or white audiences today. Lennie Bruce, the famous (or infamous) and controversial comic, who was just beginning his career in the 1950s, drew no laughs from the Casino audience, who couldn't understand what he was talking about, or understand why the pit band laughed at everything he said. Then there was Dr. Morton, the celebrated hypnotist, who put a girl in a trance. She left the theatre, calmly walked to Adams Furniture Store on Yonge Street, got into a bed on display in the front window, and slept in full view of the people in the street until he brought her out of her trance. (The people at the store, of course, were in on the act.)

I remember, as well, how pit band leader Archie Stone once told me about the stripper who "complained she couldn't walk in the key we played. We played too high for her." Archie had played with the bands of Bertram Till and Nelson Hatch in the 1920s and 1930s, before settling in at the Casino in 1940. He retired when the theatre closed its doors for the last time in 1960. In 1981, at the age of seventy-six, he quietly passed away, survived by three sons, Bert, Howard, and Fred. (Freddie Stone became a well-known jazz trumpet player and teacher, until his own untimely death in December 1986, at fifty-one.)

Coda: Barry Little on Growing Up at the Casino

When I was doing my interview on Toronto's last burlesque theatre with former manager Murray Little and his son, Barry, it became clear that Barry (who is now a practising neurologist in Toronto, but literally grew up at the Casino) had some especially interesting things to say. I came to the conclusion that I should let him tell the final installment in this particular part of my story about the Canadian music business in English-speaking Canada's largest big city — all by himself:

Our family started in the theatre business when my grandfather, who was an immigrant tailor from Poland, decided that wasn't the life for him. He was quite entrepreneurial and at the turn of the century started a chain of movie theatres in Ontario. Ultimately, he was in live theatre, but during the Depression he literally lost his shirt. He wound up owning a small burlesque house called the Roxy, which was on the south side of Queen, a couple of blocks west of Bay Street. That was in 1929. Burlesque was considered relatively smutty, but my grandfather ran it alternating with silent movies.

On March 3, 1935, my grandfather was murdered. My father, Murray, who was his son-in-law, found him in his office on the third floor of the Roxy. It was a Sunday morning. Of course, the Monday morning newspaper headlines screamed, "Manager Murdered in His Office." After a period of investigation by the police, the murder was officially declared unsolved. And that changed the course of the theatre and the course our family would take. I was three years old at the time.

After my grandfather's death, there were two men left in the family: my father and my uncle, Lou Appleby, who was a lightweight boxer. Both ran the Roxy, and much to their chagrin, discovered that a new theatre called the Casino was going up beside ours. It was owned by the Allen family, who had connections, we heard, with Hollywood. It didn't take the two partners long to decide that rather than the Roxy competing with the Casino side by side, we should join them in a partnership which lasted until the Casino closed in 1962 as the Civic Square Theatre. That partnership began in 1936.

I was around the Casino from the time I was four years old. I guess my parents wanted to know where I was at all times. Even when I grew older I used to hang around there as often as possible. I had begun studying piano and was enrolled in the Royal Conservatory, which I attended for years. So the music I heard at the Casino was wonderful for me. I remember composing a song, the first piece of music I ever wrote, which was used as an intermission piece. It was called "The Ice Cream Waltz," because we used to sell ice cream in the aisles. George Clements, the bass player, arranged it.

During the war years, when I was younger and going to public school, I was the recipient of both envy and disgust. My teachers at Clinton Street Public School would point at me and whisper, "His father's the manager of that theatre." I learned very early in life that the Casino was really a den of iniquity, and I was often hurt by those whispers. But I still liked going there, I guess because I liked seeing semi-clad girls dancing.

The story about the ordained minister who complained to the Police Morality Department because "hell" was used in a skit clearly reflected the public's attitude on what was considered acceptable then. As it was, comics never said anything more offen-

sive than "hell." "Hot damn" was a substitute for "goddammit." "Fuck" would have closed the theatre for good. Nowadays, you can find that word in the editorial pages of newspapers, and it's commonly used in most movies and television films.

There was an interesting sideline to the Casino. Because we had to be so careful of the language in the skits and the suggestive movements of the girls, my father was under considerable stress. He had to go to Buffalo every week to check out the acts that were booked for our theatre the next week. If some words were inappropriate he would tell the acts to delete them. The same caution would apply to the dancers. I would accompany him with my mom. She loved the American shopping, and I enjoyed going because it was different. Buffalo was a thriving community during the Second World War. In 1941 Bell Aircraft was there — a very busy place.

We went to the Palace Theatre where I saw much more raw — and I mean raw — burlesque. The comics said things on stage that would not be allowed in Toronto. And of course they were deleted by the time the acts came to the Casino. They generally changed their lines to get around those obscene words.

The minister who complained about "hell" may or may not have been offended by other things, too, but he came back too often after the case was closed to seem bothered by the strippers. I don't think his complaint had anything to do with the use of profanity on stage. I think he used the argument that it was corrupting the morals of our servicemen who were serving the country a little too much. But the fact that the theatre was always filled with servicemen on leave was evidence enough that the Casino's burlesque acts were a morale booster for these guys. And the theatre was constantly filled during the war years, not only with servicemen but the general public as well, including certain mobsters. Not any known Mafioso people, just local hoods.

There was a fellow who worked for us — Wally. Wally was our connection between the legitimate and illegitimate world. If we wanted to know who did a job, or who was implicated in a headline-making crime in Toronto, just ask Wally; he knew every fence. We were inundated with bookies like Joe the Goof. The place was also crawling with people from City Hall, politicians, and the odd mayor or two who loved the girlies.

Our twelve chorus girls were respectable ladies, who were either married or had boyfriends. We had gangsters from our side of the border, no American heavyweights. They didn't try to muscle in. And we had every gambler you could think of, and every local promoter and hustler anybody knew about. And then we had Osgoode Hall across the street. So we had some of the legal profession as well. In fact, everybody that had anything to do with entertainment or music or the sports world made it to the theatre. What was so intriguing about the place was that it was a focal point of so much activity that interwove with the political and social life of the city. And all because of the girls.

By 1948 burlesque had begun to lose its appeal, and we began to think of going into vaudeville. The switch took place in 1949 and much to our surprise the experiment paid off. We began bringing name acts like Victor Borge (funnier than hell), Blackstone the Magician (he was so good that my father, who used to watch from the wings, could never see how he accomplished his amazing tricks, even from that vantage point), Louis Armstrong and Ella Fitzgerald (on the same bill!), and even Rudy Vallee.

Vallee had had his heyday in the 1930s and early 1940s, when he was a huge radio star. By the late forties and early fifties his star had faded and he needed work. So he came to the Casino. I was sixteen then, working as an usher. Just before the first show one day, I was wearing my uniform and noodling on the piano backstage when he came over (I had learned to play the piano at the Conservatory). When he heard me he asked, "Hey kid, can you read?" "Yes," I said. "Keep on playing," he said, "you're pretty good. It would be kind of different having a kid like you in the act as an accompanist."

At first I thought he was a bit flaky, but when I saw who he came in with as his female companion — a gorgeous redhead — I knew he was not flaky. For some reason he presumed that I wanted to get into show business. He was an egomaniac and had to tell me all about his life. I learned later that he always sat in front of a sun lamp before each performance so that he would look just right. I didn't tell him that my father was part owner of the theatre, and that this was just a part-time gig for me. I said, "I'm not interested." He still had to tell me about his career: "When I was in show business ... " and then I heard all about Rudy Vallee's beginnings.

As a teenager I had some perceptions of what was morally appropriate, and was annoyed with my father's connection with burlesque. People often said to me, "Your father had no choice. It was a source of income for the family." I was surprised when we went "straight," went legitimate, and saw the kinds of people who began to come to the theatre — a place they wouldn't be caught dead in during the burlesque years. I was suddenly one of the most popular guys at school. (I was going to Forest Hill Collegiate at that time). Nobody seemed embarrassed any more knowing the Little family.

We brought in a lot of headliners, including Kay Starr, Frankie Lane (one of the biggest), Nat King Cole (who was not well known then, except to musicians for his piano playing. He was just beginning to sing) and Patti Page. (She was assaulted at a downtown hotel at nineteen years of age. She wasn't raped, but some guy tried to assault her. She said she would never come back to Toronto and she never did.)

With our new policy there were a few singers that we wanted to get. We decided that the best way was to book headliners only. My dad had a bit of luck with a couple of them. He got Johnny Rae, who had just recorded a hit that turned out to be number one on the American Hit Parade. The amount of business we did with him was such that the lines of people waiting to get into the theatre went around both sides of Queen Street, down York, and down Bay. I always say "Johnny Rae put me through medical school." That was in the fifties. At the time, the seating capacity of the theatre was 1,250. Rae would do an extra show, and people would stand in line for hours.

Another surprise blockbuster was Wilf Carter, the Canadian country-and-western singer. He had such a following that the people lined up on the street for hours, even before the theatre opened. The people who came to hear Carter did not ordinarily attend Casino performances, but they certainly did for this guy. They were dyed-in-the-wool *country music fans.*

One of the first acts was a group called the Page Cavanaugh Trio, who had recorded "Walking My Baby Back Home," which was a big hit. We became real celebrities in our high school because my older brother convinced Page and his guys to play the spring prom at local scale. Forest Hill Collegiate had just opened in 1949, and when this bigtime trio played, some of the school kids thought it was some sort of fraud. After all, Page Cavanaugh had been in a couple of movies and he also had several hits going for him. Why would a group of this stature play for us? We were very popular for that.

We also had a lot of name bands that played the theatre: Lionel Hampton brought in a small group, Count Basie, Duke Ellington, Cab Calloway — they all appeared. We had the Ink Spots, the Golden Gate Quartet, and the Mills Brothers. To personalize this for a moment, I had the privilege of seeing and hearing black musicians. I was backstage a lot and got to meet them. I never attended a gospel church, but I heard music at the theatre that was ear- and mind-impressing. It has stayed with me all these years. Wonderful music, wonderful musicians!

And if I told you what the musicians' union did to us you wouldn't believe me. Walter Murdoch, the union's president, had an enormous impact on our business. When American musicians came up here, they weren't allowed to appear on radio programs to advertise their product because of the protectionism of the union. A few members of the local thought it was wonderful, but it really ruined our business and caused no end of chagrin to the performers who naturally wanted to come up to Canada to let the uninitiated know about their latest record. It was an insult to them.

Though Barry Little is a practising neurologist in Toronto today, he is also a member of the Toronto Musicians' Association, Local 149 of the American Federation of Musicians of the United States and Canada, and performs from time to time as a keyboard player. As is still the case with many others among us, I suppose, when he does perform, something of the last days of Toronto's last burlesque theatre — and everything else about the time and place it was a part of itself — somehow quietly lives on.

Part Four
At the CBC

"MUSIC MAKERS" CBC TV, 1958. Jack Kane's "Music Makers" television show, which ran from September 1957 to June 1961, drew some of the largest viewing audiences in Canadian TV history. Here, Kane's thirty-piece orchestra is on set, ready to go. Trumpet section: Gordon Braund, Bernie Rowe, Ellis McLintock, and Morris Isenbaum (hidden from camera). Trombone section: Frank Reynolds, Ross Culley, Teddy Roderman, and Murray Ginsberg. Saxes: Morris Weinzweig, Benny Paul, Roy Smith, Jerry Toth, Moe Koffman, and Lew Lewis. *Courtesy Canadian Broadcasting Corporation*

I was thirty years old in 1952. It was the year that the Toronto Musicians' Protective Association first shortened its name to the Toronto Musicians' Association, and the year that saw the appointment of the first Canadian-born governor general of Canada. And it was also the year when the Canadian Broadcasting Corporation started to add a television network to its radio broadcasting services.

For a lot of us in the music business in English-speaking Canada's largest big city, the advent of CBC TV was the biggest of these events. And it came along at a good time. As Barry Little would explain when I interviewed him and his father much later, the Casino had switched from burlesque to vaudeville in 1949 because "burlesque had begun to lose its appeal. (In fact, there was some drop-off in the box office)." Once the Casino had changed its policy, the Little family discovered that some other things had begun to lose their appeal as well.

When the dawn rose in 1950, "Canada's King of Swing," Bert Niosi, had also decided to end his long association with the Palais Royale Ballroom. And he was just one of many musicians who carried on with their careers at the CBC (on television, and on the radio network that had already been in business for some two decades). A lot of what was best on the Canadian music scene had one thing or another to do with the CBC.

I wouldn't want to exaggerate this point. There was a strong side of the earlier live-music business of the golden age that would carry on for quite a while yet. Trump Davidson was showing various new and old guys how to play at the Palace Pier until 1963. Mart Kenney and Norma Locke didn't leave their ranch in Woodbridge until 1969. And the period of the 1950s was also the great age of the Colonial and the Towne Tavern on the Toronto jazz scene (and of such places as the House of Hambourg).

Yet when I think about the music I loved to play the most myself during the 1950s and 1960s, I think about jobs like the one with Jack Kane's "Music Makers" on CBC TV. When I think about what the best music in Toronto was from those days, the CBC figures prominently in the picture. Without the CBC, a lot of good music in Canada during the generation after the Second World War would probably never have happened.

Lucio Agostini (in the dark on Grenville Street)

One prominent case in point here is the career of Lucio Agostini. He had moved from Montreal to Toronto in 1943, and created some enormous excitement at the Toronto studios of the CBC. He had already conducted radio shows in Montreal. But his real success as a composer of incidental music for dramatic productions — and as a superb painter of musical portraits and landscapes — developed to it's greatest height in Toronto.

Between 1944 and 1955 he composed and conducted music for the CBC radio-drama series "Stage," produced and directed by Andrew Allen; for CBC

LUCIO AGOSTINI AND FRIENDS, 1955. The musicians who appear here are among the finest in Canada. Agostini sits in the second row, sixth from the left, between the only two ladies in his orchestra, violinist Beauna Neilson and French horn player Mary Barrow. Murray Ginsberg's teacher, white-haired Harry Hawe, is seen in top row, third from right. *Courtesy Erich Traugott*

"Wednesday Night Shakespeare" productions; for CBC Radio's "Ford Theatre" (1949–55); and for a number of variety programs, including his own "Strictly for Strings" (1951–52), and "Appointment with Agostini" (1954–55).

For musicians, his work was always a delight to play. I particularly remember his arrangement of the Howard Deitz-Arthur Schwartz masterpiece "Dancing in the Dark." We were doing a show from the Ward-Price Galleries studio on Grenville Street. The piece began with a voluptuous introduction that went on for a minute or more. The strings soared, the flutes and clarinets fluttered like birds in flight, while the horns and winds cascaded over invisible waterfalls. Then the mountain of music dwindled and faded to a guitar's single string playing the melody ("Dancing in the dark ... 'til the tune ends ... "). The contrast was startling. Lucio's musical painting conjured up a darkened ballroom, with long curtains blowing gently in the breeze from open windows — and, silhouetted against the dim light, a couple holding each other tightly, barely moving to the lovely melody.

All of Agostini's arrangements were pleasant surprises, and he never ran out of ideas. Some of his later broadcast productions included "Music Album," "Collage," and "Music to Remember."

Lucio had been born in Italy, but he grew up and studied music in Montreal. His value in the CBC studios lay in his command of musical colours, his ability to

At the CBC *117*

satisfy the dramatic requirements at hand, and his efficiency as a workman. His ability to lengthen or shorten a passage (often at the last minute) without timing the passage was uncanny.

I remember one show when, with barely a minute to go before airtime, the producer hurriedly asked for a certain cue to be lengthened by thirty-two seconds. Unruffled, Agostini looked at his score for a moment, then instructed the musicians, "Repeat the first twelve bars of 'B' and continue." There was no time to run the passage over. The red light went on; the announcer declared "CBC presents ..." Up music and voices over. When it came to the cue Lucio conducted the musicians as though nothing happened. Perfect! The producer flashed a thumbs up. The cue was right on target. Maestro Agostini allowed a smile to crease his lips, and carried the show to a successful conclusion. When I was doing my interviews for this book, the CBC studio player Morris Isen remembered:

Lucio Agostini was a strong leader, a fine musician. You gotta learn to know the man. He never insulted a guy unless he made a mistake.

My good friend, bassist Murray Lauder, actually worked as Agostini's contractor for a few years, and became close friends with him. He remembers that Lucio was a marvellous arranger:

There was nothing he couldn't do. And whoever said he was an efficient workman was right. At the same time, he wasn't the easiest guy to work for. In fact, most of the time he was a tyrant. He had little patience, but he really was a fair man.

Another of my interview informants, Frank Fusco, explained how Lucio went to Hollywood in 1955 to try his luck and stayed a year.

During that twelve-month period everybody treated him like a king. He wrote and conducted a few shows and earned the applause of a lot of people in the business. But when they learned he intended to live there, all doors closed.

To Toronto's advantage, Lucio Agostini returned in 1956, and became conductor-arranger for CBC TV's "Front Page Challenge," an appointment which lasted for twenty years. I am sad to report that he died on February 15, 1996.

The Gino Silvi Singers

I am sad as well to report the death, on July 1, 1993, of another great Canadian musician of Italian descent, who spent a lot of time at the CBC. At the age of seventy-nine, Gino Silvi, after a long battle with cancer, succumbed at 2:00 AM on Canada Day in Queensway General Hospital.

For the last two years of his life he had worn a plastic bag around his waist which drained the urine from his bladder. When I interviewed him in his Toronto condominium in January 1992, he had told me about the operation to remove the tumor in his bladder, and loosened his trouser belt to show me the bag.

Gruesome? Perhaps. But Gino seemed unbothered by his condition. "What the hell," he remarked. "This is what happens to us at this age. You just ride with the punches." That statement speaks volumes about the gentle man who rose from poverty to become an accomplished saxophonist, composer, arranger, and conductor who was held in high esteem by colleagues in Toronto and across the country.

During that January 1992 visit, despite Gino's years, I found it difficult to accept his age. He looked positively ruddy and was excited about writing some arrangements for the Encore Seniors' Band, which rehearsed every Thursday in the Toronto Musicians' Association Auditorium. We sat and joked about the good old days when we played "Laura" and "Stella By Starlight" and so many other great songs. "This garbage that passes for music today leaves me cold," Gino snorted.

Who was Gino Silvi and where did he come from? To start with, he was born in Sault Ste. Marie, Ontario, in 1914, one of five brothers and sisters. When he was just seven years old, he moved with his family to Hamilton, Ontario. Both parents were Italian immigrants who had to struggle, and life was difficult:

Our mother got sick and had to go to the hospital. My father couldn't look after us because he had a job; so all five of us were placed in different homes. I was put in a boys' foster home with my brother Guido, who was two years older than me. We were there for five years, but it felt like ten. It was pretty rough.

By the time Gino was twelve his mother's health had improved, and she came for her two sons. She had landed a job scrubbing floors in, of all places, the foster home Gino had lived in for five years.

We couldn't believe it. My brother and I kept asking each other "What have we done? Why are they kicking us out of here?" We couldn't believe she was asking for us.

But at last the family was together again, all living under one roof in Hamilton. And that was when the music started. Also living under the roof was Uncle Jack, who worked at the Dofasco steel plant. Uncle Jack had a dog. Gino had heard about a guy with a banjo for sale. He sold the dog and purchased the banjo with the proceeds.

I had no money, so selling the dog seemed the quickest way to get the banjo.

When Uncle Jack came home his fist went ka-pow across Gino's face. Back went twelve-year-old Gino with the banjo to the original owner, and back came Fido to home sweet home.

But, dammit, I still had to have that banjo. So I sold my uncle's bicycle — the one he rode to work on. That's how I got started in music, playing the four-string banjo.

Gino didn't say what happened when Uncle Jack learned that the bicycle was missing. But he did admit that as a boy he was a holy terror. Someone showed the lad some ukulele fingerings and from there he taught himself banjo fingerings. Then he bought a sheet of music with fingering symbols printed over the notes and that's when he started to learn in earnest. He was strictly self-taught, all the way.

When he was fifteen he began to experiment on a cousin's saxophone:

I was shown the fingering, and somehow I began to play, very slowly at first. I was fortunate to be able to get most of it right, instinctively — correct fingerings, getting a sound without the reed squeaking, playing a scale, all self-taught. Somebody said, "Do it this way," and I did.

Then came his first band. When leader, Stan Stephenson, asked him to join, Gino at first declined, explaining that although he loved playing the sax, he couldn't read music. "I can read banjo symbols, though." Stephenson said, "Fine. Bring both instruments." So young Gino Silvi became a member of Stan Stephenson's orchestra and, best of all, a member of the sax section, when needed. This gave the boy his first crack at improvising. He was in seventh heaven.

I played alto sax, so I'm playing banjo and the saxes are playing and the music says an ad lib solo is coming up. I put down the banjo and pick up my horn and I ad lib the solo because, all of a sudden, I knew chords. I kept on playing until it was time for me to put the saxophone down and play the banjo again. We were all about the same age — sixteen or seventeen—and we got along nicely. I really enjoyed that first solo.

Before long, other musicians had heard about the guy who could pluck a terrific banjo, lay down a good rhythm, and then switch to sax and really take off. Gino's phone began to ring, and he soon found himself in another band, playing alto sax with three other sax players:

I discovered that when they all played harmony, I could fit in my own harmony without getting in anyone's way. I sat with those guys and pretended that I was reading my part, when all I was doing was listening to the tenor harmony and fitting my own alto harmony into the music. I stayed with that band for about two years and I'm positive that none of the others had any idea that I couldn't read music.

In 1938 at age twenty-four, Gino got a chance to play tenor saxophone. Len Allen, a popular Hamilton bandleader, called Gino. "I'm starting a tenor lead band," he said. "I'd like you to join the band on tenor." (Bands that used a tenor saxophone rather than the conventional alto to play the lead melody tended to feature "sweet" music rather than swing or jazz.)

I told him I played alto, but he said he needed me on tenor and hoped I would get one. It wasn't until later that I found out he wanted me to play a harmony part. He had another guy who would play lead — two tenors and an alto. For $275 I bought a Martin tenor. It worked perfectly. It was built to last a lifetime, a collector's item. I didn't have any money, so I paid it off monthly, like everybody else.

In the Len Allen band Gino realized he couldn't go on "faking it." It was time he learned to read music. Playing simple harmony parts by ear simply wouldn't work with cleverly written arrangements. But he did somehow understand that, in the end, when he would look at a sheet of music, no matter how intricate, he would have the entire sheet memorized, and wouldn't even bother to pick the music from the folder when the leader would call out the tunes for the next set.

Some guys told me that I had a photographic memory, whatever that is. So I finally hit upon the only way I could learn to read. I bought a DeVille Method for Saxophone *— a big, thick book, one of the best. I started on page one and never repeated a page. It had everything in it on how to play the sax — a great book. I memorized the entire contents. I had no teacher. That was the way I learned to read music.*

In fact, the only time Gino ever had a teacher was years later, in the 1950s, when he was established in the upper echelon of the Toronto music community, working on jingles, recording sessions, film soundtracks, and CBC radio and television. One day, bassist Johnny Dobson told him, "You have a remarkable ear not given to many musicians. I know you want to arrange. So why don't you go to Gordon Delamont and take some tuition from him?" And although the man with the photographic memory could already arrange on a limited scale, he was aware that every musician who really wants to write must take some instruction — in composition, orchestration, and arranging — of the highest level.

Gordon Delamont, a trumpet player who jobbed around with different bands, was also a highly respected teacher of arranging and orchestration.

Gordon had a studio near the CBC on Jarvis Street, which was handy. When I rang the doorbell, Gordon opened the door and said, "Well, what can I do for the great Gino Silvi?" I could have fallen through the bloody floor. And he was serious. I began a long and happy relationship with Gord who taught me more than I'd ever hoped for.

From 1938 to 1942 Gino worked with a number of bands in Hamilton, sharpening his skills in both playing and arranging. Copying from records of such famous American bands as Tommy Dorsey, Bunny Berigan, and Benny Goodman, he began to transcribe arrangements of numbers like "Marie," "I Can't Get Started with You," and "Frankie and Johnny" to fit the instrumentation of the local bands he played with. And whenever they tried one of these arrangements, the musicians asked for more. For Gino, life took on new meaning:

I did all this by ear. I heard all the notes that each musician on the record was playing. And this is what got me going. I developed my ear so that it was razor sharp. That ear could catch anything. God gave me this gift and all I did was exploit it to the best of my ability. It was strictly something that was handed to me — a sharp ear and a good memory.

When there was a gap in jobs Gino would sometimes take a long trip north to his birthplace in Sault Ste. Marie, to visit relatives and a few friends who still lived there. On one of these trips he met and was immediately smitten by Jean Tadashore, whom he finally married, on Thursday, May 19, 1941. The wedding also took place in "the Soo."

At 2:00 PM the newlyweds boarded the train back to Hamilton. (The train ride took fifteen hours and, when I interviewed him in 1992, Gino mumbled something about how upper berths on trains were not really designed for couples on their wedding night.)

Then, in 1942, the third year of the Second World War, Gino joined the Canadian Army. At the time, when anyone in southern Ontario joined the army, they were sent to the Canadian National Exhibition in Toronto, where they were sworn in, received their serial numbers and uniforms, and took some early marching drill. Gino recalled:

So I came to Toronto and the Exhibition grounds, I figured there's nothing wrong with me; I'm a big, strong guy. I'm going to be in Europe ducking bullets in no time.

What he didn't know was that Sgt.-Maj. Bill Sharman had been told to check all incoming recruits to see if any were musicians. Sharman had been given the assignment of forming a new marching band for the Ex, to be known as District Depot Band No. 2.

When he read Gino's card he immediately called him for an interview. "How'd you like to join our band?" he asked. "We're taking the best players and you certainly fill the bill."

"Well, sir," Gino started to reply, "I'd love it, but I'm a grown man and I've got to go overseas ... "

"How'd you mean?" Sgt.-Maj. Sharman interrupted. "You can't go overseas with that sinus trouble of yours ... One whiff of that damp London air and ..."

"Sinus trouble?" Gino said. "What sinus tr ... oh, of course ... pardon me while I get another handkerchief."

And so Gino Silvi, the tenor saxophonist with a sharp ear and a very good memory, became a member of District Depot Band No. 2. The group included such well-known Toronto musicians as trombonist Jack Madden, saxophonists Jack Wachter, Jimmy O'Driscoll, and Morris Weinzweig, and bassist Howard Barnes. It marched in daily parades, played concerts, and performed an assortment of other military duties which generally kept the musicians working every day, sometimes even on Sundays. But the days usually began at 9:00 AM and ended at 5:00 PM.

Many of the musicians lived at home or rented rooms in the city and reported for duty every morning. Their evenings were free, allowing them to do as much freelance work as possible — dances, club dates, wedding, and birthday parties. Gino soon found that he was in demand by bandleaders across the city. And this led to his first CBC radio show.

Some time in 1943, he got a call from orchestra leader Samuel Hershenhorn. "Gino Silvi?" a firm voice said on the telephone. "This is Sam Hershenhorn. I understand you play tenor saxophone?"

"Yes, from Hamilton," Gino replied.

"Do you own a tenor sax? Are you a member of the union?"

"Yes, I have my own sax, and I'm a member of the Hamilton union, but not the Toronto local."

"I'd like to use you in my studio orchestra but you've got to be a member of the Toronto local."

"How do I do that?"

A pause. Then Hershenhorn said, "Look, change into civvies. Don't come in uniform, and go down to see Arthur Dowell and get your jobbing card."

Sammy told me what to say to Dowell, who was the secretary of Local 149, the Toronto Musicians' Protective Association. I went to the office, which was located on Dundas Square, at Victoria. It was up on the sixth floor of the Percy Hermant Building. I remember who I saw when I walked through the door: Walter Murdoch, the president, whose strong personality leaped out at you the moment you laid eyes on him, white-haired, bespectacled Arthur Dowell, Miss Doyle (that tall, thin fantastic woman with the uncanny memory who could always recognize telephone voices), and Mrs. Harrison, the bookkeeper, who looked like everybody's mother.

That's how it all happened. I began my CBC work in 1943 with Sam Hershenhorn. I felt pretty good about doing a big-time radio show. I found out some time later that the reason I was called was because all the good musicians were overseas. They were in the army, air force, and navy bands. I guess there was nobody left in Toronto. Sam was desperate and it was pure luck that I happened to be at the right place at the right time. One thing led to another, and I started doing a lot of work in the studios. But I was still in the army and although I had almost every evening free from military duties, I was in for the duration, and the end of the war was a long way off.

By 1946, with the war finally over, Gino had become well established with Sam

THE GINO SILVI SINGERS, 1958.
Courtesy Gino Silvi

Hershenhorn. He played all of the Hershenhorn radio shows — especially the "Wayne and Shuster Comedy Hour." It was easily the CBC's funniest series, and it went on for years. Gino played every episode. Then in 1950 Frank and Johnny decided to bring in singers. Gino had thought about writing for a vocal group of his own for years, and he was given the okay to organize such a group.

This marked the beginning of Gino's ultimate destiny at the CBC. But he was also popular with other leaders who were impressed with his playing, with his ability to compose and arrange tunes, and to rehearse and conduct a choir. One leader in particular made an enormous impact on him:

About the same time I was organizing singers for the Wayne and Shuster show, Howard Cable called me for his concert band. Howard had several shows going at the same time and a call from him was the total compliment.

And what a band that was! Everybody who was anybody in the music business in Toronto was a prominent member of that ensemble. Most of the wind players from the Toronto Symphony were included: flutists Gordie Day and Teddy Smith, clarinetist Abe Galper; bassoonist Wayland Mosher; along with the top studio players, namely Teddy Roderman, Cliff MacKay, Morris London, Ellis McLintock, Jimmy Reynolds, Harry Nicholson. The Howard Cable Concert Band had thirty-four of Canada's very best musicians.

Playing for Howard was a real challenge. He'd write a lot of his own arrangements, including a couple of original compositions on each broadcast. We'd often practise our parts at home to be ready for the next rehearsal. No way could we come unprepared.

Under normal conditions, CBC studio musicians could read anything at sight. But Howard Cable's arrangements were rigorously demanding, and the leader had little patience for anyone who could not cut his or her part.

At this point as well, away from the broadcast studios, Gino was playing with the remaining best dance bands in the city, like Ellis McLintock at the Casa Loma, and Denis Stone at the Prince George Hotel:

At that time there was so much work for everybody, we couldn't handle it all. I was starting to do jingles, recordings, and when CBC television began in 1952, I found myself playing shows on-camera, too. That was a new experience.

Gino had already had some fleeting experience writing for singers in Hamilton when he was with the Bill Andrews band:

When I copied Tommy Dorsey from records, I included all the Pied Pipers stuff. They were a marvellous quartet, with Jo Stafford singing the lead. My God, they were great. We had a pretty good girl singer in Bill's band, and three of us who played could also sing fairly well; so we copied the Pied Pipers (or made an attempt at at sounding like them) and became a quartet. That was my first experience with singing and I loved it.

It was not until 1955, however, that the real Gino Silvi Singers began their evolution, with a first appearance on the CBC "Hit Parade" radio series. On the "Hit Parade" show on the radio and "Cross-Canada Hit Parade" on television, the same song could be at the top of the charts for weeks, and every week it had to have a new arrangement, to keep it alive for the audience:

ELLIS McLINTOCK AND HIS ORCHESTRA, CASA LOMA, circa 1949. On June 2, 1944, Ellis and his dance band opened a multi-year engagement at Casa Loma. Courtesy Ellis McLintock

That was a terrific opportunity for me. I had multiple singers every week. Every week there would be a different number of vocalists, depending on the arrangement of the tune that was Number One or Two on the charts. They would tell me, "You've got four singers this week." The following week there would be thirty singers. That sort of constant writing was the best experience anyone could hope for. And that's when I got four guys and four girls who had received training at the Conservatory by professional singing coaches. I even stole one from the Leslie Bell Singers.

Leslie Bell, the director of a famous all-woman choral group, chose his singers from talented young girls in public and junior high schools, and helped train each one in the fine art of singing. Yet another seed for the Gino Silvi Singers was the "Juliette Show" in the mid-1950s:

Juliette Cavazzi, a terrific singer herself, wanted a vocal group on her show. Since she was a woman, producer Bob Gardiner thought it would make sense to have a male quartet. So we called it "Juliette and the Romeos." What else with a name like Juliette?

At this point, the Perry Como television shows in the United States were huge extravaganzas, with big choruses and an army of dancers. The CBC, whose producers were never shrinking violets, wanted to emulate the trend. Gino was asked to enlarge his chorus. The eight original vocalists were the nucleus around which Gino built his extraordinary vocal ensemble:

Some of my singers were musicians who knew a lot about singing. Alex Tichnovitch was a guitar player. Both Vern Kennedy and Rick Stainsby were trumpet players, and John Garden, who sang bass, played pretty good guitar. Angella Antonelli was a marvellous lead soprano; Fran Groat, Carol Hill, and Joyce Bertan, all just what I needed. I had twenty-four to thirty voices at times. It depended on what the script called for.

By 1956 and 1957, the CBC was impressing the world with its talent:

Every week we would see strange faces taking in the shows from the sidelines. They were usually representatives from the William Morris and other agencies from the States. When New York wanted to see what was happening with our spectaculars, they'd come to Toronto to see for themselves. Because we had it all.

Gino was in the middle of it all, doing the "Hit Parade," the "Wayne and Shuster" shows, and many, many more. But what about the tenor sax? Were his playing days over? I put this question to the big man towards the end of our conversation.

Not at all, he replied. I still wanted to keep my hand in blowing. So I'd play different jobs with only the bands I wanted to play with. And I also booked my own jobs where I could play what I wanted to play. It was a good band, too, with guys like Acey

Howard, Bill Turner, Bobby Fenton, and other fine musicians. It was a great life. I played my horn, and I had the Gino Silvi Singers on CBC.

In spite of all his other successes, one show remained closest to his heart. The fulfillment of an idea he'd had for years, "Dream Street" was a radio series that featured the incomparable Norma Locke, singing and narrating. Her voice possessed a striking clarity that mesmerized the listener. Her intonation was flawless, her musicality supreme. When she spoke, her irresistible charm held every listener spellbound. For Gino she was a dream come true.

Norma and my wonderful eight-singer group, along with a great band and terrific scripts written by producer Ken Dalziel, made this something I'll never forget

I remember myself that the show created a beautiful mood. The singing was spectacular. The arrangements by Silvi were exquisite, and the playing sparkled. No wonder "Dream Street" was closest to Gino's heart. He was big and strong — a bruiser if forced into a fight (which he never lost). But he was also the kindest and most sensitive of individuals.

I recall as well some remarks from singers I talked with, who worked on "Dream Street" and other Gino Silvi shows: "We always looked forward so much to what new and wonderful harmonies Gino would come up with. He was a marvellous arranger for voices." (Angella Antonelli); "'Dream Street' was the most satisfying program any of us were involved with. I'm so fortunate to have been a member of Gino's group. It was pure joy." (Vern Kennedy)

Gino himself deserves the last word. When I asked him, at the very end of our interview in 1992, what influences were responsible for his musical successes, he just said:

I take no credit for my accomplishments. God gets the credit.

Howard Cable

It's no accident, I think, that even the great Gino Silvi was thrilled to be asked to play in the Howard Cable Concert Band in 1950. Toronto-born Howard Cable has been the most successful conductor/composer/arranger on the Canadian music scene since the 1940s.

Not too long ago, he celebrated fifty years of making music when he conducted the Hanniford Street Silver Band's first concert of the 1994–95 season at the St. Lawrence Centre in downtown Toronto. Before a sold-out house, he introduced each piece on the program with a bit of history of his career. "My first arranging job for the CBC was for Sir Ernest MacMillan, conductor of the Supertest Concert Orchestra in 1944," he explained. By the time the 1960s rolled around he had become a household name across Canada as arranger and conductor of over a thousand CBC radio shows.

Howard became even more nationally prominent as musical director and host of some of the most popular television programs of CBC's golden age of variety shows. During the 1950s and 1960s his arrangements for wind ensembles and his direction of the Howard Cable Concert Band won him a wide following in England and the United States, through recordings and radio broadcasts. And hundreds of published arrangements and compositions for band increased his renown throughout North America.

While he has also scored over thirty films, he has had a special affinity for the musical stage. For his work with productions at Toronto's Crest and Royal Alexander theatres, the St. Lawrence Centre, and the Charlottetown Festival, he has been called "the dean of Canadian musical theatre." He was equally at home on Broadway, where he worked with Richard Rogers, Meredith Wilson, and Mitch Leigh as arranger and conductor. And his work as composer and director of intimate revues helped revitalize Canada's cabaret scene.

But it was his work on CBC radio and television in the 1950s and 1960s that made Howard Cable a familiar name in every home, office, and corporation across Canada. He wrote and conducted such radio shows as: "Canadian Cavalcade" (with Lorne Greene); "O'Keefe Hi Time", "Robin Hood Musical Kitchen", and "Esso Happy Motoring" (some of the fastest, tightest, entertainment-crammed, five half-hour shows per week in the history of the CBC); "The Howard Cable Concert Band," "Mr. Show Business," and "General Electric Showtime" featuring the Leslie Bell Singers. When TV arrived, "Showtime" went to a weekly one-hour

THE HOWARD CABLE CONCERT BAND, 1953.
Courtesy Howard Cable

128 They Loved to Play

telecast, featuring Robert Goulet and guests.

His work on CBC notwithstanding, Howard Cable has also dipped his toe into other areas of the music business and found the temperature inviting. For twelve years he was musical director of the Royal York Hotel's Imperial Room, where he worked with the likes of Ella Fitzgerald, Tony Bennett, and Peggy Lee. For more than a decade he has also appeared as a "pops" conductor with most of Canada's leading symphony orchestras.

The Hanniford Street Silver Band concert in 1994 was a great success. There were letters of congratulation from Canadian Prime Minister Jean Chrétien and former Ontario Premier Bob Rae. And before the last number, the conductor asked those in the audience who had played for him at some point in their careers to stand. More than half rose to their feet to pay tribute to the musician who had such a profound effect on their lives.

I had explored how Howard Cable got started about a year before the Hanniford Silver Band concert, during an interview in 1993. Howard, who grew up in Toronto's Parkdale neighbourhood, began by telling me:

My mother was quite musical. I was an only child so I got a lot of encouragement from her. I took piano lessons at the Royal Conservatory, dutifully, at the south Parkdale Branch. I studied with Vera M. King, not a name that's rank at the Conservatory. But anyway, I got involved with music at Parkdale Collegiate. Leslie Bell was my teacher. He said, "If you could get a clarinet; we need clarinets." So, my mother bought me a clarinet, an Albert System. I learned that and got very interested. Then he said, "You're very good on the clarinet, but how about an oboe? You think your mother and father would spring for an oboe?"

This was the middle of the Depression — 1936, 1937. My father worked at City Hall. At least he had a job. He wasn't out of work ... we didn't have any money to speak of but we were okay. They bought an oboe for me and I picked it up quite fast. I studied with Jock Hutchen. Remember Jock? He played in the symphony. And this was 1937, 1938. He was a good teacher who arranged somehow to get me a scholarship at the Conservatory on oboe. I talked to Sir Ernest who was principal of the school. And I got a scholarship and enrolled in all the courses. That was the start of it.

Prompted by Sir Ernest MacMillan, who had taken an interest in young Cable, Howard got himself a book on orchestration:

I was just a kid who played piano in a dance band and also played oboe. I wasn't really a genius of any sort, but Sir Ernest would say, "That boy! ... " He told me to look into Forsyth's Orchestration. *In fact I was fifteen or sixteen when Leslie Bell first asked me to write arrangements. I just floated into it, like fellow Torontonians Bob Farnon and Percy Faith. We all sort of floated into arranging.*

In the summer of 1937, Cable took a dance band up to Waubaushene and Honey Harbour on Georgian Bay, in the heart of Ontario's beautiful Muskoka resort district:

The guys would all go play pool or go get girls, and I'd go out and study orchestration. I'd lie in the sun and learn the Cecil Forsyth orchestration book. And I got interested in how everything's done.

Howard pressed ahead with the early parts of his story:

I remember there was a big band in the east end, George Hooey and The Modernaires. In 1938 somebody asked me to write an arrangement for this band. He wanted me to write a Benny Goodman-type arrangement. In 1938 I didn't know much about Benny Goodman, so I got some Benny Goodman records and I wrote an arrangement. He didn't like it. He played it but he said it wasn't any good. That was my first rejection.

Meanwhile I had this band. Fred Davis was my trumpet player. I grew up with Fred. We went to Parkdale together. Leslie Bell got Fred involved in music, too. Fred's father ran the meat department at Loblaw's, and he couldn't stand the idea of his son being a musician. So Fred learned on his own. He didn't take any lessons; he just learned the horn. He instinctively knew how to play jazz and he was my scat singer. He'd sing Cab Calloway and Louis Armstrong tunes.

Then in the winter of 1938 I got involved with a small band out at the Robina Hall close to St. Clair and Oakwood. It was a pickup band made up mainly of east-end kids. And later we had some gigs out on Bloor West and Runnymede at a place called the Ramona Gardens Ballroom. In those days there were little dance halls all around the city. People liked to dance in those days. It wasn't like it is now — no knives, no rumbles.

At this point I can fill in part of the story myself. In 1939, when he was nineteen years old, Cable organized a rehearsal band which met every Sunday on the third floor of Selmer's Musical Instrument Store on Shuter Street, across from Massey Hall. Most of the players were teenagers or in their early twenties — Fred Davis, Al McMullen, Al Devitt, Ray Honess, Jimmy O'Driscoll, Frank Wiertz, and myself.

We were all eager to try Howard's new arrangements, which bore strong Duke Ellington influences. Those were exciting times. Cable's energy and passion to rehearse and learn from his musical ideas — to see what worked and what didn't — was infectious. Each new arrangement was a discovery — a touch of the Duke's "Jumpin' Punkins" and "Jack the Bear," a whiff of Charlie Barnet's "Cherokee." The rehearsals ended much too quickly and we couldn't wait for the next Sunday to roll around.

As our 1993 interview progressed, Howard was drawn back to his various youthful summers in the vacation wonderland of Muskoka, and the various ways in which they ultimately shaped his musical career:

In 1932 my grandmother bought a place in Waubaushene. I used to spend the summers there. I hung around the two Waubaushene dance halls — the Bayview Pavilion and the Golden Slipper.

Waubaushene was a town of about 300 people, but the two dance halls were filled with dancers during the summer nights; people who vacationed in that part of Georgian Bay. Before I started to play — I was just a kid — I used to hang around the bands. I learned tunes and the names of tunes. They were really sweet bands. I didn't know then that they were Lombardo-ish bands.

Stan Morden ran the Bayview Pavilion. Because of that connection I learned that the owner of the Golden Slipper was looking for a band, so I applied for it and got it. Then in 1937 we got the Georgian Pavilion in Honey Harbour. Since we lived in Waubaushene we drove three nights a week over to Honey Harbour. The trip took an hour and fifteen minutes. Today you can do it in ten minutes. We played three nights a week and Fred Davis sang, and I wrote the arrangements — dinky little arrangements for trumpet, saxophone, and rhythm section ... That job lasted three years.

After three summers at the Georgian Pavilion (1937, 1938, 1939), young Howard Cable moved up. He landed a better engagement at the Chateau Gai Pavilion in Balm Beach, near Midland, in 1940 — a very big break. Unfortunately, the place burned down the first week of the job, on July 1:

I had written arrangements for the band all winter — Charlie Barnet arrangements. They all went up in smoke. Nobody had any insurance except Fred, who had his trumpet insured, because his father was a businessman and made sure Fred was covered. The whole thing was a disaster. Everybody lost their horns.

When the fire ended the job, everyone returned to Toronto, penniless. Then there was a stroke of luck. Howard received a call from Denny Vaughan — a pianist and singer he'd heard about but never met. "I heard you had a terrible problem," Denny said. "Maybe you can help me. We're looking for somebody to play in Beaumaris up in Lake Muskoka. It's a private club. Beaumaris Hotel is a very chi-chi place, and the yacht club has dances four nights a week. You live there. The hotel puts you up and you get twelve dollars a week and your board. We need a pianist and second trumpet player. Are you interested?"

As Howard explained to me in our 1993 interview:

So Fred and I go up for the balance of the summer. In the band were saxophonists Jack Taylor and Bill Carter, first trumpeter Art Oakley, and brother Vic Oakley on drums — all from the Beach, mainly a Beaches band. Fred and I were the only ones from Parkdale. Other side of the world. We never went to the east end in those days. I mean, what Toronto west-ender ever travelled past Yonge Street?

A man named Murray Morton ran the band. He wore white pants, and he looked like a 1920s kind of leader. He was the first guy I had ever met who led a band and didn't know a thing about music. Later I found out almost all dance bandleaders were like that. They don't know but they pretend. Morton ran a restaurant in St. Catharines and he knew the manager at Beaumaris and that's how he got the gig. But it was a good little band, and we had a nice summer. But we had terrible lodgings. You had to walk a long distance to get to the hall. Employees couldn't go across the lawn in front. I spent my summer sitting on the Beaumaris Yacht Club veranda with the breezes, rewriting my lost arrangements while Fred was mainly out with the girls. He was a mover.

Beaumaris was almost all American money. The head of U.S. Steel and the head of Republic Steel were there. Beaumaris was called "Little Pittsburgh." The people came in their boats to the dances. They didn't drive their boats: the chauffeurs drove, just like in an F. Scott Fitzgerald novel. They would drive up in those long Muskoka cruisers, with the guy with the cap on. And they'd get out and go to the dance while he'd wait three hours, like the livery people do. I really realized how separate the world was then — rich and poor, and middle class. I didn't know about that sort of thing until then.

Then came Jerry Dunn in Bala, "Where All Muskoka Dances." Dunn's Pavilion was where the American name bands performed, and Dunn's Pavilion was where Howard Cable played in 1941 and 1942.

My life has been a series of things happening one on top of the other; that's the way it's always been. Never really gone after things; it's come to me. I'm very lucky. It's amazing how much luck plays in a person's life. The accountant who audited the books for the Beaumaris Hotel lived in Toronto. He said he also worked for Jerry Dunn in Bala: "They're looking for a band next summer. Would you be interested in going over there?" So the next summer I get the job in Bala.

It was thirty-six dollars a week and room and board. The living conditions were bad but not as bad as Beaumaris. We were the band that played the last year of the old hall — the old 1920s hall. I closed that hall in 1941, and came back and opened the new one in 1942. Dunn called it "The Key to Bala."

The joint was packed all the time — boats parked out at the back docks. We played every night, Sunday concerts and everything. It was a six-piece band — Fred on trumpet, Jimmy O'Driscoll and Al Devitt on saxes, Frankie Wiertz on drums, Lonnie on bass, and myself on piano.

The first summer at Dunn's, a young man came looking for the bandleader. He identified himself as Robert McMichael, the aspiring entrepreneur who was organizing the *Canadian High News*. He had been asked by Lady Eaton to put a band together for "The Eaton's Young Moderns Campaign."

HOWARD CABLE, CONDUCTOR, 1970s.
Courtesy Howard Cable

He asked if I would be interested in getting a High School Super Band together and writing the arrangements. He had heard about me at Parkdale Collegiate. "We want to do a big concert for the Eaton family," he said. This was in 1941 at the start of the Eaton's Young Moderns Campaign, when they hired students to sell in the store during the summer holidays.

Howard jumped at the chance.

Bob McMichael went to Toronto to report to Lady Eaton who gave him the money. When he came back he said, "We're on!" He explained that everybody in the orchestra would have to wear a large letter on the backs of their sweaters — 'P' for Parkdale, 'H' for Harbord, 'J' for Jarvis — so audiences would recognize the schools they attended. I told him I couldn't conduct because to be in the orchestra everybody had to be in school.

I was already married and couldn't go to school ... So Fred Davis and I went into the band cottage every night with lighted cigarettes, put on some music, and I showed Fred all the beats. That's how he became the conductor. I became the music director and Fred became the conductor.

Back in Toronto auditions were held to determine who would be in "Eaton's High Time Band." Teddy Roderman, Ellis McLintock, Victor Feldbrill, Jack Groob, Victor Zuchter, Bobby Spergill, Yvonne Duncan, and Frankie Wurtz were among the chosen young giants.

Teddy, Ross Culley, and Frank Reynolds were the trombonists, and that was also when I met Jack Kane. I wrote the arrangements and we put the show on. Fred conducted everything for me.

To train Fred I'd sit in the band cottage at night, and watch him wave his lighted cigarette and say, "No, no, that's not the way to do it." I'd studied conducting at the Conservatory. Mazzoleni was my teacher — a very good teacher, very tough. Boy, he told me how to do it: really pushed me and I never forgot. (I learned that right away and he let me have the Conservatory Orchestra at the time. The first thing I ever conducted was the Borodin Second Symphony, *before I even knew what I was doing.*)

So I taught Fred to conduct and we did our big concert at Eaton Auditorium with John Knight on the keyboard playing Rhapsody in Blue. *Fred got through the Rhapsody number okay. It was amazing. We were written up in* New World Magazine. *Royce Frith, who later became Senator Frith, was in the chorus, and was also baritone soloist. It was a good orchestra — an all-star high school band. I really worked hard at the arrangements. That's when I really found out how to do it.*

Then the O'Keefe Brewery, *which owned the* New World Magazine, *decided it would be a nice idea to sponsor this orchestra on radio. They couldn't advertise beer, but they had a ginger ale in those days, which was the product they advertised. As part of the war effort people like Lillian Gish would come up and make their pitches, and the Young Moderns would play. We were on CFRB for thirteen weeks. Fred Davis conducted them all and I wrote them all ... it was a great experience.*

Not too long after this, Howard Cable did his first arranging job at CBC radio for his old teacher Sir Ernest MacMillan, conductor of the Supertest Concert Orchestra, in 1944. Somewhat more than a half-century later, after many years of helping to make his music, twenty veteran musicians who had performed with Howard Cable gathered at Louis Janetta's Place in downtown Toronto on December 16, 1996, for a luncheon to celebrate the leader's seventy-sixth birthday.

The invitation that had gone out weeks earlier read: "Howard would be delighted if you would join him, along with some of the 'Golden Era Guys,' as his guest." This particular "golden era" took in the halcyon days from the mid-1940s to the 1970s, when musicians from all parts of Canada and the world at large enjoyed the good life, performing on CBC radio and television literally from morning to night. Most musicians who played those shows are gone, but those seated at the table joined Howard when he raised a glass to the memory of all those who were no longer with us. And he paid tribute to those lucky enough to be present when he said, "You represent everything that made music work in Canada."

The list of the twenty luncheon guests — a small remnant of the dozens who ran from studio to studio to be on time for the next show during the golden era — read like a who's who of the music business in Toronto. It included Rob McConnell of Boss Brass fame, internationally renowned jazz guitarist Ed Bickert, trumpeter and songwriter Johnny Cowell, jazz pianist/composer Gene Di Novi, jazz vibraphonist Peter Appleyard, dean of Canadian composers John Weinzweig, jazz trumpeter Guido Basso, lead trumpet Erich Traugott, former Toronto Symphony principal clarinetist Abe Galper, trombonists Jerry Johnson and Lawrie Bower, composer Harry Freedman (with more than 180 published works to his credit), performer/composer/educator Phil Nimmons (of Nimmons 'n' Nine fame), ace producer Jackie Rae, French horn player Eugene Rittich, and trumpeter Bobby Herriot (also the current president of the Toronto Musicians' Association, Local 149, AFM).

Of course, stories and anecdotes of the good old days flew from everybody's lips as the pleasant luncheon progressed. A lot of them involved the sixty-piece Howard Cable Orchestra that played the annual summer Grandstand Shows at the Canadian National Exhibition, when anything and everything happened. Before the party broke up, Howard announced that he would organize a similar luncheon-meeting every year, at the same time in December. And I am very pleased to note that, at this time of reporting, a very energetic Howard Cable is still cooking.

Johnny Cowell

More than five years before Howard Cable's seventy-sixth birthday luncheon, one of his guests had already enjoyed a great commemorative event of his own. On July 18, 1991, the Toronto Symphony honoured trumpeter Johnny Cowell with a special tribute concert, to mark his retirement from the orchestra. After thirty-nine years as a member of the trumpet section, the TS management chose to roll out the red carpet for this special musician — the first event of its kind in the orchestra's history.

Why the unprecedented celebration? Simple. Johnny Cowell had brought an unprecedented degree of honour and prestige to the orchestra: not least by his ability to pack a hall when entertaining a pops-concert audience. As if his excellence in the TS trumpet section were not enough, over a career spanning more than fifty years he had also become one of Canada's top composers of popular songs. And many of his songs had become hits, recorded by more than 100 top international stars.

When tastes in music changed from the soothing love ballads to rock and roll, Johnny changed too. With such recording artists as Tony Martin and Andy

Williams no longer fashionable, Cowell turned to composing light instrumental novelties for symphony orchestra. Out of his fertile creative mind sprung the likes of *Girl on a Roller-Coaster, Famous Trumpeters,* and *Canadian Odyssey.*

The 1991 tribute was a sold-out success. Conducted by Newton Wayland, it featured most of Cowell's hit songs, as well as his later instrumental pieces, much to the delight of the audience. Many friends and colleagues were on hand, along with his wife of fifty years, Joan Mitchell Cowell. Finally, when the lights at Roy Thomson Hall were turned off, Johnny and Joan returned to their home in suburban Scarborough.

With his symphony days over, did the trumpet player quit his beloved profession? Not likely. A musician who loves to play as much as Johnny Cowell never gives up.

As I write today, he is far from retired. At a time in life when most musicians have packed away their instruments, the trumpeter still practises long hours and performs with various groups, like the Hanniford Street Silver Band, which gives periodic concerts at the St. Lawrence Centre for the Performing Arts. His mind still swims with musical ideas. And ultimately he reaches for his pen and, once again, he starts to compose.

Born in 1926 in Tillsonburg, a small town in the old tobacco-growing district of southwestern Ontario, Johnny was only six years old when, accompanied by his mother on piano, he played his first solo. His trumpet was a "battered antique" which his uncle had given him the year before. As Johnny told me in an interview in May, 1993:

It was the greatest gift I'd ever received. It was so beat up and dented that the valve caps had to be replaced with pennies. But I didn't care. I wanted to play the trumpet.

Although Tillsonburg had no professional brass teachers to speak of in 1932, Johnny's father played trombone and his uncle played trumpet in the town band.

I sort of picked it up just by watching them.

Blessed with a keen musical ear, the lad experimented with producing a sound, discovering which valves to press down to get certain notes, and how to play simple melodies:

I sort of flopped around on it and got something going.

By the time he was eight Johnny was not just a member of the Tillsonburg town band, but a featured soloist as well:

My mother wrote the arrangements for me. One year they featured me on an annual spring concert when Captain John Slatter, conductor of the 48th Highlanders Band, was the guest conductor. I played two solos with the band and Captain Slatter said he would see me again one day. He was true to his word. I met him years later when I came to Toronto and played with his band a couple of times as soloist.

Rehearsals with the Tillsonburg band took place every Thursday evening, the same night the Toronto Symphony Band performed a weekly one-hour CBC radio broadcast. The band, a thirty-five-piece ensemble, comprised mainly of Toronto Symphony Orchestra brass, woodwind, and percussion players, was conducted by "Puff" Addison, a rotund, obstreperous rhinoceros. Johnny recalls:

I used to rush home from our band practice to hear the broadcast which almost always featured their cornet soloist, Ellis McLintock, who I thought was wonderful. That was in 1941.

Little did the young Cowell realize at the time that within a year he would sit in Ellis McLintock's chair in that band. During a broadcast one evening in 1942, the announcer reported that eighteen-year-old Ellis was going into the Air Force as the cornet soloist of the RCAF Band. The Toronto Symphony Band was looking for a replacement. Cowell was fifteen at the time. He wrote a letter to Puff Addison asking for an audition, but made a point of omitting his age. The bandmaster wrote back, asking him to come to Toronto, and included his home address.

Johnny carried on with the story at our May 1993 interview:

I got a lift on an early transport truck to Toronto and took a streetcar to Columbine Avenue, in the east end, and looked for Addison's house. I knocked on the door for about five minutes before he opened it. You've gotta see Puff in his pajamas. He was madder'n hell. "Yeah? What the hell do you want?" he yelled.

"I'm Jack Cowell." (Puff later changed my name to John.) "I wrote you a letter, remember? You asked me to come on down to audition for Ellis' job."

"What? How old are you?" he asked.

"Fifteen."

"You can't audition for our band. You're just a kid. We can't even hire you. You've got to be sixteen to join the union."

"So it's a wasted trip," I said. "Well, I came all the way down here just to play for you."

"Well–ll alright, he grunted. Come on in."

I went into the house and followed him into his studio which was three by three (pretty crowded since Puff was three by three). Anyway, at nine o'clock in the morning I played some solos for him. He liked it. "Can you stay over in Toronto and come to Varsity Arena tomorrow morning? I want the guys in the band to hear you play." So he arranged to have me stay at a friend's house.

The next morning Johnny went to Varsity Arena and auditioned for the Toronto Symphony Band Committee. After hearing the first few passages they knew immediately that the young musician could fill Ellis' chair. But how to get around the union rules? Puff Addison phoned the union and explained the situation to Local 149 president, Walter Murdoch. The president quickly arranged a special "junior" membership for Jack Cowell who, with a stroke of the pen, became a union member of the Toronto Symphony Band, and a cornet soloist — all in one fell swoop. As Johnny summed things up at our 1993 interview:

That's how I got into the music business. Got Ellis' old job.

Up until the time Johnny played with the Toronto Symphony Band, he had never had a teacher. He was literally self-taught. He was playing solos and executing all the technical passages with great facility, but only as an inexperienced youngster would play them.

His life soon took a turn for the better. Harry Hawe, the principal trombonist of both the Toronto Symphony Orchestra and the Toronto Symphony Band (and, as some readers may remember, my own music teacher as well), took Johnny aside. Born in Toronto, Hawe was a master trombonist who had played and soloed with some of the world's top concert bands, including the famed Franko Edwin Goldman Band in the United States. Hawe told Johnny, "You're playing those solos really well, but your interpretation is a little bit different than what it could be. Would you like to know how to interpret them properly?"

"Sure," Johnny enthusiastically replied. So every time he had a solo to play he would go to Hawe's house for a lesson. Before the lesson began, the trombonist would play such pieces as *The Carnival of Venice*, *Bride of the Waves*, and *The Debutante*, all designed to impress the boy with how solos should be performed. He would then play a few bars of Cowell's solo and say, "This is what you're doing." Then he'd play the same bars and say, "This is the way Herbert Clarke plays it." (Herbert Clarke was a trumpet authority of the day, with whom Johnny was already familiar.) Johnny never forgot the master's advice.

By the time he was sixteen, Johnny was playing with the Toronto Symphony Orchestra:

Bert Jones, who played with the TSB, also played with the TSO. Bert was ill a lot of the time, and when he couldn't perform with the orchestra I was called to fill in. I played second trumpet to Morris Isenbaum, who had taken over from Ellis when he went into the Air Force.

Soon enough Johnny was playing with the symphony more than Bert Jones.

The following year I was offered the chance to be the soloist.

By this point the original "Jack Cowell" from Tillsonburg had already left his earlier identity behind. When he'd arrived for his very first rehearsal with the Toronto Symphony Band, Puff Addison had introduced him to the band members.

With his cigarette popping up and down and the ashes falling all over his shirt, Puff said gruffly, "Okay, gentlemen, this here's Jack Cowell. He's from Tillsonburg, wherever the hell that is. We got two Jacks in the band now. And one more Jack is just one too many. So, from now on, we're gonna call him John. It's the same as Jack; so his name is John." And from John, the guys started calling me Johnny. I really had nothing to do with changing my name.

Even with his new name, the Second World War caught up with Johnny when he turned seventeen. He joined the Canadian Navy's HMCS Naden Band as a cornet soloist, in Esquimalt, British Columbia.

While I was in the band I got to be first trumpet with the Victoria Symphony, and also got to play a little dance work. On Friday and Saturday nights I'd play with a Dixieland band, and then I joined the navy dance band. We were playing all the time — cornet solos almost daily with the navy band, playing daily and twice-daily parades, beating my Dixieland feet on the Mississippi mud of the Esquimalt jazz band on weekends, and screeching high notes in the Naden Big Band dances.

Then there was a day he will never forget: August 14, 1945 — VJ Day — the day Japan surrendered to the Allies.

I played a concert in the morning, then another concert later in the day. Then we did a parade, and still another concert, and then a second parade (three concerts and two parades), followed by a street dance at night. The gig started at 8:00 PM and went to 1:00 AM.

The next morning Johnny took his trumpet out to practise and put the mouthpiece to his lips. When he blew, to his great surprise, he found he couldn't get a sound:

I looked in the mirror and saw something was wrong with my lip. All the tissues were split.

Horrified, he went to the medical officer and told him what he had done the day before:

The doctor told me there was nothing he could do for me, but he would send me to a Vancouver specialist. After the specialist examined my lip, he looked me in the eye and asked, "How do you like it in the navy?"

"Okay, I guess," I said.
"You sure you don't want to get out?"
"How can I get out?" I countered.
"Well, you're a bandsman," the doctor said. "I can tell you you'll never play again as long as you live. All the tissues are severed. There's just a little piece of skin left. That's from playing for such a long time."

Johnny was mortified:

I didn't realize what I was doing. I was too stupid to know. I just screwed it up completely. And so, after two years of service the authorities released the nineteen-year-old from the navy, right after VJ Day.

Back in Toronto, Johnny pondered his future. The prospect of working in a factory didn't appeal to him. He tried playing again, to no avail.

There was nothing there. I couldn't get a note; so I just left it alone.

He put the trumpet in its case and tried to forget about it — a tragedy for a man whose entire existence had been music and performing. Forgetting what he loved most, however, was easier said than done. The spirit of music permeated his mind and soul:

I wanted to be in music so much that I started writing. I knew nothing about composition or orchestration, so I got a couple of scores of Beethoven's Fifth Symphony. *Then I studied them, figured them out, and wrote a* Suite for Orchestra *— for full symphony orchestra — and submitted it to the Royal Conservatory in Toronto. They thought it good enough to present me with a scholarship.*

At the Conservatory he studied orchestration with John Weinzweig, but the trumpet was never beyond his reach. Every so often he would put it to his lips and try to eke out a note. For the longest time, nothing. But he kept trying. After about two years, he began to feel a little sensitivity in his lips. One day, miracle of miracles, a note, a vibration, sounded from the bell of the trumpet. Encouraged, Johnny began to practise, slowly at first, then a little more every few days:

It got so I could play, not well, but at least something, anything, a melody or two.

He never forgot how to play. He knew all the fingerings, but his embouchure was weak. He kept trying, practising all the exercises that students practise to gain strength, like a baby learning to walk.

Then I met Don Johnson who was in the Toronto Symphony and we soon became inseparable. Don said he would get me into Stanley St. John's orchestra. I told him I couldn't play more than fifteen or twenty minutes, then I'm finished. He said, "Don't you worry, I'll carry you." This was about three years that I hadn't played. What I was getting was only a G on top of the staff; that was my highest note. But Don was such a good friend that he did exactly what he said. I'd get on the job with him and if there was any little second trumpet stuff to do and I was shot, he would cover me.

In the meantime Johnny was gaining a little more strength each time he played:

It took me quite a while to get back in shape, and I was just in the right place at the right time when my chops really started to come back. That's when Don left the symphony, which created an opening for third trumpet.

Auditions were called in 1952 and almost every trumpet player in the city applied for the position:

There must have been twenty of us waiting outside the audition room at the Conservatory to be called in. Sir Ernest MacMillan and all the principal players of each section were in there as well. Each guy would go in to Sir Ernest's office, which was a very small, crowded room, and we'd hear him play a few excerpts. Then you heard about sixteen bars of the Haydn Trumpet Concerto. *Then they would come out. And this went on and on.*

Finally it was my turn. After I played my excerpts, Sir Ernest asked, "Now we'll play a few bars of the Haydn Trumpet Concerto. *Do you know that?" After I'd played the first sixteen bars and he said, "Keep playing," I played the whole movement. When he didn't stop me I knew I had the job. I wound up playing the entire concerto, but nothing was said. Sir Ernest was such a nice guy. He wanted to be fair and allowed every trumpet player to get a crack at it.*

In the end it was weeks before the TSO personnel manager called Johnny Cowell. By then he was playing with Joe McNealy's band in Wasaga Beach for the summer. His mother took the message, and telephoned him with the good news.

After years of playing jobs, particularly one-trumpet jobs, where I was embarrassed because I would be shot at 9:15 PM, and had to suffer 'til 12:30 or one in the morning, I had finally made it. It had been a long time fighting back. I don't know why those guys ever called me again, when they knew I didn't have the chops.

While playing with Stanley St. John, Johnny had met Joan Mitchell, the band's beautiful raven-haired singer, whom he eventually married:

She was a good-looking chick. I figured I had to impress her somehow. So I started writing songs for her. She'd come over to my place and we'd play my songs. I played the piano. (I didn't have any lessons, I just picked it up.) We got going, making pretty good music together — on the couch. We got married in 1953, when I was in the Toronto Symphony.

Johnny's interests in songs and singing had already had a boost when he left Stanley St. John to play third trumpet with Art Hallman, one of Toronto's most successful bandleaders in the postwar years:

What Art really wanted was a male singer for his vocal group, not a trumpet player ... The thing that saved me was that I could sing the harmony parts without a problem, all the notes in tune. I wasn't much of a singer — Art soon found that out — but he was impressed with my ability to blend in with the other singers. I stayed with Art until 1952 when I auditioned for the Toronto Symphony.

JOHNNY COWELL, circa 1975.
Courtesy Johnny Cowell

When he became a member of the TSO, Johnny was twenty-seven. By this time his trumpet embouchure (or the strength and control in his lips) had improved significantly. In May 1993 he told me that:

My embouchure was back but not to the point that it is now. I have better endurance now, better range than I've ever had.

(Very few professional brass players who suffer total loss of an embouchure ever experience a rebirth, as I would much later learn so well myself. In this, as in other respects, Johnny Cowell was one in a million.) By this point also, the singing (or at least song-writing) part of his musical career had also taken a fresh lease on life.

I actually started writing songs in earnest when I joined the symphony. When I left Art Hallman, I went with Johnny Linden, at the Royal York Hotel. Johnny was a good-

looking guy and a terrific entertainer. The audience loved him. He and I were good friends ... That's when I started writing a lot of songs.

Someone who happened to work with Broadcast Music Incorporated in the U.S.A. heard one of the songs Johnny wrote for Linden at the Royal York (and for band vocalist Shirley Harmer), and this led to a songwriting contract with Harold Moon at BMI.

Then in 1955, Johnny was playing on the CBC's Denny Vaughan television show when Denny, a good friend, said, "I'm doing a recording session December 31. Do you have any songs I could do?" As Johnny recalls the story from here:

I brought in "Walk Hand in Hand," which he recorded and released in Canada. Everybody said it was a pretty tune but it made very little noise. Denny thought it wasn't taking off in Canada the way it should. So he took his record to Republic Music in New York, Sammy Kaye's publishing company.

As fate would have it, Sammy Kaye took the song to Archie Blyer at Cadence Records. (Archie Blyer had the band for the "Arthur Godfrey Show.") And Cadence took it to the people at RCA records, who were looking for a song for Tony Martin (whose popularity had recently taken a nosedive). RCA told Martin to record it, and his version of Johnny Cowell's song became number one all over the world, catapulting the singer to the top once more. Johnny still remembers the thrill he got when Tony Martin walked out on stage on the "Ed Sullivan Show" from New York and sang "Walk Hand in Hand." When it was released in England it became even bigger.

Then Andy Williams recorded the song, and other artists followed suit, each hoping to cash in on the hit that remained at the top of the charts for a record thirty-three weeks. Meanwhile, BMI's statements to Johnny revealed a spectacular number of performances, growing every month and followed by lucrative royalty cheques as well. Johnny told me in 1993:

I finally met Tony Martin. He said, "Hey, you got another "Walk Hand in Hand" for me?" I said, "Yeah, I got about four of them." So he took them and I never heard from him again. Nice guy. And they were good songs, too.

The climb to prominence of another of Johnny Cowell's greatest hits began when Chet Atkins phoned from New York, sometime in 1963. "Al Hirt's doing a recording session in about six weeks and we're looking for something for Al to play," he said: "something different. Your name came up, and since you're a trumpet player and a writer, would you write something for Al and send it down to us?"

Johnny went to his den and very quickly put the finishing touches on a tune he'd been calling "Long Island Sound." Usually he wrote his own lyrics, but in this case, he didn't have any lyrics for it:

I didn't have time to work on any, so I sent it off as it was.

Then Chet Atkins called from New York to ask if he could change the title.
"What do you want to change it to?" asked Johnny.
"One of our associates has come up with the idea of calling it "Our Winter Love." It's bound to get a lot of air play." Chet Atkins went on. "If it gets to be a hit, we think the title will ensure a lot of air play every year, in season."

Chet Atkins' associate was right. Every year now, for decades, just after the hectic Christmas and New Years' seasons have come and gone, pianist Bill Purcell's deeply moving rendition of "Our Winter Love" is heard on radio stations in several parts of the world. Johnny remarked during our 1993 interview:

It's incredible; those guys really think of everything. When I got my statements from the company I would see 20,000 performances in the United States in a quarter — from December through to the end of April. Then they'd drop off until the next November, when the song again got thousands of logged performances. "Our Winter Love" worked really well in the United States and England.

I can add one minor observation on the creative process here myself. Prior to a Toronto Symphony rehearsal in Massey Hall, one cold morning in 1963, when the orchestra room was a din, as musicians warmed up on their instruments, I remember seeing Johnny Cowell standing near the telephone at one end of the room.

With a cup mute in the bell of his trumpet to soften the sound, he was running over a melody he had been thinking about to see how it would fly. I realized at the time I was witness to one of the composer's moments of inspiration. That melody blossomed to become "Our Winter Love."

The vagaries of public taste have long mystified composers whose songs may be the most beautiful ever written, but for some reason never become big sellers. During his songwriting career, Johnny Cowell has written about 150 songs, of which about 100 have been recorded by different artists. A few of the recorded songs have become great hits, but most of them have fallen by the wayside (which, as Johnny says himself, "most songs do").

Apart from his initial collaboration with Chet Atkins on "Our Winter Love," Al Hirt recorded several other Johnny Cowell inventions, but "Strawberry Jam" was the only one that made it to the charts. "His Girl," a song Johnny wrote for The Guess Who's first recording session, had to rest content with "Number One in Canada," though, Johnny still likes to remember:

"His Girl" was also number one on that 1960s off-shore pirate station, Radio Caroline, in England.

Even so, it takes more than the fingers of one hand to count all the Johnny Cowell songs that have not quite fallen by the wayside. In his songwriting, as in his trumpet playing, Johnny Cowell's luck has often enough come pretty close to matching his talent. And he's still a man who never gives up.

There is, of course, giving up and giving up. And in one sense, Johnny did almost give up on writing at least certain kinds of songs:

> When Elvis Presley and The Beatles moved in with the rock stuff ... I didn't want to change my style of writing, because that's what I was good at. So I switched to writing symphonic pops and it worked out just at the right time.

As a member of the Toronto Symphony Orchestra in the 1960s he became friends with the American conductor, Eric Kunzel, who was brought in to preside over the orchestra's pops concerts. Aware of Cowell's enormous talent, Kunzel kept asking him to write something. Johnny was intrigued, but he hesitated until Seiji Ozawa, the orchestra's permanent conductor, asked for an original composition to play as an encore piece for the TSO's tour of Japan, in September 1969.

Girl on a Roller-Coaster, which featured the trumpet section executing a series of technically difficult passages, dazzled the Japanese audiences. Then when Andrew Davis replaced Ozawa, he asked Johnny to compose a piece for the orchestra's final concert at Massey Hall, on Shuter Street (before moving to its new home, at Roy Thomson Hall, on King Street West). And the resulting *A Farewell Tribute to the Grand Old Lady of Shuter Street* thrilled the audience in the TSO's home town.

Other pieces followed in a similar vein. They included *Famous Trumpeters* — a forty-minute tribute to such legendary artists as Louis Armstrong, Harry James, and Bunny Berigan, and *Canadian Odyssey* (a commemoration of the TSO's tour of Canada's sometimes forbidding but always majestic Northwest Territories).

Johnny also managed to bring some of the spirit behind his symphonic-pops writing career into his mature trumpet playing. He recorded a number of albums of "classical music hits." They were cheered and applauded by music lovers, and won praise from Johnny's peers around the world. (One morning after his album, *Carnival of Venice,* had been released, the telephone in Johnny's Scarborough home erupted in a loud ring. Wife Joan picked up the receiver. "Is Johnny Cowell there?" a voice asked. When Joan called Johnny to the phone, he asked who it was. "I don't know. Probably Doc Severenson wanting to take lessons," she joked. It *was* in fact the renowned trumpeter Doc Severenson, phoning from New York to say how much he had enjoyed *Carnival of Venice.*)

Officially, Johnny Cowell has been retired from the music business, ever since the special tribute concert of July 18, 1991, which commemorated the end of his thirty-nine years in the trumpet section of the Toronto Symphony Orchestra. But someone who loves his work as much as he does never really retires. As he explained at the end of our 1993 interview, his mind still swims with ideas, which ultimately lead him to his pen and manuscript paper. Who knows what magic musical moments he may still give us yet?

Sam Levine: A Man to Be Trusted

Johnny Cowell's struggles with his lost embouchure after the Second World War serve as a reminder that the music business anywhere can be precarious at best. (And, as I've already suggested, he has been luckier than most.) Very young arrangers, composers, conductors, and performers may not worry so much. But once you've been around awhile, you develop more appreciation for anything and anyone that can help make a musician's life a little more secure. This brings me to the special career of Sam Levine, who was instrumental in the establishment of the Organization of Canadian Symphony Musicians (OCSM), and the creation of Orchestra Openings, a service that sends bulletins announcing job prospects in Canadian orchestras to musicians across the country.

As one who received his training in the school of hard knocks at the grass roots level, and truly knew what it meant to be a musician (in the bass section of the Toronto Symphony, through years of jobbing with various bands and performing on the CBC), Sam was prompted to run for the Executive Board of the Toronto Musicians' Association in 1955. And he eventually served as vice-president for nineteen years and president for two years. Because of his dedication, he came to be recognized by friends and colleagues as a conscientious worker who toiled tirelessly on behalf of musicians — "a man to be trusted."

What was it that turned the bass player into a union activist in the first place? Part of the answer lies in his early life as a musician, having to scrape out a living playing the bass during the Great Depression. He travelled to northern Ontario in the 1930s, looking for work with any kind of band. For most musicians those years were abysmal. Scale in Toronto for a three-hour job was five dollars on Fridays and six dollars on Saturdays (when you could get a job, that is). Northern Ontario was a still colder frontier, where the difference between being punched in the mouth and getting a congratulatory slap on the back lay in your ability to make the kind of music that soothed the savage breasts of other struggling young (and old) adults, who often went to dance halls looking for fights.

On his return to Toronto in the late 1930s, Sam Levine got together with saxophonist Lew Lewis, leased a store at the corner of Church and Dundas streets, and converted it into a jazz centre called the Onyx Club, after the famous jazz spot in Harlem. Consumed by their own love of jazz, Lewis and Levine had visions of thousands of people fighting to get a seat in their new club. It featured a four-piece house band, with Lewis on tenor sax, Sam on bass, Wilf Mellor (ultimately) on piano, and Sid Shore on drums. (The band vocalist was fifteen-year-old Jackie Rae who, according to Lewis, "ate all the steaks he could find; he ate us out of the club." Jackie later joined the RCAF as a Spitfire pilot and saw action against the Luftwaffe

SAM LEVINE WITH THE JIMMY NAMARO QUARTET, 1940. Sam Levine as a young man on bass with Jimmy Namaro's group at the Royal Connaught Hotel in Hamilton. Sid Perl on drums, Harvey Silver on piano. *Courtesy Sam Levine*

over England and Europe, and then returned to Canada after the war to become one of the CBC's most successful producers.)

While it lasted, from the fall of 1938 to the summer of 1939, the Onyx Club was a meeting place for local and visiting musicians (including Duke Ellington, Andy Kirk and some of their respective band members, among others). They often came after hours to sit in with the house group and jam. What with Ontario's stringent liquor laws of the day, people usually brought their own mickeys of rye in paper bags, listened to the music, and nursed a Coke all night. Quite a few people showed up, and musically the place was a great success. But the thousands of dollars Lewis and Levine had hoped for never exactly poured in. After less than a year in business, the club was forced to close its doors.

As the 1930s led into the 1940s and the Second World War, Sam, like everyone else, joined His Majesty's Canadian armed forces and served overseas in the RCAF's Blackout Review — a concert party of thirty musicians, singers, dancers, and actors, who put on shows and helped raise the morale of thousands of fighting men, wherever they operated in England and western Europe. Back in Canada after the war, Sam, like a lot of other musicians, waited for the telephone to ring, and jobbed around with one band or another, hoping for some kind of steady income. He was now married to Tula, a devoted wife, and the couple had begun to raise two children: Michael, who would later become one-third of the rock group, Triumph; and Anita (nowadays a supervisor with the Ontario Human Rights Commission).

Sam Levine loved to play music, but he was less happy about his hand-to-mouth existence when it came time to pay the rent.

As I've already noted, during the heady period that immediately followed the war, there were quite a few night spots in Toronto. Big crowds with lots of money in their pockets flocked to these places, and for a while life for Sam took on a gentler tone. At no time, however, did Sam Levine and most other Canadian musicians live much above what would be called the poverty level today. (When he first joined the Toronto Symphony in 1949, Sam earned seventy dollars a week for a twenty-four-week season; hardly enough to raise a family.)

This was the background that Sam brought to his work on the Executive Board of the Toronto Musicians' Association, when he first became involved in the mid-1950s. He believed that, as a Board member, he would have a voice in trying to better conditions for working musicians in Toronto. How did things work out?

One big achievement was the development of the job bulletin service. As Sam explained in one of my interviews for this book:

Orchestra Openings was born out of dire necessity in the 1970s. There were orchestras looking for players and players looking for jobs, but in those days Canadian musicians were not exactly what conductors had in mind.

When a vacancy occurred in a Canadian symphony orchestra, members of some relevant Canadian locals were given the opportunity to audition. But in most cases an ad would almost immediately appear in the *International Musician* (the official publication of the American Federation of Musicians of the United States and Canada). "International" auditions were the norm; "Canadian national" auditions were rare. The process was chaotic and those who protested were given innumerable excuses about why local auditions first, to favour Canadian musicians, just couldn't be done. ("The country is just too big geographically for its population," "the distances are too vast," and on and on.)

Because the *International Musician* didn't arrive in the hands of those of us north of the undefended border any earlier than it does today, many Canadian musicians didn't know about the auditions until it was too late to apply. There was a simmering resentment, and one particular incident brought the issue to a boil. As Sam later explained to me:

A Canadian orchestra decided to hold auditions in Cleveland, Ohio, so that even local musicians had to travel there to audition for their home orchestra. I recall signing a petition with scores of names on it that eventually wound up in Ottawa. But this had no effect. Stronger action was necessary.

When the first Canadian Conference Symphony Symposium convened later that year, the delegates commissioned a report that led to he formation of a Canadian Employment Service. As Sam recalls:

For a year or two the Canadian Conference Symphony Symposium, run by me, operated a bulletin service from the office of the Toronto Musicians' Association. The service was ultimately turned over to the newly formed Association of Canadian Orchestras, which succeeded in obtaining Canada Council funds to operate the service.

Today when a Canadian orchestra has an opening it calls the service's office and gives the information. That information is included in bulletins that are circulated all over the country to union and employment offices, conservatories, music schools, and to individual musicians.

Subsequently, the bulletins have also been supplemented by the Mobility Assistance Program, a service funded by the Department of Employment and Immigration in Ottawa, which assists musicians applying for travel funds to and from auditions.

But Sam Levine's struggle to improve the working conditions of Canadian orchestra players didn't stop here:

We've had to fight for seniority pay; we've had to fight for tenure; we've had to fight for dismissal clauses. None of these things existed when I first joined the Toronto Symphony.

Following the establishment and consolidation of the Orchestra Openings and Mobility Assistance programs, orchestra musicians learned to negotiate beneficial clauses in their work agreements. For a number of years many enjoyed such benefits as longer weeks of employment, fairer auditioning procedures, health insurance, paid leaves of absence to study, and longer paid vacation weeks (particularly for string players who, because of the nature of classical music, carry more of the burden of playing constantly during performances than brass and wind players).

Looking at the music business today, there is still room for improvement. And, as in other parts of the "new economy," managements have recently discovered new means of negating earlier gains. (If musicians refuse to accept demands for such concessions as shorter work seasons which lead to lower earnings, they are increasingly being faced with threats that their orchestras will be declared bankrupt.)

The battle, it seems, is never over. But Sam Levine, now retired from the war, can look back on a lifetime of real achievement. The Canadian music scene would be much harsher than it is today if he had not been around — truly "a man to be trusted."

The Pied Piper of Canada

When many Canadians of my generation think of what's become of their country today, they also think of Bobby Gimby's great song of the 1960s, "CA-NA-DA" (one little, two little, three little Canadians). And the Leisure World Retirement Home in North Bay, Ontario, where Bobby spent his final years until his death on June 20, 1998, was never the same after he became a resident there in early 1993.

The charismatic trumpeter who came out of the west as a member of Mart Kenney's band, played with "The Happy Gang" on CBC radio from 1945 to 1955, composed and played the song that swept the nation during Canada's Centennial in 1967, and performed on CBC radio and television until his retirement.

The last time I saw Bobby Gimby was June 11, 1992. I'd heard him on a taped early morning CBC radio interview, discussing the prospect of resurrecting his "CA-NA-DA" hit for the forthcoming Canada Day celebrations. I called him at his home in Scarborough. "How about dropping over right now?" he asked. Right now? It was 7:30 AM — much too early. "How about one o'clock?" I countered. "Sure, Ginz," he said. "See you then."

I'd lost track of Bobby for a couple of years after he dropped out of sight. So it was a moment of joy when we embraced in the doorway of his apartment. We'd played together on various television shows, and on a number of gigs with his own band. Everyone who knew the lean, bespectacled trumpet player, considered him an animated musician who spoke the musicians' language: quick with a quip or a story loaded with exaggerated humour, quick to play, and happiest when jamming with the best Dixieland players in town.

BOBBY GIMBY AND EMINENT FRIENDS, 1958. Bandleader Art Hallman recorded dozens of commercials with the assistance of Dorothy Deane. A superb singer, Ms. Deane's exquisite voice was heard on over a hundred commercials over a fifteen-year period. Seen at a typical jingle session are, left to right: Hank Monis, guitar; Joe Niosi, bass; Jimmy Coxson, pianist; Bobby Gimby, trumpet; Dorothy Deane (Mrs. Jimmy Cooke); unidentified announcer, and Bert Niosi, clarinet.
Courtesy Dorothy Deane

Bobby Gimby began his musical training in in the 1930s in Vancouver, where he won a number of awards as a student musician. He jobbed around with various bands until his first big break — a chance to play lead trumpet with Mart Kenney's orchestra.

After World War II, Bobby Gimby left to form his own band in the Toronto area. Because of his exposure to so many young Canadian men and women in the wartime services, it took no time for Bobby to build a large following of devoted fans. His band was busy much of the time performing at the Brant Inn in Burlington, and soon enough the world began to open up elsewhere as well.

In 1945, Bert Pearl, host of CBC's "The Happy Gang," asked Bobby to join the show, a profitable union that lasted eleven years. When he wasn't playing with "The Happy Gang," his hours were filled with other musical activities. In 1949 he had his own western music radio program, "The Bobby Gimby Show." Between 1956 and 1960 he was the music director for "The Juliette Show" on CBC TV (which went on the air every Saturday evening, right after "Hockey Night in Canada"). In 1975 he became the musical director of the CTV musical-variety program, "Sing A Song."

Along with his conquests in Canada, Bobby travelled the world, bringing music and goodwill to foreign lands, and receiving awards and citations from grateful nations and their heads of state. In 1961 he went to London, England, to advance his musical knowledge. While he was there he was contacted by Rothman's, the international tobacco company, who found him to be just the right personality to function as a writer and musical director with special responsibilities in public relations.

Rothman's sent Bobby to Singapore in 1962, where he composed and recorded "Malaysia Forever." It became an unofficial national anthem for the new country of Malaysia. Gimby gave the anthem the special twist he would later become noted for at home by performing it first with children.

I always felt a country should honour its kids. Among those children may be the future leaders of the country.

The song became such a hit that Bobby was subsequently honoured by Tunku Abdul Rahman, then prime minister of Malaysia, and Lee Kwan Yew, prime minister of Singapore. It was also his involvement with children in Malaysia that first earned him the nickname, "The Pied Piper of Canada."

When Bobby Gimby returned home he found another honour waiting for him — a letter from the late Rt. Hon. Lester B. Pearson, then Canadian prime minister, thanking him for his services to Canada in another country.

In 1966 Bobby knew that Canada's own centennial was approaching, and his love for his country led him to search his brain for an idea; not *any idea,* but just the right one that would do justice to the occasion. About the same time the centennial commissioner, John Fisher, phoned to ask him to write a song for Canada's

100th birthday. As soon as Bobby hung up the telephone, a few words and a melody leapt into his mind. But those first impressions didn't lead to a song immediately. He needed inspiration to hit on the right idea.

He pinned a map of Canada on the wall, sat down at the piano, and went to work. After months of scribbling and rewriting, and reworking the melody half a dozen times so it would play just right, with "that certain beat," he finally knew he had the finished product.

When "CA-NA-DA" first hit the air waves (recorded with a girls' choir, and with both English and French in its lyrics), it electrified the country. When the first television show featured a caped Bobby playing the song on a special long trumpet encrusted with bangles and jewels, as dozens of singing children marched behind him in a happy parade, the song rocketed to the top of the Canadian hit parade and stayed there for the entire centennial year of 1967.

Bobby had learned his lesson well from the earlier experience with "Malaysia Forever." The success of his bilingual song about Canada owed a lot to the children who followed the trumpet-playing Pied Piper, in parades and performances from Newfoundland to British Columbia. He recalled when we last got together:

> *You know, I was in so many places across Canada, even in only one day, parading with singing kids or attending press conferences, that it all seems a blur to me now. I remember meeting Premier Joey Smallwood in St. John's one morning, and shaking hands with the premier of British Columbia that afternoon.*

He added that he probably visited every city, town, and hamlet in the entire country before the centennial year was over.

Other centennial-year compositions by Bobby Gimby included "Manitoba Hundred" and "Go British Columbia." For all his efforts, in 1968 Bobby was invested with the Order of Canada for meritorious service to his country, by Governor-General Roland Michener.

And what did he do with his share of "CA-NA-DA's" royalties? It says everything about the kind of man he was that he donated them in perpetuity to the Boy Scouts of Canada.

In later years Bobby toured the U.S.A., Germany, and Japan. Along with the Order of Canada, he received a number of other awards. In 1967 he was named Broadcaster of the Year by the Central Canada Broadcasters' Association, and that same year, he won the Lloyd E. Moffat Memorial Award for promoting Canada to Canadians.

When he lived at the Leisure World Retirement Home in North Bay, the residents and staff would go out of their way to say, "Hi Bobby," because Bobby Gimby was everybody's friend. He didn't play his trumpet much in later years. But when we said goodbye at my own last warm meeting with him, he looked to me as if he were ready to put the mouthpiece to his lips and play "CA-NA-DA," one more time.

Phil Nimmons

Another Canadian musician who came out of the west to make a distinguished career in Toronto after the Second World World is Phil Nimmons, who was born and raised in Kamloops, BC. Phil has enjoyed every day of his more than seventy years on this planet. The humble, sensitive, energetic giant loves to make music: it oozes from every pore in his body; he *loves* to play. He told me when I interviewed him in April 1997:

> *I react to it. I become so involved and react to it without thinking.*

Phil's achievements include more than 400 original contemporary classical and jazz compositions, written for stage, television, musicals, theatre, and film — in addition to hundreds of jazz arrangements. His catalogue of credentials fills five pages. Called a legend in his own time, Phil Nimmons' sixty-year career as a performer, composer, arranger, educator, clinician, and artistic director is unparalleled. He's also a brilliant jazz clarinetist and even today, in his seventies, he continues to contribute to the Canadian jazz scene.

In 1940, at the behest of his mother (but with music in his soul), Phil enrolled in a four-year premedical degree at the University of British Columbia. After graduating in 1944, however, he cast medicine aside for a musical career. He studied

NIMMONS 'N' NINE PLUS THREE, 1960s. Left to right, front row: Ted Roderman, Butch Watanabe, Phil Nimmons, Roy Smith, Jerry Toth, Jack Taylor. Back row: Vic Centro, Julius Piekarz, Erich Traugott, Fred Stone, Ron Rully, Ed Bickert, Murray Lauder. *Courtesy Phil Nimmons*

classical music at the Juilliard School of Music, in New York, and composition with John Weinzweig at the Royal Conservatory of Music in Toronto. In 1950 he married Noreen Spencer, a concert pianist. To help pay the bills for raising a family (the couple now have three children and five grandchildren), Phil started composing and playing for CBC radio shows in Toronto.

In 1952 he established the Phil Nimmons group, which performed his exciting jazz arrangements for live audiences. In succeeding years, according to requirements and the number of musicians in the group, the name changed to Nimmons 'n' Nine, Nimmons 'n' Nine Plus Six, and Nimmons 'N' Nine Minus Six (or the Phil Nimmons Quartet).

Phil is also a founding member of the Canadian League of Composers. From 1960 to 1966 he co-founded and operated, with Oscar Peterson and Ray Brown, the Advanced School of Contemporary Music. He was artistic director of summer jazz programs at the Banff School of Fine Arts, the University of Toronto, York University, the University of New Brunswick, the Courtney Youth Music Centre, the New West Jazz Clinic, and the Jazz Camp at Manitou Wabing Sports and Art Centre in Parry Sound, Ontario. He introduced the jazz program at the University of Western Ontario, and commuted from Toronto to London, Ontario, to run the program until 1992.

As a recording artist Phil has ten albums to his credit, on RCA Victor, Verve, Sackville, and CBC. They include: *The Canadiana Scene Via Phil Nimmons* (1956); *Nimmons 'n' Nine* (1963); *Take Ten* (1963); *Mary Poppins Swings* (1964); *Suite PEI* (1973); *The Atlantic Suite* (1975); and *Transformations/Invocation* (1976).

Phil has won a host of awards as well. In 1976 he received the Juno Award for Music Excellence in Jazz for his composition *The Atlantic Suite*. He won the Outstanding Success Award, issued by the Performer's Rights Organization of Canada, in 1980, and the Toronto Arts Award for Creative Excellence in Music and Contribution to Canadian Culture in 1986. His *Skyscape: Sleeping Beauty and the Lions* premiered at Expo '86 in Vancouver. In 1994 he was made an Officer of the Order of Canada and a member of the Order of Ontario.

On top of everything else, Phil has been deeply involved in fund-raising concerts for handicapped children and human rights groups. And as a tireless advocate of jazz as a significant art form, he continues to inspire young musicians. Towards the end of our interview, he remarked:

I am deeply touched and honoured. I feel a great debt to those who play my music and those musicians who play with me.

There are a lot of musicians in many parts of Canada today who would want to return the compliment. And my own reaction to Phil Nimmons' music is that the impressive weight of his awards and credentials can be misleading. In the end he's a man of inspiration. And even when he plays today, his entire being, his body, and his soul, all become a kind of musical instrument.

Norman Amadio at the Towne Tavern

For Phil Nimmons, as for so many others, the Canadian Broadcasting Corporation was very important in the 1950s and 1960s. But, as I've already remarked, it wasn't just the studios at the CBC that gave life to the Toronto music scene in the decades that followed the Second World War — when the golden age in music had its last great fling.

Norman Amadio, for instance (one of Canada's top jazz pianists), has been the quintessential musician, ever since he began to play in Toronto nightclubs in 1949. He has played everywhere; in small groups for a variety of leaders, on CBC radio and television, in recording studios, in theatres and concert halls, and as leader of his own group at jazz festivals. But one of the most interesting parts of his career was his seven-year stint with the house band at one of the two great Toronto jazz clubs of the postwar era.

Amadio began his musical career in Timmins, a mining town in northern Ontario, when he started taking piano lessons from the nuns at the local convent at age nine. After seven years with the nuns, he travelled at age sixteen to Toronto where he studied with the renowned Boris Berlin at the Royal Conservatory of Toronto.

Norm told me during an interview at his home in April 1992:

Boris Berlin straightened out a lot of things I was doing wrong. The nuns in Timmins were sweet and kind, but they didn't know too much about the piano. So Mr. Berlin helped me with my technique. Both he and I knew that I didn't want to become a concert pianist, so I used his instructions to advantage in playing popular music.

After ten months at the Conservatory, the young student travelled to Rouen, Quebec, in 1947, to continue his studies. He played in a cowboy band for four months, gaining experience. Then he returned to Toronto, by way of Timmins.

In Toronto I began jobbing with different leaders. By that time I was into jazz. I sort of leaned in that direction ... found it easy to play. In 1949 I played the cocktail lounge upstairs at the Club Norman, on Adelaide Street, with Jimmy Younger's trio, then went with Chico Vallee to the Cork Room, on Bay Street, then with Jimmy Amaro to the St. Charles on Yonge, and later with Jimmy to the Barclay Hotel, on Front Street, in early 1950.

From the Barclay Norm finally took a trio into the Towne Tavern, on Queen Street, just east of Yonge, in September of 1952, as backup house band for name acts brought in as soloists by owner Sam Berger. The house band accompanied the name acts three weeks in each month, then vacated the premises the fourth week:

NORM AMADIO, BOB PRICE, AND ALEX LAZAROFF, LATE 1970s.
Courtesy Bernie Senensky

Berger would bring in soloists because he didn't want to pay airfares for four musicians. But he'd always bring in a full American group to play the fourth week.

Norman Amadio's backup house band at the Towne Tavern remained on the job for the rest of the 1950s. The piano player was of course Amadio himself, and the drummer was Archie Alleyne (one of the noblest heirs of the unionized black music in Toronto bequeathed by Cy McLean in the mid-1940s). The original bassist, Jack Lander, left to join the Australian Jazz Quartet and was replaced by Bill Britto. Then, when Britto went home to the States, Bob Shilling, a bassist from Germany, joined the group. (Then Shilling died a few years later, while the group was playing Birdland in New York City.)

Amadio's stories and anecdotes about his many years at the Towne Tavern could easily fill a book of their own. Among the musical guests he remembers best are tenor saxophonists Bud Freeman, Lester Young, Stan Getz, and Zoot Sims, trumpeter Roy Eldridge, and singers Carmen MacRae and Mel Torme.

> The first star we played for was Bud Freeman. Bud was the nicest guy on earth. He didn't drink or smoke. He was a gentleman, a super guy, always clean, impeccably dressed, and he could play his ass off ... One night we're playing away. I had my eyes closed. Bud's sax is hot. All of a sudden he falls on one knee.
>
> I open my eyes and see a little white-haired guy on top of him, punching the hell out of him. It happened so fast I couldn't understand how the guy could get up on the stage so quickly. He had to climb over bar stools, then jump from the bar up to the stage. So I leaped up and grabbed him and pinned him down.
>
> The guy looked deranged. We found out later, after the cops tracked the story down, that he'd slipped out of the Ontario mental institution at 999 Queen Street West. He took a street car to Queen and Yonge and he saw the Towne Tavern, where a guy was playing jazz on a saxophone. He probably thought Bud was in league with the Devil, playing the Devil's own immoral music. Poor Bud. He was more shocked than hurt.

Another time, Lester Young had brought his wonderful tenor saxophone sound to the Towne. Lester's friend Roy Eldridge was appearing elsewhere in the city at the time, and paid a visit between sets. Young and Eldridge had a drink and exchanged the latest gossip, while Amadio and Archie Alleyne sat close by.

> I thought I knew a lot of the black bop language and I was positive that Archie knew a lot too. But after listening to about ten minutes of their conversation, I didn't understand a word they said. I said to Archie afterwards, "What the hell are they talking about?" He said, "I have no idea." And I thought we were hip.

Norm also recalls that Benny Winestone, the notorious Glasgow-born Toronto tenor player who seemed to know all the great jazz musicians, used to hang around Lester Young when he was in town. Benny would go home with him every night and take care of him. Lester was always depressed, Norm explained:

> He was a very private man who kept his feelings to himself. But Benny actually helped him a lot. After a few hours with the man with the heavy Scottish accent, Lester would be okay.

In 1956, Norm and his quartet went to New York City to play Birdland. This job (and the unfortunate demise of German bassist Bob Shilling) materialized after singer Mel Torme played the Towne in Toronto. Torme had packed the room with an army of elated fans for two weeks. As Amadio recalled:

Mel was easy to work with. He liked us so much that he wanted us to go to New York, not with him, but to play jazz. He gave us each a bottle of Scotch when his two-week gig was finished.

Back in New York, Torme interested an agent in booking the Towne Tavern backup house band into the famous jazz club in Times Square, in exchange for pianist Bud Powell, who went into the Towne in Toronto at the same time:

Birdland took about six months to develop. But when it did we were hired as a quartet and drove to the States in two cars.

Along with Shilling, Archie Alleyne, and Amadio, the fourth member of the quartet was Toronto guitarist Ed Bickert. Norm carried on with his story:

Because he was from Germany, I tried to sneak Shilling across the border at Niagara Falls, but the U.S. officials wanted to see our petition, a paper stating we had a contracted engagement in New York. We were afraid to show them the contract, because Shilling would be revealed as a foreign national, so we diverted to Buffalo ... At Buffalo we told the American immigration officials we were going to a jam session in Buffalo which was okay with them.

When we arrived in New York we discovered we had to be fingerprinted just like the old days with Billie Holiday and all the performers in New York. Because the drug trade was flourishing in 1956, the cops wanted to keep track of every performer by fingerprinting them. There were lineups of jugglers and singers and all kinds of people who were waiting in line for two hours and more to be fingerprinted.

When the New York official scrutinized their papers and saw they weren't right, he asked how they were able to cross the border. Amadio hemmed and hawed, and after some further checking the official said, "Okay, go and do the job and in a few days this will all work out." Amadio was worried but said nothing.

Soon enough, the plot began to thicken. The job at Birdland lasted two weeks, and Amadio's quartet played the intermission gap opposite Duke Ellington:

Whenever the Duke's band finished a set, we filled the twenty-minute gap. We'd play until four every morning. The audiences liked our music and showed their appreciation, but Shilling got in with a dealer who sold him junk, which created a problem. He kept asking me for advances, but I never realized what he wanted the money for. Had I known, I wouldn't have given him anything and we would certainly have kept an eye on him.

On the last Friday night of the engagement, Shilling didn't show up at all. Amadio borrowed Ellington's bass player until another bassist was located to fill in.

The next morning a detective phoned me. "Do you know a guy about twenty-six years old, blonde, blue-eyed, about six feet tall?" he asked. "Yeah, that's my bass player. He didn't show up last night — I'm gonna kill him," I said. The detective said, "You don't have to. He's dead. You got to come to Bellevue [hospital] to identify his body." When I got there they pulled out a drawer and that's him. He overdosed.

Meanwhile, the audiences (and more importantly, the owners) at Birdland were pleased with Amadio's quartet from Toronto. The owners suggested Norm find another bass player and stay as long as he liked. But the pianist had had enough.

"Oh no," I said. I'd already lost ten pounds worrying. "We're going back to Toronto, Monday."

Since he was also still worried that the authorities would discover Shilling was a German national, Amadio had a friend back home phone the German embassy in Ottawa to arrange for the body to be flown back to Toronto:

When we got back I found Shilling's mother had flown to Canada and was waiting for me. Then I got the surprise of my life. I learned she was a Baltic baroness, which made her son a baron. Their estates were in Estonia. Bob had never said a word about that to us.

Bob Shilling's mother wanted to know how her son had died. It was still the 1950s and Amadio was reluctant to tell her outright that Bob had overdosed on heroin. So he diplomatically borrowed the excuse the New York detective had used when he first reported the death.

I told her he was making love to a girlfriend in Harlem and had a heart attack.

Then the musicians and Shilling's mother buried the unfortunate bass player in Toronto's Mount Pleasant Cemetery, on Yonge Street, just north of St. Clair.

At this point Norman Amadio returned to the Towne Tavern to resume his career as leader of an excellent backup house band that accompanied American jazz stars. He can tell a lot of other stories about life at the Towne. And, having already heard quite a few of them, I inquired about one particular "non-musical incident" during our interview in 1992. Amadio remarked:

Non-musical is not exactly the way I'd put it. Late in 1959 Max Bluestein, a notorious gambler and who knows what else, got knifed in the lobby. I remember it was after midnight because the bar had closed and we were playing in the dining room. Someone yelled that there was a fight in the front, and I ran around to see what was happening.

I saw Leo, our night manager, trying to stop a guy who was hammering Bluestein with a blackjack. Leo was a little guy who should have known better than to try to stop three hoods from going after the gambler. They had him on the floor and were knifing him. I said, "Leo, let them go, let them do what they want." A little guy like that, what's he going to do to stop them? Anyway, in spite of his injuries Bluestein lived. He was a tough little guy, with a lot of guts. That story made the papers, but nothing really happened.

(I remember myself that there were other stories in the papers about the same gambler who had a day job running a discount appliance store on the Danforth. One time, for instance, someone put a bomb in his mattress and tried to blow him up, but he escaped with minor injuries. Max Bluestein seemed indestructible.)

In any case, Norman Amadio left the Towne Tavern in 1959 to play on CBC radio and television, and in the recording studios. And because of his fine jazz talents he was always in demand for festivals and concerts as well:

I had a little rock band for five years on CBC television's "Music Hop." I also did the "Hit Parade" series with Bert Niosi ... and a million other little shows.

He was also on the CBC's first television jazz show in 1956. Sponsored by Timex, that ninety-minute extravaganza included everybody who was anybody on the 1950s jazz scene in Toronto — the Oscar Peterson Trio with bassist Ray Brown and drummer Ed Thigpen, the Phil Nimmons Sextet, the Pat Riccio Quartet, Ron Collier, Trump Davidson's Dixieland Band, Bert Niosi and His Orchestra (with pianist Norm Amadio), the Jack Kane Orchestra, singer Annemarie Moss, and on and on.

The host was Howard Cable's boyhood friend, Fred Davis, who opened the show playing his trumpet in silhouette. (And then Fred Davis, who unhappily died in April 1996, became most famous as the host of CBC TV's "Front Page Challenge," the panel game show that lasted thirty-eight years.)

The Towne Tavern is no longer with us. But, now in his sixties, Norman Amadio is still playing piano today. When the telephone rings and someone asks if he can do a date, he says, "Let me look in my book." And then, if the date is free, Norm Amadio says, "I can do it. Where's the gig?"

Phil Antonacci: Saxophonist Par Excellence

Talking about the Canadian jazz scene in the golden age of music naturally brings me to one of Canada's most exciting jazz saxophonists, who has left musicians and listeners mesmerized by the extraordinary latitude of his improvisation — the incomparable Phil Antonacci.

When Phil joined Bert Niosi's band at the Palais Royale as a seventeen-year old, Niosi was so taken with the tenor saxophone player that he organized a quintet featuring Phil from within the larger band. And the quintet performed nightly on a separate bandstand when the other musicians took a break.

The American bands that came through the Palais every few weeks were also so impressed with the young tenorman's exceptional ability that several offered him very good jobs. He never took them up on their offers. Why?

I love to go hunting and fishing, which I couldn't do if I was touring in the States.

Toronto-born Phil Antonacci's introduction to the saxophone began at the age of ten, when his mother bought him an instrument from the music department at Simpson's, on Queen Street. It came with ten free lessons given by Charlie Banker.

I couldn't play the thing even after a couple of weeks. I knew there was something wrong; so I started filing the mouthpiece to open it up, and I finally got it working.

For a ten-year-old to recognize and actually solve such a problem was unusual, to say the least. After giving the boy a few lessons, Charlie Banker saw that Phil was no ordinary beginner. He told his mother, "You had better get a professional teacher for your son. I'm not really equipped to teach someone with his talent." Over the following three years, the next six teachers proved inadequate as well. Finally, at fourteen Phil discovered George Naylor, a schooled musician who recognized the lad's musical genius and was able to instruct him properly.

PHIL ANTONACCI AT HARBOURFRONT, MAY 1986. *Murray Ginsberg, private collection*

That's when my playing really started. He showed me everything: scales, arpeggios, all the chord progressions, how to arrange — everything I needed to be a professional.

In September of my own first year at Central Technical School, a number of students who were taking private music lessons responded to a call from George Graham, the school organist-teacher, who was organizing a school orchestra.

In 1937 there were no music classes in Toronto's high schools. Orchestras were formed only when a teacher called for students interested in rehearsing after school hours. I had been taking lessons from Harry Hawe, who suggested I should try to

At the CBC *161*

get into the orchestra. I remember meeting Phil Antonacci for the first time before we were asked to take our seats. Along with everybody else in the fledgling teenage musical aggregation, I was amazed when I heard him play. Incredibly, he was already playing jazz. We were the same age, but I couldn't do a thing. What was I doing there? No one could play like Phil. As Phil himself explains:

One day when I was about fifteen, my brother Louis and I went to a restaurant in Crow's Beach, a joint west of the Humber River in Sunnyside. They had a Wurlitzer juke box. We put in a nickel and heard Count Basie's band playing "Clap Hands, Here Comes Charlie," with Lester Young playing tenor. As soon as I heard that I ran around looking for another nickel. The guy was so great. I said, "Lou, I can do that. I can do what Lester Young was doing."

"You're nuts. You can't play like him," Lou said.

"What are you talking about. I'm telling you I know how to do that!" So after we got home he got the accordion out, and Greg got his guitar out, and we started playing a tune, and I started improvising, just like that. It just came out natural. Somebody turned the light on.

Then Phil and his brothers began to show up at some of the Toronto Catholic churches (like the popular Circolo Columbo), to join others in playing the Sunday night dances. For services rendered they each received two dollars, the usual payment for non-union musicians. Phil soon began getting other jobs. Again, it was the playing, not the money, that was important: even more than most other young musicians, he *loved* to play. And he revelled in his ability to play with abandon: testing new horizons, trying new ideas, and savouring the delight of discovering how easily the ideas flowed from his brain to his fingers.

The first guys to really recognize me were Harvey Silver and Trump Davidson.

Harvey Silver's family had a grocery store at the north-east corner of Spadina and Harbord, called Campus Grocery. They lived in a house on the north side of Harbord, where Harvey had jam sessions every week with Trump and other musicians, like pianist Johnny Burt, drummer Reef McGarvey, bassist Sam "Bozo" Weiner, and guitarist Stan Wilson.

Trump phoned me. "Hey kid," he says. "Come on over. We're having a jam session." So I walked in there and sure enough Lew Lewis is playing. First time I heard a tenor like that. I thought I'm not taking my horn out here. Man, you know Lew Lewis was a great player. And Trump was there. I never heard Trump play before either: a genius. Christ, like the guy's the greatest, right?

So Trump says to me, "Take your horn out kid, come on." I'll never forget. The first tune I played was "Avalon." So I played it and Lew Lewis was there, and I was just a skinny kid, right? Like the horn was bigger'n me.

After that Phil Antonacci's name spread like wildfire throughout the city's musical community. The Modernaires, a fine eleven-piece band that played Benny Goodman and other name-band arrangements, wasted no time in getting the sixteen-year-old into the sax section.

The young tenorman was still studying with Naylor, who also played in the band. George had shown him how to improvise, and as part of his weekly lessons, the teacher wrote out standards with the chord symbols over the music. Part of Phil's practising included improvising new variations and riffs based on the chord progressions.

> *After I joined the Modernaires, Lew Lewis and Sam Levine had the Onyx Club on Church Street. Both Lew and Trump called me to bring my horn. When I walk in I hear these two tenors, Lew Lewis and Gordie Evans. God, I'm sixteen years old. I'm not going to play with these guys. So I stick my horn under a stool. Now these guys heard about me, right? So Trump introduced me to the guys I never met before. Trump says, "This is the kid I was telling you about." Then he says, "Get your horn out and get up and play."*
>
> *I said, "No, I don't feel like playing, Trump. I'm scared." He says "Never mind, you get your horn out and start playing." Well, as soon as I got my horn out and started playing, that was it! Like nobody got on the stand. It was just Trump and myself playing. Lew didn't play and Gordie didn't play. Just the two of us and the rhythm section — Sam on bass, Sid Shore on drums, and Wilf Mellor on piano. I was sweating, I was scared.*

That Saturday afternoon the Onyx Club was crowded. After Phil played a set, the others wanted him to remain and play another set, but the boy declined.

> *I said, "No, I wanna hear you guys play."*

He began working with Trump and others, jobbing around and getting his own jobs. Then a lucky break came. Lew Lewis asked Phil to substitute for him while he attended to a matter out of town. "Who will I be playing for? Phil asked. "It's one week at the King Edward Hotel with Romanelli," Lewis replied. "Luigi Romanelli?" Phil exclaimed. "I'm going to play with the Romanelli orchestra?"

That experience was an eye-opener for the young musician:

> *You know who was in the band? Bob Farnon on trumpet, Gordie Day on alto, Reef McGarvey on drums, and trombonist Bill Dadson — guys like that. The greatest! Trump wasn't playing; he just sang. Playing with those guys was the thrill of a lifetime.*

When Romanelli heard Phil, he wanted to hire him on the spot. But after a couple of days of playing Romanelli's music, Phil had had enough. He felt the Romanelli orchestra wasn't for him: they were too square. He wanted to be in a band that played jazz. Jazz clubs and dinner/dancing spots began to feature him as the guest soloist.

Remember the bands at the Silver Slipper — Henry Kelnick and Ozzie Williams and Trump? I was a guest soloist there almost every Sunday. I also appeared most Saturday afternoons at the Club Top Hat.

One day his mother told him a "Bert Neezy" wanted him on the telephone. "Who the hell is Bert Neezy?" the son muttered and picked up the phone. A voice on the other end of the line said, "It's Joe Niosi, I'm calling for my brother, Bert. Bert wants you to come to a rehearsal at the Palais Royale, on Tuesday at 1:00 PM."
When he arrived at the Palais, Phil learned the rehearsal was in fact an audition, to fill the vacancy left by Keith Heffer:

There were five sax players auditioning. I didn't know a soul. When my turn came I climbed on the bandstand and Bert introduced himself. Holy Christ! This was the famous Bert Niosi, Canada's King of Swing. I saw Teddy Davidson — he played tenor too — trombonist George Guerrette, trumpeter Tony Ferrano, Johnny Niosi on drums, all those guys. What the hell was I doing there?

The leader picked a number and beat off the tempo. Within a minute Phil knew he had never experienced a sensation like this.

What a band! When they played you didn't have to do anything — just read the music and everything fell into place. They had everything: perfect intonation, great sound, everything. What a feeling.

Then Niosi literally threw him a part: "When you come to the solo, I'd like you to stand and play into the microphone." As the band started to play, Phil stood and aimed his sax at the microphone. He was aware that Niosi was listening intently but the leader said nothing. When the piece ended, without a word the leader pulled out another tune. Another solo at the mike, and again from Niosi the same silence.

When he didn't say anything I honestly thought I was doing something wrong.

Another few minutes of playing and Bert waved the band to stop: "Okay, guys. That's it. I've heard enough. Thanks for coming. That's it for today." The audition was over and the musicians packed their instruments into their cases and crowded around, congratulating Phil. Bert approached. "I really enjoy the way you play, kid," he said. Phil replied, "Thank you very much." He was overwhelmed. "I want you to get measured for a suit right away," Bert said. "You mean I got the job?" Phil asked, almost expecting an answer either way.

"Why? Didn't you think you were going to get it?"

"Well, with all these other guys here ... "

"Just go down tomorrow and get the suit. You start next Monday night and we've got a rehearsal on Thursday."

The Antonacci family was thrilled. Mother Antonacci told all her friends. The friends told friends, and all those friends told *their* friends. And after a couple of weeks, when they heard the radio broadcasts from the Palais Royale (and the announcer saying, "And now, featuring Phil Antonacci ... "), every night in the Antonacci neighbourhood on Henderson Street, below College near Grace Street, was cause for celebration.

Over the ensuing years a kind of love relationship developed between Phil Antonacci and Bert Niosi. Yet the elder musician never told Phil how much he admired his protégé, until very close to the end of his life. In all those years, Phil remarked towards the end of our 1992 interview:

He never said "you're a great player." Then about three months before he died we were doing a show at the Harbour Castle, and during a break Bert and I were out in the front sitting down. I'll never forget what he said to me then: "You know, Phil, I gotta tell you something. The greatest thrill I ever had in my life was listening to you play. You are the greatest tenor saxophone player I ever heard."

I said, "Please, Bert, this is the first time you ever said anything."

And he repeated, "That's the greatest thrill I ever had in my life in the music business. Ever since you joined the band — the things you played: I wish I could write them all down."

"I wish I could, too, Bert," I told him.

Others among Phil's friends did not wait as long to confess their admiration:

I was doing the Molson Jazz Festival down at Harbourfront and Lew Lewis was there. It was one of those jobs where I played with Paul Grosney first. Then Paul and his other front-liners got off the stand while I stayed on with the rhythm section. I'd become the leader, and I played. Next day Lew phoned Mary and says, "I heard Phil play yesterday with two bands. You should be proud to be married to that man. He's the greatest saxophone player I ever heard in my life." Wasn't that nice of Lew? I never heard him say things like that to other players.

When Bert Niosi reorganized his band in 1946, bringing in musicians like Ross Culley, Babe Newman, Paul Grosney, Pat Riccio, Jimmy Coxson, Howard Morris (and myself), most of the musicians became close friends. We all enjoyed playing at the Palais Royale, thrilling to the solo work of Phil and Bert (and of Babe and Pat and Jimmy — all of them). When we weren't playing at the Palais, on Sundays

Phil and I often played together on small private jobs. I always marvelled to watch him in action, on the jazz jobs where he blew everybody away, and even at all those Italian weddings.

When Phil played a song like "Sorrento" or "O Sole Mio," his sound kept getting bigger and bigger, and more beautiful. His neck would expand to allow the maximum amount of air from his lungs to create the enormous sound. And with all the spectacular verve that came to him naturally, the "Tarantella" became a performance of classic proportions.

When he played it everybody would leap to the floor and dance to the lively music; couples with hands on hips, or arms interlocked and skirts and hair flying. It was always like a scene out of a movie. And he would do it all by himself. An amazing player!

Phil Antonacci kept on receiving offers from great American bandleaders, like Les Brown, Sam Donahue, Tommy Dorsey, Coleman Hawkins, Ray McKinley, Tony Pastor ... (the list is endless). He declined every one because, as he so incredibly explains (one more time):

I don't want to leave Toronto. I love hunting and fishing too much. I can't wait for September to come. You can't take that away from me.

As our April 1992 interview drew to a close, Phil looked back on his career:

A lot has happened in fifty years, wouldn't you say? Back in the 1940s I took Lester Young with me to St. Agnes Church. Lester had his group at the Colonial for the week, so I brought him to meet my brothers one Sunday night. Tony Bennett was there, too. He was appearing at the Casino. He wasn't known then.

I said to Lester, "Prez, I gotta play with my brothers."

He said, "Go ahead, Phil. I'll stick around and listen."

He stood and watched the people dancing. Not too many people knew who he was. Then we went back to my father's house and had some wine. All the guys — Coleman Hawkins, Don Byas, Denzel Best, Thelonius Monk, Nat King Cole — came to my mother's house and my mother would come out of the kitchen with the platter and all the musicians would stand up. My mother would put the platter down and say, "You boys must not stand in front of me. You are all like my children, the same as Phil. Now you have a good time here. You don't have to stand up here."

I took Coleman Hawkins and Don Byas hunting for groundhogs. Coleman was in the back of the car. Don had a 25-calibre automatic pistol. I sneaked up on the groundhogs and he emptied his gun and never hit one.

Going after groundhogs may be Phil's idea of the good life, but his saxophone says it all. It is a toy in his hands, and when he plays he can do no wrong. Even today he really does love to play. And no one will ever be able to take that away from him.

The Colonial Tavern

As Norm Amadio has already explained, such American musical friends of Phil Antonacci as Lester Young ("the President" of the tenor saxophone, as the great Billie Holiday christened him) often played at the Towne Tavern in the Toronto of the 1950s and 1960s. Even a little more often, perhaps, they also played at the Colonial Tavern on Yonge Street, a half block north of Queen.

During its peak in popularity, some of the best names in jazz came through the doors of the Colonial. And Toronto's jazz-hungry crowds followed and filled the club, almost every night.

Purchased in 1946 by a three-way partnership, headed by Goodwin ("Goodie") Lichtenberg, what was then known as the Scholes Hotel was a standard beer joint and a ho-hum restaurant that did so-so business. But when the serving of hard liquor in public places became legal in Ontario in 1947, the partners decided to make several changes. And they altered the life of one side of Toronto for a happy generation to come.

Goodie Lichtenberg's other two partners were his brother Harvey Lichtenberg and Mike Lawrence. Alas, only Harvey was still alive when I interviewed him in 1992. As he explained, the original three partners undertook certain renovations to the old Scholes Hotel. Among other things, they turned the first floor of the building into the "drinking room," tore out the twenty-odd rooms on the second and third floors, and converted the space into a dining room (which eventually became a kind of grand balcony, from which you could look down on the first-floor bandstand below). Then they hung out an impressive sign which renamed the place the "Colonial Tavern," and applied for a liquor licence. Harvey explained:

The club didn't start as a jazz club. But, after it got a liquor licence, we were somewhat shocked to see roughnecks ... dropping in for a beer and a fight.

They speculated that good music might lure a more civilized class of customer. They contacted Cy McLean, the talented black Toronto jazz pianist (who not long before had broken the shameful colour bar in Local 149). McLean came in with a bassist and a drummer.

Cy and his musicians were decent guys whose music attracted a lot of nice people to the club. Cy ... was always cheerful and displayed a positive attitude about life in general. A wonderful guy.

When it was time to change acts, the Lichtenbergs and Mike Lawrence cast their eyes south of the undefended border. They brought in guitarist Slim Gaylord, whose hit "Flatfoot Floosie with the Floy Floy" appealed to the kind of patrons who were not used to seeing U.S. recording personalities in person.

The club did good business. But there was also a downside, Harvey explained:

Slim was a nice guy, a lot of fun, but hiring him was our first experience with booking agents. On the recommendation of bar owners in New York, my brother Goodie went to New York and contacted Joe Glazer, head of Associated Booking. That meeting was a shock. It turned out that Glazer was a hood from Chicago, and a very rough customer.

Goodie returned to New York several times in the following months to line up new acts. If Glazer happened to be in the office, the conversation always involved shouting and threats. Harvey's own first meeting in New York with Glazer months later proved just as bad:

I went into his office and was greeted by yelling and screaming and four-letter words I'd never heard before. Glazer had bandleader Phil Spitalni, leader of the all-girl orchestra, in his office. Apparently they were bitter enemies, hated each other's guts, but Glazer had Spitalni over a barrel, had him tied up with contracts. It was embarrassing to walk into a scene like that. Glazer was a gorilla.

The rough dealings with Joe Glazer, nonetheless, brought Jimmy McPartland and his band into the Colonial. And from their opening set to the last note played seven days later, they packed the club. Dozens of other American name groups followed, including Muggsy Spanier, Jack Teagarden, Phil Napoleon, Bud Freeman, Wild Bill Davidson, Mel Torme, Bobby Hackett, and Red Norvo — with the same successful results.

I remember myself that when Trump Davidson heard Phil Napoleon at the Colonial late in 1947, he raved about his playing, along with the exciting work of trombonist Nick Russo, and urged us to get down to see them. Of course, Trump and Napoleon hit it off right away. Whenever we visited the place Napoleon would sit at our table. He was a lively conversationalist who had an opinion on everything, from politics to unions, to Greenwich Village homosexuals.

Did the partners at the Colonial make any money? According to Harvey:

Well, when Muggsy Spanier came in he tore up the place. The same with Jack Teagarden, Duke Ellington, Ella Fitzgerald, and just about every jazz star of the day, all of whom packed the place, and we did make a fair amount of money. But we had our bad weeks.

When Count Basie came in with his entire band, and blew the roof off, the crowd may have roared its approval, but we didn't do too well financially. The costs of a big band were too high. We decided we had to find a way to offset costs.

When a very high-priced Benny Goodman ($5,000 per week) brought a group in the management tried to charge a small entrance fee of fifty cents:

> We decided to present several shows a night, and every person had to pay the admission fee. But when a show was finished and we asked the crowd to leave to make room for the next crowd, they wouldn't budge. We had a lot of trouble with that one, so we had to abandon the idea.

At this point, Lichtenberg paused to reflect on a wider non-financial issue:

> You know, we were really the first club to bring American jazz musicians to the city on a weekly basis. In 1947 Toronto was the most staid, conservative city in the world, and I was among the most conservative. But now, in retrospect, I feel we had a lot to do with changing the look of Toronto. The musicians who came to play for us, particularly black musicians, went back to their hometowns raving about Toronto. "Greatest city in the world," they'd say. "I can sit down and play. I can sit with people and talk." In New York and elsewhere in the United States the same musicians couldn't sit and drink with the people. In Toronto there was that freedom. Those musicians were the greatest ambassadors for Toronto, and what it stood for. And ... Toronto was never the same.

The conversation turned to Lichtenberg's remembrances of the close friends he made. He spoke about Jack Teagarden.

> He was the sweetest man you could possibly imagine. Once when I was in New York, I was taken to Basin Street, New York's most prominent jazz club at the time, to see Louis Armstrong and his band. Jack was part of that group. We arrived in time for the second show. Before it started, there was a lot of commotion on the bandstand. Jack was so drunk that Louis had to throw him off.

But when Harvey met him the next morning, Jack Teagarden was sober and quite a different man. Harvey fell in love with him right away:

> He had the disease; he was a booze fighter who was afraid to sit with anyone for fear that he would be offered a drink, which he simply could not resist. He had that fear. He used to stand in the hall where I would talk to him, until it was time to get on the bandstand. Time and again he was torn apart because of the booze. A beautiful man when you got to know him.

The Colonial, Harvey noted as well, didn't want to present just American artists. Toronto's own Cy McLean had opened the place. And from time to time after that Canadian groups like Trump Davidson's Dixieland Band were featured:

> For a while we thought we would use Canadian musicians, such as Trump, but local musicians didn't really have a chance. After Muggsy Spanier and Count Basie, nobody wanted to listen to Canadian musicians. They were really never accepted.

(I thought afterwards about what Charlie Shavers had said about Trump: "Had he been born in the United States he would be world-famous, right up there with the best of them." But Trump was born in Sudbury, Ontario, and worked in Canada almost all his life.)

I asked Harvey to reflect a little more on the personalities of some of the famous names he dealt with:

Well, let's start off with the drinkers, the lushes. Stan Getz was one. Corked all the time, but ... his playing was magnificent ... Then there was Pee Wee Russell who came with Eddie Condon's Band, which always included the same Greenwich Village and Chicago Dixieland players; guys like George Brunis, Mezz Mezrow, Vic Dickenson, and the others. Their only interest in life was booze. Pee Wee's nose got redder as the night progressed. By the time the last set started they were falling all over themselves.

I remember going to a poker game with Jimmy McPartland and Mousey Alexander, McPartland's drummer. It was late at night after they finished playing, in one of the downtown hotels, where they had a room.

Most of his musicians were there. Everybody arrived stoned, from all the customer's gifts ... As soon as the game started, out came more booze. Everybody had brought a bottle ... That's when the serious drinking began. It was unbelievable ... Interestingly enough, they could still play poker ... in spite of the fact that they were blind drunk, they could play. Every player knew what he was doing.

Other stars who played the Colonial prompted warmer memories:

I often think about Erroll Garner, a beautiful guy, and a hell of a piano player. We paid him well every time he appeared, and I really fell in love with him too. Something that stands out in my mind about Erroll is that he was the only guy that had the decency to pay the waitresses when his week was finished. He loved to spend money and was very generous.

Things did change a bit after Erroll hired a new manager, a lady named Gladys:

Because of her he became a wealthy man, investing in apartment buildings and so forth. But there was a time when a buck meant nothing to him. He literally would throw money away.

I mustn't forget Gene Krupa, who became a good friend. What a wonderful gentleman! We became so close that he had dinner with us at home on several occasions. We played baseball together. He even married a Toronto girl who he'd met at the Colonial.

Harvey had first met the great drummer himself, in the earlier 1940s before the Colonial had started (probably at the Club Esquire in Toronto).

He was stoned out of his head on drugs ... I really had no use for him.

Later on, after Krupa had reformed, the Colonial Tavern booked him for one week:

It was there that we became intimate friends. I found Gene to be a most wonderful guy. When he came to the Colonial I knew he had broken the heroin habit, was completely cured. But he couldn't escape the "dope addict" reputation which followed him wherever he went ... It ultimately killed him.

While we sat and sipped coffee, Harvey continued with his saga:

Then there was Lionel Hampton, the phenomenal Lionel Hampton. He always carried a Bible wherever he went. Lionel was deeply religious and studied the scriptures, chapter and verse, page by page, whenever there was a break in the music. He would go back to our office, which was used as the dressing room, and bury his nose in the Bible. The other musicians would sit with customers or go outside for a breath of fresh air, but Lionel had to read his Bible ... He got comfort from his religion. And everybody knows what a tremendous jazz performer he was. He was a dynamic individual.

When Artie Shaw played the Colonial, he drew huge crowds every night. His startling good looks combined with his enormous talent brought women to the club in droves. But, quite unlike what Harvey had expected, the outspoken genius on almost every subject was, strangely, at loose at ends when he wasn't performing:

You know the image that was built around him. He was world famous. He had been married eight times to gorgeous women. His book, which he autographed for me, had just come out. And yet he was a plain, ordinary sort of a guy, totally unaffected by the publicity. In the afternoons when he had nothing to do, he would come to us, looking for company. A beautiful guy.

The later part of our conversation turned to singers who appeared at the Colonial as solo acts:

Ella Fitzgerald, Sarah Vaughan, Helen Forrest, Billie Holiday — were all great. Each had her own style and charm. All brought huge crowds to the club. But I loved Ella the best. She was something special, a real show person — the-show-must-go-on type of performer. She was way ahead of everyone else.

And what about Sarah Vaughan?

To my mind Sarah's voice was a God-given gift — magnificent. But personality-

wise she was rather indifferent, insensitive. But she was very friendly with me.

And Billie Holiday?

Billie Holiday was always withdrawn, a "no relationship deal." She had a manager who ruined her, took the money and ran. She used to spend her off hours quietly in our office, which was the dressing room. Hardly spoke a word. She was sort of an "unperson." Really a shame.

Then we spoke briefly about Duke Ellington, who appeared at the Colonial with his entire band — three trumpets, three trombones, four saxes, four rhythm, and a singer:

He had a manager who was a graduate engineer. The poor guy had his hands full trying to handle the musicians, most of whom were crazy. The Duke packed the Colonial every night. People stood in line on Yonge Street, hoping to get in.

On the last night of their engagement, the manager had a bus waiting outside on Yonge Street at midnight when they finished playing. He kept yelling at them to pack up and board the bus as soon as possible, but they took their time, stopping to talk to girls who had eyed some of them, or finish a drink with a fan.

They drove the poor bugger crazy all the time. I remember him saying that when he came to play the club at 9:00 PM, it was breakfast time for him ... He'd go to bed when the sun came up.

Alas, the Colonial Tavern closed its doors in the late seventies. In 1987 the building was demolished to make way for a downtown parkette, next to the present Winter Garden Theatre.

In May 1996 Barbara Hall, the last mayor of the old City of Toronto, laid a plaque, shaped like a huge black vinyl record, on the grass. The plaque bears the names of 150 jazz artists who performed at the Colonial Tavern during its lifetime.

Toronto pianist Bill King, who was influential in having the plaque placed on the site, assembled a few local musicians who actually had appeared at the Colonial to perform at the ceremony (drummer Archie Alleyne, saxophonist Pat La Barbera, bassist Bob Price, and vibraphonist Frank Wright). For everyone who loved jazz in Toronto — and other places as well — it was a sad day.

"J.D.": More Tears (or how the golden age of music in Canada went fast-forward into the present day)

When I phoned Jimmy Dale to arrange for an interview, he suggested that he had already written a piece on his life which I might want to use. He was kind enough to send it to me and when I read it, I decided the best way to tell his story was in his very own words. So here it is:

Cut to England 1942. Wartime. Jimmy Dale starts piano instruction at age seven with a famous person whose last name is Thomas. The idea is to become a concert pianist. Father Harold pays James to practise by giving him tools every week. James likes tools. The family lives near Coventry and endures much bombing. In 1947 the family (Harold, mother Ellen, sons James and John) emigrate to Canada.

In Toronto Harold finds a job, buys a small house. James studies at the Royal Conservatory. Times are difficult, but the family survives. Clothes come from the Crippled Civilians store. Neighbours mention a talented pianist who lives nearby. James says, "He's not as good as me, you know." The other pianist is Glenn Gould.

Due to a strange Liquor Control Board of Ontario policy at the time, you need a permit to buy wine, etc., and James picks up a bottle of sherry once a week for his mother from a friend with a permit. One day he carries it in a brown paper bag to his lesson before he takes it back to the east end on the way home from the Conservatory. The teacher (a Women's Christian Temperance Union fan) sees the sherry and says, "You're out of here." So James Dale is gone from the Conservatory.

Cut to high school. J.D. quits just short of sixteen. Studies arranging with Gordon Delamont in Clem Hambourg's house at a cost of six dollars per lesson. Everybody studies arranging with Gordon Delamont. Jack Long and Jack McQuade sell instruments from a room on the second floor of the same house.

J.D. gets call from Leo Romanelli. He has had a cancellation and could J.D. play the summer at Manoir Richelieu? J.D. buys a Triumph TR3 and takes job. Leo promises eighty-five dollars a week, plus room and board. J.D. has to drive drummer Gary Lewis to the job. J.D. thinks Gary is gay and wants to stay away. They stop in Montreal overnight and Gary goes out and picks up girl and gets laid within feet of J.D. (So much for being gay.)

The Manoir job has a kind of cachet. Erich Traugott and Jerry Toth have been there in previous years. There is classical music to play, with Fred Treneer using the baritone sax as a cello, and Leo sounding like Jack Benny on a bad day. But being young makes things easier.

First payday sees only fifty-five dollars. Musicians threaten to hoist Leo on their shoulders and throw him over the cliff into the St. Lawrence. J.D at least gets some satisfaction with the promise of being the leader of the group at Tadoussac, another resort. J.D. has a sports car, kind of rare in 1956, and often goes to Quebec City to buy booze. The Manoir Richelieu is on a promontory above the St. Lawrence. J.D. drives this hill at 50 MPH and 5,000 RPM in second gear for the thrill of it. Drummer Gary Lewis goes with J.D. to Quebec City one day and asks, on return trip, to drive the last mile or so in the same fashion as J.D.

Halfway up the hill he encounters several women, children, and baby carriages, but doesn't slow down. He sounds horn, blasts through, and is arrested immediately. The PQ cop says, "I've been watching you for weeks and you're going to jail." And Gary does. J.D. tells Leo and Leo says, "Let Gary stay there." One or two days later Leo relents, pays fine, and has a drummer again. (Gary also sang.) J.D. is learning tunes along the way, of course.

In 1957 J.D. starts new career with Peter Appleyard, skirting the fringes of the jazz world. Working at the Stage Door on Yonge Street, operated by Jackie Rae, Frank Peppiatt, and Jim Karfalis — with Peter Appleyard and Steve Lawrence (and Edie Gormé), Ruth Price, and others. J.D. falls in love with Ruth Price.

J.D.'s first TV appearance is on Jackie Rae's show in 1957, where the commercials are live in a corner of the studio. Jazz looms larger with work at the Rouge in Detroit, clubs in New York, and so on. If Peter isn't busy, J.D. works in the Lux burlesque theatre on Spadina or the Zanzibar Tavern on Yonge Street.

J.D. finds time to meet and marry Irene Roncetti, secretary of Paul Simmons who manages Juliette. J.D. also works with Jack Zaza at Lichee Gardens. A conflicting career at this time: Coleman Hawkins one week and Juliette the next. At the same time friends are dying from drug use. Amadio's bass player Bob Shilling has recently died in NYC from drugs.

Television enters the picture. J.D. starts as rehearsal pianist with "Juliette Show." Has good times with Freddy Stone at this time, working the Victory Theatre, etc., and fishing.

J.D. and producer Alan Blye are sent by Canadian government to Brazil in 1966 after both write song (that Tommy Ambrose later records) called "Never Came to Be." J.D. conducts a large orchestra, meets Johnny Mandel, Henry Mancini, Bob Russell, and others. (Bob Russell had written song "Brazil" years before but had never been to country until now.)

J.D. and first wife Irene are named unofficial ambassadors for a week, and have use of the limo, which is only an Oldsmobile. They go to Madame Chiang-Kai-Shek's house in Brazil, up in the mountains and on return journey find a tree across the road. Bandits! Drive around through the brush to save lives. Lives are saved.

In 1967 J.D. goes to New York to conduct show in Central Park commemorating Canadian Confederation. First exposure to NY copyist tactics. Much extra money for three to four people working on one score, etc. J.D. works for Ricky Hyslop and then Lucio Agostini on the "Juliette Show." Lots of jobs then, and drinking and gambling at the CBC.

1967 sees J.D. working in Los Angeles for first time, and LA is impressive. Moves to LA in January 1969. Does the musical coordinator job on the "Smothers Brothers Comedy Hour," replacing Denny Vaughan, who becomes conductor on another show. Hard work being musical coordinator — twelve-hour days.

Cut to September 1969, still in LA. J.D. goes to work for Andy Williams as musical coordinator. Production manager says, "How much?" J.D. says "Scale." J.D. is conducting band by second week. Three weeks into gig production manager says, "We have to make a deal. Can't afford to pay scale." J.D. working many hours so scale is between three and four thousand dollars weekly. J.D. now called associate musical director.

Second year. J.D. goes to bandleader Mike Post, and says, "I want the title of musical director or you pay me." Mike Post pays. Big days. J.D. buys two Rolls-Royces: one black, one white, licence plates "BLOOR" and "YONGE." Meets many talented people. Many are nice.

After two years of Andy, Sonny & Cher surface. J.D. is now collecting old racing cars. Nominated for Emmy Award in 1972. Ghost-writing for H. Mancini, Jerry Fielding. Jerry is nice fellow, burdened by (they say) socialist leanings and alimony to three (or four) former wives. J.D.'s moment of fame comes when his name gets in the TV Guide crossword. Success! Real fame!

Cut to 1972. Family problems mandate return to Toronto. J.D. continues Sonny & Cher by commuting weekly from TO to LA. Fly down (first-class return $312) Wednesday AM, get to work before noon, rehearse 'til six, grab burger/fries/bottle of cold champagne, and write until midnight or after (sometimes 7:00 AM). Copyists start around 7:00 PM and finish before the 8:00 AM band call. Record music, have nice lunch, record singers, then mix. Shoot show Friday, take red-eye Friday night back to TO. No extra recompense for commuting.

Flashback to 1971. J.D. taken by George Schlatter to London and Paris for movie with Jacques Tati and Tony Curtis. Schlatter accuses J.D. of using wife as arranger to explain speed of J.D.'s writing. ("It cannot be done!") J.D. lives with this, and investigates tax status of Channel Islands. (Good food in Paris.)

Fast forward to early 1975. Schlatter calls with Cher on the phone to say there is a special to be done. If it works there may be a series. J.D. agrees to do it. J.D. takes Guido Basso, Moe Koffman, Rob McConnell, and Gary Binstead to LA.

Special is done, and GS announces that series starts next week. J.D. has no LA house now. Stays at Beverly Wilshire (forty-six dollars a night). Gets cardboard box with alarm clock, ketchup, and other silly items, which doorman stores for him each week. J.D. buys 1955 300 SL Merc Benz (rare) from Jerry Lewis' ex-copyist.

Cher series ends. J.D. drives car back to TO. Stops in Ohio to splash oil on it and drives on dusty road so he can declare low value for customs. It works, but the oil is in the paint and won't come out. (A smart-ass wielding a two-edged sword.)

Back in TO Juliette gets daytime show and J.D. does it. Guido, Moe, and Rob figure prominently. Enter Bob McLean with show that will go on for years, that has good band and, among many others, the likes of Lou Rawls, Dizzie Gillespie, Crystal Gayle, Cleo Laine, Johnny Dankworth, and Rita Moreno — all working for scale.

There is trip to New Zealand in 1978, to conduct Pacific Song Contest with Gloria Kaye (singer), Beth Harrington (composer), and Jack McAndrew (head of CBC Variety). At jam session afterward J.D. finds out that he does actually know some Rolling Stones songs, but not by title.

Then there is a call from Al Hamel for Guido, Moe, and J.D. to go to

Vancouver to play. They call it The Jazz Trio. The studio is on a mountain, away from everywhere. There is trouble with the voltage. So there are delays, but the bar is well-stocked. So The Jazz Trio is basically drunk for the three episodes.

Now it's 1980. Jackie Rae calls J.D. to do album called *Caricatures*. J.D. manages to get it called *Profiles* instead. It turns out well. Everyone plays great. Bill Richards plays violin solo on what is more or less a jazz album.

Now it's 1981. J.D. goes to Charlottetown to orchestrate *Aimee,* the main show there. An interesting experience when it seems that many people who work there have a winter wife (or girlfriend) and a different one for Charlottetown.

JIMMY DALE, 1980.
Line drawing by Dania Madera-Lerman

Cut to 1990. J.D. is hired to do an award show, either Genie or Gemini — gets mixed up since both sound the same. There is a tribute to Wayne and Shuster which requires musical background. J.D. suggests that a piano might be the best thing, but producer says that the band should play. J.D. writes background for the piece, but at the pre-record, it ends up going back to a piano background. J.D. says to producer, "If I had known you were on this job I would have refused it." Band members silently get into line and pat J.D on back.

Then, more recently still, J.D. gets talked into orchestrating a musical called *Durante.* Things work out well. Charlie Gray says to J.D.: "I never thought you were any good, but these are excellent arrangements."

Part Five
Hooked on Classics

TSO BRASS SECTION, 1962. The Toronto Symphony brass section. Horns: Art Bergin, John Simonelli, Ken Godwin, Eugene Rittich, Cliff Spearing; trombones: Gordon Pulis, Murray Ginsberg, Harry Stevenson; tuba: Hubert Meyer. (trumpets missing) *Courtesy Harry Stevenson*

My own coming of age in the music business in Toronto had everything to do with the popular or "jazz" side of the Canadian (or even North American) scene in the 1930s and 1940s. But my initial studies with Harry Hawe of the Toronto Symphony had at least introduced me to classical music. And before I was even out of my twenties, the nature of the business in Toronto had started to get me hooked on classics in a more professional way.

In 1949 I had asked Ettore Mazzoleni, conductor of the Royal Conservatory Orchestra (Royal Conservatory of Toronto, that is), if I could join the orchestra for one season. "I'm anxious to get some orchestral experience," I explained. The CBC was producing classical music radio programs and since I was being booked to play on some of them, I needed all the orchestral training I could get.

Mazz (pronounced 'matz') was most obliging. He said I would be required to play a short audition, "nothing serious, some sight reading and please bring one piece of your own choice." On the appointed afternoon, I was admitted to a small room in the Conservatory, located at that time at the corner of College Street and University, where I shook hands with Sir Ernest MacMillan, dean of the Faculty of Music, Mazzoleni, principal of the Royal Conservatory, Nicholas Goldschmidt, head of the Conservatory Opera School, and Bob Rosevear, head of Music Education. These gentlemen were the Conservatory hierarchy whom I'd actually met before, but our get-acquainted meeting that afternoon over tea and polite conversation promised a happy hour to come.

Finally, Mazzoleni suggested we begin. I took my trombone out of its case, blew a few notes to warm up, and was asked to play certain passages of orchestral works from music placed on a music stand. Mazzoleni conducted as I played the second trombone solo from Brahm's *Tragic Overture*, a section from Tchaikovsky's *1812 Overture*, and a few bars of Eric Coates' *London Suite*. No problem.

"Did you bring a piece of your own choice?" Mazzoleni asked.

"Yes, I did," I said, and produced a sheet of music titled *Sonata* by Frank Martin, a Swiss composer. I had chosen the piece because it was a simple melody, mostly whole notes (one long note equal to four beats per bar of music) which I felt would give the auditors an idea of my sound.

"Is there a piano accompaniment part?" Mazz asked.

I hadn't earlier even thought about the piano part but luckily it was in the trombone case. When I pulled it out I was shocked to see two pages black with 64th notes, in musical terms called hemi-demi-semi-quavers. "My God!" I thought, "Nobody is going to be able to play this thing at sight. It could be embarrassing if the accompanist can't play it."

Mazzoleni handed the music to Sir Ernest, who nonchalantly placed his spectacles on his nose, sat down at the piano, and scanned the music briefly. Sir Ernest turned to me and said, "Ready?" and with a nod of his head he and I began to play. I had chosen wisely: my part was easy. But the notes that flew from the piano with lightning speed and accuracy caused a couple of mouths to open in surprise. When I came to the last note of the solo (in no more than two minutes), Sir Ernest ended his accompaniment with a flourish and rose from the piano with a smile.

"Veddy good, veddy good," he said, and sat in his armchair.

Mazzoleni said, "Well, I think I can say that Mr. Ginsberg has earned a spot in the orchestra, wouldn't you gentlemen?" Flushed with a relieved degree of success I put my instrument away, shook hands with everyone, and, thanking all for their indulgence, I went home. On the streetcar I thought, "What if Sir Ernest couldn't have handled the part?" I shuddered to think what my future would have been.

As it happened, I did have a future playing classical music in Toronto. For quite a while it coexisted with my career in the more popular realms of the local scene. But then it came to be a central preoccupation. I learned a lot about classical music, and the people who played it in Canada. And it somehow seems appropriate to devote the penultimate part of this volume to the marvellous musicians I grew to know and admire so much on this side of the professional fence (which, as much else in the book so far might suggest, may never have been as high and unscalable in Toronto as it has been in some other places).

Getting to Know the TSO

About a dozen years after my audition for the Royal Conservatory Orchestra, I decided that I wanted to join the Toronto Symphony — the ultimate classical-music big time in the city then (and no doubt today as well). My experience in this case, however, was quite different from my earlier adventure.

On a sunny afternoon in August 1961 I made my way to Massey Hall, where I was scheduled for an audition with the then conductor of the TSO, Walter Susskind (who had succeeded Sir Ernest in 1956). To fortify my courage, I decided to drop in first at the nearby Silver Rail on Yonge Street. Inside I discovered that Walter Susskind had been seized by a similar inspiration. I sat down beside him and we chatted over scotches for a time. Then Mr. Susskind suggested that we go across the road to Massey Hall and attend to the audition.

This included just he and I. There was no committee as there had been at the Conservatory (and as there almost invariably is in auditions for the TSO today). Mr. Susskind and I went to the stage. I simply sat down on a chair, took out my trombone and my music, and played a number of pieces designed to demonstrate my qualifications.

"That's all very charming," Walter Susskind said. "Now," he continued, "can you play the *Bolero?*"

"No," I replied.

"Good," Susskind responded with a twinkle in his eye. "You've got the job."

Of course, I was pleased. And the job remained at the centre of my own Canadian musical career in Toronto for the next eighteen years.

Just what is it like to play in the Toronto Symphony Orchestra? To start with, the orchestra has now had eight historic conductors: Luigi von Kunits (1923–1930),

Sir Ernest MacMillan (1931–1956), Walter Susskind (1956–1965), Seiji Ozawa (1965–1969), Karel Ancerl (1969–1973), Victor Feldbrill (1973–1974), Andrew Davis (1975–1988), and Gunther Herbig (1989–1994). The ninth and current conductor, Jukka-Pekka Saraste, took up his post in 1995.

Each of these eminent maestros has contributed enormously to the growth of the orchestra. Sir Ernest MacMillan was highly respected, not only by the musicians but by the public as well. Walter Susskind, in the opinion of many TS players, was razor sharp; the most brilliant man they had ever met. Karel Ancerl was a great conductor, particularly when interpreting the likes of Beethoven and Brahms (though he did have some trouble with Stravinsky's complex rhythms). Andrew Davis was a fine conductor, who became a personal friend to many in the orchestra. Gunther Herbig was a strict disciplinarian.

It was during Seiji Ozawa's tenure between 1965 and 1969, however, that a rare atmosphere of deep respect and love developed between TSO musicians and their conductor. Though he could barely speak English when he arrived in 1965 (at age thirty-two), the bond that developed in the last half of the 1960s was unique. And for many years after, whenever Seiji would return to Toronto (for one reason or another), he would take particular pains to "meet with all my old friends again."

The deep affection for Ozawa began to develop when we travelled to Britain and France in the fall of 1965, to perform at the Commonwealth Arts Festival. It grew into a kind of party time in January 1967, when we went on a two-week tour of Florida (which was also, in the midst of the Arctic freeze of the Canadian winter, a wonderful holiday in the sun). The love affair reached its zenith in September 1969, when we travelled to Seiji's native Japan and performed in various cities over two weeks — the V.I.P. trip of a lifetime.

During my interviews for this book, a number of current and former members of the Toronto Symphony offered evaluations of their various recent conductors:

Violinist Pearl Palmason: *Walter Susskind was a great technician. He was quick with his baton, a marvellous accompanist. But most of the time when I would look at him he was looking at someone in the balcony ... Karel Ancerl was superb, the best thing that's happened to the Toronto Symphony. A pity he was not well ... Seiji Ozawa was simply marvellous! A man of great magnetism. When he came to Toronto he learned a lot with us. A great soul, quite humble ... Andrew Davis was extremely brilliant, a fine operatic conductor. He conducted many difficult works with us and was very efficient.*

Violinist Frank Fusco: *Susskind had a very sharp mind, and a wonderful talent. But he was superficial, all for the show. After he conducted the first concert, the concerts that followed were "once over lightly." They didn't seem to matter ... Karel Ancerl didn't like anyone who opposed him. At a rehearsal he once pointed down to the podium and said, "This is the last dictatorship." But (violinist) Harry Bergart stood up and told him we* live in a democracy ... Seiji Ozawa was the first dynamic personality the orchestra ever had. He was the spark plug that gave the TS something to hang on to.

Principal Trumpet Joe Umbrico: *Walter Susskind was extremely competent, an incredible accompanist. He was sympathetic to musicians' needs ... Karel Ancerl was a grand master from the old school. Wonderful interpreting Beethoven ... Seiji was magical, hypnotic — one in a million.*

French Horn Player Mary Barrow: *Susskind was a fine conductor, but lackadaisical most of the time. He liked the ladies, though. In the orchestra pit during one opera performance at the O'Keefe Centre, he noticed a gorgeous blonde in the front row. Then he turned it on. That evening the orchestra played better than it had in years.*

Principal Bassoonist Nicholas Kilburn: *Walter Susskind was the most talented conductor I've ever worked for. But he was bored most of the time. Except when he was faced with a challenge, and then he came to life. For example, when he conducted Strauss'* Der Rosenkavalier *he was brilliant ... Seiji Ozawa was the most charismatic conductor I ever knew. He would always zero in on the music and burn it out of you ... Gunther Herbig was a pedant, very autocratic. You can reason with ignorance, but you can't reason with an autocrat.*

Percussionist John Wyre: *I've gone through the gamut with Seiji. I played for him in the Toronto Symphony, and later as a member of Nexus we played for him a dozen times as guests with the Boston Symphony. Seiji is one of the most vital and joyful conductors I've ever worked for ... Ancerl was the man who challenged me the most. I could never please him. I do remember one time however, when we played the New World Symphony: after playing a certain passage, he complained about the number of times I looked up at him and saw him smiling. I guess I finally got to him ... Andrew Davis took me back to the vitality of youth. He inspired me; he was refreshingly honest.*

Exactly where a symphony orchestra performs can also have some bearing on the life of its musicians. In 1982 the Toronto Symphony moved from Massey Hall on Shuter Street (its home for almost sixty years) to the multi-million dollar Roy Thomson Hall, at King and Simcoe streets. Despite the glitzy state-of-the-art style of the new building — its beautiful auditorium, backstage rehearsal hall, and ample dressing rooms — in the opinion of several TS musicians, certain important requirements are missing.

According to former TS concertmaster Steven Staryk, the acoustics of the new hall do not compare with those of Massey Hall. During my interview with him I asked, "Do you like Roy Thomson Hall?" And he replied,

No, absolutely not. The acoustics are very trying for a string player. To begin with, he mortgages his life to a fiddle he hopes will sound, and it's very depressing when he goes out to perform and it doesn't sound. In my opinion when the hall was designed they could have chosen different acousticians.

The Calgary concert hall is excellent, as is the hall in Thunder Bay, and the hall in Dallas. The people who designed those halls and others in North America have had a good track record. Unfortunately Roy Thomson Hall was not designed by those people. It's unfortunate the Toronto Symphony doesn't have a hall which would enhance its sound and project the excellence of the orchestra.

A good sound, precision and depth in performance, strong musical leadership from an orchestra builder of the magnitude of a Fritz Reiner or a George Szell, and records distributed throughout the world give a fine orchestra its reputation. Many ensembles fall short because of a lack of one or more of the necessary requirements.

PEARL PALMASON, MID-1940s. An excellent violinist with impeccable credentials. *Courtesy Pearl Palmason*

Touring can help develop a symphony orchestra as well. And during the past several decades the Toronto Symphony has toured quite a lot. In the early 1960s under Walter Susskind's baton it visited a number of minor locales in such American states as Michigan, New York, and Illinois. During Canada's Centennial in 1967, under Seiji Ozawa, it toured from the Maritime Provinces west to Winnipeg.

As I've already suggested, the *major* tours began when Seiji Ozawa took the orchestra to Great Britain and France in 1965, and to Japan in 1969. Then, following Karel Ancerl's death in 1973, guest conductor Kasimir Kord took the orchestra to England and Germany in 1974. Under Andrew Davis the TSO toured the People's Republic of China in 1978, and the Canadian Northwest Territories in 1987. In-between these dates there was also a major European tour under Andrew Davis, which included performances in London, Amsterdam, Paris, and Prague. And in 1990, under Gunther Herbig, Toronto's symphonic ambassadors

182 They Loved to Play

performed in Australia, Singapore, Taiwan, Tokyo, and San Francisco.

Finally, a good manager can make all the difference in the lives of symphony musicians. Walter Homburger was the TSO's highly respected and internationally recognized manager, from September 1962 to 1987. To mark his retirement after twenty-five years of dedicated service, the orchestra played a special concert in Roy Thomson Hall, known as The Great Gathering. Some say the event featured so many famous international artists that it will go down in North American orchestral history as the concert of the century. (It will also go down as the longest concert in TS history. It lasted more than four hours).

Since The Great Gathering doubled as a fund-raising event for the benefit of the TSO, all guests donated their services. It says everything about the esteem in which Walter Homburger was held that many eminent international artists such as Seiji Ozawa, Jean-Pierre Rampal, Mstislav Rostopovich, Isaac Stern, and Pinchas Zukerman performed for free because of their affection for the retiring TSO manager. In the end the concert raised the quite astounding sum of $2.75 million.

Judy Loman in Concert

During my own time with the Toronto Symphony, I had the great pleasure of getting to know a number of very eminent classical musicians. One of the finest is Judy Loman, the orchestra's principal harpist since 1960.

Judy is a consummate professional, and one of the brightest stars in the international harp firmament. When she played the World Harp Congress in Israel in 1985, Jerusalem Post critic Yohanan Boehm wrote: "Miss Loman's unfailing memory and perfect control of all the intricacies of her sensitive instrument allowed her to concentrate on musical performance. She excelled in beautifully shaded dynamics, brilliant digital fluency, smooth pedal changes, and an overall elasticity that turned this recital into an unqualified pleasure."

A graduate of the Curtis Institute of Music, where she studied with the celebrated harpist Carlos Salzedo, Judy also played with the Salzedo Concert Ensemble as Salzedo's associate harpist. She was a clear favourite of the master, who once wrote, "I am always amazed when we play together: two bodies, but one mind."

Judy first met Salzedo in January 1949, shortly after her twelfth birthday, when he performed at her local high school in Goshen, Indiana. Her mother had arranged for her to have a lesson with him the day after his recital. After he heard her play Hasselmans' *La Source* and the Debussy *Danses,* Salzedo said, "I must have this child as a student."

Arrangements were made for her to study with him the following summer at his harp school in Camden, Maine. And she returned for the next five summers to sharpen her youthful talent.

When Judy entered the Curtis Institute in 1955, Salzedo covered as much repertoire with her as possible. He didn't bother to show her technique.

He basically let me do what I had been doing because it was working. He was more concerned with repertoire, phrasing, and gestures, and didn't dwell on technical points.

Several months later, Salzedo wrote to her mother, "She always was a lovely youngster, but now she is an affectionate, mature person. Her friendship is a precious gift to me ... I admire her humility and truthfulness and sense of perfection."

While at the Curtis Institute, in the spring of 1955, Judy met trumpeter and fellow student Joseph Umbrico, and they were married a year later. Their first daughter, Pennie Carlotta (named after her godfather, Carlos Salzedo) was born in 1957. Not long after Pennie Carlotta's birth, Judy Loman and Joe Umbrico moved to Toronto, where Joe took up the position of principal trumpet with the TSO.

As I've already noted, Judy herself became principal harpist with the Toronto Symphony in 1960. She has held the same position with the CBC Symphony Orchestra, the National Ballet of Canada Orchestra, and the Canadian Opera Company Orchestra. And her chamber music credits include performances with the Orford String Quartet, Toronto Woodwind Quartet, Quatuor Morency, Toronto Chamber Players, the Bach International Ensemble (Allegri String Quartet, James Campbell, Rian de Waal), and Nexus.

Since she first joined the orchestra in Toronto, Judy Loman has gone on to accumulate a formidable collection of musical credentials. Her work as a soloist has won the admiration of audiences and critics at recitals in Canada, the United States, Europe, Israel, and Japan.

The TSO has featured her as a guest soloist on three tours. She has participated in many Canadian festivals, and in Japan she performed in "Music Today," playing new works for harp by Canadian and Japanese composers. She has been a featured recitalist at several American Harp Society Conferences and the World Harp Congress as well. (She last performed with the Harp Congress in Seattle in 1996.)

An advocate of new music for the harp, Judy's more recent performances always feature new works by Canadian composers who have written for her:

Since moving to Canada I discovered a lot of good Canadian composers. It seemed natural to try to get as many of them as possible to write for the harp.

Since 1981 she has introduced several Canadian compositions on recordings and in solo recitals, inside and outside Canada. The list here includes R. Murray Schafer's *The Crown of Ariadne Concerto for Harp and Orchestra;* John Weinzweig's *Four Pieces for Harp;* and Glen Buhr's *Tanzmusik, Concerto for Flute, Harp, and Orchestra.*

Judy's performances have been heard on CBC radio, and she has recorded for RCA, Columbia, CBC, Centredisc, Aquitane, and Marquis Records. (She was also working on two new CDs for Naxos at the time this book went to press in 1998.)

Her playing has been featured in films by Rhombus Media and presented by CBC TV and TV Ontario. She has won a Juno Award and the Canada Council's Grand Prix du Disc. And she has been a guest soloist with the BBC Symphony Orchestra, the Detroit Symphony, and Canada's National Arts Centre Orchestra in Ottawa.

In the world of music education, Judy Loman today is professor of Harp at the University of Toronto, associate professor of Harp at McGill University in Montreal, and in the faculty of the Royal Conservatory of Music in Toronto. She has established a summer Harp School in Fenelon Falls, Ontario, and often adjudicates at international competitions. Her pupils come from all over the world.

I have been listening to Judy Loman myself for some forty years now. I have yet to be disappointed by any of her many performances I've heard. During one performance of *Tosca* at the O'Keefe Centre in 1976, I found myself seated directly behind Judy in the cramped quarters of the orchestra pit. The tenor was singing an aria on stage and I had a clear view over Judy's shoulder of the music on her stand as she played Puccini's accompaniment to the song. Except for Judy's harp, all other orchestra instruments remained silent. To simply say she played all the notes in the 12/8 passage would be an understatement. The absolute power of her playing, the sheer strength of her personality and her flawless rhythm, was a solo in itself. When the tenor finished his aria, the audience erupted into enthusiastic applause, not only for the tenor, but for Ms. Loman's incredible performance as well.

Ms. Loman unfailingly delivers memorable moments to her listeners. I remember a recital in May 1994 with Judy and guest artist Nora Shulman (principal flutist with the TSO), at Armour Heights Presbyterian Church in Toronto. The event was held in support of the Harp Society Scholarship Fund and an organization known as Homes for Adults with Autism and Pervasive Developmental Disorders (or HAADD: Judy herself is the mother of a young man with autism).

The recital included works by Hindemith, Scarlatti, Tailleferre, Prokofiev, and Carlos Salzedo. The featured piece was *Sonata for Flute and Harp* by Adrian Schaposchnikov. The event attracted a sold-out audience and it proved a stunning success, in a lovely little church with magnificent natural acoustics.

Judy notes that she has been lucky enough to work with really great composers, conductors, and performers, and this was a very important influence on her development as a musician. Among others, she has worked with such great composers as Stravinsky, Copeland, and Villa Lobos, and (along with Walter Susskind, Karel Ancerl, and Seiji Ozawa) such great conductors as Barbirolli and Beecham. A number of singers have influenced her as well:

I'll never forget Maureen Forrester singing Song of the Earth, *and Lois Marshall, with whom I made a wonderful recording of English folk songs.*

Ms. Loman notes that many of her colleagues in the TSO have also been an

JUDY LOMAN, 1995. Principal Harpist with the Toronto Symphony.
Courtesy Judy Loman

inspiration. And her husband, trumpeter Joe Umbrico, has been a crucial influence on both her musical development and her personal growth. After the birth of Pennie Carlotta in 1957, the couple added three more children to their family: Linda in 1961, Julie in 1963, and Joe, Jr., in 1967. Nowadays, Pennie (a highly respected artist) lives in Brooklyn, New York, with her husband and twin daughters. Linda is also married and plays viola with Orchestra London. Julie is an English teacher in Toronto. Joe, Jr., attends a day program for autistics and still lives at home. Judy and Joe, Sr., went through a period of great stress when they first became aware that their son was autistic in 1970:

At the time, my music saved me from complete depression. When I would be practising or working, my problems would recede. Eventually I was taught how to help Joey follow a step-by-step procedure in order for him to gain control over everyday life skills.

The experience ultimately helped her in her other work as a teacher.

I learned how not to jump ahead before a student was ready.

Later in the 1970s Judy Loman and Joe Umbrico bought a farm near Fenelon Falls, Ontario, about ninety miles north-east of Toronto. Joe built a main house and a guest cabin, and Judy started her Fenelon Falls Harp School. Every summer eager students come for harp lessons — and tractor rides, long evening walks, and gourmet meals.

As it happens, both Joe and Judy are excellent cooks. On the many occasions when friends from the Toronto Symphony Orchestra come for the weekend, it's wall-to-wall eating and drinking: telling and retelling stories of the early days under this or that conductor (while Joe makes pasta and gnocci on his magnificent pasta- and gnocci-making machine). Even in the midst of the party, one can never forget that Judy Loman is one of the *grande dames* of the world harp community today.

Steven Staryk

One of the TSO's most illustrious alumni is Steven Staryk (who was also born and raised in Toronto). His brilliant career as concertmaster, soloist, and teacher, for more than forty years, has prompted a generation of critics to sing his praises in unusually lofty terms. By the age of thirty-five, he had been concertmaster of three major orchestras: the Royal Philharmonic of London, the Concertgebouw of Amsterdam, and the Chicago Symphony. Even more spectacularly, he had been successively recommended for these positions by such illustrious figures as Sir Thomas Beecham, Raphael Kubelik, and George Szell.

Today in his late sixties, Staryk lives in semi-retirement in Scottsdale, Arizona, after a decade as professor of violin and head of the string division at the University of Washington's School of Music in Seattle. He was the first School of Music professor in the history of the university to receive the prestigious Distinguished Teaching Award. When he joined the faculty in Seattle, Stephen Staryk's first priority was setting up a program to prepare students for an orchestral career:

There was too much importance placed on solo playing. It still goes on in most major North American institutions — the "superstar syndrome." They have their orchestras but they are still geared to becoming star soloists.

To address the situation, Staryk runs weekly audition classes for violinists at the university. Choosing from the professor's list of numerous orchestral excerpts, students learn and perform for each other in "trial auditions." In the process they also learn from the professor's years of orchestral playing at the highest level:

When I taught at the Amsterdam Conservatory, we would have orchestral studies class every Saturday morning, where we rehearsed with the same parts used by the Concertgebouw Orchestra. At this early stage in their development the students were already being prepared for the role, stylistically and traditionally — all the little details and inflections that they would later perform in the orchestra. You don't get too much of that type of training in North American schools.

Staryk has served on the faculties of ten universities and conservatories, and has received flattering praise from violinist/colleagues David Oistrakh, Zino Francescatti, and Henryk Szeryng for "his masterful playing and decisive and everlasting contribution to heighten pedagogic standards of today and tomorrow." He has also recorded a vast repertoire of violin literature. More than 190 entries listing Staryk are found in Creighton's *Discopaedia of the Violin,* including some forty-five LPs on twenty different labels, and no less than sixteen world premieres of new music: he ranks among the most prolific of recording violinists.

Staryk's first teachers were John Moskalyk and Christopher Daffef in Toronto:

I've had so many teachers: Elie Spivak, Albert Pratz, John Dembeck, Isaac Mamot in Toronto; in the United States I studied with Alexander Schneider, Oscar Shumsky, Mischa Mishakoff. Most of what I learned about music was not from violin teachers but from good conductors and musicians who had little to do with the fiddle.

However one chooses to look at this side of his career, Stephen Staryk is the first Canadian classical musician to have held major posts in Europe and North America, and to serve on the jury of the prestigious Tchaikovsky International Competition in Moscow. He has toured Europe, the Far East, and North America, and he was a founding member of Quartet Canada and the Staryk-Perry Duo.

He has also earned such distinctions as the coveted Ukrainian Shevchenko Medal, the Queen's Silver Jubilee Medal, an Honorary Doctorate of Letters from Toronto's York University, and assorted arts awards from the Canada Council. His achievements are listed in *Grove's Dictionary of Music and Musicians,* and in various other international encyclopaedias and "who's who in music" volumes. He will be included in a new book on the great violinists by Margaret Campbell, to be released by The Strad Library in 1999. And his biography, *Fiddling with Life,* by Thane Lewis, was about to be released by Mosaic Press at the time this book went to press.

Staryk's students are found occupying positions in orchestras in Europe and North America, as well as in chamber groups and on the faculties of music institutes. In the 1980s New York critic Irving Kolodin characterized him as: "the only contemporary 'virtuoso-concertmaster' to be a star soloist." *Hi Fi Stereo* in the United States has observed that the "man's control is demonic. His playing is reminiscent of Heifetz." According to *Records and Recordings* in England, he is "one of the great virtuoso violinists of our day." *Het Parool* in Amsterdam has written that he "is not only a great violinist, but a great artist." And the *Strad Magazine* has crowned him "the King of Concertmasters."

He has accomplished more in his career than most violinists could ever hope to achieve. What led him to the Royal Philharmonic and the other major orchestras?

When he entered the Carl Flesch International Competition in London in 1956, word spread quickly about his playing. Manoug Parikian, the concertmaster of the Philharmonia, which was the rival of Beecham's Royal Philharmonic, got word to the manager of the Beecham orchestra, who contacted Staryk and arranged an audition with the maestro. The audition led to a trial period, during which Staryk was to play with the orchestra for two to three months before a final decision would be made. After four weeks he was signed:

That happened without my pursuing the position. So you see, it was Beecham who got me started. I was in the Royal Philharmonic for three years from 1956.

In 1960 Raphael Kubelik recommended Staryk for the Concertgebouw in Amsterdam. The principal guest conductor at the time was George Szell, who later recommended Staryk to the Chicago Symphony. Staryk was thirty-one at the time.

I didn't have to play in front of the orchestra committee during my audition for Beecham. But with the Concertgebouw it was a different matter. The manager of the orchestra — a violinist himself — came over to London and heard me, and set up an audition, and when I got to Amsterdam the room was filled with principals and everyone else who wanted to listen. It was a thorough and exacting audition. Eugen Jochum was the principal conductor.

In Chicago, unlike the Concertgebouw audition, Staryk only played for conductor Jean Martinon, who knew his playing from earlier collaborations:

We just got together and then I played for him. Henryk Szeryng, who also knew my playing, was a strong recommender as well.

Staryk's teaching has also complemented his work as a concertmaster:

Wherever I played I had the dual role of concertmaster and professor of violin, except in London — the pay was a pittance. From 1960 to 1963 I was with the Concertgebouw and professor at the Amsterdam Conservatory. From 1963 to 1967 I was with the Chicago Orchestra and taught at Northwestern University, as well as the American Conservatory.
Then there was the Oberlin College Conservatory and many other schools.

Staryk has played for many fine conductors from whom he has learned a lot:

As far back as 1952, I worked with Victor De Sabata and Leopold Stokowski. Both were remarkable conductors and each made a lasting impression on me. They were among the earliest highlights of my career in Toronto.

Does he have any interesting sidelights on other conductors he worked with?

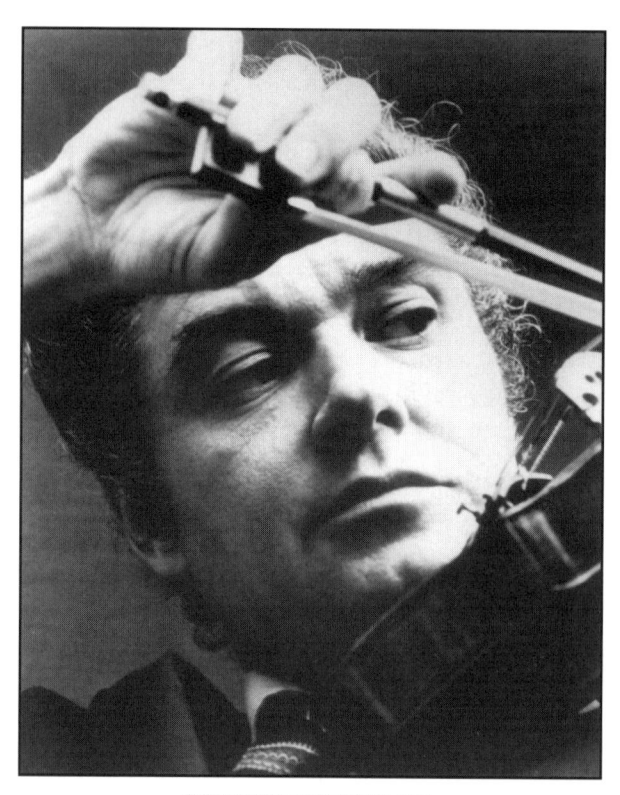

STEPHEN STARYK 1987.
Courtesy Stephen Staryk

Beecham was a witty autocrat who was always coming out with outlandish remarks, for which he was well-known. Szell ("Uncle George") was a dry taskmaster who did have a sense of humour. And he always had to have the last say on anything; a case of one-upmanship. It always had to be his story that got the last laugh.

Generally speaking, I found that almost all conductors have their party pieces. And they also have their idiosyncrasies. When you work with these types anywhere in the world, in totally different situations and atmospheres and totally different orchestras, with totally different players, these guys still do the same act. They all seem to have a fixed formula they follow (inevitably from early experiences). Their prompting, their interruptions, their instructions all come out at the same places. Not that all the orchestras have problems at the same places. It's just that perhaps the sessions with the shrink haven't resolved them yet for these conductors ... the list of conductors who influenced my musical education is long and impressive. It of course includes the bad ones as well.

Steven Staryk's amazing career has carried him to the top of the mountain and his recordings have earned him the respect of violinists and musicians around the world. Of all the 190 listings, which are his favourites?

I recorded Ein Heldenleben *in 1959 when I was with the Royal Philharmonic and Beecham, and but I like the recording of that work I did with the Toronto Symphony in 1982 with Andrew Davis conducting. In chamber music, my best works are the complete Beethoven sonatas with pianist John Perry. Others I like are the live broadcasts made into records, such as the Paganini concerto performed with NDR Hamburg Radio Orchestra in 1969, and the Kreisler album I did for the CBC. And the Prokofviev Concerto No. 1 with the Vancouver Symphony isn't bad, nor is the Shostokovitch with the Toronto Symphony, but these are now deleted and unavailable.*

In 1987 Staryk left the Toronto Symphony to join the the University of Washington's School of Music in Seattle. Since then the artist-teacher's influence has nonetheless inspired dozens of young violinists in many parts of the world on their way to the top of the mountain. And who better to show them than Steven Staryk, who has already been there?

Nexus

One thing I've learned about the contemporary classical music scene myself is that it can be a lot more lively and innovative than is sometimes thought. A case in point is the percussion group Nexus, which originated in Toronto and has been captivating audiences with an eclectic mix of music from all over the globe, ever since its first concert in 1971.

The five original members, John Wyre, Bob Becker, Bill Cahn, Robin Engelman, and Russell Hartenberger, continue to perform a repertoire that includes contemporary percussion masterworks, ragtime, world music, group improvisations, and compositions by the members themselves. The ensemble's virtuosity, innovative programming, and insatiable curiosity have inspired compositions from some of the greatest present-day composers.

The group's performances of Toru Takemitsu's *From Me Flows What You Call Time*, composed for Nexus and the Boston Symphony Orchestra under the direction of Seiji Ozawa, and commissioned by Carnegie Hall for its 1990–1991 Centennial celebration, won immediate international acclaim. The world premiere was given by Nexus with the Boston Symphony under Ozawa's direction at Carnegie Hall in October 1990. Subsequent performances have featured the percussion quintet with the New Japan Philharmonic, the Orchestré National de Lyon, the combined orchestras of Kitchener-Waterloo and Orchestra London, the Rochester Philharmonic, the Buffalo Philharmonic, and the Chautauqua, Louisville, Milwaukee, Pacific, and Toronto Symphony Orchestras. The quintet's distinctive repertoire for percussion and symphony orchestra has led as well to appearances with the New York Philharmonic, the Cleveland Orchestra, and the orchestras of Anchorage, Atlanta, Colorado Springs, Detroit, Dallas, Kingston (Ontario), Memphis, and St. Paul.

What does the name Nexus mean? The word dates back to the ancient Romans, and points to "a connection or tie between the members of a group or series." (The music of percussion instruments forms the connection between the five members of the ensemble.)

As the critic Bill Tilland has explained: "Nexus treats the definition of 'percussion' with a certain latitude, and includes not only a variety of tuned mallet instruments (marimbas, xylophones, and vibraphones), but also zithers, harmonicas, flutes, primitive accordions, and so on." The group's programs for children, teenagers and young adults introduce the broad and colourful range of percussion music in a delightful and entertaining style. Its recent CD release, *The Story of Percussion in the Orchestra,* features Nexus with PBS journalist Bill Moyers and the

Rochester Philharmonic. Other Nexus performances have been recorded on compact discs.

Nexus created and performed the music for the Academy Award winning film *The Man Who Skied Down Mount Everest*. It has been featured on CBS Television's "Sunday Morning," with Charles Kuralt and Eugenia Zuckerman. The quintet has been travelling extensively since 1975, including tours of Australia, New Zealand, Asia (it was the first Western percussion group to perform in the People's Republic of China), Scandinavia, and other parts of Europe. It makes regular appearances throughout the U.S.A. and Canada, and has given workshops and master-classes at universities around the world.

Nexus has also been featured at the Adelaide Festival, the Holland Festival, the Budapest Spring Festival, the Tanglewood, Ravinia, and Blossom Music Festivals, the Los Angeles Festival, the Houston International Festival, the Toronto Festival, the Forum des Percussions in Paris, the British Percussion Festival, the Southbank Festival and BBC Proms in London, the Music Today and Music Joy Festivals in Tokyo, and World Drum Festivals in Vancouver, Brisbane, and Calgary.

The master percussionists are the 1997 recipients of the Banff Centre for the Arts National Award, for their "constant and joyful commitment to the development of the next generation of musicians and audiences," and "as superb musicians, with a following around the world." (In its own hometown, Nexus also won the Toronto Arts Award for 1989.)

I've known John Wyre for many years now, and I had the pleasure of working with him in the Toronto Symphony. He joined the orchestra in 1967 and stayed for some fifteen years. John was the tympanist in the TSO — a far cry from a jazz drummer. But I particularly remember one demonstration of his striking versatility. In 1970 Karel Ancerl conducted a memorable three-week Beethoven Festival at the O'Keefe Centre in Toronto. After each concert the audience was invited to join a party down in the cocktail lounge, where I had a quintet that played for dancing. This group was made up mostly of Toronto Symphony musicians who had also played in dance bands (drummer Don Wherry, trumpeter Johnny Cowell, bassist Sam Levine, and the late pianist Herby Helbig (Herby was our one ringer who was not in the TSO), and I, of course, played trombone.

One night drummer Don Wherry became ill and couldn't play. Who could I get at the last minute? Phoning a replacement at 10:30 PM to come to the O'Keefe was impossible. Then John Wyre stepped into the breech. "Let me do it," he suggested. Somewhat apprehensive about whether he could play that kind of music, I agreed to let him sit in. But did he know anything about a high-hat cymbal? Did he know how to handle brushes? Did he have any conception of "getting a beat?"

While the audience in the foyer discussed the marvellous concert they'd just heard, before they sauntered downstairs to the lounge, John sat on Don Wherry's special drummer's stool to get the right feel, to test the right height. Then he got up, adjusted the height to his comfort, sat down again, tried the brushes on the snare drum, and then he nodded to me, as if to say, "Don't worry, Murray. I think I've got it." And, well folks, I better make it clear that we were treated to a performance of drumming that night that lifted the entire group right off their derrières. It was one of the most amazing performances I ever saw. It didn't matter what the tune or the tempo was; John Wyre was simply a genius.

In fact for many years John has been on a musical journey that has taken him from rock and roll to jazz and classical music, through free improvisation, contemporary compositions, and world music.

Along with Nexus and the TSO, he has been a part of the Marlboro Music Festival and a member of the Boston Symphony Orchestra. His compositions have been performed by the New York Philharmonic, the Cleveland Orchestra, the Japan Philharmonic, and (of course) Nexus. He is artistic director of World Drums, which has presented international drum festivals since 1984.

Like John himself, the other members of Nexus are not just passable percussionists. Each is a master in his own right. Bob Becker's performing experience spans nearly all of the musical disciplines where percussion is found. Considered by many to be one of the world's premier virtuoso performers on xylophone and marimba, he also appears regularly as an independent soloist and clinician.

William Cahn has performed with composers, ensembles, and popular artists representing diverse musical styles. In 1985 Cahn wrote and produced a classical music video entitled *March to the Scaffold,* featuring the Rochester Philharmonic Orchestra. The six-minute video has been seen on public television stations in the U.S.A. and Australia, and in August 1987 it was featured on the CBS News "Sunday Morning" national broadcast.

Robin Engelman has taught percussion at Ithaca College, Eastman School of Music, York University, and the University of Toronto. He has performed at the Marlboro Music Festival, New Hampshire Music Festival, and appeared as a soloist with symphony orchestras and music festivals worldwide.

Russell Hartenberger is professor of percussion at the University of Toronto and performs regularly with the Steve Reich ensemble. He holds a PhD in world music from Wesleyan University, where he studied the mrdangam with Ramnad Raghavan of Madras, India. He has been a featured performer with the New York Philharmonic, the Boston Symphony, and with other leading North American orchestras.

In the end it is impossible to listen to these master percussionists — especially when they combine to perform as Nexus, accompanied by a major symphony orchestra — and still imagine that contemporary classical music is something trapped in a European time warp somewhere in the eighteenth or nineteenth or even early twentieth centuries.

Albert Pratz

No matter how innovative it might be, of course, the string family of musical instruments — and especially the violin — remains at the centre of classical music. As I noted earlier on, in the 1930s and 1940s there were many more fine violinists emerging in Toronto than a city of its size should normally produce. And Albert Pratz was one of them. He is one of the finest violinists Canada has ever produced, ultimately rising to the top of his profession to become the concertmaster of the Toronto Symphony Orchestra

Born in Toronto on May 13, 1914, in his youth Pratz studied the violin in the city of his birth with Broadus Farmer and Luigi von Kunits. In 1933, at twenty-nine, he studied in the United States with Michel Piastro and Mischa Mischakoff. In 1936–37 he also spent some time in Europe, studying with William Primrose. He had begun his professional career in Toronto, when he joined a CFRB radio orchestra under Alexander Chuhaldin in 1929. And he made his solo debut at Varsity Arena in 1937 in the Tchaikovsky *Concerto for Violin* at the Promenade Philharmonic concerts under Reginald Stewart.

From 1933 to 1941 he was a member of the Toronto Symphony Orchestra, and played radio shows on CFRB as well as with CBC orchestras conducted by the likes of Geoffrey Waddington, Rex Battle, and Percy Faith. From 1940 to 1943 he worked as music director of CBC Winnipeg.

After the United States entered the Second World War, Pratz enlisted in the American army and performed in an army band between 1943 and 1946. In 1946, the year of his discharge from the army, Pratz joined the NBC Symphony Orchestra under Arturo Toscanini. He remained with this ensemble until it was disbanded in 1953. During the same period he worked extensively in New York radio and recording studios. Pratz later used to say that when the New York musicians of that era had a day off some of them went to the race track:

We had a fool-proof system where we couldn't lose. Every horse that the newspaper handicappers said would run third, we bet it to come first. Nine times out of ten we were right. We started by betting two dollars on the first race, four dollars on the second race, eight dollars on the third, and so on. Somewhere along the way we had a winner. But once we won, we left the track. We didn't want to jeopardize our chances by continuing to bet. It was all a matter of luck, which can go either way.

I once tried Pratz's system at Greenwood Race Track in Toronto and lost a bundle. I also remember how mesmerized some of my Toronto musical colleagues and I were by the television broadcasts of the old NBC Symphony Orchestra under Arturo Toscanini. We watched the concerts from New York religiously, every Saturday at 6:00 PM, only somewhat frustrated by the early small-screen TV sets, with everything in black and white.

When the show came on, we'd crowd around the set trying to recognize the faces of such orchestra members as Albert Pratz. The opening shots were always of the entire orchestra playing the theme (something by Wagner, I think). While the music played, the program items would be flashed on the screen — an overture, a short orchestral work, or a guest soloist, then a major symphony: Brahms, Beethoven, or Mozart. When the opening credits and announcements, timed to fit the length of the theme, were finished, the camera rested on Toscanini and remained that way until the end of the program. You might occasionally catch a small glimpse of the orchestra members, but mostly, you saw the great conductor.

My own experience was that watching Arturo Toscanini became an obsession. The television screen, no matter how small, picked up every frown — every flicker of an eyebrow, twitch of the moustache, curl of the lip — and the orchestra responded magnificently. It included some of the world's best musicians. I often wondered whether they followed maestro Toscanini's baton or his face, as with each facial expression the music grew louder here, softer there, bolder, quicker, slower. It was pure magic. Charismatic Arturo Toscanini had one of the most fascinating faces I have ever seen.

ALBERT PRATZ, 1975.
Courtesy National Youth Orchestra of Canada

Albert Pratz returned to Toronto in 1953. That summer he played with Glenn Gould and cellist Isaac Mamott in the Festival Trio at the first Stratford Festival.

When Geoffrey Waddington organized the CBC Symphony in 1955, Pratz became a member of that "virtuoso" orchestra. The ensemble presented live weekly broadcasts with famous guest conductors (Sir Thomas Beecham, Sir John Barbirolli, Sir Colin Davis) from the Parliament Street studios in Toronto.

Although it has been written that Albert Pratz served as concertmaster of the CBC Symphony from its beginning in 1955 to 1961, the facts are that Hyman

Goodman was in the concertmaster's chair at the very start, and Pratz sat on his left. There was a change, however, early on in the orchestra's life, when Pratz one Saturday morning sat in Goodman's chair, and remained there. As a result, Goodman left the orchestra that very day. (As an original member of the group, I witnessed that incident.)

At the time Pratz also conducted his own radio show called "Let's Make Music." Rod Coneybeare was the narrator, and the weekly program dramatized the lives of such famous songwriters as Irving Berlin, George Gershwin, and Rogers and Hammerstein.

From 1964 to 1966 Pratz taught at Brandon University in Winnipeg, where he organized the Wawanesa String Ensemble for on-campus concerts. He also served as concertmaster of the Buffalo Philharmonic under conductor Lukas Foss from 1965 to 1969. Then he returned to Toronto once again, where he served as concertmaster of the Toronto Symphony Orchestra from 1971 to 1979.

From 1961 to 1963 Albert Pratz was also a member of the Faculty of Music at the University of Toronto, and he continued to teach privately after that. On his retirement he coached National Youth Orchestra of Canada violinists during the summer months at Queen's University. He died on March 14, 1995, two months before his eighty-first birthday.

Hyman Goodman

Another imposing figure from Toronto's age of emerging fine violinists in the 1930s and 1940s was Hyman Goodman, who occupied the concertmaster's chair of the TSO from 1947 until his retirement in 1967. Like Albert Pratz, Hyman Goodman was born in Toronto. He received his early training at the city's Royal Conservatory of Music, and then later studied in New York with Vladimir Graffman and D.C. Dounis.

Goodman was recognized early amongst the extraordinarily large number of excellent Toronto violinists of his time. He was already performing in shows and concerts during the first days of CFRB and CBC radio. Sir Ernest MacMillan was also impressed with his playing and in 1931 hired him to play with the Toronto Symphony — for fifteen dollars a week. During this early period as well the young violinist performed with Percy Faith, Rex Battle, and Geoffrey Waddington in various local theatres and hotels.

Hyman Goodman's Second World War years, from 1942 to 1946, were spent as an RCAF flight-sergeant bandsman in the Air Force Music Group. On discharge in 1946 he rejoined the Toronto Symphony and became its concertmaster in 1947. He remained in the position until 1967, when he left the TSO to take up a new career in Los Angeles.

I've already alluded to the conflict between Goodman and Pratz, in the CBC Symphony Orchestra organized in 1955 under Geoffrey Waddington, head of music for the English language radio network. And I can't quite resist elaborating a little more. As I said earlier, when the "virtuoso" orchestra first started, Hyman

HYMAN GOODMAN, circa 1967.
Courtesy Erica Goodman

Goodman was sitting in the concertmaster's chair.and Albert Pratz sat next to him on his left.

Some time between 1956 and 1957, I recall coming to the studio for the Saturday morning rehearsal, taking my trombone out of its case, and seeing Albert Pratz sitting in the concertmaster's chair. I realized then that an altercation might soon break out. Other musicians coming from the street spotted it immediately as well. (Musicians, I suppose like any other human beings, do not take kindly to being removed from a locked-in position, especially without prior warning.) I raised the matter with my seat-mate, Teddy Roderman, who was the principal trombonist of the CBC Symphony. Teddy's only comment was: "The shit is about to hit the fan."

When Hyman Goodman arrived at the rehearsal, he must have sensed what was in store for him. He removed his hat and coat, took his instrument out of its case, and approached Pratz, who looked straight ahead. No one heard the conversation, but whatever transpired between the two, Albert Pratz did not move.

Hyman then spoke to Harry Bergart, the contractor. Whatever passed between the two remained a secret. But it was obvious that Pratz had received permission, or demanded permission, or complained about his seating arrangements, with the result that he didn't budge from the concertmaster's chair. (The only person with the authority to make such a change would have been the head of music for the English language network of the CBC.)

At this point Hyman put on his coat and hat, returned his violin to its case, and walked out of the studio onto the street. No one said a word, but many shook their heads at the injustice. And many silently applauded Hyman Goodman for having the courage to walk out of the studio that morning.

In the early 1960s, while still based in Toronto, Hyman spent several summers teaching at the American Federation of Musician's Congress of Strings, first in East

Lansing, Michigan, and then in Los Angeles. After he moved to Los Angeles in 1967, he played in the studios under such illustrious conductor/arrangers as Percy Faith, David Rose, and Henry Mancini. His violin can be heard on the soundtracks of a number of 1970s television programs (including "Little House on the Prairie"), and in the film *The Godfather*. He also toured Japan three times as concertmaster for the Percy Faith Orchestra.

Throughout his life Hyman was an inveterate letter-writer. Violinist Agnes Roberts, one of Toronto's busiest musicians, was one of his most ardent correspondents. The two violinists exchanged letters frequently, and Agnes would often pass along his humorous stories to me. Eventually I came to correspond with him myself. His quietly hilarious anecdotes about the world of music could fill several volumes in their own right.

For the last quarter-century or so of his life, Hyman lived in Encino, California, with his second wife Sylvia. I am sad to report that, ultimately, severe arthritis prevented him from playing his beloved violin. Then, after the January 1994 California earthquake, he experienced traumatic shock which affected him until his death on March 27, 1994. He was a gentle man of high intelligence and high principle, and he won respect from *almost* everyone he met. For me he came to stand for a great deal of what is best about music and the people who love to play it. (And, as some readers may remember, it was Hyman Goodman who first inspired me to settle down and write this book.)

Mary Barrow

As I look back on everything I've written so far, it strikes me that there have been rather fewer women musicians in my story than I would like. And I think this has a lot to do with the plain fact that, apart from singers, there just weren't very many women musicians in the more popular branches of the business during the golden age of music. As my references to Judy Loman and Pearl Palmason have already suggested, however, in classical music women seem to have secured a somewhat stronger foothold earlier on.

Another case in point here is Mary Barrow, who was introduced to the French horn just before she became a teenager and was playing principal horn with the Toronto Symphony at the age of eighteen. Mary told me during our interview:

> *When I was twelve, a friend of my father's, who had three daughters who played clarinet, bassoon, and oboe, wanted someone to play French horn with them. He talked my father into getting me to play it. Bert Barrow, my future husband's father, showed me how to produce a note on the horn. I had never seen a French horn before, but I hit a note right at the beginning.*

Recognized as a "natural" right from the start, a month later Mary played a small solo in her school. At fourteen she started taking lessons at the Conservatory from the elder Barrow and was playing solos regularly in other Toronto schools.

She graduated from the Conservatory at sixteen. Under normal conditions any youngster studying a brass instrument must develop an embouchure in order to play properly. A proper embouchure (the manner in which the lips and tongue are applied to a mouthpiece along with correct articulation and breath control) can take years to develop. Only on rare occasions will a gem like Mary Barrow emerge to play with a perfect embouchure right from the start.

Even beyond such rare occasions, to sit in the principal horn hot seat of the TSO a mere five years after she hit her first note was something of a miracle. (And, at the age of eighteen, the young lady who had begun her life as Mary Robb also married the French horn player Reg Barrow, whose father had already helped her produce her first musical note.)

Mary Barrow's working career on the Toronto music scene actually began even before she joined the Toronto Symphony. It takes in an intriguing piece of the city's musical history — involving the "Proms" concerts at Varsity Arena that an orchestra originally organized by Reginald Stewart used to give in the 1930s.

In 1935, just after Mary had graduated from the Conservatory, she was told that the Proms needed a horn player. She went down to Varsity Arena and auditioned successfully for Reginald Stewart, and was then appointed principal horn for the rest of the season.

Just as I was leaving the audition room, Sir Reginald said, "I suppose you find it difficult as a woman to get a job." His question caught me by surprise. That was the first time I'd ever auditioned for anything.

The Proms concerts had their origin in an agreement between Reginald Stewart and Walter Murdoch of the Toronto Musicians' Association. Under the agreement Stewart organized the Promenade Philharmonic to perform summertime concerts in Varsity Arena "which would offer musicians the opportunity to play and at the same time earn some money." (Like so many others in the 1930s, Toronto classical musicians welcomed any opportunity for employment.)

The agreement allowed the players to perform and receive whatever money came through the sale of tickets. On most concert nights Varsity Arena was packed. After guest artists and conductors were paid, and such expenses as ushers and cleaners had been covered, the remaining money was divided equally among the eighty or ninety musicians in the orchestra. The later TSO stalwart Harold Sumberg remembers that "some nights we received only enough money to buy a streetcar ticket." Nights of this sort, however, usually had a lot to do with bad weather, or bad programming and an unattractive guest artist. As Mary Barrow herself recalls:

While Stewart was there we received between eight and ten dollars for a pair of concerts. But after a few years as conductor, he left to become principal of the Peabody Conservatory of Music in the States. At the same time he also became the conductor of the Baltimore Symphony.

In another of my interviews, bassist Sam Levine, who also played in the Promenade Philharmonic, helped shed a little more light on the departure of Reginald Stewart:

He was unhappy with some of the musicians who played the Proms. He complained to Walter Murdoch a number of times that he wanted the same players every week, and only those whose performing abilities satisfied him. But Murdoch, as president of the union, wouldn't agree. "The Promenade Concerts," he said, "were a summertime make-work project and he had to be fair to all TMA members. When Stewart finally decided he'd had enough, he resigned and went to the States. But it wasn't all bad for the Proms. They began bringing in conductors like Beecham, Kostelanetz, and other renowned personalities. The music lovers of Toronto flocked to Varsity Arena after that.

Alas, the rise in attendance to Varsity Arena did not exactly improve the circumstances of all the musicians. Mary Barrow remembers:

After Stewart left, conditions changed considerably. All of a sudden they said they weren't taking in enough money, although the arena was always jammed. When we lined up on Thursdays to collect our money, Ernest Johnson, the contractor, sat at a table with a pile of dollar bills next to a box with coins in it. As we moved up to the table he paid us one dollar, which we had to sign for. Then he said, "Oh Mary, you're first chair. Here's an extra payment," He handed me a dime from the box. We couldn't believe it.

The disappointed first-chair musicians held a meeting and decided to approach Walter Murdoch, to protest the shoddy practice and see what could be done. Murdoch herded them into a room and told them to sit around a table. Then he said, "If you don't agree to the conditions that have been laid down, you can leave right now. But you'll never work in the city again." According to Mary:

I was against it. The rest didn't know what to do. Old Leo Smith, the cello player said, "Well, if Mary thinks she's better than the rest of us and deserves more than the rest of us, let her go ahead. But as for me, I'll be content to take what we are getting." I resigned right then.

Before she left the Promenade Philharmonic, Mary had a chance to work under guest conductor Sir Thomas Beecham. Hundreds of anecdotes about the crusty British maestro are still being told around the coffee dispensers of every orchestra room in the English-speaking world. And Mary Barrow has her own contribution:

When Beecham first came here and saw me, he raised his eyebrows. He had never seen a woman in an orchestra. He stopped the orchestra and turned to Elie Spivak, the concertmaster. Elie said, "Let her play. I'm sure she'll play the part to your satisfaction." At one rehearsal we were doing Brahms' Second Symphony, *and it was freezing in the arena. Cliff Spearing, the third horn, kept messing up his part. After a third try, Beecham said, "First horn, take your section off and rehearse them, and don't come back until they can all play the part." So we went around the back and Spearing said, "He's got me nervous. I'll never play the part." So I said, "Since the rest of us don't play there — it's your solo — we can all play it, and that's the way we will do it." When we returned to our seats Beecham never said a word; he never mentioned it at all.*

That evening, just before the concert, somebody came to the girls' room and said, "Sir Thomas wants to talk to you." So I went to his dressing room and knocked on the door. "Come in," a voice said. I opened the door and saw him in his undershirt bent over with his rear end to me, tying his shoes.

"You wished to talk to me, Sir Thomas?"

"Oh yes, what are you doing about that horn part?"

I told him what we were doing and he said, "That's fine," and never moved from that position. I shut the door and he was still bent over. Beecham took his time coming to the podium. The audience had to wait a long time while he went to the washroom. But he finally came out and conducted the concert. After that he left Toronto.

It was not long after Mary Barrow became first horn in the Promenade Philharmonic that Sir Ernest MacMillan asked her to join the Toronto Symphony, where she was appointed principal horn as well:

Whenever a new first chair player came into the orchestra MacMillan had them play every solo in the repertoire. So I played every solo that year. I did the Nocturne in the Midsummer Night's Dream, *the solo in Tchaikovsky's* Fifth Symphony, *every one.*

Audiences were taken with the beautiful young auburn-haired woman in the horn section. The musicians also found her to be affable and easy to get along with, never an unkind or nasty word passing her lips. Guest conductors and soloists, too, found her attractive (along with the other great TSO beauty of the day, Pearl Palmason: some offered invitations to their dressing rooms, but the ladies always stayed clear).

When Mary and Reg Barrow were married in 1938, Sir Ernest Macmillan played at their wedding.

He played every piece that had a horn part in it.

Already, word of Mary's unusual ability had begun to spread. She was invited by Leopold Stokowski to join his All-American Youth Orchestra, touring the U.S.A. and South America. Two other Canadians, Toronto trumpeter Ellis McLintock, and Zara Nelsova, the Winnipeg cellist, accepted similar invitations.

I had to decline. I had just gotten married and a tour was the last thing I wanted.

MARY BARROW AND HUSBAND REG, circa 1952.
Courtesy Mary Barrow

To Toronto's great benefit, Mary Barrow remained in town. Soon enough, arrangers and commercial leaders began calling her. They knew she was reliable; a professional to the core. She began doing radio shows with leaders like Lucio Agostini, Sam Hershenhorn, Howard Cable, and Geoffrey Waddington. When television came to the CBC in 1952 she was seen on many shows that aired from coast to coast. She finally left the Symphony in 1953 to work as a freelance musician, a very lucrative part of the music business for those who can perform at the top of their class. At the height of her freelance career, Mary recalled:

Things got so busy I had to take a breather for a while. It was too much.

She had four shows on Sundays. Then she had at least one show every weekday, which caught her running from studio to studio for an entire season. That same season she was called to do every jingle session imaginable. And she played the CNE Grandstand shows, afternoons and evenings. She also spent the occasional week or two in the orchestra pits of the O'Keefe Centre and the Royal Alexandra Theatre.

A little further down the road, Mary Barrow, who had become principal horn with the Toronto Symphony Orchestra when she was only eighteen, became an important member of Rob McConnell's Boss Brass, Toronto's superb jazz orchestra of the later twentieth century. Playing in the Boss Brass was an eye-opener.

That job was entirely different from all the musical assignments I had ever done. There is a thing about perfection in music today. At a session music is recorded over and over until the finished product is perfect. There's a lot of tension in a recording studio.

But playing with jazz musicians is easier. There never is any tension. Jazz players are more relaxed, happier, particularly when they are playing a solo. Unlike performing in a symphony orchestra, which is rigidly controlled, the sky is the limit in a jazz solo. Whatever comes into the musician's mind is transmitted immediately to his fingers, pressing the keys of his saxophone, or the valves of his trumpet. It's a happy way of life.

By the 1980s the time had come for Mary to retire. She lives today in the most northern part of the new city of Toronto with her second husband, Art Rogers. It is a happy circumstance that she is certainly not the last supremely talented and successful female musician in Canada. But (I think it's fair enough to say) she was among the first.

Victor Feldbrill

Of course, even today men still account for the majority of performers in classical music. This is especially true among the ranks of orchestra conductors. And it should come as no surprise that the one young symphonic conductor who emerged from the Toronto classical music scene of the 1930s and 1940s is Victor Feldbrill.

When Victor was just sixteen years old, and concertmaster of the All-Ontario Secondary School Orchestra (comprised of the province's best high-school musicians), he boldly knocked on the door of TSO maestro Sir Ernest MacMillan, and announced that he would like to become a conductor. Sir Ernest, who was also principal of the Royal Conservatory of Toronto at the time, smiled at the young man's enthusiasm and said, "There may not be enough orchestras to go around." But Victor replied, "Oh, I think I'll take my chances."

Sir Ernest saw something interesting in the sixteen-year-old and had him enroll in the Conservatory, where Ettore Mazzoleni began teaching him the art of conducting. Two years later both Sir Ernest and Mazzoleni felt that Victor had progressed enough to allow him a spot with the orchestra.

At the age of eighteen, the young Feldbrill mounted the podium on the stage of Massey Hall to rehearse a five-minute Strauss waltz. When Sir Ernest handed him the baton he said, "You have twenty minutes." Enthralled to be in such an enviable position, Victor found himself conducting and offering direction to some of the country's finest violinists.

Many years later again, on January 15, 1992, a white-haired Victor Feldbrill mounted the podium at Roy Thomson Hall to conduct the Toronto Symphony, in celebration of his fiftieth anniversary as one of Canada's respected conductors. Much had happened to Feldbrill in the intervening half-century. And his association with the TSO has been a close, ongoing one, during his entire career.

While he was studying with Mazzoleni at the Conservatory in Toronto, Feldbrill was also studying violin with Bobby Steinberg. During the Second World

War, when Sir Ernest learned Feldbrill was going overseas to London as a member of the Royal Canadian Navy, he gave him a letter of introduction that opened doors in the most amazing places. In London Victor met Sir Thomas Beecham and Sir Adrian Boult, both of whom left indelible impressions of what great conductors do to achieve the ultimate in orchestral performance.

At war's end, while Feldbrill was still in England, Boult offered him a conducting post with a British orchestra. Victor reluctantly declined because he missed his family and his city and wanted to go home. Back in Canada he began to champion young Canadian-born artists and composers. From 1949 to 1956 he played in the TS violin section, and conducted the orchestra several times under the watchful eye of Sir Ernest MacMillan. When he left the TSO he began to appear with other major orchestras in the country, often accompanied by new Canadian performers. Many of his programs featured new Canadian works, along with Beethoven and Mozart symphonies. His face became more and more familiar to orchestra patrons across the country.

VICTOR FELDBRILL. On January 15, 1992, a white-haired Feldbrill appeared at Roy Thomson Hall to conduct the Toronto Symphony, in celebration of his fiftieth anniversary as one of Canada's respected conductors. *Courtesy Victor Feldbrill*

For ten years he was music director of the Winnipeg Symphony Orchestra. In 1973 he was appointed resident conductor of the Toronto Symphony, and in 1974 he organized the Toronto Symphony Youth Orchestra. In 1979 he left Canada to become the music director of Japan's Geidhai Philharmonia (at Tokyo's University of the Arts) and he remained at his post in Japan for the next seven years.

By 1990 Feldbrill had returned to Canada, and taken up the conducting reins of the Hamilton Philharmonic Orchestra. At this point the Hamilton organization was much in need of fresh morale and enthusiasm. He immediately set about righting all wrongs. By the time he departed at the end of the 1992–93 concert season, he had, as *Hamilton Spectator* music reviewer Hugh Fraser observed, "transformed the orchestra."

Less than a year before, during the celebration concert of January 15, 1992, at Roy Thomson Hall in Toronto, Max Tapper, the TS's managing director, had stepped forward to announce the establishment of the Victor Feldbrill Scholarship, to be awarded annually to a promising member of the Toronto Symphony Youth Orchestra. Tapper also confessed that it was Feldbrill who had introduced him as a child to the world of symphonic music.

Is Victor Feldbrill retired today, and just resting quietly on his many laurels, as he has every right to do? Well ... let's say he is semi-retired. From time to time he is still called upon to perform a special service with one orchestra or another.

In the fall of 1997 he conducted the National Arts Centre Orchestra in Ottawa, in a series of concerts devoted to music composed and arranged by Toronto-born Robert Farnon (of whom I have already had quite a lot to say in other parts of this book). Bob Farnon himself flew to Ottawa from his current home in Guernsey in the Channel Islands, to be present at the concerts. That was another tribute to Victor Feldbrill's long and honourable career. And there are probably a few more still to come.

The Enchanted Strings

The particular cause of women in the Canadian music business in Toronto received a boost after the Second World War, when Trump Davidson added five classically trained female violinists to his band at the Palace Pier in 1950.

The original group included Billie Buschert, Irene Mokry, Ohulani Otbo, Josephine Toth, and Erica Zentner (who later became Trump's wife). But there were assorted comings and goings over the years. Others who played in the female violin section in Trump's band were Mary Carr, Elsie Dunlop, Florence and Andrea Hansen, Lillian Nickoloff, Olga Priestman, Lois Thomas, and Dolores Vann.

The key figure for my particular story here is Elsie Dunlop, an attractive classical violinist who also played dance music for Trump Davidson at the Palace Pier and other local bandleaders as well. And as Elsie explained to me not too long ago:

The trouble with playing for Jimmy Davidson was that it was only during the fall and winter months. During the summer months it was difficult finding work.

So what did the lady do?

On the many private parties I played over the years, I remember thinking how effective a strolling string group might be during dinner when dance music stopped, to allow the waiters to serve. With that in mind and to drum up some work during the summer months, some of us organized a group of four violinists — Lois Thomas, Erica Davidson, Lillian Nickoloff, and myself — as a strolling quartet to play popular songs and medleys during dinners. We called the group the Enchanted Strings.

THE ENCHANTED STRINGS, 1950s. Lois Thomas, Erica Davidson, Lillian Nickoloff, and Elsie Dunlop. *Courtesy Erica Davidson*

At first, putting the idea into practice wasn't easy.

We had to rehearse as much as possible. All the music had to be memorized, and since we had arrangements written by a number of the best arrangers in the city, learning the individual harmony parts presented a challenge. It was a case of constant repetition, memorizing each note and bar until we had a tune down pat; then on to the next, and so on. Our act took about thirty minutes, and that's a lot of music to learn from memory. We also had to learn how to walk and how to smile.

The members of the Enchanted Strings brought in the CBC choreographer Len Starmer, to show them the proper steps, when to turn, when to kneel, and above all, how to smile — all important prerequisites for a top-flight act. (Len, by the way, would go on to become the permanent producer of the Wayne and Shuster TV shows.) They also had several special gowns made:

My mother made us gowns and cocktail dresses, which saved us money. We played Blue Tango, Jealousy, Pizzicato Polka, Hora Staccato, *and* Czardas. *We also had special choreography for every arrangement, and we changed gowns after each number.*

In the end, it all paid off.

Edna Slatter at the CBC helped the group find jobs: Edna saw us perform on one of our early engagements, and liked what she saw. She had connections which led to a number of successful engagements. In fact, she got us a series called "A Date with Frosia," a popular CBC television show in the fifties. Sam Hershenhorn also called us to do some television shows on which he conducted the orchestra ... It really developed into a fascinating and enchanting floor show.

As the ladies in the quartet honed their act, they also found themselves playing shows at the Elmwood Casino in the border city of Windsor, Ontario (which regularly attracted a large crowd from Detroit, Michigan, just across the river), and at night clubs in Detroit, Cleveland, and Montreal. They played the Club Norman in Toronto as well. They also did a date on the "Arthur Godfrey Show." Towards the end of our conversation, I asked Elsie: Did everything always go as rehearsed?

Well, there were a few funny things, she said. On one "A Date with Frosia" show, we were coming down some stairs when a prop pillar began to topple beside Lois Thomas. The poor girl had to stand beside the column to keep it from toppling over and play at the same time right on camera until a stagehand straightened it out.

Another time at the Club Norman we were performing on a small dias with little room to manoeuvre. At the end of the act we kneeled to take a bow ... Lois kneeled on a hot light, which melted her stocking. The pain must have been terrible, but Lois just stayed in that position, smiling, until the blackout allowed us to get off.

Ultimately, the Enchanted Strings had enough material in their repertoire for quite a wide variety of engagements. And the group gained particular fresh insights playing on the nightclub circuit.

We were actually able to provide the proper music for whatever type of party or club we found ourselves doing. We would see the professional chorus girls drinking a lot of milk in their dressing rooms. The girls said that drinking milk made the boobs bigger.

A little down the road, the wandering violinists attracted the attention of bandleader Moxie Whitney, who brought them in to enhance his Imperial Room Orchestra at the Royal York Hotel in 1958. In those days the Imperial Room in Toronto often featured such American television and recording stars as Tony Martin, Peggy Lee, and Ella Fitzgerald. Elsie Dunlop, Erica Davidson, Lillian Nickoloff, and Lois Thomas often served as the string section for the shows that featured these big-name stars from out of town.

When other musicians, in Toronto and other parts of Canada, saw how successful the group had become, they began to organize similar ensembles. None, however, could finally match the special showmanship of Elsie's quartet. It did not last forever, but then nothing does. Like some other people my age in the Toronto music business, I still can't quite forget the Enchanted Strings today. And I don't think I ever will.

Once Upon a Time in the TSO: Tales from the Catacombs

As I think I've alluded to several times now, in the midst of all its formality and discipline, the world of classical music is also full of its own kind of lighter moments and comic relief. Before leaving the subject of my rather lengthy excursion into this world, I thought it might make some sense to recall a few of my own encounters with its lighter human side.

My main problem here is that I could go on about such things almost forever. I have been advised to stick to the top ten anecdotes on a much longer list. A lot of the top ten, I realized once I'd selected them, have to do with the Toronto Symphony Orchestra under the baton of Seiji Ozawa, in the 1960s. And there are, no doubt, good reasons for this.

ONE

On October 23, 1965, the Toronto Symphony played a concert at Cedarbrae Collegiate in the Toronto suburb of Scarborough, with Seiji Ozawa conducting. Ozawa had only recently joined the TSO at this point. It would be years before he was recognized as a world-class conductor of symphony orchestras.

The trombones didn't have anything to play until the last piece on the program, Brahms' *Symphony No. 4*, which was scheduled right after intermission. I left what was then my home in Downsview for the drive to Cedarbrae at 8:00 PM, in enough time to be in my chair for the downbeat at 9:15. In the Brahms' *Symphony No. 4* the trombones are actually silent for the first three movements, but they begin the fourth movement with a beautiful chorale.

Our regular Massey Hall Tuesday and Wednesday night concerts always began at 8:00 PM. It was customary for orchestra members to arrive at least a half hour before the concert, in order to change into stage attire (black tailcoat and trousers, white tie and vest), warm up on their instruments, and get ready to go on. Some who weren't required to play the first half chose to arrive around 8:30 PM.

On October 23, 1965, wearing my working clothes (black tailcoat, white tie, etc.), I arrived in the Cedarbrae parking lot at ten minutes to nine — more than enough time before the twenty-minute intermission would be over. When I entered the school, however, I was surprised to hear the orchestra playing the third movement of the Brahms.

With a start I realized I'd forgotten that the Cedarbrae concert had actually begun at 7:30 PM. I was so used to the Massey Hall 8:00 PM concert time that I instinctively assumed it applied to the Cedarbrae concert as well, even though we were told weeks in advance of the earlier time. (My God, how could I do such a stupid thing?) I rushed to the right stage door. Locked! I flew to the left door. Also locked. Where the hell was the janitor, the keeper of the keys? The guy was nowhere to be found. With a pounding heart I heard the orchestra playing the last passage of the third movement. There was little time left, and the question was: how to get on stage?

I noticed the huge barn-sized door along the hall behind the stage, which was used when large scenery, pianos, and the like were brought in. There was usually a portable staircase rolled into position to allow such equipment to be moved down to the stage. When I slid the door open, I was shocked to see a nine-foot drop to the stage floor. There were no stairs in sight. (No time to waste: only bars to go before the end of the third movement.)

To avoid making any noise, I removed my shoes, then took out my trombone, leaving the case and my coat on the hall floor. Then I lowered myself with my left arm, the white-knuckled fingers of my left hand clinging to the floor-edge of the opening, supporting the full weight of my body, while my right hand held my shoes and trombone. My left arm stretched painfully to the limit, I dangled a brief moment and looked downward. At least three feet of air separated me from the stage floor. It might as well have been three thousand feet. Should I or shouldn't I?

With my heart in my mouth I let go and hurtled floorward. It took a split second for my full 190 pounds to land with a shattering jolt on the soles of my stockinged feet. The pain was excruciating. I felt I'd broken every bone in both legs. In a panic I slipped into my shoes and hobbled to the velvet curtain, which acted as a backdrop behind the orchestra. The third movement ended. In a stage whisper to the brass section, sitting directly in front of the curtain (a whisper which I'm sure everybody in the audience also heard, along with the earlier shattering jolt of my 190 pounds), I croaked, "Quick, where's my seat?"

Not a word from anyone in the trumpets or trombones, except for some snickering. (Oh God, he's going to start the fourth, gotta get into my chair!) In a lightning move born of desperation, I crawled under the curtain where I thought my chair should be. It was! And I sat down, just as Seiji brought his baton down to begin the last movement.

Personally, I thought the trombones were magnificent in the chorale. But I was aware of a muttering in the audience. For a symphony musician, my approach to reaching my seat in time to play my part was just not acceptable. The expression on Seiji's face told me I would be beheaded, Samurai-style, right after the concert. And of course, when the concert was over I was ribbed mercilessly by my fellow musicians. To say I suffered untold embarrassment would be the greatest understatement of my entire musical career.

TWO

I am happy to report that I was not the only symphony musician who suffered embarrassment of this order during my time with the TSO. On another occasion during the regime of Seiji Ozawa, in 1967, the featured work at a series of Massey Hall concerts was *Turangalila-symphonie*, a composition in ten movements by

Olivier Messiaen. We were told that the composer would be travelling from France to attend the opening concert.

During the many rehearsals for the piece, at the end of the fifth movement the conductor instructed the string players to keep their bows on their instruments, to "retain the mood of tranquility in the music." They were to remain perfectly still, until he signalled them to lower their instruments. He wanted the feeling of serenity to remain, he explained, so "don't nobody move." We rehearsed the quiet pause several times each day to make sure everybody knew exactly what to do.

On opening night the concert began with Monsieur Messiaen (the composer) sitting prominently in the audience. In front of a sold-out house, Seiji was at his best as he conducted the orchestra through the varied rhythmic complexities of the difficult work.

Just as the fourth movement began, as luck would have it, a string on principal cellist Peter Schenkman's instrument broke with a snap. Peter immediately turned around to the cellist behind him sitting on the second stand, whose name for the sake of this story shall be Zorgay, and handed him his cello. Peter told Zorgay to pass the cello back to Georgina, the last cellist in the section, and have her pass her instrument up to Peter so he could continue playing.

The relationship between the principal cellist and Zorgay was, to say the least, frigid. Zorgay was scared to death of Peter for a number of reasons and was eager to ingratiate himself. No matter how hard he tried to please the leader of his section, the principal persisted in ignoring him or waving him into oblivion. Zorgay took Peter's cello, and handed him his own, saying, "Use mine. I will put a new string on yours myself."

With no time to argue, Peter turned back to face the conductor who had waited for everyone to settle down. But just as Seiji brought the baton down to begin the fifth movement, Zorgay chose to climb over second-stand partner David Hetherington, who was trying to play and follow the conductor's beat. Despite the close quarters in the section, Zorgay accomplished the feat somewhat on the order of a bull in a china shop, with a maximum of clattering bows and cellos jarring music stands. Then he marched off the stage, through the stage door beside the trombones and tuba. For a moment the conductor's eyes went from oriental to occidental as Zorgay clomped down the metal stairs to the orchestra room, making noises that were clearly audible to everyone in the hall.

Then, instead of changing the string in the orchestra room, where no one could see him, Zorgay reappeared through the stage door to our left, and in full view of the audience, balanced himself on one leg (his right), while he supported Peter's cello on his left knee and proceeded to fit a new string through the peg box in the scroll at the end of the fingerboard and attach it to a peg. Visibly proud of himself, Zorgay waited for the fifth movement of Monsieur Messiaen's composition to end, so he could return to his seat.

The movement ended and, as rehearsed, the string players kept their bows on their strings, while the rest of the orchestra sat perfectly still, in playing position —

to "retain the mood of tranquility in the music." Zorgay found himself faced with a dilemma. Although the conductor had instructed the musicians not to move until his signal, Zorgay had to get back to his seat before the next downbeat. He decided he had no choice but to forge ahead.

Carrying Peter's cello over his head to much tittering from the audience, he clomped across the stage to the cello section, climbed over David Hetherington (more clattering of bows and music stands), and sat in his seat. Recognizing that "the mood of tranquility" had now been irretrievably shattered, the conductor signalled the musicians to lower their instruments, just as Zorgay tapped Peter on the shoulder and handed him his restrung cello.

When the concert was over, followed by a smattering of polite applause, Zorgay was the first to hurry off the stage. As the other musicians descended the stairs on their way to the orchestra room, he stood at the bottom to receive their jeers. ("Attaboy Shmorgay, nice going ... you should get a medal for that.") After the last musician mockingly patted him on the back for a job well done, the embarrassed cellist muttered, "Jesus Christ, you try to do a guy a favour and all you get is shit."

THREE

Have you ever found yourself in a roomful of people, all chattering away enthusiastically, when for some reason all noise stops for a split second, and then begins again as quickly as it stopped? The experience may be somewhat rare, but it does happen, doesn't it?

In the early 1960s the famed Igor Stravinsky was in Massey Hall in Toronto, to record a considerable number of his compositions with the CBC Symphony Orchestra. He had gallantly said that the musicians assembled were the fastest readers of all the orchestras he had ever dealt with. Even so, we spent long, sometimes tedious hours rehearsing or checking difficult passages. (It was not unusual for players in even the finest orchestras to raise questions about the many time-changes and complex harmonies in Stravinsky's music during rehearsals.)

Late in the afternoon of one very long Sunday rehearsal of this sort, cor anglais player Harry Freedman was at the podium, checking a passage in his music with the maestro's score. With his spectacles perched on his forehead, Stravinsky was peering back and forth from score to part, trying to determine a correct note. Elsewhere the stage was in an uproar, as everyone practised difficult or favourite passages, screeched high notes, or exchanged jokes with restless colleagues.

Then suddenly, for a split second, all noise in the auditorium stopped dead. The silence was shattering. And at that precise moment one of the group innocently raised one buttock and released the loudest fart ever heard in the Old Lady of Shuter Street. The explosion startled everyone: Stravinsky's head jerked up, causing his glasses to drop to his nose; we musicians looked suspiciously at one another. Then, as suddenly as it had stopped, the uproar on the stage began again.

Had the eruption occurred at any other time, it would have gone unnoticed. But it did happen at the precise moment of silence, as though on cue.

More than once since that very long Sunday rehearsal, I have pondered the explanation of this incident. Was it just a one-in-a-million random phenomenon? Or had it somehow been created by some incorrigible god (perhaps even the type of god one might expect would preside over Igor Stravinsky's marvellous music)? None of us on stage that historic afternoon will ever know.

FOUR

In June 1965 the Finnish architect Viljo Revell's new Toronto City Hall was officially opened in Nathan Phillips Square (on the north side of Queen Street, immediately west of Bay). To help celebrate, there was a week of musical entertainment on the site, during noon hours from Monday to Friday. After three days of jazz, rock, and country, the fourth day was dedicated to classical music. The Toronto Symphony under Seiji Ozawa, the National Ballet of Canada dancers conducted by George Crum, and the Canadian Opera Company singers conducted by Ernesto Barbini were the featured artists.

The stage was a three-foot-high platform erected in front of the new City Hall's doors, large enough to hold all 106 musicians, instruments, and music stands. On the south side of Queen Street (opposite the new City Hall), the construction site of what would become the new multi-storied Sheraton Centre hotel was a hive of activity. From our vantage point, we classical musicians could see huge cranes moving up and down everywhere, carpenters sawing and hammering, and buckets lifting tons of cement from the street level up to the roof, where dozens of tiny construction workers emptied the containers and spread the cement across the rooftop.

In any event, after the Orchestra played its opening overture at the City Hall celebration, four singers — two men and two women — took centre stage. When conductor Barbini brought his baton down, the orchestra went into the introduction of Verdi's *Quartet from Rigoletto*. And as soon as the singers launched into the four-part song, the cranes and cement buckets across the street stopped in mid-air.

Then the tiny figures on the Sheraton rooftop stopped working, doffed their caps, and joined the orchestra and quartet in singing Verdi's opus. Miraculous tiny voices singing the Italian lyrics drifted down and across Nathan Phillips Square to the City Hall stage.

When the quartet was finished, the cranes and the buckets and the carpenters started moving again. How marvellous that Toronto's vibrant Italian community was once again just in the right place at the right time.

FIVE

Touring with a symphony orchestra can lead to various adventures. And in my own classical music career nothing was quite like touring with Seiji Ozawa in the 1960s.

After one concert in Fort Meyers, during our tour of Florida in January 1967, Seiji and assistant conductor Nicholas Weiss came back to the hotel, changed from their tails into nothing but shorts (because it was so hot that night), and went in

Seiji's rented Cadillac looking for a bar. The shorts were all they had on: they weren't even wearing shoes. And neither could speak English very well at the time. (Seiji was still relatively new in North America, and Weiss spoke with a heavy Swiss-German accent.)

They drove down one street, zigzagging from one side of the road to the other, checking out the storefronts that looked like possible bars. Then they found themselves driving around a one-way circle but facing in the wrong direction. When he realized his mistake Seiji put the car in reverse and backed his way in the direction they had come from. Suddenly a state trooper wearing a Stetson hat, goggles, and holstered gun stopped them.

"Hey, boy," he said, "where you think you going?"

"I conductor of Toronto Symphony," said Seiji.

"Yah, iss correct," said Weiss.

The cop looked at the two scruffy individuals and said, "Yeah, and I'm Abraham Lincoln. Let's see your identification."

As neither had anything but the shorts they were wearing, the cop arrested them and took them to the local jail. All the pleading about being with the Toronto orchestra didn't move the sergeant at the station. To add to their woes, the state trooper kept saying to Weiss, "You better hope your buddy is telling the truth." All Seiji and Weiss could understand from the cop's southern accent was some horrifying reference to "*your body.*"

Finally, the police allowed Weiss to go back to the hotel to get their passports and other identification, but insisted on keeping Seiji in the lockup. When Weiss returned around 2:00 AM with the necessary documents, the troopers escorted both culprits back to the hotel, warning them to carry identification and to wear more clothes the next time they went for a drink.

During the earlier concert in Fort Meyers (again because of the excessive heat), all the doors of the high-school auditorium where we played were kept open — even the doors to the stage. Seiji had just started conducting Verdi's *I Vespri Siciliani* when a small bassett hound wandered through the doors onto the stage.

Right after the opening drum roll in the introduction, there was a slight wavering in the orchestra as the dog sniffed his way from music stand to music stand. What could Seiji do? The show had to go on.

He continued conducting as the hound proceeded to the podium and sniffed the conductor's legs, which caused the audience to break up with laughter. Finally the unconcerned dog made a slow exit stage left, but not before dropping a calling card against the last music stand of the cello section. The concert continued to a glorious finale.

At the end of the Florida tour the orchestra was informed it had to remain one more day, because an ice storm in Toronto prevented any planes from landing. The orchestra was staying at The Tides in St. Petersburg, a beautiful motel complex that stretched along the white sandy beach. Seiji immediately went to the manager of the motel bar, dumped a wad of bills on the counter and said, "We have party tonight after concert." The musicians of course were delighted.

After the concert everyone changed into civilian clothes, crowded into the lounge, and began lubricating their tonsils. Some of musicians brought their instruments and launched into a jam session, encouraging the rest of the orchestra members to get up and dance. Hours later, after all the food and liquor had been consumed, some performers, feeling no pain, stripped and jumped into the pool.

Concertmaster Hyman Goodman who was still in his tails, stood at the pool's edge watching the fun. Suddenly he found himself flying through the air and dropping into the water, fully clothed, with a splash. Someone had pushed him. To this day no one really knows who, but suspicious fingers point in one direction. Was it the conductor? We'll never know.

SIX

In 1967 the Toronto Symphony also celebrated Canada's Centennial by going on a tour of the great Canadian wilderness in Northern Ontario. On a day off in North Bay, some 250 miles north of Toronto, some of the musicians organized a fishing party for Seiji on Lake Nipissing. Seiji of course was the only one to catch a fish, a Great Northern Pike. On the way back into town the party drove past a Chinese restaurant.

"Stop the car!" ordered Seiji. Out he jumped with the fish and into the restaurant. Some moments later he emerged: "We have dinner here this evening. I spoke with chef who say he will cook fish." Later that night the party returned to the restaurant for a sumptuous banquet of Northern Pike in sweet-sour sauce, chicken wings in black bean and oyster sauce, dim sum, chicken soo gai, pork fried rice, and other oriental delicacies, accompanied by the appropriate lubrication — all as guests of maestro Seiji Ozawa.

SEVEN

The TSO's greatest adventure with Seiji Ozawa was its two-week tour of his native Japan, in September 1969. He was so eager to show-off his orchestra to the people of his country (and vice-versa) that he planned a vast assortment of activities for the musicians and accompanying entourage, taking us far beyond the musical engagements that were the ostensible chief objectives of our tour.

Prior to leaving Canada, and then on the long flight to Japan, he painted messages in Japanese on large three-inch buttons, for every one of the more than 100 musicians to wear on his or her sweater or jacket. The messages announced the

ON THE ROAD AGAIN, 1969. Walter Homburger, Seiji Ozawa, and Murray Ginsberg board plane. *Murray Ginsberg, private collection*

Toronto Symphony's tour of Japan, and asked every citizen to help the Canadians in any way they could. All the citizens of Japan we subsequently encountered responded gladly.

In Japan itself Seiji pulled enough strings to provide us with a guided tour of the grounds of the Imperial Palace (a place ordinarily closed to everyone, except for the most very special guests.) And on a side-trip to Kyoto, a site of much historical significance, he was able to arrange to have the theatre open for a performance of a traditional Japanese play — in the off-season and just for the entertainment (and education) of Toronto Symphony musicians.

In Tokyo Seiji organized a marvellous party for us in the city's renowned Ueno Park. While we sat at open tables amid beautiful gardens in bright Saturday-afternoon sunlight, geisha girls barbecued an immense array of culinary delights. When the feasting was done, the Emperor's Court Musicians, a small orchestra dressed in traditional costumes and playing traditional Japanese instruments, put on a concert for our particular pleasure. We learned that the group usually played only for the emperor, but Seiji Ozawa had somehow managed to arrange this unique event. I had never before felt that I was being treated as such a very important person (and I never would again).

EIGHT

For me, the climax of our 1969 tour of Japan was another special party given by Seiji and some of his closest friends, in the yard of a Bhuddist temple in Tokyo.

The party took place in the temple yard because the house of Madame Tsuruta across the road was too small to accommodate the more than 120 musicians and TS Association members. The hosts were Madame Tsuruta (who owned a steel factory and was the head of the Japan Biwa Society), Seiji himself, his very good friend Takao Miyazaki, and Yokayama (a Shakuhachi player who would perform at Massey Hall in Toronto a year later). The event was the culmination of long months of dedicated planning.

We were treated to a spectacular evening, replete with every imaginable form of food and entertainment. Cooks stood at their hibachis barbequing a dazzling assortment of viandes and seafood. Huge vats of warm saki were there for the quaffing. On a stage erected for the occasion geisha girls performed traditional dances to music played by a Japanese orchestra. A magician cut true-to-life silhouettes of TSO orchestra members out of black paper with only a pair of scissors.

For Seiji and his partners the long-anticipated celebration had come to fruition at last. Each of the hosts who had waited so long and now had the joy of seeing their Canadian friends finally in Japan savoured the emotional moment. As the party was winding down, I wandered away from the fun to a dark corner of the temple yard and suddenly became aware of anguished wailing and crying. In the darkness I peered at the fence in the corner. There stood Seiji and Takao, both clinging to one another, crying their eyes out. And somehow I realized that what I was seeing was not unhappiness, but tears of joy.

NINE

In a number of respects the 1978 TSO tour of the Peoples' Republic of China was my own swan song with the orchestra. And on Monday, January 30, with Andrew Davis on the podium, we performed a concert in Peking's packed-to-the-rafters Min Zu (National Minorities) Concert Hall. The program was dominated by Brahms, Liszt, and Beethoven, but it also included a Chinese poem, Nanniwan, set to music and sung by the great Toronto contralto Maureen Forrester.

Nanniwan tells the story of a beautiful village, filled with flowers and singing birds and happy people. Evil landlords come and desecrate the land and drive the birds away, and the flowers die. The people are oppressed and unhappy in the barren land. Then in the nick of time, Red soldiers arrive to drive the evil landlords away: the land is restored; the birds and flowers sing and bloom again; and the villagers are happy once more.

The poem is written in Mandarin Chinese, and Ms. Forrester had to learn the lines phonetically. Since she understood not a word of Mandarin, she had the word-sounds and syllables written out in English *sound*. After the orchestral introduction, her song began well enough, but in the course of shifting a page, she unwittingly (and understandably enough) mixed the order of verses and out came:

> Nanniwan was a beautiful village of flowers and singing birds,
> Then the brave Red soldiers came and desecrated the land,
> And drove the villagers away.

This brought spontaneous and uproarious laughter from the packed auditorium. Embarrassed audience "coaches" ran through the hall shouting: "Stop laughing, you fools!" But all too many long minutes passed before order was restored.

Ms. Forrester is of course recognized as one of the world's leading contraltos, and she works very hard. She has proved her great talent many times in international performances, and she continued to prove it many times more on our TSO tour of China. Magnificent singer that she is, however, the phonetics for Nanniwan had proved just impossible to understand. The language barrier was just too great to overcome. (Or, you can't win them all: and this is something I still sometimes think about today, when I hear someone talking a little too much about Marshall McLuhan's global village.)

TEN

For reasons that should become clear shortly, my last tale from the catacombs strays somewhat from the subject of the Toronto Symphony Orchestra, narrowly defined, and goes all the way back to the early 1950s, an era of assorted new beginnings on the Canadian scene, musical and otherwise. The particular occasion I have in mind was the CBC's first television broadcast, on September 25, 1952.

Most of Canada's finest performers appeared in this live broadcast, and it went on for over two hours. As might be expected on a first-ever show in a new medium, there was the odd goof (stagehands running across the studio floor in full view of the audience at home, scenery falling over, and so on). Such things were not uncommon on live television everywhere in those days, and there was nothing on the inaugural broadcast of CBC TV to make the home audience switch to another channel in utter disgust. But my own involvement in the festivities did have a lighter side that I will never quite forget.

Several Toronto studios were used to accommodate the large number of acts involved. The especially renowned Canadian musicians, ballerinas, actors, and singers who performed included such figures as soprano Lois Marshall and pianist Glenn Gould. My own modest role was in the only item that featured trumpets and trombones; a brass sextet heralding the "two solitudes" of "the English" and "the French" in Canada.

Trumpeters Ellis McLintock, Morris Isenbaum, and Don Johnson, along with trombonists Teddy Roderman, Harry Stevenson, and myself, had agonized through many hours of rehearsal before Geoffrey Waddington, head of the English CBC's music department, was satisfied with the work of this brass sextet. The piece that we played — a fanfare by Canada's dean of composers, John Weinzweig — was difficult, but in the end we were ready to go on.

Our turn to perform came about halfway through the telecast, right after pianist Glenn Gould had performed. Already in position, we waited for Glenn to finish before the camera trained its lens on us. The particular studio we were in had been painted to resemble a marble palace. The palace floor was covered with large black and white tiles. Marble columns — really tall sixteen-inch-diameter self-standing cardboard cylinders, of the sort used by carpet stores to roll their merchandise around, but painted to look like authentic marble — stood at intervals throughout the "palace stateroom."

When he finished playing, Glenn stood beside the piano and bowed. The scene faded and the announcer introduced the next act: "Happy to present ... a work by John Weinzweig performed by the CBC Brass Sextet, Geoffrey Waddington conducting." Lights. Camera. We were on. About fifteen feet from where we were playing, Waddington stood beside the camera and conducted from the score on a music stand. We trumpeters and trombonists, garbed in long black gowns that reached to our ankles, stood on a fourteen-inch riser. Directly in front of us on the studio floor, two actors — one a blonde lad with a Union Jack emblazoned on his tunic; the other, a black-haired boy sporting a fleur-de-lis — stood with their arms entwined, drinking from the "common cup of Canadian comradeship."

As we played we could see Glenn Gould, about thirty feet behind the camera, watching the scene with fascination. He became so engrossed that, without realizing what he was doing, he leaned against one of the "marble" columns, which immediately began to topple over. In a state of shock Glenn began to wrestle with the clumsy cylinder to keep it from crashing to the floor. Don Johnson and I (and perhaps a few more) began to snicker (which is actually very difficult to do while playing a brass instrument). Geoffrey Waddington's face took on a purple hue.

Well ... in the end he managed to get the column standing again, and we finished John Weinzweig's fanfare to Canadian comradeship. When the performance ended Waddington snarled at us, "Extremely unprofessional to say the least." I was convinced that my last day at the CBC had come. Fortunately, I was quite wrong.

Glenn Gould

There seems to be some agreement, in some parts of Toronto at least, that the ever-curious Glenn Gould was in fact the greatest musician in the European classical tradition that Canada has yet produced. And, while I can't pretend to have been a colleague of Glenn's myself, it only seems fitting to conclude this section with some brief account of his career and undoubted enormous talent.

When he died of a stroke in 1982, at fifty years of age, he was already a legend. The Toronto-born pianist was considered by thousands around the globe as one of the world's top-ranking musicians. At the height of his career, the American music critic B.H. Haggin (the Toscanini idolater whose articles often appeared in *The Nation*) wrote of Gould's standing among twentieth-century pianists:

> This young Canadian stands out above all other pianists young and old. The playing style, with its powerful note-to-note continuity of shape and tension, is like no other. So is what it produces — the object in sound completely formed and completely achieved to the exact sonority of the last note ... one's mind is seized by the very first sounds, with their electrifying authority and force, and is held fascinated by the continuous coming into existence of the remainder of the musical object.

The earliest beginnings of Glenn Gould's musical career are now quite well known. At age eleven he entered the Royal Conservatory of Music in Toronto, where he studied piano with Alberto Guerrero, from 1943 to 1952.

He first appeared with an orchestra on May 8, 1946, when (at thirteen) he played the first movement of Beethoven's *Concerto No. 4* with the Conservatory Orchestra under Ettore Mazzoleni. Reviewing the performance, Edward W. Wodson of the *Evening Telegram* observed how the very youthful pianist "showed the music lover that scale passages and arpeggios on the humble piano may have spiritual as well as technical beauty and character. His phrasing was as eloquent as poetry chanted by the poet himself."

On January 14, 1947, Gould performed the entire Beethoven *Concerto No. 4* with the Toronto Symphony Orchestra conducted by Bernard Heinze, in a concert for high school pupils in the city. Shortly after his fifteenth birthday (on September 25) Glenn played his recital debut in Eaton Auditorium, on October 20, 1947.

Because Glenn died some considerable time before I even thought about writing this book, there was no point in even thinking about interviewing him. Since I never knew him very well myself, I interviewed two Toronto musicians who did — Nicholas Kilburn, former principal bassoonist with the Toronto Symphony, and Nick's younger brother Paul, who plays the piano. Nick told me:

> *I first met Glenn when we were twelve years old. He was only a few months younger than me. We both played piano but when I heard him perform in a cello-violin-piano trio, I decided the piano was not for me, so I meandered over to the bassoon. We didn't have much contact after that for a few years, but when we were sixteen or seventeen Glenn's parents invited me up to their cottage on Lake Simcoe, in the summer of 1948.*
>
> *We did a lot of silly things, the sort teenagers do, a lot of rowing and fooling around. One day we were out in the boat and Glenn was swooping and swamping all over the*

lake while his father had an 8 mm camera shooting the world's greatest pianist for posterity, with North America's greatest bassoonist.

Glenn's parents wanted their son to take part in some sort of physical exercise. They thought Nick, who was into tennis and skiing, would be a good influence.

During my visit to the family cottage Glenn suggested we play a game of horseshoes. I'd played this game before but I never considered it a particularly vigorous form of exercise. Well, Glenn came out and he devastated me. There wasn't a point he couldn't beat me on. At the end of the game he said, "Now I'm going to throw a leaner." And he threw a leaner. Then he said, "Now I'm going to throw a ringer inside that leaner." And he threw a ringer. It was the most incredible thing. It was as though he had that tactile sense that he knew exactly what to do to accomplish those feats.

Nick's younger brother Paul, a pianist, remembers that while he was studying at the Royal Conservatory between 1955 and 1958, he and Glenn drank a lot of coffee together in the Conservatory cafeteria:

One day I'd mentioned that they'd got a new grand piano up in the Concert Hall. Glenn said, "Let's go try it." So we went upstairs to the Concert Hall and there was this spanking brand new Steinway on the stage. We went to try the piano but the lid was locked. Glenn saw an old Steinway was open nearby, so he casually sat down at that one and began to play. In one second his entire focus was on bringing this phrase, this passage out. It was the most mesmerizing thing I'd ever seen. He was amazing. I was riveted to the spot, right by the piano. Then he came to the end of the phrase and he looked at me and said, "My back is killing me." Glenn had been sitting on a normal piano bench but he was used to sitting quite low. He had to crouch low in relation with the piano keys in order to perform to his satisfaction.

Gould's playing posture was of crucial importance to him. Several years later, after he had rocked the music world with his astonishing talent, he was appearing with the Cleveland Orchestra. During a rehearsal, he took long minutes turning the seat of the piano stool clockwise and counter clockwise, trying to adjust to the right height. After a few minutes of this exercise an impatient conductor George Szell said, "Mr. Gould, if I shaved an inch off your ass would that satisfy you?"

Paul Kilburn also remembers:

In the summer of 1954 at a party that Nick had, attended mostly by orchestra players, Glenn showed up in his father's truck with "Thomas G. Gould Furs" displayed on its side. There was this fur truck parked on Strathallan, where we lived. As always happens when musicians get together, the talk soon degenerated into shop talk about their horns and what horn player said so-and-so to the conductor and so on. A lovely girl named Maureen, who had come with a musician, had met everyone, and everyone in the room commented on how charming and beautiful she was, but she knew nothing about music or even who Glenn Gould was.

Maureen listened respectfully to the comments and eventually asked Glenn, who had been casually lying on the sofa, "And what instrument do you play?"

Without batting an eye Glenn said, "I've been studying bassoon with Nick Kilburn." No one said a word or let on who he was. A little while later Nick asked Glenn, "Why don't you go home and bring back some of your records?" Glenn immediately leaped up, got into the truck with Mike Kilburn, another brother, and drove to the Beaches where his family lived. Within an hour they were back stacked with records.

While they were away, Maureen asked my mother, "Why does Nick want them to get records when you have all the records anyone needs right here?" But mother didn't let the cat out of the bag. Then Glenn and Mike came in loaded with records and scores — The Goldberg Variations, the CBC recording of Survivor from Warsaw, Schoenberg's Piano Concerto, and things like that. We started putting the records on and Glenn was talking about the Goldberg. He had his tattered score of the piece, which was all in sheets, and Glenn said, "You know, I took an aspirin before I did this recording, and halfway through the piece I started to perspire: my hands got sweaty and the keys got slippery. I messed up a whole run completely." He split one note in the run. That to him was complete ruination.

By the time he was twenty, in 1952, Gould had toured Canada, east and west, as a soloist with symphony orchestras, and played a number of recitals of music by Bach, Beethoven, Brahms, Webern, Berg, and Schoenberg. (And, as I've already noted, he had appeared on the CBC's first television broadcast from Toronto.)

He made his American debut on January 3, 1955, when he played at the Phillips Gallery in Washington. The next morning *Washington Post* reviewer Paul Hume wrote: "I suppose it's a little early in the year but I think I just heard the recital of the year." As Nick Kilburn pointed out:

Paul Hume was so taken with Glenn's performance that he insisted the Columbia Records people attend his recital in New York.

Only eight days later Glenn played at Town Hall in New York. And the next day he signed a contract with Columbia Records. The enthusiastic critical response to the Town Hall recital catapulted Gould to nine years of generally very well-received concert and recital tours. In 1957 he made his European debut with the Moscow Philharmonic, gave recitals of music by Bach, Beethoven, and Berg in Moscow, Leningrad, and Vienna, and played with the Berlin Philharmonic under von Karajan. (Glenn was one of the first Canadian cultural figures to visit the old U.S.S.R. after the start of the Cold War.)

In 1958 he appeared with the Concertgebouw Orchestra under Dimitri

Mitropoulos at the Salzburg Festival, and with the Hart House Orchestra under Boyd Neel at the Brussels World's Fair. And he also gave eleven performances in eighteen days that year in Israel.

After his first public performance of the Brahm's *Concerto No. 1 in D Minor*, with the Winnipeg Symphony Orchestra under Victor Feldbrill in 1959, Peggie Sampson wrote to Kenneth Winters: "Gould played the Brahms' D Minor ... It was marvellous. No, more than that: it was so clear!"

Glenn repeated the work in 1961 at the Vancouver International Festival under Zubin Mehta, anyone, but his ideas on how the music should be played were changing. When he played it on April 14, 1962, with the New York Philharmonic, conductor Leonard Bernstein, in an announcement prior to the performance, dis-associated himself from Gould's radical ideas (exemplified by a slow tempo in the first movement). Bernstein declared that he would go ahead with conducting the New York Philharmonic for Gould's interpretation only because he felt Glenn's ideas on the subject ought to be demonstrated. The performance embodied, perhaps, Glenn's penchant for upsetting or flouting conventionally held attitudes on music which interested him.

In 1964 Glenn Gould made his historic announcement that he would retire from the concert stage, and concentrate on electronic communication through recordings alone. Here again, Paul Kilburn had some interesting observations on this aspect of Gould's career:

> *Glenn was the recording industry's equivalent of "box office." And that wasn't lost on Leonard Rose, the famous cellist. He did the Beethoven* A Major Sonata *with Glenn at the Stratford Festival, and was terribly uncomfortable playing it with him. And yet years later, Rose approached Glenn with the idea of the two of them recording all of the Beethoven Sonatas. I think it was because he and Glenn had recorded all of the Bach Viola di Gamba Sonatas together. That recording probably outsold any other that Rose ever made. And he was a great cellist. He had recorded all the major cello repertoire: he did the Brahms'* Double Concerto *with Isaac Stern. The rest of his recordings weren't exactly chopped liver.*

In the end, opinions about Gould's interpretations vary considerably, but there is a measure of agreement about his personality, enigmatic though it may have been. Knowledgeable observers seem to agree on his craving for control, his mixture of serious conviction and playful speculation on the one hand, and of logical insight and rationalization on the other, along with his need for physical privacy and his ultimate passion for electronic communication.

Unlike the performance of a soloist in a concert hall, where the audience savours the music as it is played, Gould felt that a soloist in a recording studio must make conscious use of all the technical devices — position of the microphones, editing of tape during the playback stage to check loudness, balance, tempo, and the dozen other requirements necessary to achieve the perfect recording.

Part Six
Silver Threads Among the Gold

MURRAY LAUDER, 1990. Murray Ginsberg's long-time friend.
Courtesy Murray Lauder

One day in September 1978, I descended the elevator from the fifth floor offices of the Toronto Symphony at 215 Victoria Street, my mind reeling with the stark realization that my playing days were over. I had just come from a fateful meeting with TSO managing director Walter Homburger and musical director Andrew Davis, both of whom, after hearing my plea, agreed that I should leave the Toronto Symphony as soon as possible. The fact of the matter was I couldn't play my trombone any more.

After a career that spanned forty-three years, eighteen of which had been spent as a member of the TSO brass section, my embouchure had weakened to the point that the tiniest amount of air that passed between my lips into the mouthpiece forced the lips apart, preventing them from producing a sound. That afternoon, my mind a kaleidoscope of images, I wandered aimlessly north on Victoria Street, along Davenport Road, and up Yonge Street, thinking all the time that the beloved instrument I had performed on for more than four decades was of no further use to me. I can't remember how many hours went by but I ultimately found myself in my apartment in north Toronto. I had walked some seven miles, unmindful of the fact that I had left my car in the parking lot near Massey Hall.

Walter Homburger and Andrew Davis, both kind and considerate gentlemen, allowed me to remain on the orchestra's roster until such time as I found employment somewhere else. They were kind enough to see that my salary continued, a gesture for which I will always be grateful.

In any event, it had become painfully clear that I needed some kind of new career. (I was still only fifty-six years old at the time — a little early, especially in those days, for any serious, secure retirement.) And I spent the next several months trying to find one.

The Union Keeps Us Strong

As it happened, the Canadian music business in Toronto wasn't quite through with me yet, even though I'd lost the physical capacity to play the musical instrument of my choice. On April 1, 1979, after a series of interviews with a committee headed by then president J. Alan Wood, I was hired as a business representative of the Toronto Musicians' Association, a job that included checking on orchestras' performing engagements around the city.

A year later, after J. Alan Wood had become the vice-president from Canada of the AFM International Executive Board, the new Local 149 president, Sam Levine, created the TMA Recording Department and asked me to overlook its operation. Far from leaving the music business, I had just walked through a door into another room and was now attending to the affairs of my fellow musicians. That job was to last fifteen years.

Then on January 1, 1995, I was elected secretary of the Toronto Musicians' Association, and began to wear two hats — recording department supervisor and secretary. Either job was more than enough for one man.

Instead of retiring at the sensible age of sixty-five, I had chosen to continue on and become embroiled in the politics of the union, thus compounding the work load. As the months passed, it became evident that I simply couldn't handle the impossible task of wearing both hats. I was tired.

What do you do when you can't play your instrument any more? Following the precedent of my meeting with Walter Homburger and Andrew Davis years earlier, you leave the orchestra. In mid-May of 1995, I handed my letter of resignation to President Bobby Herriot. I announced I would vacate my position on the TMA Executive Board and that of recording department supervisor effective July 31.

My New Old Romance

At the beginning of August 1995, I passed through another door on to another planet: I moved to London, England, to live with the lady I'd met during the Second World War, when I was a twenty-one-year-old soldier in the Royal Canadian Army Show, and she was an eighteen-year-old beauty across the sea. Our subsequent meeting again fifty years later, in December 1994, changed our lives forever. We are living together, happily, for the rest of our lives.

Does Fate play a part in what happens to us, or do we just exist from day to day and take each day as it comes? Back when we parted company during the war, I never expected to see Myra Rosengarten again. But twenty-two years later, in September 1965, when the Toronto Symphony performed in England for the British Commonwealth Arts Festival, we met for a brief hour in the bar of the Cumberland Hotel in Marble Arch in London. I was then forty-four, married with two children, had lost all my hair, and put on a few pounds "from living the good life of a musician."

She was forty, a ravishing beauty, also married with two children (and now known as Myra Davis), and she showed up at the Cumberland without her husband, which I found strange. Our meeting was very formal. Not a word about the times twenty-two years earlier when we held one another tightly and kissed in the London moonlight.

She spoke confidently with a soft London accent. She still exuded that fresh girlish fragrance I remembered so well. For a brief hour we exchanged photographs of our kids, had one drink each, and made small talk. Then with a kiss on the cheek and a handshake, we each went our separate ways. I floated on a cloud back to our hotel and told my friends in the orchestra about our meeting. "It was a Noel Coward *Brief Encounter*," some said. I thought about Myra a lot over the next several days, but when the TSO's two-week tour of England and France came to an end, I returned to Canada and my wife and children.

Back across the ocean, I didn't think much about the incident for a long time. Then, one night in late October 1994, I received a telephone call from a young man who had just arrived from London to work in Toronto. He said his first duty was to bring regards from Myra Davis, his grandmother's best friend.

"Myra Davis! I haven't thought about Myra in years," I said. "How is she?"

"Her husband died a few years ago," the boy replied. "She wasn't sure you would still be here."

"Oh, I'm very much alive," I said. "Do you have her address? I'll try to write her." About two weeks slipped by before I had the time to sit down and write a long letter to the lady who meant so much to me when we were still kids, fifty years before:

November 6, 1994

Dear Myra:

Imagine my surprise when a young man with an English accent phoned a few days ago to bring regards from Myra Davis. He said his name was Darren Tessler and he was in Toronto to work for some Canadian insurance company.

You may be surprised to see the enclosed photo. Think of it! You gave it to me fifty years ago when I was twenty-one and you were eighteen. I've kept it in a drawer along with many other photographs of my life, you might say. I hardly ever look at them, but I've kept them there because I don't like throwing things away. Of course, they bring back memories of years past. There are snapshots of my years in the army — in Canada, England and in Europe — and other photos of my life as a musician. I was surprised, in fact I was more than surprised to realize that the photo of you on a bicycle taken in Bournemouth (I think you told me) when you were seventeen had remained in my drawer for fifty years!

When Darren phoned, the first thing I did was search for the photo. How that picture brought back memories of those lovely days during the war after I met you at that Swing Club on Oxford Street. I remember your family and some of your relatives, particularly the very good-looking Aunt Betty who scared the hell out of me when she began using expressions like "marching down the aisle to the altar." She was a blonde, I think. I remember your father, a generous man, who always treated me kindly, and your mother, a nice-looking lady who didn't care for me very much, I'm afraid. I remember your sister and little brother who became a doctor? To reminisce about those days would fill volumes.

And 1965 was a precious moment for me, too, when I was with the Toronto Symphony in London and met you for a brief hour in the bar of the Cumberland Hotel in Marble Arch. What a trip that was, twenty-two years after the war, London was beautiful — no blackouts, no bombs, no sandbags. The world was at peace again ... and then I saw you, fortyish and very chic, and I was forty-four, and much too overweight.

Of course, you produced snapshots of your husband and children, and I brought out photos of my daughters. That was a sweet moment, almost like a Noel Coward playlet, a sort of Brief Encounter. (That was during the British Commonwealth Arts Festival.)

After London, we played concerts in Paris and Lyon, and then it was back to Canada, to my wife and daughters. And of course, back to my life as a musician in the symphony, and doing all sorts of other work, including radio and television shows, recording sessions, and whatever else musicians do to earn a living.

I was divorced in 1970, and after a brief separation from my daughters (they lived with their mother for about eight months) they came to live with me. Susan was fifteen at the time, and Barby ten. Today, Susan is forty-three and married to Stephen, and they have two beautiful little girls — Leigh Erin, who is five, and Melanie Nicole, who will be three in May. Barby is thirty-seven, not married, and just broke up with a nice guy, an accountant who is divorced. What else is new?

My life as a playing musician came to an end on March 31, 1979. For a couple of years my embouchure — that's what brass players call the muscles around the lips that allow the player to control the sounds coming out of the instrument — was failing. I ultimately lost all control and couldn't play any more. After forty-three years as a musician, it all came to an end.

But the day after my release from the orchestra, on April 1, I was hired by the musicians' union as a business representative to check on our member musicians to see that they receive proper payment for their performing services wherever they play an engagement, sort of a musical policeman. Since I had played on almost every type of musical engagement during my career, the union president thought I knew enough about the business to do a creditable job.

And that's what I have been doing since that time. My department covers anything that involves recording of any kind — phonograph recording sessions, commercials, television films, motion picture soundtracks, etc.

Also, since I couldn't play any more, I turned to writing. That began in 1978 when I realized my playing days were coming to an end. I took courses at the university on creative writing, journalism, and so on. It's almost the same as music. Instead of dealing with harmonies and chord progressions, I now enjoy the shape and shade of words and their various meanings.

I've been writing a book for the last couple of years (which I should be doing right now, but I'd rather be writing this letter). The book is an account of the musicians who played in Canada — Toronto, mostly, because it's the largest city in the country — from the 1920s to the present. I've interviewed some seventy musicians over sixty-five years of age, who are still walking on this planet. Their stories are all remarkable.

I turned seventy-two on October 4 and I certainly don't look anything like I did when I was twenty-one. It's time I retired but can't bring myself to doing so. I'm going to have to make a decision soon. And I do want to finish the book.

I was sorry to hear about the death of your husband. That's a part of life we must all bear, and carrying on during one's bereavement can be very difficult. Please accept my sympathy.

The chances of our meeting seem remote at this time, but it would be nice to see you again. Imagine, a voice from the past, after fifty years, bringing back all sorts of pleasant memories. I've often thought of flying to England for a fast weekend to interview Bob Farnon for the book, but so far have not made any plans. He's from Toronto, but remained in England after the war. He's a famous composer of movie music and has written more than a hundred scores for major Hollywood and British films. As well, he has recorded every major American and British (and European) artist from jazz to classical. Bob's life in the 1940s would be right for the book. Maybe that's the excuse I need to see you again.

Myra, it would be nice if you would write. It's 1:30 AM and time to call it a night.
Sincerely yours,

Murray

A few weeks later, I received a reply:

November 13, 1994

Dear Murray:

It was wonderful to receive your very informative letter, with all your interesting background. Darren is my best friend's grandson. We have been friends since 1940 and she remembers coming to see you in Godalming with me. Yes, we met at the Swing Club, 100 Oxford Street (it is still going). I hope Darren finds a job. Please help him if you can.

I am enclosing two photos taken this year. I was sixty-eight in September. My dear husband died in May 1992 after forty-three years of a very happy and loving marriage. I am sad and miss him so much. I have a daughter, Caroline, forty-three, and a son Richard, thirty-nine. I have three grandsons: Robert, twenty-two, Andrew, nineteen, and Dean; twelve, and a granddaughter, Cassie, eight. I also have wonderful friends of forty to fifty years and we keep together (widows).

Regarding music. I do know of Bob Farnon. He is a wonderful composer. I am an Andrew Lloyd Webber fan. I love his songs and play the tapes from his shows, which are all winners. Murray, what can I tell you in a letter after twenty-nine years when I last met you in London. Please send me a photo. You can telephone me, but it would be very nice to see you. Come to London.

I am very fortunate. I have a lovely family. My sister Pat and two brothers, Terry, a doctor, and Bruce who was born in 1947. But at the end of the day, I am on my own. Looking forward to hearing from you.
Sincerely yours,

Myra

I telephoned Bob Farnon in the Channel Islands and asked about an interview for my book. He said come any time in December. Glad to help. I made plans with a travel agent to leave Toronto on December 12th and arrive at Heathrow the following day. Then I phoned Myra to tell her I'd see her after I'd seen Farnon.

Then began a series of phone calls back and forth across the ocean. At first, they were sporadic calls every second or third day; then one a day, then two a day, and finally ten a day and to hell with the telephone bill. With each call I became more enamoured with Myra (although we'd exchanged photos, hers made me wonder if I was doing the right thing; mine were ten years old and we really didn't know what the other looked like). But her voice had that freshness I remembered so well. With each succeeding day Myra and I grew closer. I called Farnon to cancel our appointment. He said he really never expected to see me after I had told him about Myra. (We met later in Miami, in 1995, where he was doing a recording session.)

When December 12 finally arrived, I arose bright and early. I had a speech memorized that would sweep her off her feet when we finally met. The plane flight was the usual long, dreary, half-asleep, half-awake sort of flight. I went through immigration at 7:00 PM, and took a cab to the Grim's Dyke Hotel in Harrow, near

MYRA, 1944.
Murray Ginsberg, private collection

where Myra lived. An hour later I called her from the hotel. "Meet me in the parking lot at nine," she said.

At 9:00 PM, a blue Honda pulled into the Grim's Dyke parking lot. I saw a lady in a mink coat, wearing a new hairdo and dark glasses. I approached her car. We stared at one another. ("Oh my God. Are you the man I talked to on the telephone?" her eyes seemed to say.) My tongue was stuck to the roof my mouth. I had never been so petrified.

Finally I was able to squeak out an embarrassing falsetto: "It's me."

"Get in the car," she said. She drove through the narrow winding streets like an Italian race car driver. I tried to think of something funny to say, something about driving on the wrong side of the road, but nothing seemed funny. Myra said nothing. Finally she pulled up at the curb outside her flat. We got out of the car and into the flat, where she poured a large Scotch into a glass. I downed it immediately; then another. Then, at last, peace returned to the universe.

Myra Davis and I are now living in Middlesex, with occasional trips back to Canada to visit my family and friends. Life couldn't be better. So does Fate determine our lives? Myra and I met at the beginning of our productive years, but marriage wasn't in the cards. We parted after about a year together. Twenty-two years later in mid-life we were brought together for a brief hour. Was it a portent of something beautiful yet to be completed? Twenty-nine years later we met again — and this time lived happily ever after, for the rest of our lives.

MURRAY, 1944.
Murray Ginsberg, private collection

Silver Threads Among the Gold

Memories, Memories

Over in England today (a place that, in one way or another, had so much to do with the Toronto in which I grew up) I have a lot of memories about my Canadian musical career in Toronto. And when I'm back in town, I can see again, even though rock and roll and everything that followed has fundamentally changed the face of the landscape, that there are still musicians in Toronto playing the kind of music on which I cut my own musical teeth (or at least a kind of music that follows more logically from what I grew up with than rock and roll does). And there are a number of marvellous musical personalities I feel compelled to talk a little bit more about, now that I'm almost at the very end of my book.

Eddie Graf

Though I never got married overseas during the Second World War, thinking about my life today reminds me of someone who did. On January 1, 1945, at nine o'clock in the morning, our Unit A saxophonist Eddie Graf married Bernice O'Donnell in a church in Whitley, Surrey, England. The fact that the marriage took place on New Year's Day was significant. The couple wanted to start their life together at the earliest hour on the first day of a new year when the promise of a long life filled with joy and happiness was strongest: a noble thought indeed.

As I was honoured to be the best man, it was my duty to get all the groom's invited guests out of bed, dressed, shaved, hair-combed, and on the troop carrier that would take them to the church on time. Then, after the marriage vows were exchanged, I had to get the same gentlemen to the hotel where the wedding breakfast would take place.

Since the evening before had been New Year's Eve, everybody in the Royal Canadian Army Show had celebrated into the wee hours of the morning — jamming, dancing, drinking the night away, and finally dropping into their bunks around 4:30 AM. Trying to wake them generated a few punches in the groin (mine) and much yelling and shouting to "get lost!" It was touch and go before the dozen or so soldiers of the King's Canadian Forces were seated in the truck. They may not all have been shaved and otherwise groomed, and they may have resembled a motley crew of sleepy lowlifes, ready to kill, but they *were* on the vehicle, and away we went to Whitley, some twenty miles away.

In the end, the wedding went off without a hitch. Eddie and Bunny became man and wife. Every unshaven mother's son sitting in the pews congratulated the couple and kissed the bride. Then off we went to the Lion's Head Hotel for the wedding breakfast. As I write today Eddie and Bunny Graf are still very much alive. Eddie still plays his saxophone and writes his arrangements, and mother Bunny attends to the family of five sons and two daughters. Of course they are all adults now, and most (though not all) are musicians or musically trained.

I first met Eddie in 1944 when he was transferred from Captain Bob Farnon's Canadian contingent of the Armed Forces Network stationed in London. Bob's brother Brian, who'd played lead alto in the Unit A orchestra, was sent back to Canada and Eddie was brought in to fill the gap. Eddie fit in like the proverbial glove with all the guys — Murray Lauder, Freddie Powell, Bob Kinsman, Denny Farnon, Denny Vaughan, and on and on. It didn't take him long to learn the parts of our show, particularly the Tramp Band act which had everybody cavorting on stage: playing, jumping, dancing, singing.

We played "C Jam Blues" and "King Porter Stomp" — a lot of jazz that the soldiers enjoyed. The girls sang or danced, contortionist Penny Brander tied herself up in knots daily (except when we played a matinée, then twice daily), and Don Hudson performed his magic act with finesse. It was a good show that helped keep morale high. Bunny O'Donnell was in a related Army Show unit called "Fun Fatigues." At the base in Guildford all the units would sometimes come together, returning from the many runouts to all parts of southern England. And that's how Eddie and Bunny met, fell in love, and eventually became man and wife.

Back in Canada after the war, Eddie and Bunny settled down in a house in Toronto where they began to raise their family. And Eddie, a magnificent alto sax player, jobbed around with various bands, including his own. But, most importantly, he started arranging for a wide assortment of other bandleaders.

One was Horace Lapp, who called Eddie to ask if he would do seven or eight arrangements for his big band. He complied and sent the finished charts to the bushy-haired leader. Eddie recalled when I talked with him recently:

One day Graham Topping came round to the house with a cheque for me from Horace. Graham said it was for the arrangements. I looked at the cheque. It was made out in my name and signed by Horace, but no figure had been attached to it. Graham told me Horace said to fill it in yourself, whatever figure you think appropriate. Imagine a guy doing that.

I actually got started in Kitchener, as a kid. My two brothers played: one played the fiddle, the other played piano and fiddle, and I played a clarinet. So I wrote arrangements for that little group and we'd try them over. When I was sixteen or seventeen in Kitchener, I got a book out of the library on traditional harmony and I did the exercises and hoped I was doing them correctly. The book was by Kitson. I had no teacher. Years later in London I took an arrangement to Bob Farnon and asked him to check it out. You know Farnon's dry sense of humour. He played the chart and it sounded nice. He said, "Not bad for the first book of Kitson. How did he know?

Eventually the little group that started with Eddie and his brothers grew to a fairly big band: four saxes, three brass, and a rhythm section. Eddie kept writing and moved to London, Ontario, where he lived for two years. In London he did a lot of writing for local bands as well as other bands around Kitchener. He joined the army in 1942 and played in the Royal Canadian Regiment band in London for a couple of years until he was transferred to the Army Show in Toronto. Then he went overseas to London, England, with the Canadian contingent of the Allied

Expeditionary Forces under Captain Robert Farnon. Then he was transferred to our Unit A band in Guildford. Then, like me, he remained with Unit A (which later became Swing Patrol) until we returned to Canada.

When I came back, I studied with quite a few different people, like Tony Bradon. We got together a few times, and then I studied with Oscar Morawetz at the Faculty of Music. Then I went to Phil Nimmons and I also did a whole course on harmony and orchestration with John Weinzweig. Later I studied with Gordon Delamont, we did harmony and counterpoint.

Eddie made a connection with Ivan Romanoff, a fine violinist who had been a member of the Navy Show orchestra in Meet the Navy. Ivan had heard Eddie's arrangements on a CBC radio program called "Continental Café," and liked them so much that he asked Eddie to write for his new show, "Songs of My People." The flavour of the show was mid-European music — Hungarian, Ukrainian, gypsy airs, waltzes — music to attract postwar Canada's increasingly large ethnic audiences. Ultimately, the show went to television and the named changed to "Rhapsody."

Ivan was a good connection. I wrote for him for more than ten years. Among other shows, I did "Juliette" for eight years. The first year after I got out of the army, in 1946, Sinatra came to town. He was going to play the Mutual Street Arena. He had some Sy Oliver arrangements but they were written for a smaller band. He called me and asked, "Would you add parts to these arrangements?" So I got the scores and filled them out and made them into big-band arrangements. That's when I wrote for Frank Sinatra.

In fact Eddie Graf's arrangements may have been played by more bands in Canada than those of any other arranger.

In the 1950s I had a notion that dance bands across the country would like some special arrangements, instead of playing stocks. I thought I would write a series of arrangements, photostat them, then sell them for a nominal fee. I sent out a form letter with a list of tunes, and before I knew what was happening the requests began to roll in. I had so many bands in Montreal that it seemed as though everybody in the city wanted my arrangements. I met a trumpet player one day who said, "Eddie Graf! I played your arrangements." I asked, "Whose band?" And the guy said, "All of them."

Today in the 1990s, of course, tastes in music have changed dramatically. It's a rock and roll world out there. Yet there are still some bands from Halifax to Vancouver that insist on playing Eddie Graf charts. Eddie himself has embarked on a new career. His latest inspiration is writing for concert bands:

Next to a symphony orchestra, the concert band is the most rewarding. In the last year I've written eight or nine compositions, and get a tremendous bang out of it.

EDDIE GRAF, circa 1990.
Courtesy Eddie Graf

Nowadays, Eddie Graf sits in with the Encore Band, an ensemble of senior musicians who rehearse every Thursday morning in the auditorium of the Toronto Musicians' Association. John Riddell is the conductor who gets the most out of the group. The intonation must be right, and the dynamics are very important. It's great therapy for the players who eagerly look forward to their Thursday mornings. And Eddie also rehearses with Bobby Herriot's Royal Canadian Artillery Band, which holds its practices at the Armouries in Toronto.

I think it's the best concert band in the city. There's a core of militia guys who just want to play. The band has a terrific bassoonist and a great solo clarinet. And there is a girl who plays beautiful French horn. A very good band.

Eddie says it's been a new lease on life for him, an energizing "labour of love."

Moe Koffman

When Moe performs on his alto saxophone, or on any of his seven flutes, there is no mistaking his artistry as a fine jazzman or a top-calibre studio musician. Everywhere he plays, whether in Europe, Australia, Japan, or North or South America, he is acclaimed for his distinctive brand of music.

Born in Toronto in 1928, Moe Koffman was a teenage saxophone prodigy who went to the United States to work in big bands, led by the likes of Jimmy Dorsey, Sonny Dunham, and Charlie Barnet. In New York in the 1950s he studied flute with Harold Bennett and clarinet with Leon Russianoff. When he returned to Toronto in 1957 he quickly gained a reputation as a peerless studio musician who could play anything. Although he is recognized internationally for his jazz flute, he also ranks among the very best alto saxophonists. No one need be prodded to pay attention to any of his solos, say, on Boss Brass records. They leap out at you.

While driving from the airport one late night some years ago, I turned the dial of the radio and almost jerked off the road when I heard a huge band on a Detroit

MOE KOFFMAN, LATE SEVENTIES. *Courtesy Bernie Senensky*

station playing a blazing "I Got Rhythm," at a very fast clip. All the solos were spectacular, but when the alto stepped into the breech, the player's peerless technique and heart-stopping improvisations generated the same excitement as watching boxer Sugar Ray Robinson demolish an opponent with one punch. Of course, the band was Rob McConnell's Boss Brass and the alto soloist Moe Koffman. Another heart-stopping Koffman sax solo can be heard on the BB's rendition of "All the Things You Are." What a saxophonist! What a band!

During the 1950s and 1960s, Moe and almost everyone else mentioned in this book played together on many CBC television shows. On Jack Kane's weekly "Music Makers" show, so many fine instrumentalists were featured every week, but Moe's solos seemed to stand out more than any of the others. In 1958 he wrote and recorded a simple riff that became a bestseller, titled "Swinging Shepherd Blues" (which also received the BMI Award for one million performances logged in 1992). Later on, Moe was one of the first to experiment with electronic woodwinds and to play two saxes at the same time, in a kind of R&B jazz-influenced rock. He has been featured at the Toronto and Montreal jazz festivals, and made guest soloist appearances with Benny Goodman, Quincy Jones, Woody Herman, and Dizzy Gillespie's United Nations Orchestra.

One Moe Time, Moe-Mentum, Moe Koffman Plays, and *Oop-pop-a-da*, featuring Dizzy Gillespie, are only a few of Moe Koffman's many popular jazz albums. He has received the prestigious Harold Moon Award for "outstanding contribution to the international music scene." In 1991 he was a Juno nominee for Instrumental Artist of the Year. In the same year he was cited by the jury that awarded him the 1991 Toronto Arts Award as the "personification of excellence." He has been the orchestra contractor for Andrew Lloyd Webber's Toronto production of *The Phantom of the Opera* at the Pantages Theatre. And his recording, *Music for the Night,* features his multi-reed artistry in symphonic, chamber music, and pop interpretations of the music of Lloyd Webber.

Among those who really love music, Moe Koffman is justly celebrated for his renowned Moe Koffman Quintet. Moe and guitarist Ed Bickert, bassist Patrick Collins, keyboard player Bernie Senensky, and drummer Barry Elmes have toured almost everywhere and garnered high praise. In the world at large as it is today, however, Moe is probably still most famous for his "swinging shepherd" piece of 1958. When he went into the studio to record the tune, he was still calling it, for want of a better name, "Blues à la Canadiana." At the end of the recording session the producer opened the door of the control booth and asked, "What do you call this thing?" When he heard Moe's answer, he said, "Naww, that's not right for this kind of cute melody. Why don't you call it … uhhm, let's see … why don't you call it "Swinging Shepherd Blues?"

In any case, the piece took off and was heard around the world. On the TSO's trip to the People's Republic of China in 1978, during a banquet in Shanghai, one of the after-dinner entertainers was a native flutist who played a number of Chinese songs on a marvellous bamboo instrument. When the orchestra members gave him a standing ovation, as an encore he launched into Moe's famous composition. We'd heard that the Chinese people were forbidden to listen to Western radio, and asked the flutist how he knew the piece. In hand-signal dialogue he told us, "I listen to Western radio. I hear that music all the time. Easy to play." (And that, I thought, is the price of fame.)

Oscar Peterson

Think of a "stroke" and what it means. It's an aneurysm — a sudden loss of brain function caused by a blockage or a rupture of a blood vessel to the brain. It's paralysis. Now think of a hip replacement. It hurts. And now think of being seventy years old. Combine these handicaps and you get an idea of what Oscar Peterson has been going through in the last few years.

Under normal circumstances it's enough to keep a man in bed for the rest of his life. But think of Oscar Peterson and his enormous power. Think of those individuals in history who rose above adversity through the human spirit, the spirit of man. In his seventies, Oscar is no ordinary man. So much has been written about the world-famous Canadian jazz pianist that trying to concoct new superlatives becomes almost an impossible exercise. Since he broke onto the world scene when he performed at Carnegie Hall in 1949 with Norman Granz's *Jazz at the Philharmonic*, the great Montreal-born musician (who now lives in the so-called "Greater Toronto Area") has been up there with the gods.

How he still performs, given his handicaps, is a mystery. In an October 1997 article in the *Sunday Times* in London, Clive Davis wrote: "That he is playing in public at all is no mean achievement. At one point, he says, he was convinced that he would never perform again; it took long bouts of physiotherapy before he was able to fight his way back. As he observes, with characteristic understatement, 'I've learned something about patience.'" Davis added, "it was impossible not to be moved by the sight of Peterson, now in his seventies, walking onto the stage for a tribute concert at New York's Town Hall in October 1996, three years after suffering a serious stroke. His gait was still laboured, his left arm still hung awkwardly at his side."

Clive Davis' article prompted me to think about a younger, very exciting Oscar Peterson, when he played at the Paddock Tavern on Queen at Bathurst in the Toronto of the 1950s. The joint was always packed. Oscar in those days was a magnificent reminder of the great Art Tatum, and I remember that he also appeared at the Colonial and the Towne Tavern in Toronto. And of course he has played everywhere. He has dazzled audiences throughout the U.S.A., Europe, Japan, Australia, and South America. His more than 200 album releases are a legacy that will remain available to everyone well into the next century.

Clive Davis also wrote: "The album that documented the October 1996 concert, *A Tribute to Oscar Peterson: Live at the Town Hall,* may not become an all-time Peterson hit if only for the reason that the star of the evening was confined to a supporting role for substantial portions of the concert." But fans will still have concrete proof that despite his handicaps the man could still hammer it out in the best Petersonian tradition.

Many today would be inclined to argue, I suspect, that Oscar Peterson is to jazz what Glenn Gould is to classical music in Canada; simply the greatest musician of his sort that the country has yet produced. (And as an old Toronto boy myself, I am of course willing to forgive the fact that, even though Oscar now lives in Toronto, he was born and raised in Montreal.)

Jimmy Namaro

I've had occasion lately to think of another star figure who used to haunt the Toronto music scene and finally wound up in the greater Vancouver area, in Richmond, British Columbia. After a career spanning a stupendous sixty-eight years, Jimmy Namaro celebrated his eighty-fourth birthday at a big surprise party in Richmond, on April 14, 1997. And even in his mid-eighties (and on both piano and vibes), he never missed a beat when he joined his old partners, bass player Peter Trimble and drummer Don Fraser, to entertain 200 longtime friends and colleagues who gathered to wish him well.

Jimmy's beautiful wife, Anne-Marie, had asked the guests to keep mum about the party. As she put it, "the element of surprise was the greatest gift, seconded by the realization of my gift to him — that he play again to an appreciative audience with a trio." Among those on hand were Canada's great bandleader Mart Kenney, eighty-six, and one of the early singers with Mart's Western Gentlemen, Judy Richards. The congratulatory telegrams included messages from Canadian Prime Minister Jean Chrétien, BC Premier Glen Clark, and singer Frankie Laine (Jimmy Namaro had served as musical director for him in an earlier incarnation).

Jimmy Namaro got his start in 1928, at age fifteen, when he played the marimba on a radio station in Hamilton, Ontario. He remembers:

That was before I was old enough to join the union. When I turned sixteen the next year I joined the union in Toronto. I've been a member ever since.

A few years later, in 1933, Jimmy was assistant conductor and sole Canadian member of a 100-piece marimba band featured at the Chicago World's Fair.

In spite of the Great Depression, Jimmy worked throughout the 1930s. He appeared on NBC radio's "Kate Smith Hour" in 1934, and in 1935 he was the first artist engaged to do solo work on the CRBC, the forerunner of the CBC. In 1936, while working on CBC radio as a xylophonist, vibraphonist, and pianist, he formed his first band, which performed in many top hotel ballrooms in eastern Canada. In 1940 he produced shows for Famous Players Theatres, and in 1941 broadcast twice weekly on the Mutual Network in the United States. In 1942 he joined Bert Pearl and "The Happy Gang" on CBC radio in Toronto, and remained with this venerable Canadian institution until it went off the air in 1959.

JIMMY NAMARO, 1997.
Courtesy Jimmy Namaro

After "The Happy Gang," Jimmy fronted a wide assortment of musical groups at elegant hotels and became a familiar figure on Canadian television. Then in 1977 he moved to San Diego, where he met singing personality Frankie Laine. Laine signed Jimmy as his pianist/conductor/arranger, and the resulting ensemble successfully toured North America and the United Kingdom. The tour included performances with symphony orchestras, and the highlight for Jimmy Namaro came when he conducted the symphony orchestra at Royal Albert Hall in London.

In 1987 the Namaros moved from San Diego back to Canada, to their present home in Richmond, BC. Jimmy continued to work with Frankie Laine by commuting to concert locations in various parts of North America. At the end of our August 1993 interview, he explained that he was still ready and willing to perform:

Anywhere, anytime ... I haven't turned anything down yet.

(And at his big surprise party, about three-and-a-half years later, he showed that he could still put together some pretty potent musical brews.) Not long before my book went to press, I read in the *Globe and Mail* about his unhappy death from a heart attack, on April 25, 1998, just two weeks after he turned eighty-five.

Hagood Hardy

Thinking about Jimmy Namaro also reminds me of the Toronto-based vibraphonist, pianist, and composer Hagood Hardy, whose catchy tune "The Homecoming" brought him international fame. Alas, Hagood died of cancer on January 1, 1996, at the tender age of fifty-nine. About a year and a half before his unhappy death, however, I'd had what struck me as an unusually interesting interview with him. And as I was putting this last part of my book together, I found myself wanting to get at least a fair bit of our talk down on the record.

"The Homecoming" jingle, written in 1972 for a tea commercial, was just one aspect of Hagood Hardy's multifaceted career. He was also a respected jazz musician, the composer of numerous movie and TV soundtracks, and an Ontario Liberal Party candidate who ran unsuccessfully against former premier Bob Rae in the 1995 provincial election. (And in fact, I finally discovered, Hagood's grandfather, Arthur Sturgis Hardy, had actually served as Liberal premier of Ontario in the last years of the nineteenth century, around the time when my book on the Canadian music business in Toronto might be said to begin.)

Although born in Angola, Indiana, in the U.S.A., Hagood Hardy grew up in Oakville, Ontario, a town not far west of the actual city of Toronto. And, as a member of the Toronto Musicians' Association, he built his career as a jazz vibraphonist and pianist during the 1950s, while studying political science and economics at the University of Toronto.

In 1959 he moved to the United States with his wife, Martha, shortly after their marriage. Here he spent seven years performing with such luminaries as Herbie Mann and George Shearing. By 1967 he returned to Toronto and a new phase in his career — travelling with a small pop group, The Montage, and writing television jingles and more than fifty scores for movie and television productions.

I grew up in Oakville. I studied conservatory piano ... up to the equivalent of Grade 9 or 10; then about age thirteen or fourteen I discovered jazz. I always listened to a Niagara Falls, New York, radio station, WHLD, which featured Joe Rico's show, "Jump for Joe." I used to take my radio to bed with me every night. Most kids would take a comic book to bed, but I always had my radio with me and listened to Joe Rico. He was great. In 1950–51 I discovered the George Shearing Quintet. And I really fell in love with the sound of the vibraphone. So in 1953 when I went to private boarding school in Port Hope, I got a set of old xylophone keys, built myself a frame, and started to play with mallets. I had no instruction; I just picked it up on my own.

Jazz changed the impetus for me. Whereas classical music is mainly an interpretive art, jazz is definitely a creative art. It was something that expressed who you were. And that really captured my imagination. At the time no one was teaching popular music. My instruction was classical (on the piano, not the xylophone). I was into Liszt's Hungarian Dances and Rachmaninoff and other classical composers. But I made myself figure out how chords were constructed — A Minor, C Major. It was just like somebody opening a door for me. Suddenly, I could play my own version of things.

In the last year of private school, 1954–55, I started playing the vibraphone: "It was a tiny instrument and sounded more like a glockenspiel than a vibraphone. But God, I was in absolute heaven. And when I went to the University of Toronto I bought Peter Appleyard's old Ajax vibraphone and we had a band that played all up and down university row for a year. I was already into jazz. People asked me "How do you improvise?" I told them I didn't know. I guess it's the search for melody.

That's what paid off for him, Hagood told me. It was the melodies in pop music that supported him:

Improvisation is an attempt to create an evocative melody. It's not just running scales and chords. There's a danger that some of the people coming along today put more notes in their music than I ever played in my life. The people who can't get in touch with the deeper sense of the music are going to fall by the wayside. No matter how many notes you put in a bar, it doesn't really matter unless they mean something.

Hagood joined the union in 1956 when Walter Murdoch was still president.

I felt I was going up before the Supreme Court when I went into that office. There was a certain aura around the Toronto Musicians' Association that was rather fearsome.

As a member of the TMA he could play with anyone he wanted, so long as they were members as well. He played with Jack Zaza's band at the Orchard Park Hotel on weekends. Jack initiated him into the gentle art of drinking beer:

I was nineteen at the time and I didn't really like beer, but I forced myself and got high on half a glass. Gordon Lightfoot played drums in that band and Vic Centro on accordion made it a great little band. We had a lot of fun there.

Around the winter of 1956 and the spring of 1957, Hagood discovered the House of Hambourg. That was the beginning of a new phase in his life:

That's where I started to have opportunities and learned a lot ... One night I went in and Moe's group was playing. Bickert had been detained: in fact he never got there. Moe said, "Hey, why don't you sit in?" I sat at the piano and we played "Gone With the Wind." Clem Hambourg took an interest that night. ("University student, clean cut, veddy nice, veddy nice. Bring a nice feeling to the place.") So he introduced me to Ed Bickert, and I told Ed about the ideas I had for a vibes, bass, guitar, and drums thing.

I tried to explain that I wasn't really a piano player; my instrument was the vibraphone.

At that time, Ed Bickert (who would subsequently develop into a superb jazz guitarist) was living in Clem's attic. And Clem picked up Hagood's ideas about a new group immediately.

ED BICKERT, LATE SEVENTIES. At Bourbon Street.
Courtesy Bernie Senensky

Soon I had my own quartet there on Friday nights, with Ed on guitar, Ron Rully on drums, and Bob Price on bass. It worked out pretty good. We played Friday nights, ad infinitum.

Of course, other groups played Clem's House of Hambourg in that era as well. Sunday nights featured the Ron Collier Quintet, with trombonist Collier, Carne Bray on bass, Jack McQuaid on drums, Ed Bickert on guitar, and Bernie Piltch on alto. And trombonist Collier was also a talented composer/arranger whose charts always pleased. Ron ultimately taught at Humber College and turned out an extraordinarily large number of excellent arrangers.

This was the environment I was fortunate enough to be in. Saturday nights Clem had the hard swinging stuff playing — guys like Norm Amadio, Archie Alleyne, and Ernie Osachuk, who came up after they finished playing the Towne Tavern downtown. Sometimes tenorman D.T. [Don Thompson] was there blowing up a storm. Gradually, I started playing all the nights there — Fridays, Saturdays, and Sundays. It wasn't open Sundays, originally, until Clem started to say, "Well, we can have three floors of music and three nights of music." We played an early set on Fridays and Saturdays, then went upstairs and played the later set with Bernie Piltch and bassist Bill Britto: We had a nice trio there — vibes, alto, and bass.

In its location on Cumberland Street, the House of Hambourg was an old cellar. (And it was another old cellar when it later moved to Grenville Street.) When you walked in you were greeted with some rickety old steps that led up to the kitchen, or went down to the basement. In the basement were beautiful old brick arches, the kind one finds in old wine cellars. You would walk from one charming room "as old as time" through an arch into another ancient charming room.

Clem and Ruth Hambourg did it all up with candles. They made the best damn pizza you've ever tasted. It was a deep dish small pizza. And Ruth, in her own way, was every bit as remarkable as Clem. I lived there in the summers up in Ed's garret apartment; he had moved out. When he and Madeleine got married, I took over the attic.

Clem and Ruth were the same age, and they never aged. To my way of thinking Clem would be considered eccentric. But Clem's eccentricity came from the fact that he was always thinking so far ahead of everything that was going on. To me he was a strange sort of visionary, and often expressed some wonderful ideas about the way things should be and how they were going ... He took chances. He would try anything.

Eventually, the Toronto press discovered Clem and Ruth's House of Hambourg, and people began to flock to the after-hours jazz club. It was not unusual to see line-ups waiting outside. At first Clem hardly ever opened before 11:00 PM. But with the growing crowds, he decided to open earlier, and patrons rushed to grab seats wherever they could.

Before long, with everyone raving about the wonderful jazz vibraphonist at the House of Hambourg, Hagood Hardy was discovered by the CBC. For the next few years he made a substantial number of appearances on CBC television. He knew he was a good jazz musician who could meet every challenge head-on. He had confidence that he could always get work. Like others before and since, he began to wonder if it would be as easy south of the border, and that drove him to New York. He and wife Martha hit on a five-year plan:

Let's give myself five years in New York to see if I can really make this thing work.

They gathered the savings they had in the bank, borrowed some money from friends, and, with their baby daughter, took off to the United States. Hagood travelled with the family to Virginia, where his parents lived, and left Martha and baby daughter there for a spell. With his vibraphone in tow, he took a bus to New York. A friend who was going on tour with Peter Appleyard rented him an apartment.

A union regulation prescribed that new musicians seeking work in New York had to wait six months before they were allowed to play: so jazz musician Hagood Hardy shovelled snow for eighty cents an hour for the city government. Having served his snow-shovelling apprenticeship, and with a list of people he intended to meet in his hand, he headed first for the Five-Spot, a club in lower Manhattan, where Gi Gi Gryce was playing.

It had been snowing all day and the roads were next to impossible to navigate with a car. When I introduced myself to Gi Gi, he asked me to sit in, because Eddie Costa, who played vibes for Gi Gi, was snowed in at home. So I played the whole night with him. The next day he came to the apartment, took me to the union, got me my card, and I started with him that night at the Five-Spot.

I worked a month at the Five-Spot for eighty-six dollars a week. I took it home in my sock because when the job finished at 3:30 AM, I used to ride the subway every night from the Bowery all the way up to West 72nd Street. I'd be in the subway all by myself waiting for fifteen to twenty minutes before a train would come along. It was really something. Then the night Gi Gi closed, Herbie Mann came in to listen to the band: His vibraphone player was leaving. He hired me to start with him the next night at the Village Gate. So I started working with Herbie — he had the greatest reputation. He would work six months of the year in New York. Nobody could do that. But between the Half Note, where we would spend six weeks, and the Village Gate, where we'd spend six weeks, and dates the rest of the time at the Apollo up in Harlem, I did all right.

Herbie Mann's group performed at the Apollo in Harlem. They also played Chicago, Philadelphia, and Washington.

In those days I had no problem with being received by the blacks ... I'd go up to Count Basie's Bar in Harlem and sit in and play, night after night. I used to play all over Manhattan, anywhere there was an opportunity. That was the only way to get known. You really had to get out and fight for it. I'll never forget the night we played the Showboat in Philadelphia. The police raided our dressing room, made us line up against the wall, and roll up our sleeves, looking for needle marks. This was the week after Art Blakey and his Jazz Messengers had been there. For a while it got pretty scary. But thank God everybody was clean.

Towards the ends of 1961, I had become a familiar figure in New York jazz circles. People knew me. I was able to bring my wife and daughter up from Virginia. In January 1962 Martha gave birth to a baby boy, and we named him David. We moved into a little apartment in Inglewood, New Jersey. I was playing all the time. Symphony Sid used to phone me to get a band together for Monday nights at Birdland. I got people like Walter Bishop, Jr., Charlie Percip, Ron Carter, Mal Waldren, and that job would stretch out to five or six Monday nights. And in would walk Paul Chambers and Philly Jo Jones and sit in the whole night. I was in heaven. It was just a wonderful thing for me. Playing Birdland made me feel I had put down roots there.

The Toronto vibraphonist was making it in New York clubs that were part of the history of jazz. In the spring of 1962, while he was still working with Herbie Mann, Hagood received a call from Martin Denny, who led a somewhat exotic show band and had a hit record called "Quiet Village" on the charts.

I was making $106 a week. When Herbie was off, I played at the Metropole on weekends with Saul Jaeger and his Dixie Mets ... I used to fill up my time as much as I could. But Martin offered me forty-eight weeks with a guaranteed salary of $300 a week, living in Honolulu six months of the year, and travelling to the major show places in the States. His vibraphone player played marimba, xylophone, vibraphone, chimes, and other sound effects as well. I hated to leave New York. I hated to get out of the jazz idiom. But $300 a week for a family of four! That was a lot of money in 1962.

So Martha and Hagood had a garage sale and sold everything they owned in their New Jersey apartment. Then they packed their car and drove to San Francisco, and from there they made their way to Honolulu. Hagood worked with Martin for a year and nine months. Then one night, while listening to the music, he decided he'd had enough. He didn't want to luxuriate in Hawaii for the rest of his life, playing marimba, xylophone, chimes, and all sorts of sound effects.

We saved up enough money and I gave Martin my notice. We flew to California, where we picked up a car and decided to go on the road. We lived on the road for three months, all over the southwest. I played a lot in Las Vegas at the Sands. Getting a booking there was easy: we could sit down for six weeks at a time.

In 1962 and 1963 Las Vegas was still in its mythic earlier phases, and all the hotels were one-storey buildings.

Those were the days when Frank Sinatra, Joey Bishop, Sammy Davis, Jr., and Dean Martin would all come up on stage just before our show and do a couple of numbers. It was magic. Nat King Cole was there all the time at the tables, gambling after his show. It was great to have been in on all that stuff.

Hagood used to sit in with the band that alternated with him after his shows.

Buddy Rich usually came over when he had finished the evening with Harry James' Band. I've never experienced anything like it ... I would play piano, and with Buddy on drums the band would lift right off the floor: the feeling was incredible.

When Martha gave birth to their third child, Jennifer, in 1964, she took the baby and the other children back to Hagood's parents' place in Virginia, and she and the family lived there while her husband continued on the road, sessioning with Pete Jolley, Chuck Berghoffer, and Lou Levy. Eventually they moved to Los Angeles where he did a lot of recording sessions as a percussionist.

In the year and nine months I'd spent with Martin Denny, I learned to play all the percussion instruments and became quite adept at it. I did record dates with The Supremes and Cannonball Adderley. We lived in the Valley — Martha, our three kids, and me. Victor Feldman was a close friend and he helped me tremendously.

(I remember myself that when Murray Lauder and I went to the Feldman Swing Club, on Oxford Street in London during the war, a very talented ten-year-old, Victor Feldman, would sit in on drums with the "big-time jazzmen." Victor was the club owner's son. Whenever he was on the bandstand, his father beamed with pride. He'd nudge a few people sitting at a table and say, "That's my son." Victor Feldman grew up to become one of the finest percussionists in Los Angeles.)

HAGOOD HARDY, 1982. The Ontario Science Centre.
Courtesy Hagood Hardy

Victor was a great help. We had this little house in Woodland Hills, and he and his family lived close by, near the freeway. He used to have us down for barbeques and we'd get together with two vibes. I'd bring my vibes over and we'd practise Bartok's String Duets. *When we weren't working we'd get together all the time. Victor was a great guy.*

At this juncture George Shearing, who had just taken a year off to rest, decided to reform his quintet. He asked Victor Feldman to go with him, but Victor was too busy with his own engagements; so he recommended Hagood Hardy. Shearing hired Hagood on the spot.

For the next while Hagood either played with Shearing all the time, or packed a steel lunchbox, like Victor would do, and worked every day running from recording studio to studio. The pace became quite hectic.

It got to the point that Martha and I didn't like my schedule. We'd just gone through the Watts riots where they had snipers on the Ventura Freeway. You couldn't move anywhere without the threat of violence. We figured it was time to move. Our daughter was in Grade 1 and our little boy hadn't quite started school ... When I finished with Shearing in 1967, we moved back to Toronto.

Back in Toronto Hagood formed a jazz trio and played the Dell Tavern for awhile. Then the trio went into Sutton Place, at Bay and Wellesley, from 1967 to 1968. But he grew tired of playing jazz with nobody listening. He added two girls to the group (Lynn McNeil and Stephanie Taylor) and The Montage was born.

That was the band that toured all over Canada and the United States. Our first job, a two-week engagement, was in a club called the Living Room, in Rochester, New York, where we got paid in a brown paper bag with one-dollar bills and endorsed Social Security cheques.

I was convinced the owners were criminals who were going to lay in wait for us on our trip back to the hotel and rob us.

244 They Loved to Play

After Rochester The Montage played the Virginian in Cleveland, opened for Victor Borge at the Waldorf Astoria in New York, played the Sahara in Las Vegas, and the London House in Chicago. They played in Miami Beach and Puerto Rico and toured American Air Force bases in Europe. Then, after five years, he figured it was time to move on. Hagood had formed his own jingle company in 1968 and it became the new focus of his musical career.

It lasted until 1983, and I operated it out of the basement of my house. It gave me a degree of financial security. I had the Kellogg's account for ten years: It was the first real taste of money that we ever had.

In August 1972 he wrote "The Homecoming" for a tea-company television commercial. The beautiful melody was infectious, and a lot of people found the commercial delightful. It showed a station wagon with wood sides pulling up to a nice old frame house, with the grandparents welcoming the family for a reunion.

I wrote the eight bars of music to last twenty seconds for this scenario. Then I orchestrated it. I didn't have the budget to use more than twelve to fourteen strings.

The response to "The Homecoming" was startling. Taken with the melody, people started calling the ad agency about the music in the commercial. The agency wanted Hagood to release a record because of the product identification.

About that time the Canadian content regulations came in; so it was feasible that I record the piece. With regulations in place "The Homecoming" could get a lot of airplay, which wouldn't hurt the tea company's sales. When we made the record for release, "The Homecoming" was played by four violins, two violas, and two cellos. David Green, the sound engineer in the control booth, made it sound like a huge orchestra.

"The Homecoming" also gave rise to the one period of real bitterness in Hardy's musical career. He was stunned when he received a lawyer's letter informing him that a client claimed Hagood had stolen the melody and was suing him.

The original complaint was left in a plain envelope on my vibraphone one September night in 1980, at George's Spaghetti House on Dundas ... The court trial was painful as hell ... when somebody is calling you a thief and a liar in the Supreme Court of Ontario, that's a bit much.

The cost alone was unbelievable, because the guy didn't have any money. I won everything but I bore the brunt just to defend myself.

The trial ended in July 1982. In the meantime the plaintiff had died. But his second wife (he had left his widow and five children to marry her), arrived in court every day dressed all in black, complete with veil.

It was such a cut-and-dried case that it should never have gone to court. Seventy-five thousand dollars to defend myself at a trial that, as far as most people were concerned, should never have gone to court. It was unconscionable and outrageous.

One of the last things Hagood talked about during our interview in 1994 was how amazed he was to hear young lawyers say to him, "Oh, we studied your case in school. It's really written up." I thought about all this again when I heard of Hagood Hardy's untimely death — about a year and a half later. There can be many hard sides to a musician's life. I wondered if Hagood's experience with his lawsuit in the early 1980s had anything to do with his decision to follow in his grandfather's footsteps and try his hand at politics, in the mid-1990s: a mere six months before he died.

Teddy Roderman

I've already talked about the superb Toronto trombonist Teddy Roderman. But there's another story about him that I sometimes especially remember nowadays.

Teddy was playing radio shows when he was seventeen. Lucio Agostini loved him, not only for his playing but also for his friendship. Teddy played for Sam Hershenhorn, Howard Cable — all of them. His sound was spectacular. He was truly one in a million. He had a sense of humour that had us laughing most of the time. But his humour could also be acerbic (and, in one case that touched me quite directly, prescient as well).

My wedding day was June 3, 1954. The celebration took place at the Prince George Hotel, located at the south-east corner of York and Richmond streets. The wedding ceremony was

TEDDY RODERMAN, 1969. *Courtesy Teddy Roderman*

246   They Loved to Play

in the ballroom, which had been converted into a temporary chapel. The guests were seated on chairs on either side of the aisle. And the aisle was covered by a long, red carpet that ran the full length of the room — from the doors to the canopy under which the vows were to be exchanged.

The ceremony had begun. The bride and her maid of honour were standing under the canopy, waiting for me and the best man, who was my good friend Teddy Roderman. When the signal was given, while everybody turned to watch, we proceeded in a dignified manner along the red carpet towards the bride, maid of honour, and the parents.

With almost every step forward, Teddy would whisper loudly in my ear, "Look, it's not too late, I've got a cab waiting outside. We can nip out through one of these doors. Think of what you're getting into."

"For Christ's sake, shut up," I would say.

"I'm not kidding. You're walking to your doom. Let's go now, that door there. The cabbie's got his motor going."

"For God's sake, will you shut up!"

"In America today almost every marriage winds up in divorce. Quick! Through the door." Teddy kept up the barrage until we'd reached the canopy.

In the end I was married that day and the party was memorable. Friends, relatives, all the guys — Ellis McLintock, Hank and Helen Rosati, Murray and Yvonne Lauder, all of them — everybody had a ball. My new wife, Rosanna, and I spent our honeymoon in Miami and Cuba. Very romantic.

I should have listened to Teddy and gotten into the cab.

Paul Grosney

Thinking of weddings reminds me of trumpeter Paul Grosney as well. The first time I met Paul was at an army hostel in London, called Cartwright Gardens, in 1944. One day as I entered the building, I could hear music coming from the ballroom, just to my right. I pushed open the louvred saloon-type ballroom doors and heard Paul playing "How High the Moon." I couldn't help being moved by his golden tones.

On the same bandstand was the great tenorman Bob Burns, pianist Neil Chotem, drummer Lee Raeburn, and bassist Sam Levine. The musicians were all in RCAF uniform. As what remained of the war progressed, Paul and I became good friends. A spectacular musician, his connections in Las Vegas and Hollywood have given birth to dozens of stories about him .

I have a Paul Grosney story of my own that demonstrates his fearlessness in coming to the aid of a friend. Sometime in the 1950s, when I was leading a band at a wedding party at the House of Righteousness, in north Toronto, I was accosted by a guest. He'd had too much to drink, and he told me my band stunk. Since I, too, had copious amounts of firewater coursing merrily through my veins, I invited him to join me in the privacy of a room on the right side of the stage behind closed doors. Once inside we exchanged such harsh words as "Oh Yeah?" and "What the hell do you know about music?" This led the guest to punch me in my mouth. (It was a lucky shot, to be sure: I could have demolished him with my little finger.) And as all members of the breed are very aware, hitting a brass player in the lip is a very bad thing to do.

Suddenly from out of nowhere, a huge shape flew through the air from the direction of the stage. It proved to be trumpeter Paul Grosney. While still aloft he brought both his clenched fists down on my assailant's head. The inebriated music critic was knocked cold,

PAUL GROSNEY, LATE SEVENTIES.
Courtesy Bernie Senensky

while my arms held him so he wouldn't crumple to the floor. Suddenly the unconscious man's beautiful wife was in the room, screaming for me to take my hands off her husband. A certain Mrs. Bergman was shouting, "Stop fighting! This is a house of worship." And Paul was yelling at the top of his lungs, "Call the police! Call the police!" Right then and there I knew that's what you call a true friend.

Rob McConnell

Rob McConnell is another Toronto brass player. I've known him for more than thirty years, and from our first meeting I sensed he had what it took to become a top jazz artist. History has borne out my humble prediction. His arrangements have been recognized and applauded by musicians and other arrangers, throughout North America, as brilliant, inventive, inspired, and exciting.

When Rob formed his spectacular Boss Brass in 1968, the band was composed of brass players alone (musicians who only played trumpets, trombones, and French horns), along with an excellent rhythm section. (At the time the word "boss" was indigenous to the Toronto jazz community; it was tossed around as a synonym for great, wonderful, altogether out out this world, and so forth.)

The band's first major gig was at the Savarin Restaurant (and cocktail lounge). After the impact of its exciting music hit Toronto like an exploding ten-ton bomb, saxophonist Moe Koffman and about two dozen local reed players entered the packed-to-the-ceiling Savarin and marched up on stage carrying placards that proclaimed, "Rob McConnell and the Boss Brass Unfair to Woodwinds. We Want In!"

(As Moe has subsequently explained: "Just organizing every sax player in the city to carry a placard down to the Savarin was something else!")

Shortly afterwards Rob agreed that there was certainly room for saxophones, and began to write parts for a five-saxophone section. The resulting twenty-piece band really began to catch public attention. The band appeared at jazz festivals, played many different Toronto clubs, and recorded for the likes of the California-based Concord label.

In 1981 the Canadian Department of External Affairs kicked in some money which helped Rob McConnell and the Boss Brass to fly to Los Angeles and to appear at Carmello's jazz club in Sherman Oaks. In 1984 Rob's brass players (and saxophones) returned to Los Angeles and performed at Dante's in Hollywood. The band may not have been a household name in Canada, but it certainly was in some parts of Los Angeles: crowds waiting to get in Carmello's and Dante's were lined up around the block for hours.

Rob McConnell himself is a valve trombonist with a warm, robust sound. His brilliant and polished improvisations have been titillating listeners and musicians for years. Among his best friends and fans he is also well-known for his extraordinary sense of humour. And one can see this at work (along with certain other aspects of the fate of the golden age of music in Toronto today) in a flyer-letter sent to loyal Boss Brass followers, prior to a late-1980s appearance of the band at the Limelight Dinner Theatre:

Hello Friends:

It's time for another try at playing for the paying public, and we hope that you're still one of them. Over the years we have played many places in Toronto ... it's not that the bandleader has had fights with all owners.

The Savarin. Our start in 1968 — a good place and nice people (Eddie Assaf). We were playing pop music in those days, so it's questionable how a jazz band would have done. After a few good years Eddie (owner) died, the building was sold ... no more Savarin.

The Colonial. We played The Colonial twenty years ago. The club was in flux at that time, re: the entertainment policy, and the regular clientele was a trifle questionable. I've told the story before, but if you haven't heard it ... The Colonial was a strip joint with a large marquee out front (So & So and Her Twin 44s, etc.) "The Boss Brass" was on the marquee when we started, but by about Wednesday the 'ss' in Brass had fallen off. A number of disgruntled regulars stumbled in looking forward to the the new Act, and were noticeably disturbed to see a twenty-piece jazz band on the scene

Basin Street/Bourbon Street. We always had an excellent time working for Doug Cole — at one time he had all the jazz going in town at Bourbon Street, Basin Street (main floor), and at George's. Jazz musicians (over forty-five) miss Doug, Dorian, Kenny, Tony, Leo, Erminio, Mafundsalow, etc.

Bamboo. Basically a good joint, but not a jazz place and not in the right place. Also a good idea to bring a tape recorder to meetings with management.

The El Mocambo. Played here in 1981–82 and were treated very well. The set-up of the room was really not good for a large jazz band though. We took so much room from the wall that we literally

ROB MCCONNELL, LATE SEVENTIES. *Courtesy Bernie Senensky*

played for two rows in front of us — everyone else was on the sides.

The Pilot. A pretty good joint, but unfortunately had disagreements with management over business matters. Why, when a club has a very successful first engagement, they decide to change everything the second time — reservations, prices, times, etc., is a mystery. Good-bye Pilot.

The Limelight Theatre, March 28–April 1. Our good friends Paul Simmons, Don Harron, Catherine McKinnon and Dave Broadfoot bought the place last fall (Paul booked us at The Colonial but we won't hold that against him). It is a very nice theatre, nice neighborhood, seating 200 or so. Everybody has excellent sight and hearing lines to the stage — the audience sits at tables that are tiered to the back of the room. The band and audience are looking right at each other, and people at the back are not that far away, the theatre being a square shape. Also, no stand-up bar at the end of the room containing various drunks and (band members sometimes) discussing why we will never make it without some Stan Kenton charts, who was the third trumpet in the Second Herd (I know), and so on. They have a good sound system, lighting, nice piano, and (fanfare here!) a dressing room!

All in all, I think it looks good ... one small downtick — it's almost impossible to find a parking spot. The subway is a smart move — exit at Davisville and walk north two short blocks. Dave Broadfoot in his Act does a long bit about all the miracles in our lives ... one of them (when he's at The Limelight) is that he found a parking spot that was only a ten-dollar cab ride to the theatre!

We have a lot of new music and look forward to seeing you there!

Erich Traugott

Thinking a little more about great Toronto brass players inevitably brings me to Erich Traugott. When Erich showed up at a rehearsal of the CBC's "General Electric Showtime" in Studio 4 on Yonge Street, and sat in the first trumpet chair, nobody introduced him. I thought this was strange. Howard Cable just started the rehearsal by asking for the first number on the music stands and away we went.

When the orchestra came to the last chord, Erich played a magnificent high 'C' ("Hey man, that was great," the musicians shouted.) When we played the arrangement for a second time, Traugott ended on a nose-bleeding high 'E,' one third interval higher. And that did it. He had all the musicians in the orchestra in his pocket. The Kitchener-born trumpet player became a fixture on CBC radio and television shows And he became a key figure in Phil Nimmons' Nimmons 'n' Nine Plus Six (or Plus Three or Four, or whatever else it was called from time to time to time again).

Oddly enough, as a child Erich studied the trumpet with Nathaniel Stroh, a flutist with the Kitchener Symphony Orchestra. But by the time he was eleven years old, he had won some fifty medals in competitions throughout Ontario, including the CNE and the Stratford and London Music Festivals. At twenty he won a three-year scholarship at the Peabody Conservatory of Music in Baltimore. While at Peabody he played with the Baltimore Symphony Orchestra conducted by Reginald Stewart (who, some readers may recall, had conducted the Promenade Philharmonic Orchestra in the Toronto of the 1930s).

ERICH TRAUGOTT, circa 1970.
Courtesy Erich Traugott

Despite his brilliance, Erich has always been a quiet, unassuming, well-liked guy who never (so to speak) blew his own horn. After many years of quietly demonstrating his enormous talent, he quietly retired on December 31, 1988.

Bernie Piltch

Along with all the other wonderful woodwind players I've talked about in this book (and others about whom lack of space and time have compelled me to remain silent), I think in particular of my friend Bernie Piltch. A highly respected and versatile alto saxophonist and clarinetist, he died April 7, 1983, at fifty-five years of age, following a heart attack while working at a CBC recording studio.

Born in Montreal, and conservatory-trained in Toronto as a clarinetist, Bernie began his career at sixteen, playing alto saxophone in Toronto dance bands. In the 1950s, he played in jazz groups led by Norm Symonds and Ron Collier, and others, and became established in the radio, television, and recording orchestras that dominated his career in the 1960s and 1970s. His alto work may have reached its highest level when he appeared as a bebop jazz soloist on records by Ron Collier and Paul Hoffert.

At the other end of the musical spectrum, Bernie Piltch was the saxophonist-on-call with the Toronto Symphony from 1968 to 1975. (The saxophone is not an instrument regularly called for in the classical repertoire, but Bernie also worked in other classical music situations that did require a saxophonist's services.)

One thing I especially remember is that, along with a number of other CBC players, Bernie was an ardent fan of American humourist S.J. Perelman, who wrote such gems as *Chicken Inspector No. 23, Dawn Ginsbergh's Revenge, The Rising Gorge,* and *The Swiss Family Perelman.*

BERNIE PILTCH, circa 1950. *Courtesy Susan Piltch*

From time to time, Bernie Piltch, Teddy Roderman, Lew Lewis, Moe Weinzweig, a few others, and I would get together at somebody's house and take turns reading the author's hilarious stories ("Eine Kleine Mothmusik," "La Plume de Mon Ami Est dans le Flapdoodle," "Nobody Knows the Rubble I've Seen/Nobody Knows but Croesus.") After a couple of drinks we'd be rolling around on the floor, howling with laughter.

S.J. Perelman, who wrote for the Marx Brothers in the 1930s and penned several Broadway hits, was a cult hero to Bernie and the rest of us. One day CBC producer Andrew Allan invited him to appear in a radio interview in Toronto.

When he alighted from the cab outside the doors of the CBC Radio Building on Jarvis Street, the short, moustached, bespectacled Perelman was surprised to be greeted by about fifteen applauding musicians and actors. And the great alto saxophonist Bernie Piltch was in the front row, applauding louder than the rest.

At the Boss Brass' first gig at the Savarin in 1968, Moe Koffman's placard-waving saxophonists made it clear that it is important for brass players not to be "Unfair to Woodwinds." And as I think about this, I'm also reminded that Moe himself was not the only great saxophone player during the later days of the golden age of music in Toronto. There were other saxophone players who made their mark as well, such as Roy Smith, Pat Labarbera, Phil Antonacci, and of course Bernie Piltch.

Archie Alleyne

I couldn't do even very rough justice to the subject of jazz in Toronto during the last half of the twentieth century (or Canada at large, for that matter) without talking a little more than I have so far about the superb Toronto-born drummer, Archie Alleyne. A kind of heir of the pathway cleared by Cy McLean during the Second World War, Archie is one of the most significant figures in recent African-Canadian music — and a man of many talents.

Along with his long stint at the Towne Tavern with Norm Amadio in the 1950s and his after-hours appearances at the House of Hambourg, Archie has played with such illustrious performers as Billie Holiday, Carmen McRae, Illinois Jacquet, Lester Young, and Mel Torme. From 1964 to 1966 he was one-third of the Teddy Wilson Trio, playing Antigua in the West Indies. And he toured Canada and the United States with pianist Marian McPartland in the 1960s as well.

In addition to his very active musical career in the 1970s, Archie became a co-owner of The Underground Railroad, a Toronto soul food restaurant that enjoyed much popularity for thirteen years, until a series of uncontrollable circumstances in 1983 forced the owners to close down. He has appeared on CBC radio and television countless times, and recorded extensively with the likes of jazz singer Ranee Lee, Detroit's George Benson, Faith Nolan, and Jay McShann.

In 1981 the Canadian Black Music Awards recognized the artistry of Archie Alleyne by presenting him with the Canadian Black Music Pioneer citation. As evidence of his wider links with contemporary African music, he was honoured in Nigeria as First Grand Patron of the Peter King College of Music in Lagos, when he toured Africa with pianist Oliver Jones in 1988.

When Canadian Prime Minister Brian Mulroney welcomed Nelson and Winnie Mandela to Ottawa in June 1990, the state dinner that followed featured the Archie Alleyne-Frank Wright Quartet. Wright and Alleyne had earlier performed at state dinners for the president of Iceland, the president of Israel, and the Duke of Edinburgh. (And, thus, Archie was on hand to witness the conversation between this particular duke and Frank Wright that, as some readers may recall, has already been reported on in this book.)

To mark his debts to the wider African experience in world music, Archie has also been involved in such successful musical productions as *Madame Gertrude*, *A Tribute to Ma Rainey*, *Lady Day*, and *Many Rivers to Cross*. A more recent project has been *The Evolution of Jazz*, a narrated musical chronicling the origins of jazz from its earliest roots to its emergence as a distinctive present-day art form.

The show traces a musical path which begins in West Africa, and then wends its way through the West Indies and the United States, before its introduction to Canada in the early years of the twentieth century. As part of the Canadian Artists Network/Black Artists in Action programming for 1991, *The Evolution of Jazz* with a cast of thirty musicians and performers was first presented in November 1991 at the University of Toronto's Convocation Hall. A reduced shorter version has been playing in Toronto schools.

Archie is a man who never stands still. With so many ideas buzzing around in his head, there just isn't enough time in a day to get them all out in front of the public. In the most recent past, his many persistent local fans and warm admirers have been able to catch him playing around town with the Toronto Jazz Quartet (or, as the group sometimes appears, Quintet), on the new and increasingly interesting local jazz scene that has been developing quietly in Toronto during the last years of the twentieth century. It is a fact that Archie Alleyne is one of the surviving great gentlemen of the Canadian music business in Toronto today. And (who really knows?) this may even be a hopeful sign that the golden age of music 'ain't' quite dead yet.

ARCHIE ALLEYNE, MAY 1983. At the Sheraton Centre.
Courtesy Archie Alleyne

Ron Collier

Late in the 1960s, Ron Collier's compositional and arranging ability caught the astutely discriminating ears of Duke Ellington. The Coleman, Alberta-born Collier went on to work with the great American on a number of high-profile commissions that came late in Duke's life. In Ron's own words:

> *In 1966 when Lou Applebaum was head of the Canadian Association of Publishers, Authors and Composers (CAPAC), he struck a deal with Decca Records where they would make non-jazz records of original Canadian compositions. CAPAC would pay for the sessions and Decca would pay for the packaging, promoting, and recording.*
>
> *After they made one record of music by Harry Freedman, Harry Somers, and others, Lou thought he would like to do something with jazz, so he sounded out Norm Symonds, Gord Delamont, and myself: "Would we like to do a jazz album?" When he added, "I think we would need somebody of international recognition. How about Duke Ellington?" we all said, "Terrific!" Lou had known the Duke from Stratford, where he had performed earlier and got him to agree.*
>
> *A year later, during Expo '67, the Duke came to Toronto for two days, working just*

for scale and expenses. "We had sent him the music months before, but we weren't sure he had received the material, and weren't terribly sure how good a reader he was."

The first thing Simon, Delamont, Applebaum, and Collier did the morning of the sessions was go to the King Edward Hotel, where he was staying. They knocked on his door, and after some delay the Duke finally opened the door and stood in the doorway, stark naked. "You caught me with my charisma showing," he said.

We eventually got to the studio and learned that he hadn't seen the music. It's amazing. Here was a guy who had written mounds of music and could hardly read a single note. So we did the album down at the old Hallmark Studios, on Sackville Street. He just played piano, I conducted, Roy Smith was the engineer, and it all came out.

But the great composer had more for Ron to do.

In 1969 I was at his apartment in New York when he said, "I wonder if you could do this?" He was doing a ballet with Alvyn Ailey called "The River." He sits down at the piano with a lead sheet which says "Lake," which is one of the three or four movements. It's just a few lead lines and a couple of changes. He says, "Would you like to do it?"

I asked him, "What do you want me to do with it?"

"Well, you know what to do with it."

So I thought, it's a ballet, and there's going to be a pas de deux. So I finished this thing in Portland and we're in Chicago and he says, "Are you ready for tomorrow?"

I asked, "What's tomorrow?

"Well, we're going to record "Lake" tomorrow."

I stayed up all night and wrote and wrote and wrote. I wrote it for a small group and it's a long piece. Then I started copying the parts myself. When I got to the rehearsal I got bassist Joe Benjamin to copy some parts. They needed something to send to the choreographer so that they could work. Then they would tape it and Joe would send it off to the choreographer, Alvin Ailey, who would work with the tape.

Then I had to orchestrate the entire ballet for the New York City Ballet Orchestra. I also composed a symphony for him for the Jacksonville Symphony Orchestra. On his seventy-fifth birthday we played both works with a symphony-size orchestra comprised of the best Toronto players at the Ontario Science Centre. That concert was taped and broadcast later over CJRT-FM. I sent him the tape; he was very excited about getting it. He called me from the hospital but he passed away in 1974 before the tape arrived.

Collier notes that Ellington never used a piano book in his band.

The music was all in his head. Any time I wrote anything for him, he told me, "I don't want a piano part, don't write anything for me." I'd say, "Look, Duke, just a couple of changes, a tinkle here, a tinkle there."

In 1972 when Ellington was at the Royal York Hotel, Collier, who had just started teaching at Humber College, asked him whether he would come to the college and talk to the music students.

I drove him out and he spoke for a good hour and a half and played the piano. The whole lecture theatre was packed, much more than just music staff. Then I saw the Duke in Montreal shortly after. He called me up and said, "I wonder if you could go to Portland, Oregon, for me? There's a black girl who lives in a Benedictine monastery on a hill, who had been a dancer, but got polio, which finished her career. She's sort of composer-in-residence there."

The girl had vocalized some original music which she had put on a tape and convinced Ellington that a band should play it for the dedication of the newly built library at the monastery. This was fine, except there wasn't one note written on paper. The Duke agreed to do it at his own expense. So I went to Portland and hung out in this monastery for two weeks while a piano player, who couldn't read or write a note of music, played the piano, and she sang and I wrote a lead sheet. Two weeks in a monastery! First of all I panicked. "Where can I get a drink?" I asked. Next thing I know a priest comes in with a big twenty-sixer of rye and a case of beer.

After that, I had to return to Toronto and arrange the music for Duke's orchestra. And in the midst of it all, I had to chase the band around. When they were in Chicago, I chased them and rehearsed them a bit. Then back to Toronto for more writing, and I had to get it all copied. In the middle of all this, Johnny Hodges died.

Another time around 1973 when the Duke left the King Edward Hotel, the band boy, Jimmy Lowe, called me up to say, "Get down here right away. Duke's got something for you." I went down there and found his Wurlitzer electric piano waiting for me. I put it in the back seat and drove home. That piano is now at my cottage up north. I use it for writing when I'm there. It was really a nice gift.

When he died the band still had gigs to do in Bermuda, and they had to have a piano player who would play his part. They had to get records of his music where someone lifted his distinctive piano parts off each disk and created a piano book for the Duke Ellington Orchestra. It was quite an experience working with him. He wanted me to go with him, but it was the same year I began at Humber.

Gene DiNovi

The last of the musical personalities about whom I want to say a few final words — the Brooklyn-born pianist Gene DiNovi — may point to another kind of small but hopeful sign for the golden age of music. Gene moved to Toronto in the 1970s. In 1983 he married Deirdre Bowen, a casting director in the city, and the happy couple have subsequently been raising a son, William. But Gene DiNovi remains a staunch American. And it came as a pleasant surprise when he learned recently that the Smithsonian Institute has "archived" his life in music in the National Museum of American History in Washington. In leading a nationwide effort to preserve and celebrate jazz as a national treasure, the Smithsonian has been promoting and presenting America's classical music with travelling exhibitions, live performances, recordings, and ongoing research projects that entertain and educate audiences across the country. In November 1997, sixty-nine-year-old DiNovi received a letter from program coordinator Matt Watson, informing him that through the America's Jazz Heritage partnership with the Lila Wallace-Reader's Digest Fund, the Smithsonian wanted to document his life story, from his early musical training and influences to his current projects and new directions.

A few weeks later Smithsonian representative Peter Pullman came to Toronto. He conducted lengthy interviews with the pianist, and learned about the details of Gene's long career in jazz, and in the allied popular music that had so much to do with jazz during its earlier development. Pullman heard DiNovi tell of the time in 1944 when, at age sixteen, he sat in with the band of the fabled Dizzy Gillespie. He heard him tell of the times he played with Art Tatum, Lester Young, and the legendary Charlie Parker. The great alto saxophonist Charlie Parker, of course, was also known as "Bird," and, as he once recounted in an article in John Norris' Toronto-based *Coda* magazine, Gene remembers how, in the mid-1940s:

Bird was starting to exercise his place in music. He'd say, "Hey, I dig your watch. Lay it on me." So you gave it to him; he was Bird. He played with every necessary element of great music: humour, passion, drive, technique, gentility, sensitivity, finesse, taste, love. I'm eternally grateful that I was there when he was.

Pullman heard how, by 1948, Gene DiNovi was playing with the bands of Buddy Rich and Benny Goodman, and how he went on to accompany such singers as Tony Bennett, Peggy Lee, and Dinah Shore, and serve for more than five years as musical director for the wonderful Lena Horne. He heard how Gene DiNovi's subsequent career has been as varied and colourful as a rainbow; how Gene went to Hollywood and became pianist-arranger for all the television shows produced by Danny Thomas, and composed and scored music for the Dick Van Dyke and Andy Griffiths TV shows.

He also heard how in October 1971, while on tour with the superb singer Carmen McRae, Gene DiNovi came to Toronto. Gene looked around the city and loved it so much that he decided to make it his home in 1972. In Toronto he became well known through his appearances on CBC radio's "Morningside." He also kept busy composing for film and television. Not long after he first arrived in the city he appeared in a delightful thirteen-week television series on TV Ontario called "The Music Room," where he played and sang and interviewed film composers (Henry Mancini, Harry Warren, Bronislaw Kaper, Sammy Cahn), who told some fascinating stories about their careers and the music they wrote.

Gene also performed in the Consort Lounge of the King Edward Hotel. His extraordinary talent as a pianist who could turn the beautiful songs of the 1930s and 1940s into veritable concertos attracted hundreds of listeners daily. Because of

DiNovi's artistry, the Consort Lounge sold a lot of booze, but a lot of people — including the middle-aged trombonist Murray Ginsberg — came to enjoy the music and not necessarily to drink. ("Oh, I guess I'll have a little one ... uhh, wait, you better make that a double.")

From his base in Toronto, Gene kept on performing (and recording) elsewhere in the world in such places as Scandinavia, Switzerland, Holland, France, and England, to the delight of his many fans. In 1985 he teamed up with classical clarinetist James Campbell to perform as a "classical-jazz duo" called Clarinet Contrasts, that played music by Brahms, Bartok, Von Weber, Michael Baker, Phil Nimmons, and George Shearing.

By 1990 Gene wanted to return to his jazz roots. The opportunity to begin this project came with an invitation to play at the Ontario Pavilion at Expo 1990 in Osaka, Japan. Gene's gig there led to engagements at Japanese jazz clubs and his first trio recording session in years. As he recalled when I interviewed him in June 1993:

> When GAMI, the management company, was pitching Jim Campbell and myself to go to Osaka '90 in Japan, Jim couldn't go, so I went. As a result I played two weeks at Osaka '90, lived in an apartment there, rode the train — it was great. My first time in Japan. So Mark Gardner, a fine English jazz writer, told Mitsuo Jofu about me. Jofu owns a clothing store in Yokahama but has a record company called Marshmallow.
>
> They put me on the bullet train to Yokahama, where I was picked up, treated like a king (as they always do), and I did a trio album with two very good Japanese players — Yukio Kimura and Kohji Tohyama. Yukio was the drummer and Kohji the bass player. And we made an album called "Precious Moment." Back in Toronto [the CBC radio hostess] Vicky Gabereau played this on the air and she said, "Kohji Tohyama on bass and Yukio Kimura on drugs." So I got some Japanese stationery and I wrote back, "I played drums, not drugs." So she wrote a card back, "I knew you'd be listening."

As it happens, I was listening that day, too. I remember how I thought that having an artist like Gene DiNovi from Brooklyn in Toronto in the 1990s was at last some kind of compensation for sending geniuses like Bob Farnon to London and Percy Faith to Chicago, New York, and Los Angeles, a half-century or so before. And as I've thought about this in my present circumstances, I've begun to wonder whether Fate may be something that affects cities, as well as individual lives.

The Changing Fate of Toronto

For better or worse, at least a part of this book has been about the fate not just of the Canadian music business in Toronto, but of Toronto itself — the place the rest of Canada loves to say it couldn't care less about. Nonetheless, the city, in its broadest sense, finally replaced Montreal as Canada's largest metropolis in the 1970s — not long after Gene DiNovi came to town, and just before I began the final phases of my Canadian music career. So nowadays, Toronto isn't just English-speaking

Canada's largest big city; it's Canada's largest big city, period!

In 1935, when we lived on Euclid Avenue, near Harbord, I was playing baseball, on a *Sunday*, in the lane between Palmerston and Euclid, with Eddie Matheweski, Norm Binstock, and a few other boys. One of us was the pitcher, one the catcher, and the others "out in field," while the guy at bat had to either smash a home run over a backyard fence or strike out, which automatically moved everybody up one position. (Some readers may remember this game themselves.)

We had been playing about an hour when, from out of nowhere, a ten-foot-tall policeman wearing a bobby's helmet appeared on a bicycle with notebook in hand. "What do you think you're doing, playing baseball on the Lord's Day?" he asked sternly. We were twelve years old and scared to death. And although we recited the Lord's Prayer every morning in Clinton Street Public School, we had no idea what he was talking about. He wrote each boy's name and address in his book and told us, "You'll have to appear in court with a parent to answer to the charges."

We returned to our homes, still frightened, and when I told my parents, they were frightened as well. Within a few days a letter arrived from City Hall informing my parents that they would have to take me to court on the appointed day. As it turned out, the judge roundly admonished the fathers of the boys (there were five of us) and dismissed the case with a warning: "Playing sports on the Lord's Day is forbidden in Ontario. You should teach your sons to respect the law. You'll be held responsible and severely dealt with if they are caught playing again."

Nothing quite like this ever happens in the much larger and more diverse and varied and even more interesting Toronto of today. And I can't think of anyone I know who is unhappy that this side of the city has disappeared. On the other hand, fifty years ago a stroll, day or night, on any Toronto street was considered safe for almost every citizen. Today, certain shopping malls and subway stations can be meeting places for gangs of hooligans.

In March 1998 the newspapers reported that the Kennedy subway station had a problem with hordes of teenage gangs, who posed a threat to law-abiding citizens. How to get rid of the problem? Some clever official at the Toronto Transit Commission hit on the bright idea of piping polite classical music by Bach and Mozart through the station's PA system. Within minutes, apparently, the station emptied of the unruly youth, who couldn't stand "the noise." (And who says classical music is an impractical, dying art?)

In fact when I moved to England in 1995, I had no further use of my car; so I gave it to my daughter, Susan. No sense letting it stand idle in the garage six months at a time. When we return to Toronto every six months or so to visit family and friends, I sometimes borrow the car when Susan isn't using it. But I don't really need to: I've rediscovered the wonderful system of public transportation operated by the Toronto Transit Commission (or TTC), and it suits me just fine.

A half-century ago, before I got my driver's licence in January 1950, I used the TTC to get to the CBC radio building on Jarvis Street, or the Palais Royale, or the Palace Pier, and the other places my engagements took me. Travelling by street car never bothered me then. And I've found that I like travelling by bus or streetcar or subway today. You get to see so much more of the city than you do by car. (On occasion, while riding the subway today, I remember walking out of the Colonial Tavern every night of a week-long gig with Trump Davidson in the early 1950s and facing a huge excavation on Yonge Street — which is where the subway began.)

I have a lot of warm and vivid memories of Toronto when I was a teenager and a young man, in the 1930s and 1940s. I remember St. Clair Avenue when it was a cobblestone road. The north side of the street bordered on farmers' fields, and the sight of grazing cows was commonplace. The eight-inch-high streetcar tracks were laid, as I recall, on wooden ties, and people climbing onto a streetcar had to raise a toe quite high to reach the first step. When you boarded a streetcar you didn't drop your ticket into a box when you passed the driver: you paid it to the ticket collector who sat in the middle of the vehicle.

I remember when popsicles were three cents each, corned beef sandwiches at Shopsy's on Spadina were five cents each, and a hot beef sandwich at Bassels at Yonge and Gerrard was about fifty cents. Somewhat later, when I was married in 1954, we paid $13,200 for a five-room bungalow on Laurelcrest Avenue, in Downsview. We had a 4 percent NHA mortgage. When our second daughter was born in 1960, we looked for a larger house but were appalled to find mortgages had risen to 7 percent; so we decided to build on to the existing bungalow.

In the 1930s our telephone number on Euclid was Melrose 3953. Those quaint names have long since vanished, replaced with area codes, and seven-digit numbers. Even fifty years ago who thought of fax machines, calculators, computers that can almost think, or satellite television that brings Middle East wars with "smart bombs" into your home? In Toronto today you can watch the news in Paris and Rome on cable channels. It is not unusual to have the prime minister of Britain, the president of France, Nelson Mandela of South Africa, Suharto of Indonesia, or even UFOs from outer space visiting your living room, day and night.

In 1899 the new City Hall with its soaring clock tower opened for all of Toronto's citizens to view with pride. About a hundred years later the building still stands, but it is no longer the City Hall. Today there is Nathan Phillips Square and the new City Hall (though even this is now more than thirty years old, and as I write no one seems quite sure just where the city hall of the new city of Toronto in the twenty-first century is going to be). The downtown Toronto skyline today is dominated by the CN Tower, SkyDome, First Canadian Place, the Toronto-Dominion Centre, Commerce Court, BCE Place, the Royal Bank Plaza, Scotia Plaza, Roy Thomson Hall, and on and on and on. It's all quite different than it used to be, but somehow it's still the place where I grew up and lived my life in music. I've enjoyed living in England in the most recent part of my life today. But I still enjoy coming back to Toronto. There's no place like home.

CODA

Where Is Music Going?

THE ELECTRONIC MUSIC STUDIO, McGILL UNIVERSITY, MONTREAL, 1998.
Courtesy William MacDonald White

One of the things I like best about periodically coming back to Toronto, Canada, from London, England, in my life today, is getting together again with my old friends from the music business. They are the friends I learned the business with, some two generations ago, and they share so many of my old memories, and, no doubt as well, my present-day attitudes, as a man in his seventies who is not getting any younger. One of the subjects we always seem to talk about is the future of music today. And quickly offering a few of my own instincts about this subject somehow seems to me the best way to end this book.

For quite a while now, of course, at least the "popular" musical universe that my old friends and I grew up with has been a thing of the past. (Classical music is somewhat different in this respect, though in its own way even it has changed.) The kind of Canadian music scene in Toronto in which my friends and I came of age and finally "made it" has changed into something quite different, in so many different respects. For many of our generation this is something to be lamented, and I know what they mean. But in the end I guess I like to remember that the American astronaut-politician, John Glenn, is in his seventies nowadays as well. And as I write, he is scheduled to make one last trip to the moon.

It helps to remember, I think, that in the 1920s the sound of voices and music was introduced to the motion picture industry. Almost overnight thousands of musicians who had enjoyed reasonable employment performing background music in the silent movie houses across North America were thrown out of work.

"It's the end of the music business," many cried. But, as the world soon learned, the music business did not end; it continued as a viable product when the best musicians moved from the orchestra pits into the recording studios to record the music tracks for the thousands of films produced in Hollywood and in other centres around the world.

In 1942 AFM President James Petrillo led the entire AFM membership through a strike against the phonograph record companies, because he predicted correctly, the day when records played by individuals (now known as disc jockeys) would replace live music at parties, shows, nightclubs, and radio stations. The successful result of that strike led to the establishment of the Music Performance Trust Fund, and subsequently to the Phonograph Record Manufacturers' Special Payments Fund. Both funds provide money to musicians. The MPTF pays for musicians who perform free concerts for the public in parks, in schools for children, and in hospitals for patients and visitors. The Special Payments Fund is a pension fund paid by employers and producers into individual musicians' pension plans.

Unfortunately, I agree, the threat to musicians' employment at the edge of the twenty-first century is worse than when sound came to the movies in the late 1920s. The latest phenomena today are the electronic music devices (EMDs) that have been increasingly replacing live music on television, in motion pictures, in commercials, and in virtually all other areas of the recording industry.

When the television series "Miami Vice" became a mega hit some years ago, the trend among TV and motion picture producers and many others was to go the "Miami Vice" route — to use synthesizers and other electronic music devices instead of live musicians. And to expect technology to stop in its tracks in order to accommodate musicians would be comparable to one man standing on the beach with his arms outstretched trying to hold back a tidal wave. The use of electronic music devices has continued to increase. For some younger people they are at the heart of the future of music. And, it does seem to me that, as we've learned time and time again in the last few hundred years, you can't stop technology.

I am happy to note that there also seem to be some strong recent moves back to the use of large orchestras in recording studios, combined with the use of assorted EMDs. (After all, there is nothing in recorded music to compare with "a thousand soaring violins" played by live, breathing violinists.) I don't have much doubt myself, however, that, in one way or another, electronic music devices are here to stay, as an increasingly important segment of the music industry of the future.

Steve Webster: A Wizard of EMD

It was with all this in mind that, in one of the last interviews I did for this book, I found myself in the rocket-ship studio of Steve Webster, trying to learn more about the mysterious new musical universe of EMDs.

Born in Toronto, Steve began his musical career as a bass player in rock bands. He's played with Allanah Myles, Parachute Club, and Lisa del Bello, and he toured extensively with Billy Idol. Nowadays he is a member of Rosnick-MacKinnon Productions, a firm of many faces at Church and Wellesley Streets in downtown Toronto.

To illustrate his work, Steve took me through the creation of a Bell Canada commercial that was playing on Canadian television at the time. His studio is in the basement of the Rosnick-MacKinnon building. It's a small room banked by every kind of electronic equipment: computers, samplers, synthesizers, and what-not — all far too numerous to list in any short and simple space.

Steve did his best to tell me what his musical work is all about:

I use a combination of the traditional-style synthesizers, samplers, hard disk recording, and computer-based sample players and editors. Most of this stuff is interconnected via traditional MIDI and SCSI lines, which allow me to transfer sounds from one unit to another. For example, I can record a singer, then import that digital recording into a sampler and play it as if it were an instrument, or manipulate it, or time-compress it, or what have you.

The equipment is worth about $60,000 to $80,000. As Steve explained:

Aside from the retail value of the items, putting it together carries a large price tag, which increases the value. Expensive, but nothing compared to a Stradivarius violin.

What did it take to put the Bell commercial together, I wondered? And Steve obliged:

I started that spot by working with a vocalist named Amy Sky. She and I got together, working around a piano, basically, and we came up with an idea for a melody. At that point I arranged the piece, and did it all on synthesizers.

The intention here was to create a quick mock-up of the idea which Steve presented to the clients, who said they liked the general flavour.

At that point we went into a studio and began replacing and adding to what we had. Originally, there was a certain amount of synthesizer stuff that was kept from the mock-up, but then we added it and also brought in nine string players who doubled the melody that was already on the synthesizers.
Percussion on the tape was replaced when we brought in top percussionist Brian Leonard, who played a multiple number of instruments to which we added a guitar and an electric, fretless bass. And that was it for the actual instrumentation.

What about the vocal lines?

Since we had been working together on the melody, Amy Sky and myself recorded

STEVE WEBSTER, circa 1995. Electronic Music Wizard,
Courtesy Steve Webster

all the vocals here in my studio directly to hard disk. Rather than record them in a large studio, we just transferred them from the equipment in my office.

In addition to that, I created a vocal part out of a couple of syllables that she recorded. We used the technology quite effectively in that we manipulated a lot of live musicians and a lot of live vocal performers, and combined it with synthesizer, and then overlaid people in a natural performance-type setting.

Steve went on to explain that he would be doing the same spot again, only changed to a thirty-second version of the original sixty-second piece. But rather than go in again to record the same stuff again, he'd had it stripped off the master tape at the studio on to a Digital Audio Tape (DAT) and imported it into his sequencer. As for percussionist Brian Leonard's original track, Webster said he would edit this down to a thirty-second format, saving Rosnick-MacKinnon a lot of money that would otherwise be spent in renting a large studio to record Leonard's live performance again.

There's really no need to try to chase these things down — because you never know if you can capture the same quality on another day. When you're working in the jingle field, you're moving so fast that it would be impossible to get the same exact microphone position, or perhaps the drums might react differently on another day.

This way we're using the technology in a way that's not really replacing people, but rather taking advantage of the technology and trying to enhance the performance that the musicians give.

On other jobs, Webster also notes, he frequently uses Ron Allen, a contemporary Toronto reed player (saxes and flutes).

Ron is particularly adept at playing Middle Eastern-type bamboo flutes. Aside from being a terrific sax player, Ron has recently moved into the area of ethnic wooden flutes, which create a wonderful sound. He is not only a wonderful musician but he is also a great improviser.

Webster's command of his equipment is uncanny.

Working in a thirty-second format, I find it somewhat restricting to have Ron get all of his ideas in just such a way so it will relate to the picture at a specific time. So I get him to improvise while I record his playing. Then I edit him in my equipment later to match what he's doing to the picture on the monitor.

Rather than restrict his performance, I let him do his thing, then after he's packed his instruments and gone home, I'll manipulate his music so that it does what I need it to do for the picture.

(Readers, are you still with us?)

Steve has been working with electronic musical devices for a number of years now. And he has become quite successful in manipulating his new musical "tools." In the year immediately before my interview with him, in the mid-1990s, he had created and produced over 170 jingles and commercials for such organizations as Bell Canada, American Express, Arm & Hammer, Bank of Montreal, Canadian Airlines, and Labatt's Beer.

Now in his forties, Steve Webster is also one of the brightest individuals I have ever met. And he has his own ideas about the Canadian music business in Toronto today.

I know there is a certain type of musician who may be resentful of this kind of production. There is no question that with the addition of synthesizers and the sophistication of the latest equipment today, the music business is not the same as some years ago, when a lot of musicians would move into the studios. A lot of their employment has been curtailed, which is an unfortunate reality in the music world. So much advertising reflects popular culture, and people who are involved in the popular music scene have embraced this technology.

But it goes through cycles. There was a time a few years ago when everything one heard was played by synthesizers. But now, most of the young bands are eschewing that stuff completely, and are working with traditional rock and roll instruments. But the reality is that this stuff is here to stay. It's pretty much integrated, and it's a foolish musician who doesn't accept the reality of it.

In Steve's view as well, in the very end, the new technology is complementary to live musicians.

It does things that live musicians cannot do, which is not a criticism of anybody's abilities. It's merely another instrument to be played. Embrace it and accept it; it's not an enemy any more.

After I'd left Steve Webster's up-to-the-minute basement studio at Church and Wellesley, in the middle of the 1990s — so long away from the 1930s, when I began my own musical career (and longer still of course from the 1880s, when the Toronto Musicians' Protective Association was first established) — I found myself thinking about another conversation I'd had recently with the very talented Toronto saxophonist of my own generation, Hart Wheeler.

(And Hart, you may recall, began his own career playing an Albert System clarinet: so right from the start he had some first-hand experience with the meaning of technological obsolescence in the music business of the twentieth century.) I had asked Hart why he "loves to play," and his answer was direct and to the point.

It's tied up with emotion; it's tied up with ego; it's an artistic endeavour where your output is immediate. A lot of artistic output can take years to realize, or weeks, or days, depending on what the finished product is — a photograph, a painting, a novel, or a motion picture. None are as immediate as music.

When you play an instrument, it's not just your eye and your hand painting a picture. It's the immediate result that pleases the senses. It's a continuing, revolving beautiful experience.

It struck me that, no matter what happens to the technology, there will always be some pretty crucial senses in which all this is still true. Electronically or acoustically or any other way, there will still be musicians who love to play for the same reasons Hart Wheeler summarized so well.

That's what's been most important about my own memories of the way it was, in one part of the world we all live in today. And whatever making it in music exactly becomes in the future, it will still be what is most important at that time.

In the future, as in the present and the past, the greatest thing anyone will be able to say about musicians anywhere is that they love to play.

List of Interviews

The earlier parts of the list include interviews I conducted in connection with my "Canadian Scene" column in the *International Musician* magazine.

Again, I would like to thank all those who shared their time and experience so generously in all the interviews, and all those who helped in transcribing the interviews for publication.

Along with the taped interviews (and my own recollections), the book also draws on less-formal conversations with musicians I have worked with (some of whom are, alas, no longer with us), from the late-1930s down to the present. In this connection I would particularly liked to acknowledge my debts to Lucio Agostini, Archie Alleyne, Peter Appleyard, Jimmy Dale, Jimmy (Trump) Davidson, Elsie Dunlop, and the charming members of the Enchanted Strings, Bob Farnon, Moe Koffman, Horace Lapp, Murray Lauder, Judy Loman, Rob McConnell, Babe Newman, Bernie Piltch, Teddy Roderman, Joe Umbrico, and John Wyre.

In various places as well the book draws on the records of the Toronto Musicians' Association (Local 149 of the American Federation of Musicians of the United States and Canada), with which I became familiar during my sixteen years as an Association employee.

M.G.

1980 May 16	Murray Little	1992 July 20	Henry Wright
		1992 July 27	Henry Wright
1987 March 1	Pearl Palmason	1992 August 3	Bill Richards
1987 July 12	Stephen Staryk	1992 September 12	Jimmy Cooke
1987 July 18	Stephen Staryk	1992 September 12	Dorothy Deane
		1992 November 14	Paul Grosney
1989 December 31	Pearl Palmason		
		1993 February 9	Bob Burgess
1990 July 13	Albert Pratz	1993 February 20	Frank Bogart
1990 July 26	Hyman Goodman	1993 March 6	Paul Grosney
		1993 March 7	Paul Grosney
1991 March 14	George Horvath	1993 March 8	Paul Grosney
1991 December 5	Bill Richards	1993 March 28	Barry Little
		1993 April 18	Ron Collier
1992 January 6	Art Hallman	1993 April 28	Howard Cable
1992 January 11	Gino Silvi	1993 May 13	Johnny Cowell
1992 January 18	Gino Silvi	1993 May 23	Lloyd Richards
1992 January 25	Frank Fusco	1993 June 7	Gene DiNovi
1992 January 25	Gino Silvi	1993 August 9	Jimmy Namaro
1992 January 31	Lou Applebaum	1993 September 27	Harvey Perrin
1992 February 9	Pearl Palmason		
1992 March 11	Sam Levine	1994 April 23	Robert Plunkett
1992 April 4	Gordon Evans	1994 May 10	Hagood Hardy
1992 April 4	Hart Wheeler	1994 May 16	Billy O'Connor
1992 April 12	Hank Rosati	1994 May 16	Harvey Silver
1992 April 20	Harvey Lichtenberg	1994 May 28	Sam Levine
1992 April 23	Phil Antonacci	1994 November 7	Steve Webster
1992 April 25	Lew Lewis		
1992 April 26	Nat Cassells	1995 January 28	Jackie Rae
1992 April 27	Norman Amadio	1995 February 4	Jackie Rae
1992 May 7	Harold Sumberg		
1992 May 8	Lew Lewis	1997 April 8	Phil Nimmons
1992 May 9	Eddy Graf	1997 April 8	Erich Traugott
1992 May 9	Ellis McLintock		
1992 May 13	Victor Feldbrill	1998 March 9	Nicholas Kilburn
1992 May 16	Ellis McLintock	1998 March 14	Paul Kilburn
1992 June 11	Bobby Gimby	1998 March 15	Mary Barrow
1992 June 17	Mart Kenney	1998 March 29	Percy Faith Family
1992 July 16	James Amaro, Jr.	1998 March 31	Stephen Staryk
1992 July 20	Frank Wright		

Index

Adamson, Ken, 73
Addison, Puff, 49, 137
AFM Congress of Strings, 197
Agostini, Lucio, 69, 116–118, 174, 202, 246
Ailey, Alvin, 255
Alda, Alan, 109
Alda, Robert, 109
Alexandra Ballroom, 9, 65, 66
All-Star Band, 89
Allen, Andrew, 116, 252
Allen, Len, 120, 121
Allen, Ron, 265
Allen Theatres, 24, 25, 111
Alleyne, Archie, 88, 240, 253, 254
Amadio, Norman, 155, 156, 158, 160, 240, 268
Amaro, Jr., James, 268
Amaro, Jimmy, 44
American Federation of Musicians, 15, 85, 114, 123
Ancerl, Karel, 180
Anderson, Cat, 94
Andrews, Bill, 125
Andrews, Ted, 33
Antonacci, Greg, 162
Antonacci, Louis, 162
Antonacci, Phil, 41, 51, 64, 75, 77, 79, 161-63, 165, 268
Antonelli, Angella, 126, 127
Apollo Theatre, 242
Applebaum, Lou, 255, 268
Appleyard, Peter, 86, 174
Arcadian Court, 44
Armstrong, Louis, 113, 169
Army Show, 53, 54, 56, 58, 59, 230
Arthur, Jack, 17, 29
Association of Canadian Orchestras, 149
Atkins, Chet, 144
Auditorium, The, 22
Auld, Georgie, 58

Baker, Kenny, 55
Banker, Charlie, 161
Barber, Jimmy, 50
Barbini, Ernesto, 212
Barbirolli, Sir John, 195
Barnes, Howard, 123
Barnet, Charlie, 233
Barraca, Russ, 44, 50
Barrow, Bert, 198
Barrow, Mary, 117, 181, 198, 199, 268
Barrow, Reg, 199, 202
Basie, Count, 76, 83, 114
Bassel's Restaurant, 72, 260
Bates, Mary, 73
Battle, Rex, 61, 196

Beales, Ruth Ann, 6
Beasley, Bill, 93, 94
Beaumaris Hotel, 131
Beck, George, 107
Becker, Bob, 191
Bedlington, Harry, 74
Beecham, Sir Thomas, 188, 195, 200, 204
Beiderbecke, Bix, 99, 100
Bell, Gordie, 94
Bell, Leslie, 125, 128–130
Bennett, Harold, 233
Bennett, Tony, 60, 129, 166
Benson, George, 253
Benson, Ivy, 63
Bergart, Harry, 197
Berger, Sam, 155
Berigan, Bunny, 40, 41, 58, 121
Berlin, Boris, 155
Berry, Chu, 37
Bertan, Joyce, 126
Bickert, Ed, 158, 240
Birdland, 159, 242
Bishop, Jr., Walter, 242
Blackburn, Don, 45, 46
Blakey, Art, 242
Blue, Al, 71, 94
Bluestein, Max, 159
Blye, Alan, 174
Bogart, Frank, 48, 78, 89–91, 93–95, 97
Borge, Victor, 105, 112
Boss Brass, 234, 248
Boulevard Club, 48, 102
Boult, Sir Adrian, 204
Bradan, Tony, 55, 232
Brander, Penny, 54
Braund, Gordon, 96, 115
Bray, Carne, 240
Brethour, Eldon, 36
Bridle, Augustus, 20
Britto, Bill, 240
Broadfoot, Dave, 250
Broderick, Joe, 74, 76, 93
Brown, Bobby, 84
Brown, Les, 79, 101
Brown, Ray, 154
Bruce, George, 52
Burgess, Bob, 268
Burns, Bob, 247
Burns, Louise, 32
Burt, Johnny, 25, 27, 41, 97
Buschert, Billie, 205
Busseri, Frank, 48
Butterfield, Billy, 40
Buttons, Red, 105

Cable, Howard, 48, 69, 124, 125, 127-31, 202, 246, 250, 269

Calloway, Cab, 41, 76, 83, 106, 114
Campbell, Bruce, 23
Campbell, Howard, 94, 97, 101
Campbell, James, 258
Campbell, Norman, 62
Canadian Academy of Music, 20
Canadian Broadcasting Corporation, 9, 23, 25, 38, 43, 59, 61, 62, 78, 80, 95, 96, 98, 116, 118, 121, 123, 237
Canadian National Exhibition, 16, 29, 41, 63, 80, 93, 122
Canadian Radio Broadcasting Commission, 23, 38, 67
Caplan, Dave, 23, 87
Flesch, Carl, 52, 53
Carlyle, Charlie, 45
Carney, Bill, 45
Carny, Joe, 103
Carrington, Don, 81
Carter, Bill, 45
Carter, Wilf, 113
Cartright Gardens, 55, 247
Casa Loma Orchestra, 16, 76
Casino Theatre, 84, 104–114, 166
Cassells, Nat, 7, 10, 11, 17, 18, 21, 22, 25, 26, 268
Cassidy, Frankie, 54
Cavazzi, Juliette, 126
CBC Brass Sextet, 218
CBC Symphony Orchestra, 195, 197, 211
CBC Television, 29 45, 72, 80, 234
Centro, Vic, 153, 239
CFCA, 22, 25
CFRB, 87
Chandler, George, 66
Charles, Bill, 54, 55
Chiaschini, Ned, 55
Chicago Symphony, 187
Chisholm, George, 55
Chotem, Neil, 247
Chycoski, Arnie, 101
CJOR, 66
CJRT-FM, 255
CKEY, 40
Claxton, Thomas 14
Clements, George, 107, 111
Club Embassy, 48, 93
Club Esquire, 48, 85, 92, 93, 94, 102
Club Kingsway, 74

Club Norman, 72, 207
Club Top Hat, 48, 78, 85, 89, 93, 94–96, 164
CNRO, 38
CNRT, 23
Cohen, Harold, 63
Coker, Raymond, 81
Cole, Nat, King, 113, 166
Colin, Charles, 58
Collier, Ron, 240, 252, 254, 269
Colonial Tavern, 72, 85, 86, 99, 100, 116, 166, 167,169, 171, 236
Concertgebouw, 187
Condon, Eddie, 170
Cooke, Jimmy, 29–32, 37, 50, 268
Corio, Ann, 105
Cornfield, Bobby, 48
Cortese, Larry, 25, 26
Cowell, Johnny, 135, 138–140, 142, 268
Coxson, Jimmy, 64, 77
CRBC, 23, 24, 25, 61
Crosby, Bob, 76, 100
Crum, George, 212
Crystal Ballroom, 26
Culley, Ed, 22
Culley, Ross, 77, 115, 165
Curry, Jack, 25, 26
Cuthbert and Deller, 39, 75, 76
Cuthbert, Bill, 74

Daffel, Christopher, 188
Dale, Father James, 42
Dale, Jimmy, 173–76
Dalziel, Ken, 127
Damone, Vic, 106
Dardanella Ballroom, 19, 103
Davidson, Jimmy (Trump), 25, 27, 35, 48, 73, 94, 95, 97–104, 116
Davidson, Teddy, 75, 97, 99
Davis, Andrew, 145, 180, 190, 216, 224
Davis, Fred, 71, 130, 160
Davis, Myra, 225
Davis, Sr., Sammy, 84, 106
Davis, Jr., Sammy, 84, 106
Davis, Sir Colin, 195
Day, Gordon, 25, 27, 31, 124, 163
Deane, Dorothy, 150, 268
Deitz, Howard, 117
Del Greco, Enrico, 26
Delamont, Gordon, 94, 100, 121, 232, 255
Delaurentis, Willie, 35, 103
Deller, George, 74
Denny, Martin, 242

Desser, Isadore, 31, 32
DiNovi, Gene, 256, 258, 268
Dobson, Johnny, 75, 77, 78, 121
Dojack, Charlie, 55
Donahue, Sam, 55
Dorsey, Jimmy, 39, 40, 76, 101, 106, 233
Dorsey, Tommy, 40–42, 63, 64, 95, 100, 101, 106, 121
Dounis, D. C., 196
Dowell, Arthur, 50, 123
Downes, Wray, 88
Doyle, Rex, 109
Duchin, Eddie, 76, 90, 91, 93
Dumbells, 17, 18
Dunham, Sonny, 233
Dunlop, Elsie, 205
Dunn, Jerry, 132

Eaton's Music Department, 46
Eaton's Young Moderns Campaign, 133
Edinborough, Arnold, 20
Edison, Harry "Sweets," 72
Edison Hotel, 99
Eldridge, Roy, 37, 58, 157
Electronic Music Studio, 261
Ellington, Duke, 41, 76, 83, 94, 101, 106, 109, 114, 172, 254–56
Elmwood Casino, 207
Emel, Ed, 65
Emperor's Court Musicians, 215
Enchanted Strings, 205, 206
Encore Band, 119, 233
Engelman, Robin, 191
Evans, Gordon, 27, 37, 79, 163, 268
Evans, Jack, 39, 40, 44, 50
Everett, Ted, 77

Faith, Percy, 9, 23, 24, 27, 38, 59, 61–63, 78, 129, 196, 198
Fallingbrook Pavilion, 48, 74, 81, 83
Farlow, Tal, 86
Farmer, Broadus, 194
Farnon, Brian, 54, 55, 59
Farnon, Denny, 54, 55, 59, 231
Farnon, Robert, 9, 59–61, 129, 163, 205, 228
Farr, Russ, 73
Feldbrill, Victor, 52, 134, 203, 222, 243, 268
Feldman Swing Club, 55
Fenton, Bobby, 127
Ferguson, Bob, 110
Ferrano, Tony, 75, 77
Figelski, Cecil, 23, 25, 26
Fink, Max, 75
Fitzgerald, Ella, 64, 113, 129,

171
Five Spot, 241
Flaherty, Cliff, 73
Fonger, David, 86
Ford, Freddie, 47, 48,
Forrest, Helen, 40
Forrester, Maureen, 185, 216, 217
Foss, Harry, 18, 22
Foss, Lukas, 196
Fraser, Don, 236
Freedman, Harry, 73, 255
Freeman, Bud, 102
Freeman, Earl, 42
Fritzlay, Gene, 25, 26
Fry, Jimmy, 44, 50
Fusco, Frank, 55, 118, 268

Gaiety Theatre, 14
Gallagher and Sheen, 14
Gallagher, Howard, 43
Galper, Abe, 124, 135
Garden, John, 126
Gardiner, Bob, 126
Garner, Erroll, 170
Garvey, Marcus, 83
Gaylord, Slim, 168
George, Colonel Victor, 54
George Hooey, 130
George's Spaghetti House, 88, 245
Getz, Stan, 157, 170
Gimby, Bobby, 10, 150, 151, 268
Gino Silvi Singers, 124, 126, 127
Ginsberg, Murray, 55, 99, 115
Ginzler, Seymour "Red," 25, 27
Glazer, Joe, 168
Gleiser, Carl, 41
Glover, Elwood, 95, 96
Golden Gate Quartet, 114
Golden Slipper, 131
Goldhawk, Gordie, 107
Goldschmidt, Nicholas, 178
Gooch, Vern, 107
Goodman, Benny, 30, 38, 40, 42, 51, 95, 101, 121, 130
Goodman, Bobby, 109
Goodman, Hyman, 8, 32, 52, 195, 196, 214, 268
Gordon, Don, 44
Goring, Vic, 79
Gould, Glenn, 217–19
Gould, Morton, 62
Graf, Eddie, 54, 230, 233, 268
Graffman, Vladimir, 196
Graham, Vern, 73
Grand Opera House, 17
Granite Club, 47, 89, 91, 93, 96, 97
Gray, Charlie, 176
Gray, Harold, 75

Green, Charlie, 23
Greenberg, Max, 23
Gregory, Chuck, 107
Griffiths, Glen, 65
Groat, Fran, 126
Groob, Jack 54, 55, 57–59, 134
Grosney, Paul, 77, 79, 96, 165, 247, 248, 268
Gryce, Gi Gi, 241, 242
Guerrero, Albert, 219
Guerrette, George, 75, 97

HAADD, 185
Haggin, B.H., 219
Hallman, Art, 65, 142, 150
Hambourg, Clem, 24, 87, 239, 241
Hambourg Conservatory of Music, 87
Hambourg, Jan, 24
Hamilton Philharmonic Orchestra, 204
Hampton, Lionel, 114, 171
Hanniford Street Silver Band, 127, 129
"Happy Gang, The," 59, 80, 151, 237
Hardy, Hagood, 87, 238–44, 268
Harmer, Shirley, 143
Harmony Grill, 45
Harron, Don, 250
Hartenberger, Russell, 191
Hatch, Nelson, 48, 110
Hawe, Harry, 36, 53, 63, 117, 138, 177
Hawkins, Coleman, 37, 72, 94, 95
Hawkins, Earl, 48
Hebert, Paul, 35
Hemmings, Jack, 65
Henderson, Fletcher, 37
Herbig, Gunther, 180
Herriot, Bobby, 225, 233
Hershenhorn, Leonard, 54
Hershenhorn, Sam, 23, 52, 59, 123, 246
Hetherington, David, 210
Hill, Carol, 126
HMCS Naden band, 139
Hoffert, Paul, 252
Holiday, Billie, 72, 172, 253
Homburger, Walter, 183, 215, 222
Horace Heidt Orchestra, 81
Horne, Lena, 257
House of Hambourg, 87, 116, 239–41
House of Righteousness, 247
Houston, Ken, 47
Howard, Acey, 64, 126, 127
Hudson, Don, 54
Hume, Paul, 221
Hurley, Doug, 75
Huston, Art, 94

Huston, Walter, 94
Hutchen, Jock, 129
Hutton, Ina Ray, 63
Hyslop, Ricky, 174

Imperial Room, 30, 31, 48, 89, 96, 129
Imperial Theatre, 29
Ink Spots, The, 114
Isen, Morris, 61, 115, 118
Isenbaum, Morris, 217

Jack Kane's Music Makers, 115
Jackson, Arthur, 60
James, Harry, 101
Jardine, Jack, 49
Jemet, Clyde, 84
Johanus, Leo, 37
Johns, Charlie, 46
Johnson, Don, 140, 217
Johnson, Ernest, 200
Johnston, Merve, 95
Jolley, Pete, 243
Jones, Oliver, 253
Jones, Philly Jo, 242

Kane, Jackie, 42, 43, **94, 95**
Karr, Harry, 67
Katz, Jack, 107, 108
Kaye, Sammy, 41, 79
Kelnick, Henry, 37, 48
Kennedy, Vern, 126, 127
Kenney, Mart, 9, 48, 65–70, 116, 268
Kenton, Stan, 79
Kilburn, Nicholas, 181, 219, 221, 268
Kilburn, Paul, 220, 222, 268
Kimura, Yukio, 258
King, Bill, 172
King Edward Hotel, 11, 25, 26, 29, 41, 44, 47, 48, 72, 100, 102, 103, 255
King, Wayne, 67
Kinsman, Bob, 54, 231
Kirby, John, 100
Kirk, Andy, 37
Klein, Daddy, 82
Koffman, Moe, 88, 106, 115, 233, 234, 248, 252
Kondaks, Steve, 54
Konjalava, Tad, 54, 55
Kostelanetz, Andre, 62, 200
Krupa, Gene, 42, 101, 170
Kunits, Luigi von, 19, 20, 36, 178, 194
Kunzel, Eric, 145

Laine, Frankie, 113, 237
Lander, Jack, 156
Lanin, Lester, 96
Lapp, Horace 26–34, 37, 48, 50, 231
Lauder, Murray, 10, 43, 54–58, 118, 223, 231, 247

270 Index

Lazaroff, Alex, 156
Lee, Bill, 87
Leech, George, 54
Leigh, Mitch, 128
Leonard, Brian, 264, 265
Levine, Michael, 147
Levine, Sam, 35, 97, 103, 146–48, 224, 247, 268
Levy, Lou, 243
Lewis, Gary, 173
Lewis, Lew, 24, 27, 41, 47, 55, 96, 100, 115, 147, 162, 268
Lewis, Savoy, 94
Lewis, Ted, 18, 67
Lichtenberg, Goody, 167
Lichtenberg, Harvey, 167, 169, 268
Linden, Johnny, 48
Lister, Bert, 65, 67
Little, Barry, 106, 107, 110, 114, 268
Little, Lou, 53
Little, Murray, 105, 106, 110, 268
Locke, Norma, 65, 69, 70, 96, 116, 127
Loman, Judy, 183–86
Lombardo, Carmen, 41, 90
Lombardo, Guy, 41, 77, 90
Lombardo, Lebert, 41, 9
London, Morris, 124
Long & McQuade, 86
Lowe, Ruth, 63–65
Lustig, Nathan, 107

MacCallum, Hec, 65
MacDonald, Jimmy, 48
MacIntyre, Hal, 101
MacKay, Cliff, 98, 124
MacMillan, Sir Ernest, 20, 36, 52, 127, 129, 141, 177
Madden, Jack, 54, 55, 123
Mancini, Henry, 198
Mann, Herbie, 238
Manoir Richelieu, 7, 24, 25, 173
Marsden, Albert, 81, 82, 84
Marshall, Lois, 185, 217
Marshall, Red, 110
Martin, Larry, 77
Martin, Tony, 135
Mason, Betty, 54
Massey Hall, 20, 52, 61, 72, 178, 208, 211
Mathe, Blaine, 47
Mathe, Charles, 47
Mathews, Mr., 68
Mayers, Al, 81
Mazzoleni, Ettore, 177, 178, 219
McAndrew, Jack, 175
McCauley, Bill, 97
McConnell, Rob, 59, 248–50
McDougal, Dick, 40, 41
McGarvey, Reef, 97–99

McGuiness, Scotty, 39
McKinnon, Catherine, 250
McLean, Bob, 175
McLean Brothers, 66, 67
McLean, Cy, 9, 81, 83–85, 167
McLean, Reg, 81
McLintock, Ellis, 28, 36, 38, 49, 115, 124, 125, 201, 217, 247, 268
McMichael, Bob, 133
McNealy, Joe, 141
McPartland, Jimmy, 168
McPartland, Marian, 253
McQuaid, Jack, 240
McRae, Carmen, 253
McShann, Jay, 253
Meechim, Bert, 46
Mellor, Wilf, 163
Mends, May, 54
Messiaen, Olivier, 210
Mezzrow, Mezz, 170
Miller, Glenn, 59, 60
Mills Brothers, 114
Mince, Johnny, 55
Minevitch, Bora, 110
Mingus, Charlie, 86
Mitford, Bert, 102
Miyazaki, Takao, 216
Mobility Assistance Program, 149
Modernaires, 73, 130, 163
Moe Koffman Quintet, 235
Moir, Mary, 43
Mokry, Irene, 205
Mole, Miff, 42
Molson Jazz Festival, 165
Monarchs of Melody, 25, 28, 41
Monis, Hank, 99, 150
Montage, The, 244
Montreal Jazz Festival, 234
Moon, Harold, 143
Morawetz, Oscar, 232
Morris, Howard, 77
Mortimer, Mark, 71
Morton, Gav, 75
Morton, Murray, 132
Moscow Philharmonic, 221
Mosher, Wayland, 124
Mosher's Arcadia Ballroom, 18, 22
Moskalyk, John, 188
Mowry Ferdy, 44, 48, 90, 93
Murdoch, Walter, 49, 50, 82, 106, 114, 123, 138, 200, 239
Muse, Bob, 71, 73
Music Performance Trust Fund, 262
Mutual Broadcasting System, 61
Myles, Allanah, 263

Namaro, Jimmy, 236, 237, 147, 268

Napoleon, Phil, 72, 100
Naylor, George, 73, 161
NBC, 23, 25, 96
NBC Symphony Orchestra, 10
Neilson, Beauna, 117
Nelsova, Zara, 201
New Symphony Orchestra, 19, 20, 21, 36
Newman, Babe, 55, 57, 77
Nexus, 191–93
Nicholson, Harry, 37, 124
Nickoloff, Lillian, 205
Nimmons, Phil, 153, 154, 232, 251, 268
Niosi, Bert, 48, 74, 75, 77-80, 96, 98, 116, 164, 165
Niosi, Joe, 97, 99, 150
Niosi, Johnny, 75, 77
Nixon, Pat, 77
Noble, Ray, 102
Norvo, Red, 86, 94

O'Connell, Helen, 40
O'Connor, Billy, 269
O'Donnell, Bernice, 230
O'Keefe Centre, 202
O'Toole, Dick, 41
Oakley, Art, 54, 71
Ontario Place Forum, 62
Onyx Club, 146
Orchestra Openings, 148
Orpen, Abe, 88
Osachuck, Ernie, 240
Oxford Street Swing Club, 226
Ozawa, Seiji, 145, 180, 191, 208, 209, 212, 213, 215

Page Cavanaugh Trio, 114
Page, Patti, 113
Paisley, Lew, 45
Palace Pier, 73, 74, 88, 97–101, 103, 116
Palace Theatre, 112
Palais Royale, 10, 39, 44, 74–76, 77, 79, 80, 85, 93, 101, 164
Palmason, Pearl, 182, 268
Pantages, 17, 29
Parker, Charlie, 72, 257
Parnes, Earl, 33
Pasternak, Percy, 23, 61
Pastor, Tony, 40
Patterson, Roy, 73
Paul, Benny, 23, 47, 115
Paul, Jimmy, 97
Peabody Conservatory of Music, 199, 251
Pearl, Bert, 59, 80
Percip, Charlie, 242
Percival, Lloyd, 87
Perkins, Tiny, 41
Perl, Sid, 35, 103
Perrin, Harvey, 36, 268
Peterson, Oscar, 154, 235

Petrillo, James, 262
Pied Pipers, 63, 125
Pied Piper of Canada, 150, 152
Pier, Bob, 41, 73
Pilot Tavern, 72
Piltch, Bernie, 240, 251, 252
Plunkett, Captain Merton, 17, 18
Plunkett, Robert, 269
Powell, Fred, 54
Powell, Ruth, 89
Pratz, Albert, 8, 10, 32, 52, 194–97
Price, Bob, 156, 240
Priestman, Olga, 205
Prima Louis, 76, 101
Primeau, Joe, 40
Professor Glass' Juvenile Band, 18, 19, 25
Promenade Philharmonic Concerts, 194, 200
Promenade Philharmonic, 199
Pullman, Peter, 257
Purcell, Bill, 144

Queen's Hotel, 16, 26
Queensway Ballroom, 97

Rae, Jackie, 135, 269
Rae, Johnny, 113
Rand, Sally, 105
Record Manufacturers' Special Payments Fund, 262
Red Norvo Trio, 85
Reed, Bubs, 41
Reiner, Fritz, 182
Reischman, Leo, 90, 91
Reynolds, Frank, 115
Reynolds, Jimmy, 41, 47, 124
Riccio, Jimmy, 83
Riccio, Pat, 77, 78, 83, 160
Rich, Buddy, 243
Richards, Bill, 38, 176, 268
Richards, Lloyd "Steve," 43, 71, 97, 268
Richardson, Jack, 64
Richardson, Sammy, 81, 84
Roberts, Agnes, 198
Roberts, Floyd, 94
Roberts, Vivian, 81, 84
Roderman, Teddy, 36, 53, 94, 97, 115, 124 218, 246, 247
Rogers, Richard, 128
Romaine, Doug, 97, 98
Romanelli, Don, 13, 22
Romanelli, Leo, 173
Romanelli, Luigi, 11, 24–29, 37, 41, 48, 61, 99
Romanoff, Ivan, 232
Rosati, Hank, 47, 49, 58, 77, 247, 268
Rosevear, Bob, 177
Ross, Harold, 37

Index *271*

Rostopovich, Mstislav, 183
Rowe, Bernie, 115
Roxy, 104, 107, 111
Royal Albert Hall, 237
Royal Alexandra Theatre, 86, 128, 202
Royal Canadian Artillery Band, 233
Royal Canadian Regiment Band, 231
Royal Conservatory of Music, 61, 69, 86, 111, 129, 155, 177
Royal London Philharmonic, 187, 189
Royal York Hotel, 9, 11, 26, 29, 31–34, 44, 47, 48, 68, 70, 72 89, 103
Rully, Ron, 240
Russianoff, Leon, 233

Saila, Bill, 41
Salmon, Lloyd, 81, 84
Salzedo, Carlos, 183, 184
Samborsky, Peter, 107, 108
Sampson, Peggie, 222
Sanborn, Eddie, 55
Sandler Family, 64
Saraste, Jukka-Pekka, 180
Savarin, 48, 72, 248
Saville, Reg, 35, 103
Schafer, R. Murray, 184
Schenkman, Peter, 210
Schertzer, Hymie, 95
Schlatter, George, 175
Scholes Hotel, 167
Schwartz, Arthur, 117
Sea Breeze, 39, 48, 73, 74
Secondary School Orchestra, 36, 203
Sedgwick, Joseph, 105
Seth, Ben, 25,
Shakuhachi, 216
Sharman, Bill, 122
Shavers, Charlie, 100, 170
Shaw, Artie, 39, 40, 76, 171
Shea's Hippodrome, 29, 84, 102
Shearing, George, 86, 87, 106, 238, 244
Sherman Oaks, 249
Sherman, Paul, 32
Shilling, Bob, 157, 158
Shore, Sid, 163
Silver, Harvey, 35, 97–99, 103, 268
Silver, Nibsy, 106, 107
Silver, Sam, 48
Silver Slipper, 37, 48, 51, 85, 164
Silvi, Gino, 69, 118–25, 127, 268
Simmons, Paul, 250
Sinatra, Frank, 41, 63, 64, 101, 232
Sinclair, Peter, 31, 55, 97, 98

Sky, Amy, 264
Sky Club, 93
Slatter, Captain John, 137
Slatter, Edna, 207
Smith, Gladys, 24
Smith, Roy, 115
Smith, Teddy, 124
Southern, Georgia, 105
Spanier, Muggsy, 168
Spearing, Cliff, 47, 201
Spitalni, Phil, 63
Spivak, Charlie, 102
Spratt, Rudy, 44
St. Cyr, Lily, 105
St. John, Stanley, 46–48, 141
St. Lawrence Centre, 127, 128,
Stafford, Jo, 63
Stage Door, 174
Stainsby, Rick, 126
Standard Theatre, 83
Standish Hall Hotel, 35, 103
Stanwyk, Al, 45
Stanwyk, Jack, 45
Starmer, Len, 206
Starr, Kay, 106, 113
Staryk, Steven, 181, 187–90, 268
Statler Hotel, 84
Steinberg, Bobby, 47
Stephenson, Stan, 120
Stevenson, Harry, 218
Stewart, Reginald, 194, 199
Stokowski, Leopold, 201
Stone, Archie, 104, 106, 107, 110
Stone, Dennis, 126
Stone, Freddie, 110
Stovin, Horace, 67, 68
Stratford Music Festival, 195, 251
Stravinsky, Igor, 10, 211
Stroh, Nathaniel, 251
Stroud, Eddie, 44
Sturn, Vaughan, 23
Sumberg, Harold, 61, 268
Supertest Concert Orchestra, 127
Susskind, Walter, 178, 180
Sweeney, Fred, 90
Swing Patrol, 57
Symonds, Norman, 252, 255
Symphony Symposium, 148
Szell, George, 182, 190, 220

Tadashore, Jean, 122
Takemitsu, Toru, 191
Tapper, Max, 205
Tasker, Stan, 54
Tatum, Art, 236
Teagarden, Jack, 42, 72, 169
Teddy Wilson Trio, 253
Thomas, Danny, 257
Thomas, Lois, 206
Thornhill, Claude, 102
Tichnovitch, Alex, 126

Till, Bertram, 110
Titmarsh, Gurney, 25
Tjaeder, Cal, 86
Topping, Graham, 231
Torme, Mel, 106, 158, 253
Toronto Jazz Festival, 234
Toronto Jazz Quartet, 254
Toronto Musicians' Association, 9, 14, 15, 72, 114, 119, 224, 225
Toronto Musicians' Protective Association, 15, 49, 50, 82, 85, 116
Toronto Symphony Band, 137
Toronto Symphony Concert Band, 49
Toronto Symphony Orchestra, 8, 10, 20, 36, 38, 52, 62, 142, 144, 177, 190, 224
Toscanini, Arturo, 10
Toth, Jerry, 115, 153
Toth, Josephine, 205
Town Hall, 45, 46, 221
Towne Tavern, 72, 87, 116, 155, 156, 160, 236
Tramp Band, 54, 231
Traugott, Erich, 101, 153, 250, 251, 268
Treneer, Freddie, 31
Tri-Bell Club, 42, 43, 83
Trimble, Peter, 236
Turner, Bill, 127

U.N.I.A., 83
Umbrico, Joe, 181, 184
Unit A Orchestra, 231, 232

Vallee, Rudy, 113
Vancouver International Festival, 222
Varsity Arena, 138, 199
Vaughan, Denny, 30, 54, 55, 57, 59, 96, 231
Vaughan, Sarah, 72, 171
Venuti, Professor, 90
Victoria Theatre, 25, 54, 59

Wachter, Jack, 98, 99, 103, 123
Waddington, Geoffrey, 56, 61, 196, 218
Wagner, Ollie, 81
Waizman, Louis, 61
Wallace, Steve, 88
Waller, Fats, 40, 42, 80, 94, 95
Watanabe, Butch, 153
Watson, Homer, 73
Wayland, Newton, 136
Webster, Steve, 263–66, 268
Weiner, Sam "Bozo," 97
Weinzweig, John, 140, 218, 232
Weinzweig, Morris, 55, 115,

123
Weiss, Nicholas, 213
Weitz, George, 24
Welsman, Frank, 19, 61
Whaley Royce, 37, 38, 46
Wheeler, Hart, 6, 37, 51, 266–68
Wheeler, Stan, 35, 97, 103
White, Bill, 101
White, George, 24
Whiteman, Frank, 19
Whiteman, Paul, 76, 99
Whitney, Moxie, 48, 207
Whittaker, Byng, 69, 95
Wilf Marsden Trio, 84, 85, 106
Williams, Joe, 87
Williams, Ozzie, 48
Williams, Wilf, 81, 84
Wilson, Meredith, 128
Wilson, Stan, 41
Winestone, Benny, 58, 94, 95, 157
Winnipeg Symphony Orchestra, 222
Winston, Maurice, 107, 108
Winters, Kenneth, 222
Wood, Alfie, 47
Wood, J. Alan, 224
Woodcock, Glen, 60
World Harp Congress, 184
Worrell, Roy, 81, 84
Wright Frank, 81, 85, 86–88, 268
Wright, Henry, 81, 83, 84, 268
Wyre, John, 181, 191

Young, Lester, 72, 157, 166
Youngman, Henny, 105

Zaza, Jack, 239
Zeigfield Follies, 14
Zene, Moe, 97, 101
Zentner, Erica, 205

110th Irish Regimental Band, 18
48th Highlanders Band, 54